# Significant Changes

## TO THE *NEC*® 2014

IN PARTNERSHIP WITH

CH 3
A 344
P II
S
chapter
1
2
3 Build chapter

This book conveys the information related to each change as of July 26, 2013, but does not reflect any subsequent appeal or other action taken by the NFPA Standards Council. The changes covered in this textbook that could be impacted are identified with the following text:

**Subsequent NFPA Standards Council Action Pending**

This text appears in the Code Language segment of any such change that could possibly be affected by such actions incorporated into the Code AFTER the printing of this textbook.



1 2 3 4 5 6 7 8 9 – 14 – 9 8 7 6 5 4 3

Printed in the United States of America

# Contents

## Chapter 1

# Contents

## Chapter 2

# Contents

## Chapter 2 (continued)

# Contents

## Chapter 3

Articles 300-393 .......................................... **98**

### Wiring Methods and Materials

# Contents

## Chapter 3 (continued)

## Chapter 4

# Contents

## Chapter 4 (continued)

## Chapter 5

### Special Occupancies

# Contents

## Chapter 5 (continued)

# Contents

## Chapter 6

# Contents

# Chapter 6 (continued)

# Chapter 7

# Contents

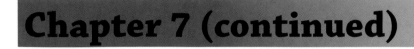

## Chapter 7 (continued)

## Chapter 8

### Articles 800-840 ..................................................................... 280
### Communications Systems

## Chapter 9

### Tables, Examples, Annexes ..................................................... 288

# Introduction

The *National Electrical Code®* (*NEC®*) is the most widely used electrical installation standard in the United States and North America. In fact, the *NEC* is being adopted more globally as electrical codes and standards evolve internationally. It is a living document, and is in a continuous state of evolution. As new technologies, equipment, wiring methods and industry needs evolve; the *NEC* must stay current to effectively address essential installation and safety requirements. An established three-year revision cycle effectively facilitates a dynamic and timely development process. The *NEC* is integral to the electrical business and used daily by electrical contractors, electricians, maintainers, inspectors, engineers and designers.

The *NEC* development process begins with submission of public proposals. There were 3,745 proposals submitted this cycle. The deadline for proposals to change the 2011 *NEC* was November 4, 2011. In January 2012 the technical committees met to act on all proposed revisions and new requirements. After the committee meetings and final balloting is complete the results are made publically available on the internet and in a printed document titled *National Electrical Code Committee Report on Proposals*. This document is more commonly known as the *ROP*. The public then has an opportunity to modify or reverse the actions initially taken by the technical committees by submitting public comments on any proposal(s). The comments were accepted up until October 17, 2012. There were 1,625 comments submitted this cycle. In December 2012 the technical committees met to act on all comments submitted. After the meetings and final balloting is complete on the comments, the results are made available to the public on the internet and in printed form in a document titled *National Electrical Code Committee Report on Comments*. This document is more commonly known as the *ROC*. Throughout this entire process, the *NEC* Correlating Committee reviews the work in the *ROP* and *ROC* stages to ensure that there were not conflicting actions between the work of the technical committees, and that all revisions conform to the *NEC Style Manual* and NFPA Regulations Governing Committee Projects. Once the *ROC* is published, there is a final opportunity to submit a notice of intent to make a motion (NITMAM) directed at any revision accepted during this process. Actions on these motions are made during the Technical Session at the NFPA annual meeting. The NFPA Standards Council reviews these motions and all that are in order become certified amending motions (CAMs). At the NFPA annual meeting, the work of the technical committees can be modified by such motions, if accepted. The NFPA annual meeting for the 2014 NEC was held in Chicago, IL in June 2013. Appeals can be submitted to the NFPA Standards Council from any individual or any organization. The Standards Council met in Boston in August 2013 to hear appeals. After appeals are heard and acted upon, the Standards Council issued the 2014 *NEC*.

This open consensus revision process provides all users of the *NEC* with an opportunity to mold the next edition through individual and organizational participation. As you read through these significant changes for the 2014 *NEC*, be sure to note your ideas for an improved *Code* and submit them as proposals for the next edition.

# About This Book

This text is written to inform electrical contractors, electricians, maintenance personnel, inspectors, engineers, and system designers of the most significant revisions and new requirements in the 2014 *National Electrical Code* (*NEC*). The coverage of each change provides readers with an authoritative review by providing insight and detailed information about the reasons for the changes and how these changes impact the industry and one's daily work and business operations. The information in this book is a must for active electrical contracting businesses that need to stay current on the installation requirements they manage every day. This textbook is used most effectively in conjunction with the actual 2014 *NEC* textbook.

# Features

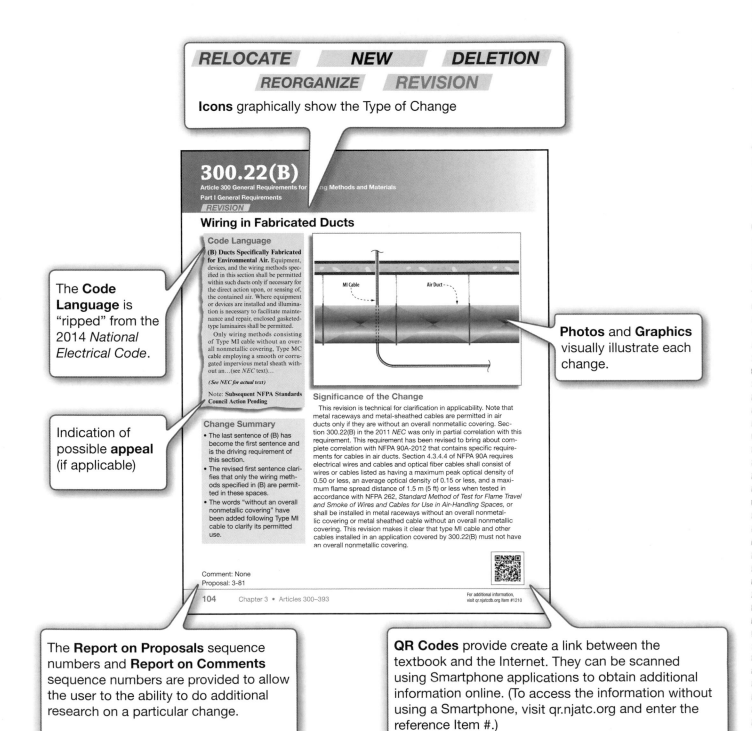

RELOCATE   NEW   DELETION
REORGANIZE   REVISION

**Icons** graphically show the Type of Change

## 300.22(B)
Article 300 General Requirements for [.....]ng Methods and Materials
Part I General Requirements
**REVISION**

### Wiring in Fabricated Ducts

#### Code Language

**(B) Ducts Specifically Fabricated for Environmental Air.** Equipment, devices, and the wiring methods specified in this section shall be permitted within such ducts only if necessary for the direct action upon, or sensing of, the contained air. Where equipment or devices are installed and illumination is necessary to facilitate maintenance and repair, enclosed gasketed-type luminaires shall be permitted.

Only wiring methods consisting of Type MI cable without an overall nonmetallic covering, Type MC cable employing a smooth or corrugated impervious metal sheath without an...(see *NEC* text)...

*(See NEC for actual text)*

Note: **Subsequent NFPA Standards Council Action Pending**

The **Code Language** is "ripped" from the 2014 *National Electrical Code*.

Indication of possible **appeal** (if applicable)

#### Change Summary

- The last sentence of (B) has become the first sentence and is the driving requirement of this section.
- The revised first sentence clarifies that only the wiring methods specified in (B) are permitted in these spaces.
- The words "without an overall nonmetallic covering" have been added following Type MI cable to clarify its permitted use.

MI Cable     Air Duct

**Photos** and **Graphics** visually illustrate each change.

#### Significance of the Change

This revision is technical for clarification in applicability. Note that metal raceways and metal-sheathed cables are permitted in air ducts only if they are without an overall nonmetallic covering. Section 300.22(B) in the 2011 *NEC* was only in partial correlation with this requirement. This requirement has been revised to bring about complete correlation with NFPA 90A-2012 that contains specific requirements for cables in air ducts. Section 4.3.4.4 of NFPA 90A requires electrical wires and cables and optical fiber cables shall consist of wires or cables listed as having a maximum peak optical density of 0.50 or less, an average optical density of 0.15 or less, and a maximum flame spread distance of 1.5 m (5 ft) or less when tested in accordance with NFPA 262, *Standard Method of Test for Flame Travel and Smoke of Wires and Cables for Use in Air-Handling Spaces*, or shall be installed in metal raceways without an overall nonmetallic covering or metal sheathed cable without an overall nonmetallic covering. This revision makes it clear that type MI cable and other cables installed in an application covered by 300.22(B) must not have an overall nonmetallic covering.

Comment: None
Proposal: 3-81

104   Chapter 3 • Articles 300–393

For additional information, visit qr.njatcdb.org Item #1210

The **Report on Proposals** sequence numbers and **Report on Comments** sequence numbers are provided to allow the user to the ability to do additional research on a particular change.

**QR Codes** provide create a link between the textbook and the Internet. They can be scanned using Smartphone applications to obtain additional information online. (To access the information without using a Smartphone, visit qr.njatc.org and enter the reference Item #.)

# Features

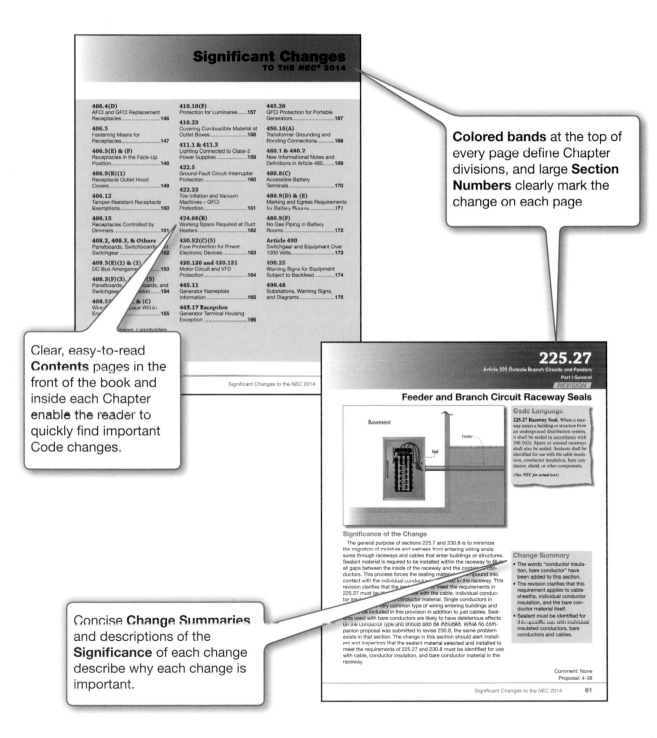

**Colored bands** at the top of every page define Chapter divisions, and large **Section Numbers** clearly mark the change on each page

Clear, easy-to-read **Contents** pages in the front of the book and inside each Chapter enable the reader to quickly find important Code changes.

Concise **Change Summaries** and descriptions of the **Significance** of each change describe why each change is important.

# Acknowledgments

**Michael J. Johnston,** NECA
**Joseph V. Sheehan,** NJATC

Bill McGovern, City of Plano, TX
Chris Bayer
Christopher Edwards, Illustrations
Cogburn Brothers, Inc.
Cooper Bussmann
Donald Cook/IAEI
Eaton Corporation
Eaton's Cooper-Bussmann
EMerge Alliance
ERICO International Corporation
EVSE, LLC
FRE Composites
General Electric, Industrial Solutions Business
General Cable
Harger Lightning and Grounding
Hubbell Incorporated.
Independence LED Lighting, LLC
International Association of Electrical Inspectors
John E. Kelly & Sons, Inc.

Leviton Mfg. Co.
Milbank, Kansas City, MO
National Electrical Contractors Association
NECA (iStock Photo & Rob Colgan)
Pass and Seymour Legrand
Panduit Corp.
PDE Total Energy Solutions
Rick Maddox, Clark County, NV
San Diego Electrical JATC
Schneider Electric USA, Inc.
Shermco Industries
Simplex Wire and Cable Co.
TE Connectivity Enterprises Network
Thomas & Betts
Tim Arendt
Tom Garvey
VITALink MC Cable by RSCC Wire & Cable LLC
Wirecon Division of Hubbell Incorporated
YESCO

# Contributing Writers

**Michael J. Johnston** is NECA's Executive Director of Standards and Safety. Prior to working with NECA, Mike worked for the International Association of Electrical Inspectors as the Director of Education, Codes and Standards. He also worked as an electrical inspector and electrical inspection field supervisor for the City of Phoenix, AZ and achieved all IAEI and ICC electrical inspector certifications. Mike achieved a BS in Business Management from the University of Phoenix. He served on *NEC* Code-Making Panel 5 in the 2002, 2005, 2008 cycles and has chaired the Code-Making Panel 5 representing NECA during the 2011 *NEC* cycle. He currently chairs the *NEC* Correlating Committee and serves on the NFPA *NEC* Smart Grid Task Force. He is also currently a member of *NEC* Code-Making Panel 1. Among his responsibilities for managing the codes, standards, and safety functions for NECA, Mike is secretary of the NECA Codes and Standards Committee. Mike has been a consistent contributor to the NJATC curriculum, authoring titles such as the *Health Care Systems, Hazardous Locations, Applied Grounding and Bonding,* and *Significant Changes to the NEC*. Mike is a member of the IBEW and has experience as an electrical journeyman wireman, foreman and project superintendant. He has achieved journeyman and master electrician licenses in multiple states. Johnston is an active member of IAEI, ICC, NFPA, ASSE, SES, the NFPA Electrical Section, Education Section, the UL Electrical Council, and National Safety Council.

**Joseph V. Sheehan,** NJATC

# 2014 NEC® Code-Wide Revisions

## Informational Note – Placement and Revisions

The *NEC* Correlating Committee activated the Usability Task Group to update the *NEC Style Manual* since the last update occurred in 2003. As a result, the technical committees were able to incorporate the latest style manual requirements into the 2014 *NEC* development process. As various task groups and work were being assigned, the Correlating Committee chair also directed each *NEC* panel chair to incorporate 2011 *NEC Style Manual* compliance in their editorial work. Section 3.1.3 of the revised *NEC Style Manual* requires informational notes to immediately follow the rule to which they apply. Informational notes cannot contain any requirements or mandatory text. If an informational note is needed to provide additional explanation or guidance for users, consideration should be given to incorporating it into the requirements. Each technical committee included this editorial work as part of their work on the 2014 *NEC*. As a result, many informational notes were relocated to follow the rule to which they applied. It was apparent that over the years, some informational notes (formerly Fine Print Notes) had shifted and were no longer immediately following the provision to which they applied. During the course of the process, many of the technical committees either deleted informational notes completely because they were no longer necessary, or incorporated them into the text of the *Code*. These *Code*-wide revisions were primarily editorial in nature and some even involved developing panel proposals to accomplish the assignment.

## Voltage Thresholds – Increased from 600 Volts to 1000 Volts

The *NEC* Correlating Committee reactivated the High Voltage Task Group for the 2014 *NEC* development process and provided a specific assignment to review the entire *NEC* and submit proposals that raise the 600-volt threshold to 1000 volts. The reason behind this global effort relates primarily to some output circuits from renewable energy sources often exceeding the 600-volt level. The problem is significant enough that the *NEC* Correlating Committee determined the need to consider proposing increasing the long-standing 600-volt threshold to 1000 volts, *Code* wide. The Task Group submitted proposals to each technical committee to consider and act on in the 2014 *NEC* development cycle. As these proposals were addressed by each committee, it became clear that many proposed revisions would have no impact, and were accepted. However, some technical committees determined these proposed changes would require substantial work that would require much more time and research to complete than the 2014 cycle would permit, accordingly they rejected the proposals. The result in the 2014 *NEC* is that in many rules, where the voltage level was previously 600 volts, it has been changed to 1000 volts. The *NEC* Correlating Committee understands that these revisions are necessary as the industry is evolving, however, concedes this project is extensive and will extend into the 2017 *NEC* cycle and perhaps beyond. The assigned High Voltage Task Group also continues to be active in incorporating many other new medium and high voltage requirements throughout the *NEC* to close gaps and incorporate adequate *NEC* provisions for those installations and systems that are no longer governed by the National Electrical Safety Code® (NESC®) or applicable Utility Regulations. Wiring and equipment installed on the line side of the service point is typically not covered by the *NEC*, while electrical installations on the load side of the service point are usually covered by the *NEC*.

## Switchgear Terminology *Code* Wide

The title of the definition of the term *Metal-Enclosed Switchgear* has been changed to simply *Switchgear* resulting in more expanded application of this term. The revised definition also allows for inclusion of the term *switchgear* in existing *NEC* rules that only include the term *switchboards*, but both types of equipment are covered by that requirement. The last sentence of the existing definition is more informative than descriptive and accordingly has been crafted into an informational note following this definition. All switchgear covered by the *NEC* rules is intended to be metal-enclosed types. As revised, the definition now applies to all switchgear types such as metal-clad switchgear, metal-enclosed switchgear, and low-voltage power circuit breaker switchgear as indicated in the new informational note. Action by CMP-9 on Proposal 9-104a results in a change in the title of Article 408 from Switchboards and Panelboards to Switchboards, Switchgear, and Panelboards and the scope was revised to include switchgear. Article 490 was also completely revised to incorporate the term *switchgear* in place of the term *metal-enclosed*

*Courtesy of Donald Cook/IAEI*

*switchgear*. Other *NEC* revisions have been made to replace the term *metal-enclosed switchgear* with *switchgear*. It should be noted that while the definition of switchgear is located in Article 100, CMP-9 maintains technical responsibility for this definition and its use through the *NEC*.

## Direct Current (dc) Rules in the NEC

Prior to the start of the 2014 *NEC* development process, a special Task Group was specifically assigned to review the existing direct current (dc) requirements in the 2011 *NEC* and identify any gaps in these requirements. The Task Group was also charged with developing recommendations and proposals for specific new *Code* requirements to fill any of those gaps or provide any needed revisions to existing requirements. The work of this group included researching a number of areas that may be in need of additional dc requirements, such as in Articles 240, 300, 410, 480, 645, 690, and 694. This *Code*-wide effort involved the participation of members from the appropriate *Code*-making panels. The work of this assigned Task Group resulted in revisions to existing dc requirements in the *Code* and various new rules where needs were identified. Examples include the new dc provisions in Article 408 and 480 and new Article 393 that covers low-voltage suspended ceiling power distribution systems and equipment that can be ac or dc. With the expanded use of dc power from renewable energy sources, and in efforts to reduce energy use and to address long-range smart grid initiatives, the *NEC* is expected to see continued expansion of dc wiring rules. Use and installation of dc microgrids is a good example of gaps that still need to be filled in the *NEC*. It is anticipated that the work of this dc Task Group will continue into to 2017 *NEC* development process.

### Article 393 Low Voltage Suspended Ceiling Power Distribution Systems [ROP 18-10a]

This new article covers the installation of low voltage suspended ceiling power distribution systems. These electrical systems also serve as structural supports for a finished ceiling surface. They consist of a busbar and busbar support system to distribute power to utilization equipment supplied by a Class 2 power supply. These systems operate at not more than 30 volts ac and not more than 60 volts dc and are required to be listed as a complete system that includes all associated fittings and required power supplies.

### Article 646 Modular Data Centers [ROP 12-147]

This new article covers modular data centers including the definition of, the nameplate data for, and the size and overcurrent protection of supply conductors to modular data centers. This article also covers the equipment, electrical supply and distribution, wiring and protection, working space, grounding, HVAC and the like, located in or associated with a modular data center.

### Article 728 Fire Resistive Cable Systems [ROP 3-170]

This new article covers the installation of fire resistive cables, conductors and other system components used for survivability of critical circuits to ensure continued operation during a specified time under fire conditions as required in this *Code* and in other NFPA Standards. Fire resistive cables, conductors and components are tested as a complete system. These systems shall be listed and are not limited to low-voltage systems. The cables, conductors and components are designated for use in a specific system and shall not be interchanged between systems. Cables, conductors and components shall be suitable for use in accordance with the wiring methods described in the *NEC*.

### Article 750 Energy Management Systems [ROP 13-180]

This new article applies to the installation and operation of energy management systems. Performance provisions related to energy management and conservation in other codes, such as energy codes developed by other model code groups, establish prescriptive requirements that may further restrict the requirements contained in this article. The *NEC* provides users with a baseline that establishes general requirements for energy management systems and provides a list of loads that should not be controlled by energy management systems.

### Annex J ADA Standards for Accessible Design [ROP 1-191]

Informative Annex J is new and titled ADA Standards for Accessible Design. This informative annex is not a part of the requirements of the *NEC*, but is included for informational purposes only. The provisions cited in this Informative Annex are to assist the users of the *Code* in properly considering various electrical design constraints of other building systems and are part of the 2010 *ADA Standards for Accessible Design* and are the same as those found in ANSI/ICC A117.1-2009, *Accessible and Usable Buildings and Facilities*.

# Chapter 1

## Articles 90, 100, and 110
### Introduction, Definitions, and Requirements for Electrical Installations

# Significant

**REVISION** | **RELOCATE**

# Practical Safeguarding and Purpose of the *Code*

## Code Language

**(A) Practical Safeguarding.** The purpose of this Code is the practical safeguarding of persons and property from hazards arising from the use of electricity. This Code is not intended as a design specification or an instruction manual for untrained persons.

*(See NEC for actual text)*

*Courtesy of NECA*

## Change Summary

- Section 90.1(C) has been deleted and the text has been relocated as a second sentence in 90.1(A).
- The purpose of the *Code* is now consolidated into a single paragraph that indicates both its purpose and limitations of its use and intent.
- The revision corrects the inconsistent context in former subdivision (C).

## Significance of the Change

This is an editorial change only. Former subdivision (C) in 90.1 was titled Intent yet the sentence included in this subdivision essentially had nothing to do with the intent of the *Code*. Instead this section described how the *Code* was not intended to be used and applied. This revision removes the inconsistency between the title of subdivision (C) and the contained text removing the negative context that did not explain anything about the intent of the *NEC*. The title of subdivision (A) remains as Practical Safeguarding and continues to allow for broad and expanded text that also describes the purpose of the *Code*, which has not been changed, and still provides limitations on *NEC* application relative to design specification use and use as a training program or manual for untrained persons. Clearly the *Code* is not intended to be used as a design specification however electrical designs and engineering generally use the *NEC* rules as the minimum when developing designs for electrical systems and installations. While the *Code* is used as the basis for various *NEC*-based training materials, it is incomplete relative to comprehensive training for electrical workers that builds all the necessary electrical trade qualifications and skills.

Comment: 1-1
Proposal: 1-3

# Number of Circuits in Enclosures

*Courtesy of Tom Garvey*

## Code Language

**(B) Number of Circuits in Enclosures.** It is elsewhere provided in this *Code* that the number of wires and circuits confined in a single enclosure be varyingly restricted. Limiting the number of circuits in a single enclosure minimizes the effects from a short circuit or ground fault.

*(See NEC for actual text)*

## Significance of the Change

This section provides users with an indication that various rules throughout the *NEC* limit the number of circuits and conductors (wires) in raceways, boxes, or other enclosures. The second sentence is more advisory in that the effects of down time and damage can be minimized by limiting the quantities of wires and circuits in the same enclosure. This also reduces heating effects and eases installation process and provides for better workmanship. The revised second sentence provides a clarification about ground-fault and short circuit events not being limited to just one circuit. The previous text in this section indicated that this type of fault was limited to only one circuit, which was never the intent. These types of events could happen to more than one circuit in the same enclosure and could also occur simultaneously or as the result of one such occurrence that causes damage to other circuits and circuit failure. As revised, the section now aligns with how electrical circuits are actually installed in the field, but continues to advise users about minimizing the consequences of ground-faults or short circuit events that could happen to one or more circuits installed in the same enclosure.

## Change Summary

- This section has been revised editorially with technical meaning.
- The words "in one circuit" have been deleted from the second sentence.
- The revision clarifies that limiting the number of circuits in enclosures minimizes the effects of ground-fault or short circuit event(s) that could occur in one or multiple circuits contained in that enclosure.

Comment: None
Proposal: 1-19

# Definition of Accessible, Readily

## Code Language

**Accessible, Readily (Readily Accessible).** Capable of being reached quickly for operation, renewal, or inspections without requiring those to whom ready access is requisite to actions such as to use tools, to climb over or remove obstacles, or to resort to portable ladders, and so forth.

*(See NEC for actual text)*

## Change Summary

- This definition clarifies what constitutes *readily accessible* for operation, renewal, or inspection.
- This definition has been revised by adding the words "to actions such as" and "to use tools."
- The revision clarifies that use of tools to render access is not *readily accessible* condition, but can only be considered and qualify as *accessible*, by definition.

## Significance of the Change

Three levels of accessibility are defined in Article 100: accessible pertaining to equipment, accessible pertaining to wiring methods and the most restrictive, readily accessible. This definition has been revised to provide clarification about what constitutes a condition that qualifies as readily accessible. The existing definition indicated that readily accessible was capable of being reached quickly for operation, such as in the case of a required disconnecting means, circuit breaker, and so forth. Information in the substantiation indicated that some integral disconnecting means provided with equipment, such as HVAC units, may have to be accessed by use of a screw driver or other tool(s). This additional action to gain access does not constitute a condition that qualifies as readily accessible, even though the requirements in 440.14 specifically call for the required disconnect to be within sight from and *readily accessible* from the air-conditioning or refrigerating equipment. Where *NEC* rules require ready access, tools cannot be used to accomplish such access because use of a tool is an additional action that would impede or delay the necessary ready access intended. The revised definition should help users and enforcement more effectively and accurately apply the various *NEC* requirements that include the term *readily accessible*.

Comment: 1-13

Proposal: 1-24

**RELOCATE | REVISION**

# Adjustable Speed Drive/Adjustable Speed Drive System

*Courtesy of Bill McGovern/City of Plano, TX*

## Code Language

**Adjustable Speed Drive.** Power conversion equipment that provides a means of adjusting the speed of an electric motor.

Informational Note: A variable frequency drive is one type of electronic adjustable speed drive that controls the rotational speed of an ac electric motor by controlling the frequency and voltage of the electrical power supplied to the motor.

**Adjustable Speed Drive System.** A combination of an adjustable speed drive, its associated motor(s), and auxiliary equipment.

*(See NEC for actual text)*

## Significance of the Change

Panel action on Proposal 11-75 resulted in revisions to the existing 430.2 definitions of the terms *adjustable speed drive* and *adjustable speed drive system* for clarity and completeness. The second part of this revision involves relocating both definitions to Part I of Article 100. The original proposal was to include (duplicate) the 430.2 definitions of these terms in 440.2. These terms are used in both article 440 and 430 and other locations in the *Code* such as 110.28. Section 2.2.2.1 of the *NEC Style Manual* generally requires that Article 100 contain definitions of terms that appear in more than one article. The revisions to each definition actually simplify the meaning and broaden them for more global application where the terms are used throughout the *NEC*. The new informational note following the definition of *adjustable speed drive* clarifies that variable frequency drives (VFDs) are a type of electronic equipment that adjusts the motor rotational speed controlling the frequency and voltage of the motor supply circuit. The difference between these two definitions is that one describes just the drive itself and the other describes a system that includes a drive unit, the motor and any accessory or auxiliary equipment necessary for operation.

## Change Summary

- Definitions of the terms *adjustable speed drive* and *adjustable speed drive system* have been relocated to Article 100.

- A new informational note describing a variable frequency drive (VFD) has been added following the definition of *adjustable speed drive*.

- The revisions clarify and simplify the definitions and the relocation complies with the *NEC Style Manual*.

Comment: 11-1
Proposal: 11-75

**RELOCATE** / **REVISION**

# Cable Routing Assembly Usage Expanded

## Code Language

**Cable Routing Assembly.** A single channel or connected multiple channels, as well as associated fittings, forming a structural system that is used to support and route communications wires and cables, optical fiber cables, data cables associated with information technology and communications equipment, Class 2 and Class 3 cables, and power-limited fire alarm cables.

*(See NEC for actual text)*

## Change Summary

- The definition of *Cable Routing Assembly* was expanded and moved from Article 770 to Article 100.
- Moving this definition from Article 770 to Article 100 now permits the definition to apply to Article 90 and Chapters 1 through 8.
- The usage of the word "channel" within the definition differentiates this routing assembly from cable tray.

*Courtesy of Panduit Corp.*

## Significance of the Change

According to the 2011 *NEC Style Manual*, 2.2.2.1, Article 100 contains definitions of terms that appear in two or more other articles of the *NEC*. Since 90.3 refers to *NEC* requirements, and definitions are not requirements of the *NEC*, the definitions of Article 100 apply generally to all chapters, articles and annexes throughout the *NEC*, unless specifically amended elsewhere. The original definition was located in 770.2 For the 2014 *NEC*, specific requirements for cable routing assemblies were added or modified in Articles 725, 760, 770, and 800. As a result of this expansion, the revised definition was moved from 770 to Article 100 to comply with the *NEC Style Manual*.

Cable routing assemblies used for general purpose must be resistant to the spread of fire and if used in risers, they must have adequate fire-resistant characteristics capable of preventing the carrying of fire from floor to floor. And, if they are used in plenum applications, the cable routing assembly must have adequate fire-resistant and low smoke-producing characteristics. Each of these particular assemblies must pass the appropriate requirement(s) within UL 2024, *Signaling, Optical Fiber and Communications Raceways and Cable Routing Assemblies* and must be listed.

Comment: 16-5
Proposal: 16-23

# Definition of Charge Controller and Other Definitions

Courtesy of PDE Total Energy Solutions

## Code Language

**Charge Controller.** Equipment that control dc voltage or dc current, or both, and that is used to charge a battery or other energy storage device.

*(See NEC for actual text)*

Note: Other definitions relocated to Article 100.

## Significance of the Change

The definition has been revised by combining the 690.2 and 694.2 definition of the same term. The definition in 690 addressed a charge controller for a battery while the definition in 694 addressed both a battery and other storage devices. Combining the two definitions results in more broad meaning of the same term that can be applied to the term as used in multiple *NEC* articles. The definition of the term *charge controller* is also one of several existing definitions that have been relocated to Article 100 to comply with the *NEC Style Manual*. Section 2.2.2.1 of the *NEC Style Manual* generally requires that Article 100 contain definitions of terms that appear in more than one article. Action by several Code-Making panels results in defined terms formerly located in the .2 section of the respective articles are now located in Article 100. It should be noted that while these definitions have been relocated to Article 100, the responsibility for revisions to these terms remains with the applicable assigned *NEC* committee. The following are examples of relocated definitions:

Adjustable Speed Drive [ROP 11-75]

Adjustable Speed Drive System [ROP 11-75]

Ground Fault Current Path [ROP 5-13]

Hermetic Refrigerant Motor Compressor [ROP 11-6]

Industrial Control Panel [ROP 11-7]

Substation [ROP 4-10]

## Change Summary

- The definitions of *charge controller* in Articles 690 and 694 have been combined into a single definition.
- The combined definition as revised has been relocated to Article 100 to comply with the *NEC Style Manual*.
- The revised definition has broadened its application to all *NEC* rules where the term is used.

Comment: None
Proposal: 4-4

# Use of Communications Raceway Expanded

## Code Language

**Communications Raceway.** An enclosed channel of nonmetallic materials designed expressly for holding communications wires and cables, typically communications wires and cables and optical fiber and data (Class 2 and Class 3) in plenum, riser, and general-purpose applications.

*(See NEC for actual text)*

## Change Summary

- For the 2014 *NEC*, the definition of *communications raceway* was revised and expanded to include CATV and optical fiber cables.
- Since the definition now permits the use of both Chapter 7 and 8 cables, the definition was moved into Article 100.
- Listed communications raceways are available as general-purpose, riser and plenum raceways.

## Significance of the Change

For the 2014 *NEC* cycle, CMP-16 submitted a group of coordinated proposals to align definitions and requirements within Chapter 8. Some Chapter 8 definitions were expanded for use in other chapters. The definition of *communications raceways* was expanded beyond communications cables and now, as a raceway, is permitted to carry cables other than communications cables including optical fiber cables, CATV, Class 2 and 3 data cables. The definition was revised to mention these items. Since the installation of these cables is now covered by both Chapter 8 Communications and Chapter 7 Special Conditions, the definition had to be moved from Chapter 8 to Chapter 1, Article 100 according to the *NEC Style Manual*. Interestingly, the word "expressly" was added to this definition to correlate with the general definition of *raceway* from Part I of Article 100. This revised text illustrates the types of wires and cables that may be used within communications raceway without placing requirements within a definition.

Comment: 16-8

Proposal: 16-85

# Definition of Control Circuit

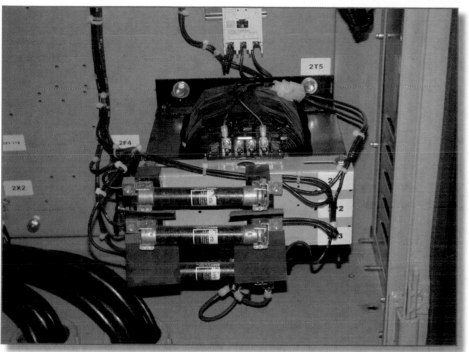

## Code Language

**Control Circuit.** The circuit of a control apparatus or system that carries the electric signals directing the performance of the controller but does not carry the main power current.

*(See NEC for actual text)*

## Significance of the Change

Section 2.2.2.1 of the *NEC Style Manual* requires that Article 100 generally contain definitions of terms that appear in more than one article. Action by CMP-11 relocates the defined term *motor control circuit* from 430.2 to Article 100. The word *motor* has been removed from the definition expanding the application of this defined term beyond just Article 430. The key features of this definition are that these circuits only direct the performance of the controller to which they are connected. As defined, control circuits do not make and break the power circuit. One example of a control circuit used for other than motor control is a thermostat that controls fixed electric space heating units covered in Article 424. In many cases the thermostat directs the performance of a contactor that controls the power to the heating load. Article 725 provides requirements for Class 1, 2, and Class 3 remote-control, signaling, and power-limited circuits. Control or signaling circuits can be those covered in Article 725 and those covered by other *NEC* articles. To correlate and avoid duplication of the same defined term, action by CMP-11 on Proposal 11-5 removes the definition of control circuit from 409.2.

## Change Summary

- The definition of the term *motor control circuit* has been relocated to Part I of Article 100.
- The word "motor" has been removed from the term *motor control circuit*.
- Control circuit is now defined in Article 100 and applies to *NEC* rules containing the term *control circuit*.

Comment: None
Proposals: 11-8, 11-5

# Definition of Coordination, Selective

## Code Language

**Coordination (Selective).** Localization of an overcurrent condition to restrict outages to the circuit or equipment affected, accomplished by the selection and installation of overcurrent protective devices and their ratings or settings for the full range of available overcurrents, from overload to the maximum available fault current, and for the full range of overcurrent protective device opening times associated with those overcurrents.

*(See NEC for actual text)*

## Change Summary

- The definition has been revised to clarify what constitutes *selective coordination*.

- The word "choice" has been replaced by the words "selection and installation" to clarify it is selection and installation of overcurrent protection that achieves selective coordination.

- As revised, this definition makes it clear that selective coordination is across the "full range" of available overcurrents.

## Significance of the Change

The revisions to this definition were made only to clarify the meaning of this term, not to change the meaning at all. The word "choice" has been replaced by the words "selection and installation" basically because it is not a choice that achieves the selectivity required, but rather the installation. Information provided in the substantiation indicated that there has been some confusion, primarily initiated by those opposed to full selective coordination. As revised, it is clear that where the term selective coordination is used within *NEC* requirements, it is intended to mean full selectivity across the full range of overcurrent protection applied in the system. The idea is to localize offending faults to the lowest level, especially in systems that require greater continuity of service and reliability, such as essential systems, crritical operations power, and emergency systems. The *NEC* remains the principal document where the term selective coordination was originally defined and related rules were initially developed. This is an electrical system safety issue, and while the existing definition served the industry well for years, it became clear that was necessary to clarify the definition reflect what was always intended by the term *selective coordination* as it appears in *NEC* rules.

Comment: 10-2

Proposal: 10-5

# Definition of Device

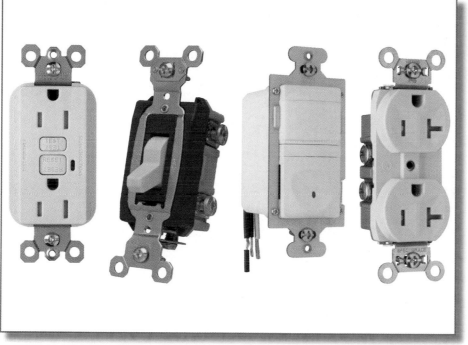

*Courtesy of Pass and Seymour Legrand*

## Code Language

**Device.** A unit of an electrical system, other than a conductor, that carries or controls electric energy as its principal function.

*(See NEC for actual text)*

## Significance of the Change

The definition of the term *device* has been revised by adding the words "other than a conductor" after the word "system." This revised definition provides a clear differentiation between what constitutes a device and what is considered a conductor. Information in the substantiation indicated that several *Code* rules refer to devices and conductors and that the existing definition of device could be interpreted as including conductors. Electrical devices such as switches, receptacles, and so forth include conductive materials that serve as a conductive path through the device, but devices are not conductors as the *NEC* refers to conductors. Three forms of conductors are addressed in the *NEC* and are defined in Article 100; they are bare, covered, or insulated conductors. These definitions do not include electrical devices. Electrical devices are manufactured to meet product safety standards and provided with electrical current ratings and conductive terminals or leads to which electrical conductors (usually wire type) are connected. The ampacity of conductors on the other hand, are determined by application of *NEC* requirements, specifically in Article 310. The revised definition provides a distinction between electrical devices and electrical conductors promoting more consistent application and enforcement of *Code* rules that include these terms.

## Change Summary

- The words "other than a conductor" have been added to the definition of the term *device*.
- Devices carry current through a conductive component of the device, not a conductor.
- Ratings of devices are determined from product standards while the *NEC* covers conductor ampacity.

Comment: None
Proposal: 1-31a

# Definition of Effective Ground-Fault Current Path

## Code Language

**Effective Ground-Fault Current Path.** An intentionally constructed, low-impedance electrically conductive path designed and intended to carry current under ground-fault conditions from the point of a ground fault on a wiring system to the electrical supply source and that facilitates the operation of the overcurrent protective device or ground-fault detectors.

*(See NEC for actual text)*

## Change Summary

- The definition of *Effective Ground-Fault Current Path* has been relocated to Part I of Article 100.
- The definition has been revised by removing the words "on high-impedance grounded systems."
- The effective ground-fault current path facilitates ground-fault detector operation on high-impedance grounded systems and other systems such as ungrounded systems.

## Significance of the Change

Section 2.2.2.1 of the *NEC Style Manual* requires that Article 100 generally contain definitions of terms that appear in more than one article. While the term is used most often in Article 250, it is also used in a few other articles of the *NEC*. Action by CMP-5 on Proposal 5-6 relocates the defined term *effective ground-fault current path* from 250.2 to Part I of Article 100. The words "on high-impedance grounded systems" have also been removed from the definition resulting from a Panel 5 action on Proposal 5-46. This revision clarifies that ground detection systems are required on more than just high-impedance grounded systems as covered in 250.36. Ground detection systems are also required on ungrounded systems as provided in 250.21. The previous definition could have been interpreted that ground detection systems were only required on high-impedance grounded systems, even though definitions cannot include requirements, but rather descriptions. The revision to this definition clarifies that the effective ground-fault current path functions to facilitate both overcurrent protective devices and required ground detection systems during a ground fault event.

Comment: 5-3
Proposals: 5-6, 5-7, 5-46

# Definition of Grounding Conductor, Equipment (EGC)

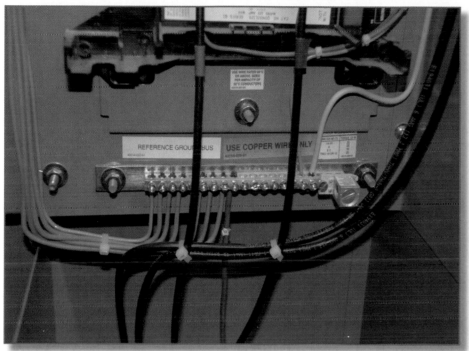

## Code Language

**Grounding Conductor, Equipment (EGC).** The conductive path(s) that provides a ground-fault current path and connects normally non-current-carrying metal parts of equipment together and to the system grounded conductor or to the grounding electrode conductor, or both.

*(See NEC for actual text)*

## Significance of the Change

This revision provides a more complete description of the functional aspects of the equipment grounding conductor (EGC). Essentially, equipment grounding conductors perform three functions in the grounding and bonding schemes. First, they perform grounding functions. In other words, when an equipment grounding conductor is connected to equipment, the equipment becomes grounded. When installing equipment grounding conductors, they connect normally non-current-carrying parts together which is performing bonding functions. The revision adds the third performance function into the definition which is to provide an effective ground-fault current path to facilitate overcurrent device operation during ground fault events that may occur. Several acceptable equipment grounding conductors are recognized in 250.118. Each must be able to perform all of the functions described in the definition as revised. Although the term *bonding* is not included in the definition, bonding functions are integral to the equipment grounding conductor by means of its use in connecting parts together. Informational Note No. 1 following the definition is clear that equipment grounding conductors are recognized as performing bonding functions, in addition to grounding functions. This revision, although relatively minor, provides additional clarification about the performance aspects of the equipment grounding conductors installed in electrical systems.

## Change Summary

- The definition has been revised by adding the words "provides a ground-fault path and."
- The revision clarifies additional performance functions provided by the EGC.
- The EGC provides a connection to ground for equipment, connects equipment together, and provides an effective ground-fault current path.

Comment: None
Proposal: 5-14a

# Definition of Premises Wiring (System)

## Code Language

**Premises Wiring (System).** Interior and exterior wiring, including power, lighting, control, and signal circuit wiring together with all their associated hardware, fittings, and wiring devices, both permanently and temporarily installed. This includes…(See *NEC* for full text)

Informational Note: Power sources include, but are not limited to, interconnected or stand-alone batteries, solar photovoltaic systems, other distributed generation systems, or generators.

*(See NEC for actual text)*

## Change Summary

- A new informational note has been added to the definition of *Premises Wiring (System)*.
- No changes have been made to the definition itself and it continues to address permanently and temporarily installed wiring.
- The new informational note provides some examples of what constitutes premises wiring systems (sources) and is non-inclusive.

## Significance of the Change

The new informational note following the definition of *Premises Wiring (System)* provides clarification as to what qualifies as premises wiring. Information in the substantiation indicated that some contend stand-alone generators, including portable generators, are not considered premises wiring. It really depends how the generator is connected to the premises wiring systems and if a generator is used in a manner covered by *NEC* rules. The definition clearly addresses all interior and exterior wiring "both permanently and temporarily installed." Portable generators are not installed, they are utilized. Issues clarified by this are if a portable generator connects to the permanent or temporarily installed wiring, then the applicable *NEC* requirements apply. First, generators are manufactured to applicable product safety standards that include installation and use instructions. The second issue relates to how and if a generator is connected to the premises wiring system. If connected to the premises wiring system through suitable transfer equipment, *NEC* requirements apply. If portable generators are used for connection of cord- and plug-connected equipment and temporary use, then only the provided *NEC* requirements for portable generators apply. Examples of generators used as premises wiring covered by the *NEC* are provided in 250.34, 590.6(A) and 702.5 and 702.11.

Comment: None

Proposal: 1-61

# Definition of Retrofit Kit

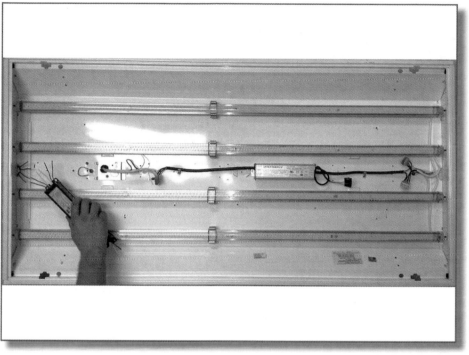

*Courtesy of Independence LED Lighting, LLC*

### Code Language

**Retrofit Kit.** A general term for a complete subassembly of parts and devices for field conversion of utilization equipment.

*(See NEC for actual text)*

## Significance of the Change

A new definition *Retrofit Kit* has been added to Article 100. New provisions have been added to Articles 410 and 600 that use this new term. Section 2.2.2.1 of the *NEC Style Manual* requires that Article 100 generally contain definitions of terms that appear in more than one article. The new definition is necessary and applies to equipment being commonly used to update lighting and sign systems for energy efficiency purposes. A common form of retrofit is changing a conventional fluorescent luminaire to a luminaire that incorporates LED technology. This involves use of a listed kit that replaces the fluorescent tubes and ballast(s) with LEDs and associated power supplies. The new definition provides correlation with the new *NEC* rules in Article 410 and 600 that specify use of listed retrofit kits for such conversions. One important aspect of the revised rules addressing retrofit kits is that these kits be listed subassemblies. This aligns with the product safety standards that have been developed for manufacturing lighting and sign retrofit kits. The new definition clearly describes what a retrofit kit is and the *NEC* requirements that address them require that they be listed which assists both installers and enforcement.

### Change Summary

- A new definition of *Retrofit Kit* has been added to Part I of Article 100.

- There are new requirements added to Articles 410 and 600 that include the term *Retrofit Kit*.

- The definition clarifies what constitutes a retrofit kit for use in electrical signs and luminaires.

Comment: 18-4
Proposal: 18-9

# Definition of Separately Derived System

## Code Language

**Separately Derived System.** An electrical source, other than a service, having no direct connection(s) to circuit conductors of any other electrical source other than those established by grounding and bonding connections.

*(See NEC for actual text)*

## Change Summary

- The definition has been revised by combining two sentences into one.
- Separately derived systems are electrical sources other than the electrical service.
- The revised definition clarifies that there is no direct connection to circuit conductors of any other electrical source other than those established by grounding and bonding connections.

## Significance of the Change

Separately derived systems are common in premises wiring and come in various forms such as batteries, photovoltaic systems, wind turbines, generators, and transformers. Action by CMP-5 simplifies the definition of separately derived system into a single sentence that includes the concepts previously addressed using two sentences. The previous definition addressed separate aspects of what constitutes a separately derived system in two sentences. Sentence one dealt with these systems being a source of energy supplied from other than a service. The second sentence addressed the concept of no direct connections between the circuit conductors of one system to another, other than those established through required grounding and bonding. Whether a separately derived system is required to be grounded, or permitted to be grounded is determined from the provisions in 250.20 and 250.21 respectively. If grounded, the system must comply with 250.30(A). Section 250.30(A) provides necessary details about required grounding and bonding connections that sometimes establish a connection between the circuit conductors of another system, especially if the system (source) is a transformer with a primary (input) and secondary (output) that is grounded. The revised definition takes a simplified approach and just describes a separately derived system enhancing clarity and usability.

Comment: 5-6

Proposal: 5-20

RELOCATE / REVISION

# Definition of Substation

iStock Photo Courtesy of NECA

## Code Language

**Substation.** An enclosed assemblage of equipment (e.g., switches, interrupting devices, circuit breakers, buses, and transformers) through which electric energy is passed for the purpose of distribution, switching, or modifying its characteristics.

*(See NEC for actual text)*

## Significance of the Change

There are requirements in the *NEC* other than in Article 225 that use the term *substation* such as Article 250 and Article 490. Section 2.2.2.1 of the *NEC Style Manual* requires that Article 100 generally contain definitions of terms that appear in more than one article. The *NEC Style Manual* also prohibits requirements from being included within definitions. The words "under the control of qualified persons" clearly provide a requirement within this definition and accordingly have been removed as part of this change in the *NEC*. The requirements for substations being under the control of qualified persons are appropriated for rules for substations other than the definition. A significant part of this change is that the definition now addresses indoor and outdoor substations. Previously, because it was included in 225.2 only, it applied to substations outdoors, since Article 225 applied only to outside branch circuits and feeders. As defined, the term appears to apply to both indoor and outdoor constructed substations as well as unit substation installations. Use and installation of listed unit substations are covered in the *UL Guide Information for Electrical Equipment (White Book)* under categories YEFR (600 volt or less) and YEFV (over 600 volts).

## Change Summary

- The definition of the term *substation* has been relocated from 225.2 to Part I of Article 100.
- This definition has been revised by removing the words "under the control of qualified persons" to comply with the *NEC Style Manual*.
- The definition now applies throughout the *NEC* where rules include the term *substation*.

Comments: 9-5, 9-6
Proposals: 9-8a, 4-9, 4-10

**NEW** / **REVISION**

# Definition of Switchgear

## Code Language

**Switchgear.** An assembly completely enclosed on all sides and top with sheet metal (except for ventilating openings and inspection windows) and containing primary power circuit switching, interrupting devices, or both, with buses and connections. The assembly may include control and auxiliary devices. Access to the interior of the enclosure is provided by doors, removable covers, or both.

Informational Note: All switchgear subject to *NEC* requirements is metal enclosed. Switchgear rated 1000 V or less may be identified as "low-voltage power circuit breaker switchgear." Switchgear rated over 1000 V may be identified as "metal-enclosed switchgear" or "metal-clad switchgear." Switchgear is available in non–arc-resistant or arc-resistant constructions.

*(See NEC for actual text)*

## Change Summary

- The definition of *Metal-Enclosed Power Switchgear* has been revised by changing the title to Switchgear and removing that word from the first sentence.
- The last sentence of the existing definition has been relocated in the new informational note.
- The informational note provides information about identification for switchgear rated 1000 volts and below.

## Significance of the Change

The definition of *Metal-Enclosed Power Switchgear* has been revised and broadened to cover all types of switchgear covered by the *NEC*. The title of the definition is changed to simply Switchgear which results in more expanded application of this term. The revised definition also provided opportunities for inclusion of the term *switchgear* in existing rules that previously only included the term switchboards, but both types of equipment are covered in that requirement. Action by CMP-9 on Proposal 9-104a results in a change in the title of Article 408 from Switchboards and Panelboards to Switchboards, Switchgear, and Panelboards and the scope was revised to include switchgear. The last sentence of the existing definition was more informative than descriptive and accordingly is more appropriate as an informational note to this definition. All switchgear covered by the *NEC* rules are intended to be metal-enclosed types. The revisions expand the definition to apply to all switchgear types such as metal-clad switchgear, metal-enclosed switchgear, and low-voltage power circuit breaker switchgear as indicated in the new informational note. It should be noted that while the definition of *switchgear* is located in Article 100, CMP-9 maintains technical responsibility for this definition.

Comments: 9-2, 9-3
Proposals: 9-7, 9-104a

For additional information, visit qr.njatcdb.org Item #1206

# Equipment Interrupting Ratings

## Code Language

**110.9 Interrupting Rating.** Equipment intended to interrupt current at fault levels shall have an interrupting rating at nominal circuit voltage sufficient for the current that is available at the line terminals of the equipment. Equipment intended to interrupt current at other than fault levels shall have an interrupting rating at nominal circuit voltage sufficient for the current that must be interrupted.

*(See NEC for actual text)*

## Significance of the Change

During extended discussions in the proposal stage of the process CMP-1 discussed the option of revising 110.9 to improve clarity. After meaningful input by multiple panel members, it was clear that the rule could use an editorial revision for improvement. Action by CMP-1 resulted in the development of a panel proposal that addressed the concerns expressed during the meeting. The result is a revision that reverts back to the text of 110.9 used in the 2008 edition with minor editorial revisions. The concept of "ratings not less than the nominal voltage" has been replaced with "ratings at nominal circuit voltage." As revised, both sentences in the rule now include this language. As a result, equipment must have an interrupting rating at nominal circuit voltage sufficient for the current that is available at the line terminals and equipment intended to interrupt current at other than fault levels must have an interrupting rating at nominal circuit voltage sufficient for the current that must be interrupted. For example, if 65,000 amperes of available fault current is available at the line terminals of a 208Y/120-volt, 3-phase, 4-wire service, the equipment must have a 65K AIC rating at the nominal circuit voltage of 208Y/120 volts.

## Change Summary

- This editorial revision is intended to improve clarity and usability of this requirement.
- This section essentially reverts back to the 2008 language by replacing "ratings not less than the nominal voltage" with "ratings at nominal circuit voltage."
- The section has also been revised to incorporate a parallel structure between the two sentences in the rule.

Comments: 1-36, 1-37

Proposal: 1-85a

# Arc-Flash Hazard Warning

## Code Language

**110.16 Arc-Flash Hazard Warning.** Electrical equipment, such as switchboards, switchgear, panelboards, industrial control panels, meter socket enclosures, and motor control centers, that are in other than dwelling units, and are likely to require examination, adjustment, servicing, or maintenance while energized, shall be field or factory marked to warn qualified persons of potential electric arc flash hazards. The marking shall meet the requirements in 110.21(B) and shall be located so as to be clearly visible to qualified persons before examination, adjustment, servicing, or maintenance of the equipment.

Informational Note No. 1: NFPA 70E-2012 provides...practices, arc flash labeling, and selecting personal protective equipment.

Informational Note No. 2: ANSI Z535.4-1998, *Product Safety Signs and Labels,* provides guidelines for the design of safety signs and labels for application to products.

*(See NEC for actual text)*

## Change Summary

- The revision clarifies that the marking applies also to switchgear and it can be either field applied or applied at the factory.
- The words "meet the requirements in 110.21(B) and" have been added in the second sentence.
- Informational Note No. 1 has been revised to include the words "arc flash labeling."

Comments: 1-47, 1-52, 1-53, 1-54, 1-56

Proposals: 1-102, 1-105, 1-107, 1-109, 9-14a

*Courtesy of Tom Garvey*

## Significance of the Change

This section has been revised and its application broadened to include switchgear in the requirements and to incorporate language that allows the warning marks to be applied either in the field or by the manufacturer at the factory. Prior to the 2014 *NEC*, the markings required by this section were required to be field applied. Although not a requirement, some manufacturers have been including multiple hazard markings including arc-flash hazard warnings that conform to the ANSI Z535.4 standard. This section has also been revised to include additional requirements for arc-flash hazard markings or labels by referencing a new section 110.21(B). New subdivision (B) in 110.21 includes specific requirements for caution, danger, and warning markings and provides an important reference to ANSI Z535.4 *Product Safety Signs and Labels*. Action on Proposal 1-109 results in a revision to Informational Note No. 1 to include the words "arc-flash labeling." This is significant and necessary due the expansion of information on arc-flash hazard warning labels required by NFPA 70E-2012 *Standard for Electrical Safety in the Workplace*. Section 130.5(C) of NFPA 70E provides specific requirements for information that should be included on the equipment labels.

# Field-Applied Hazard Markings and Labels

Field-Applied Hazard Warning requirements have been added in 110.21(B).

Applies where the signal words "danger", "warning", or "caution" are used in NEC rules.

New informational notes refer to ANSI Z535.4 for marking or label development criteria.

Note: The signal word communicates the degree of hazard. The other label components provide the specific hazard, instructions, and could also include a graphic (See ANSI Z535.4-2011).

## Code Language (in part)

**(A) Manufacturer's Markings.**

**(B) Field-Applied Hazard Markings.** Where caution, warning, or danger signs or labels are required by this *Code,* the labels shall meet the following requirements:

(1) The marking shall adequately warn of the hazard using effective words and/or colors and/or symbols.

...(See *NEC* text)...

(2) The label shall be permanently affixed to the equipment or wiring method and shall not be hand written.

*Exception: Portions of labels or markings that are variable, or that could be subject to changes, shall be permitted to be hand written and shall be legible.*

(3) The label shall be of sufficient durability to withstand the environment involved.

Informational Note: ANSI Z535.4-2011, *Product Safety Signs and Labels,* provides guidelines for the design and durability of safety signs and labels for application to electrical equipment.

*(See NEC for actual text)*

## Significance of the Change

The existing text of 110.21 is retained in subdivision (A) and is titled Manufacturers Marking. A new subdivision (B) is added and is titled Field-Applied Hazard Markings. The new rules for field-applied markings require effective and consistent hazard warnings using appropriate colors, words, or symbols. These markings are generally not permitted to be hand written, with an exception for portions of the markings or labels that are variable or subject to change such as those required by 110.24 or 110.16. Hand-written portions must be legible. The markings in (B) must also be durable for the environment where they are installed. Important aspects of this revision are references to the ANSI Z535.4-2011 standard titled *Product Safety Signs and Labels* from two informational notes following list items 1 and 3. ANSI Z535.4-2011 uses a standardized approach and specific development criteria for labels and signs that include the signal words danger, warning, and caution. Many existing *NEC* rules use these signal words in marking and label requirements. These existing rules have been revised to reference 110.21(B). The change promotes a more consistent approach in developing and application of the hazard markings, labels, and signs for wiring methods and equipment that exist throughout the *NEC*.

## Change Summary

- A subdivision (B) titled Field-Applied Hazard Markings is added to Section 110.21.
- Specific requirements now apply to field-applied hazard markings or labels using signal words "danger", "warning", or "caution" as provided within many *NEC* rules.
- New informational notes reference ANSI Z535.4-2011 for guidelines on consistent and effective markings and labels.

Comments: 1-59, 1-60, 1-61
Proposal: 1-114

# Engineered and Tested Series Combination Systems

## Code Language

**(B) Engineered Series Combination Systems.** Equipment enclosures for circuit breakers or fuses applied in compliance with series combination ratings selected under engineering supervision…with a series combination rating. The marking shall meet the requirements in 110.21(B) and shall be readily visible and state the following:

…(See *NEC* text)…

**(C) Tested Series Combination Systems.** Equipment enclosures for circuit breakers or fuses applied in compliance with series combination ratings marked on the equipment by the manufacturer…with a series combination rating. The marking shall meet the requirements in 110.21(B) and shall be readily visible and state the following:

*(See NEC for actual text)*

## Change Summary

- The words "meet the requirements in 110.21(B) and" have been added to the last sentence in subdivisions (B) and (C).
- Referencing 110.21(B) places additional requirements for equipment marking specified in this section.
- Section 110.21(B) includes specific requirements for caution, danger, and warning markings and provides a reference to ANSI Z535.4 *Product Safety Signs and Labels*.

Caution markings required in 110.22(B) and (C) must meet the requirements in 110.21(B).

Applies where the signal words "danger", "warning", or "caution" are used in NEC rules.

Informational notes reference ANSI Z535.4 for marking or label development criteria.

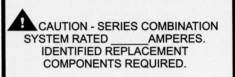

⚠ CAUTION - ENGINEERED SERIES COMBINATION SYSTEM RATED _____ AMPERES. IDENTIFIED REPLACEMENT COMPONENTS REQUIRED.

Marking required by 110.22(B)

Marking required by 110.22(C)

⚠ CAUTION - SERIES COMBINATION SYSTEM RATED _____ AMPERES. IDENTIFIED REPLACEMENT COMPONENTS REQUIRED.

Note: The signal word communicates the degree of hazard. The other label components provide the specific hazard, instructions, and could also include a graphic (See ANSI Z535.4-2011).

## Significance of the Change

The revisions to subdivisions (B) and (C) place additional specific marking and label requirements for the markings required in this rule. The reference to new 110.21(B) is being incorporated *Code*-wide in *NEC* provisions that use the words danger, caution, or warning. These are signal terms that according to ANSI Z535.4 *Product Safety Signs and Labels* include specific criteria that must be followed in developing signs or markings. Examples of criteria that must be met are content of the label of marking, size of the font, colors to be used based on the signal word used. As an example the markings required by these two subdivisions use the signal word "CAUTION" which requires the color yellow to be used. In addition to 110.22(B) and (C), there are many other labeling and marking requirements throughout the *NEC* that specify use of a signal word such as danger, caution, and warning. For consistency and improved clarity throughout the *NEC*, the marking and labels are required to meet 110.21(B) and are generally not permitted to be hand written. The informational notes provided in 110.21(B) provide effective guidance and assist users by reference to the appropriate guidelines for developing such labels and markings.

Comment: None
Proposal: 1-117

# Available Fault Current Marking for Equipment Rating

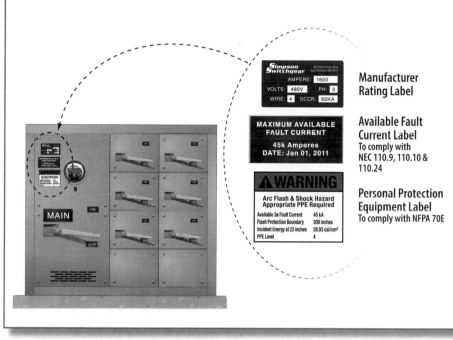

**Manufacturer Rating Label**

**Available Fault Current Label**
To comply with NEC 110.9, 110.10 & 110.24

**Personal Protection Equipment Label**
To comply with NFPA 70E

## Code Language

**110.24 Available Fault Current.**

**(A) Field Marking.** Service equipment in other than dwelling units shall be legibly marked in the field with the maximum available fault current. The field marking(s) shall include the date the fault current calculation was performed and be of sufficient durability to withstand the environment involved.

Informational Note: The available fault current marking(s) addressed in 110.24 is related to required short-circuit current ratings of equipment. NFPA70E-2012, *Standard for Electrical Safety in the Workplace*, provides assistance in determining the severity of potential exposure, planning safe work practices, and selecting personal protective equipment.

*(See NEC for actual text)*

## Significance of the Change

The marking required by 110.24 relates to equipment ratings. Service equipment must be suitable for the maximum available fault current at the line terminals of the equipment, without exception. Section 110.24 is a marking requirement that demonstrates compliance with 110.9 and 110.10 for both new installations and modifications in existing systems that increase the available fault current beyond existing equipment ratings. Equipment can be supplied with any level of fault current that is equal to or less than the manufacturers marked short-circuit current rating of the equipment. Determining incident energy levels (arc flash intensity) is primarily dependent on the value of available fault current, the overcurrent device clearing time and the working distance to live parts. Higher fault current usually causes faster clearing times resulting in less incident energy than for lower fault current values. Time is a big factor and longer times can result in higher incident energy levels. Some commercially available methods of determining incident energy recommend that calculations using both the highest and lowest fault current values are performed and then the highest incident energy level determined is selected. Using the maximum value to determine incident energy can provide incorrect (lower) levels for selecting arc flash protective equipment resulting in insufficient protection.

## Change Summary

- A new informational note has been added following 110.24(A).
- The note clarifies that marking requirements in 110.24 relate to equipment fault current ratings and compliance with 110.9 and 110.10.
- The maximum available fault current value required by 110.24 is not intended to be used for performing incident energy analysis.

Comments: 1-64, 1-66
Proposals: 1-124, 1-121, 1-125

# 110.25 & Exception

Article 110 Requirements for Electrical Installations

Part I General

## Lockable Disconnecting Means

### Code Language

**110.25 Lockable Disconnecting Means.** Where a disconnecting means is required to be lockable open elsewhere in this *Code*, it shall be capable of being locked in the open position. The provisions for locking shall remain in place with or without the lock installed.

*Exception: Cord-and-plug connection locking provisions shall not be required to remain in place without the lock installed.*

**(See NEC for actual text)**

### Change Summary

- A new section 110.25 titled Lockable Disconnecting Means and exception have been added to Part I of Article 110.
- The new section consolidates the provisions for lockable disconnecting means into one location.
- Previous *NEC* requirements that dealt with lockable disconnecting means will now reference 110.25 for consistency and uniform application of the requirements.

### Significance of the Change

Section 110.25 resulted from work of the Usability Task Group assigned by the *NEC* Correlating Committee. Requirements for disconnecting means to be lockable in the open position existed in numerous sections in previous *NEC* editions. This new section consolidates identical requirements for disconnecting means required to be "capable of being locked in the open position" in a single section for clarity. This new section is intended to facilitate a lockout tag-out scenario consistently. It is equally important to ensure that the means for placing the lock remain in place with installed equipment. The concepts included in the proposal provided correlation throughout the *NEC* with respect to the capability of placing a lock on a disconnecting means to secure it in the open position. To effectively correlate these requirements *Code*-wide, the Task Group developed companion proposals that removed all existing lockable disconnecting means provisions and replace them with a reference to 110.25. Action by CMP-1 on Comment 1-76 results in an exception that relaxes the requirements for cord-and-plug connection locking means where the provisions for adding a lock would not have to remain with the cord cap or attachment plug when the lock is not installed.

Comment: 1-76
Proposals: 1-130, 1-116

## Personnel Doors

### Code Language

**110.26(C)(3) Personnel Doors.**
Where equipment rated 800 A or more that contains overcurrent devices, switching devices, or control devices is installed and there is a personnel door(s) intended for entrance to and egress from the working space less than 7.6 m (25 ft) from the nearest edge of the working space, the door(s) shall open in the direction of egress and be equipped with listed panic hardware.

*(See NEC for actual text)*

### Significance of the Change

The revisions to this section addressing personnel doors for working spaces have been expanded to apply to equipment rated at 800 amperes or more rather than the 1200 ampere value in previous editions. Information provided in the substantiation indicated that action in the 2002 revision cycle on Proposal 1-260a to include panic hardware and doors that open in the direction of egress was based upon the action to accept in principle proposals 1-247, 1-248 and 1-249. The committee did not base these actions on a 1200-ampere threshold; it was based on a requirement for doors. Information in the substantiation also demonstrated that the need for lowering this value was significant in that personnel egress through panic hardware equipped doors is essential at lower equipment ratings. CMP-1 acted favorable to the personnel safety concerns provided in the substantiation and reduced the 1200 amperes to 800 amperes. The other revision to this requirement removes the previous remedial solutions for accomplishing simple pressure release for doors by just requiring listed panic hardware on doors. The change reduces inconsistencies in application of this provision and aligns with the requirements in applicable building codes that use the term *listed panic hardware*.

### Change Summary

- The value "1200 A" has been lowered to "800 A" expanding requirements for panic hardware on egress doors.
- The words "panic bars, pressure plates, or other devices that are normally latched but open under simple pressure" have been replaced with "listed panic hardware."
- Listed panic hardware is required on personnel doors addressed by this section.

Comment: None
Proposals: 1-143a, 1-145

# 110.26(E)(2)(a) & (b)

## Dedicated Equipment Space Outdoors

### Code Language

**(2) Outdoor.** Outdoor installations shall comply with 110.26(E)(2)(a) and (b).

**(a)** *Installation Requirements.* Outdoor electrical equipment shall be installed in suitable enlosures and shall be protected from accidental contact by unauthorized personnel, or by vehicular traffic, or by accidental spillage or leakage from piping systems. The working clearance space shall include the zone described in 110.26(A). No architectural appurtenance or other equipment shall be located in this zone.

**(b)** *Dedicated Equipment Space.* The space equal to the width and depth of the equipment, and extending from grade to a height of 1.8 m (6 ft) above the equipment, shall be dedicated to the electrical installation. No piping or other equipment foreign to the electrical installation shall be located in this zone.

*(See NEC for actual text)*

### Change Summary

- This section has been rearranged and renumbered into a list format to meet the *NEC Style Manual*.
- A new list item (b) has been added and is titled Dedicated Equipment Space.
- The requirements for dedicated space for equipment installed outside are similar to the dedicated space requirements for equipment located indoors.

Comment: None
Proposals: 1-155, 1-154

### Significance of the Change

*Courtesy of Tom Garvey*

Action by CMP-1 on Proposal 1-155 adds requirements for dedicated equipment space for equipment installed in outdoor locations. For indoor installations, the *Code* is clear as to the dedicated spaces required for electrical equipment. For equipment outdoors there previously were no dedicated space requirements. The result is items such as gas piping, water piping, mechanical refrigeration lines, irrigation equipment, phone equipment, air lines, and so forth installed in what would normally be dedicated space for electrical installations. These items impede worker access to these normally dedicated spaces. The hazards and access problems and need for dedicated space requirements are the same for equipment located outdoors as they are for indoor electrical equipment. With many designs specifying placement of all equipment in one location, the dedicate space problems are exacerbated. The problems are compounded in that other items are located in close proximity to the electrical equipment and in dedicated spaces create a hazard when servicing electrical equipment. As revised the requirements for dedicated equipment space will apply to equipment located indoors and outdoors resulting in consistency for installers, designers, and *Code* enforcement officials. The new requirements also correlate with the same requirements in 110.26(E)(1)(a) for indoor equipment.

# Guarding of Live Parts

Courtesy of YESCO

## Code Language

**110.27 Guarding of Live Parts.**

**(A) Live Parts Guarded Against Accidental Contact.** Except as elsewhere required or permitted by this *Code*, live parts of electrical equipment operating at 50 volts or more shall be guarded against accidental contact by approved enclosures or by any of the following means:

**(1), (2) and (3).** ...(See *NEC* text)...

**(4)** By elevation above the floor or other working surface as shown in 110.27(A)(4)(a) or (b) below:

a. A minimum of 2.5 m (8 ft) for 50 to 300 volts

b. A minimum of 2.6 m (8½ ft) for 301 to 600 volts

...(See *NEC* text)...

*(See NEC for actual text)*

## Significance of the Change

Section 110.27 includes provisions to guard live parts against accidental contact. Subdivision (A) sets basic guarding requirements for voltage parameters of 50 volts or more. The methods of guarding against contact if other than containment inside an enclosure are by locating live parts in a vault, room, or similar enclosure accessible only to qualified persons. Other methods are to provide separation by suitable partitions or screens (fences) restricting access to unqualified persons. Live parts can also be isolated by installation on a suitable balcony, gallery, or elevated platform arranged that only qualified persons can access them. List item (4) in this section is modified by this revision. In previous editions of the *NEC*, the height of 2.5 m (8 ft) applied to all voltage levels above 50. The change to this section introduces two distinct elevations based on the voltage of the live parts required to be guarded. A minimum of 2.5 m (8 ft) is required for voltages 50 to 300, and at least 2.6 m (8-1/2 ft) is required for live parts at voltages of 301 through 600. The revision establishes more consistent alignment with similar *NESC* provisions dealing with elevation as the method for guarding against contact.

## Change Summary

- List item (4) to Section 110.27(A) has been revised and expanded to include new list items (a) and (b).

- The revision provides minimum vertical clearances to live parts operating at 50-300 volts and those operating at 301 – 600 volts.

- These provisions align with similar requirements in Rule 124 of the *National Electrical Safety Code (NESC)*.

Comment: 1-94
Proposal: 1-158

## Personnel Doors

### Code Language

**(3) Personnel Doors.** Where there is a personnel door(s) intended for entrance to and egress from the working space less than 7.6 m (25 ft) from the nearest edge of the working space, the door(s) shall open in the direction of egress and be equipped with listed panic hardware.

*(See NEC for actual text)*

### Significance of the Change

The revisions to this section address the means of release (opening) personnel doors for entrance and egress to working spaces for large equipment over 600 volts. The requirements for personnel doors apply where the door(s) is located less than 7.6 m (25 ft) from the nearest edge of the required minimum equipment working space. Where a personnel door is installed, it must swing in the direction of egress travel, in other words away from the working space and equipment. This revision provides a more consistent and uniform requirement for listed panic hardware to be used on doors so located. The items identified as panic bars, pressure plates, or other devices that are normally latched but open under simple pressure have been deleted from this section. These various remedial solutions for accomplishing simple pressure release for doors are now limited to doors equipped with only listed panic hardware. The change reduces inconsistencies in application of this provision and aligns with the requirements in applicable building codes that use the term *listed panic hardware*. This revision correlates with a similar change in 110.26(C)(3) dealing with personnel doors for working space egress for large equipment rated a 600 volts and less.

### Change Summary

- This revision correlates with the same revision in Section 110.26(C)(3) dealing with personnel doors.
- The words "panic bars, pressure plates, or other devices that are normally latched but open under simple pressure" have been replaced with the term *listed panic hardware*.
- Listed panic hardware is required on personnel doors addressed by this section.

Comment: None
Proposal: 1-169a

# Locked Rooms or Enclosures – Signs

*iStock Photo Courtesy of NECA*

## Significance of the Change

This revision to subdivision (C) places additional specific danger signs required in this rule. The reference to new 110.21(B) is being incorporated *Code*-wide in various *NEC* provisions that use the signal words danger, caution, or warning. These are signal terms that according to ANSI Z535.4 *Product Safety Signs and Labels* include specific criteria that must be followed in developing signs or markings. Examples of criteria that must be met are content of the label of marking, size of the font, colors to be used based on the signal word used. As an example the markings required by this rule use the signal word 'DANGER" which requires the color red to be used. In addition to this sign requirement in (C), there are many other sign, labeling and marking requirements throughout the *NEC* that specify use of a signal word such as danger, caution, and warning. For consistency and improved clarity throughout the *NEC*, the signs, markings and labels are required to meet 110.21(B) and are generally not permitted to be hand written. The informational notes provided in 110.21(B) provide effective guidance and assist users by reference to the appropriate guidelines for developing such labels and markings.

## Code Language

**110.34 Work Space and Guarding.**

**(A) Working Space.** ...(See *NEC* text)...

**(B) Separation from Low-Voltage Equipment.** ...(See *NEC* text)...

**(C) Locked Rooms or Enclosures.** The entrance to all buildings, vaults, rooms, or enclosures containing exposed live parts or exposed conductors operating at over 600 volts, nominal, shall be kept locked unless such entrances are under the observation of a qualified person at all times. Permanent and conspicuous danger signs shall be provided. The danger sign shall meet the requirements in 110.21(B) and shall read as follows: DANGER — HIGH VOLTAGE — KEEP OUT

*(See NEC for actual text)*

## Change Summary

- The words "meet the requirements in 110.21(B) and" have been added to the last sentence in (C).

- Referencing 110.21(B) places additional requirements for equipment marking specified in this section.

- Section 110.21(B) includes specific requirements for caution, danger, and warning markings and provides a reference to ANSI Z535.4 *Product Safety Signs and Labels*.

Comment: 1-104
Proposal: 1-175

# Chapter 2

## Articles 200–285
## Wiring and Protection

# 200.4(A) & (B)

Article 200 Use and Identification of Grounded Conductors

## Neutral Conductors

### Code Language

**200.4 Neutral Conductors.** Neutral conductors shall be installed in accordance with 200.4(A) and (B).

**(A) Installation.** (See *NEC* text)

**(B) Multiple Circuits.** Where more than one neutral conductor associated with different circuits is in an enclosure, grounded circuit conductors of each circuit shall be identified or grouped to correspond with the ungrounded (See *NEC* text).

*Exception No. 1: The requirement for grouping or identifying shall not apply if the branch circuit or feeder conductors enter from (See NEC text).*

*Exception No. 2: The requirement for grouping or identifying shall not apply where branch-circuit conductors pass though (See NEC text).*

**(See *NEC* for actual text)**

### Change Summary

- This section now includes subdivision (B) *Multiple Circuits* and is arranged in a list format.

- If more than one neutral is in the same enclosure, grounded and ungrounded conductors of the same circuit must be grouped.

- Two exceptions relax grouping requirements for cables and raceways if the grouping is obvious and for unspliced loops in conduit bodies or boxes.

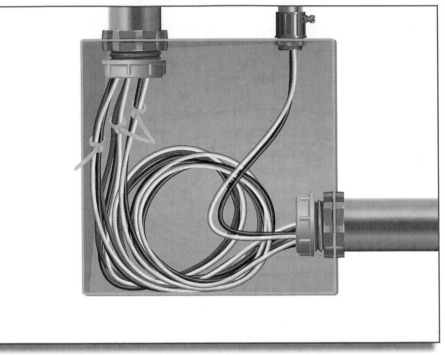

### Significance of the Change

This section has been revised into a list format and has been expanded to require grouping or identification where multiple circuits with neutral(s) are installed in the same enclosure(s). The grouping or identification must be accomplished using suitable identification means, cable ties, or similar means at least once in the enclosure to establish grouping of neutral conductors with their associated ungrounded conductors of the circuit(s). Two exceptions have also been added to (B). Exception No. 1 relaxes the grouping requirement for cables where the cable installation makes the grouping obvious. Exception No. 2 relaxes the grouping requirement for un-spliced loops in conduit bodies or boxes as provided in 314.16(B)(1). This revision results in an enhancement for identifying neutral conductors with their corresponding ungrounded circuit conductors enhancing safety and the quality of multiple branch circuit installations within the same enclosure(s).

Comments: 5-10, 5-11
Proposal: 5-29

# Means of Identifying Grounded Conductors

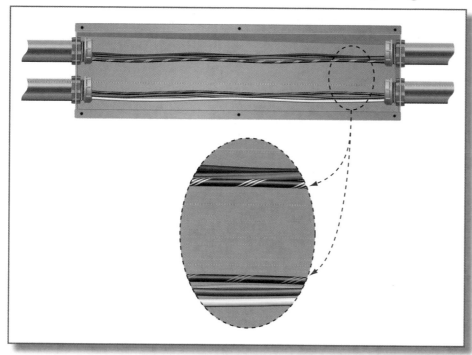

## Code Language

**Each identified section is revised as follows:**

**200.6(A)(3)** …three continuous white or gray stripes…,

**200.6(B)(3)** …three continuous white or gray stripes…

**200.6(E)** …three continuous white or gray stripes…,

**200.7(title)** …three continuous white or gray stripes…,

**200.7(A)(2)** …three continuous white or gray stripes…,

**200.7(C)** …three continuous white or gray stripes…

**200.7(C)(1)** …three continuous white or gray stripes…,

**200.7(C)(2)** …three continuous white or gray stripes…

*(See NEC for actual text)*

## Significance of the Change

This revision occurs in several locations within Section 200.6 and 200.7. The words "or gray" have been added to complete the phrase "three continuous white or gray stripes." The result is that identification with continuous stripes along the entire length of the conductor can be accomplished using white or gray stripes. Manufacturers can now use this option when producing conductors and cable assemblies that have integral identification. The substantiation indicated that because of several improvements in compounds and coloring methods, white and gray skim coats and stripes are now easily differentiable. The color gray is often installed by choice or by specification for grounded conductors of 480Y/277-volt systems. Gray stripes are a natural addition to the acceptable means of identification for grounded conductors. This additional option also makes it easier to comply with the requirements in 200.6(D), which requires identification by phase and system where multiple systems are installed. The use of gray stripes as an identification method can be useful where multiple branch circuits or feeders supplied from different systems are installed in the same enclosure. The revisions to these sections provide an additional identification method to achieve compliance for grounded conductor identification.

## Change Summary

- The words "or gray" have been added in several locations within 200.6 and 200.7.

- The identification using three continuous white stripes is expanded to include three continuous gray stripes.

- The revision provides additional means for manufacturers to assist installers in meeting the identification requirements for grounded conductors.

Comment: None
Proposals: 5-31, 5-33, 5-34, 5-35, 5-36, 5-38, 5-40, 5-41

# Line-to-Neutral Loads

## Code Language

**210.4 Multiwire Branch Circuits.**

**(A) General.** Branch circuits recognized by this article shall be permitted as multiwire circuits. A multiwire circuit shall be permitted to be considered as multiple circuits. All conductors of a multiwire branch circuit shall originate from the same panelboard or similar distribution equipment.

Informational Note No. 1: A 3-phase, 4-wire, wye connected power system (See *NEC* Text)

Informational Note No. 2: See 300.13(B) for continuity of grounded conductors on mutiwire circuits.

*(See NEC for actual text)*

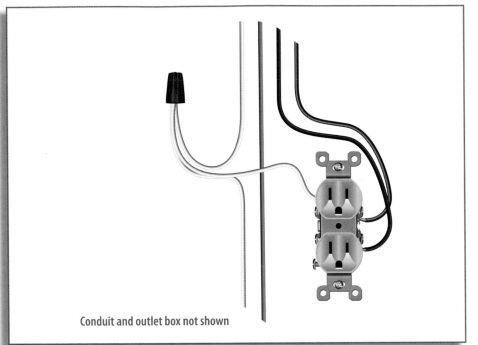

Conduit and outlet box not shown

## Change Summary

- Informational notes are required to be located directly after the rule to which they apply.
- The Informational Note following 210.4(C), Exception No. 2 has been relocated to comply with 3.1.3 of the *NEC Style Manual*.
- The informational note applies the general requirements in 210.4(A) rather than to following 210.4(C), Exception No. 2.

## Significance of the Change

The revision relocates the informational note following 210.4(C), Exception No. 2 to follow the general requirement in 210.4(A) because that is the text it applies to, not the exception. The *NEC* Correlating Committee activated the Usability Task Group to revise the *NEC Style Manual*. As a result, the technical committees have incorporated many of the latest style manual requirements into the 2014 *NEC* development process. As in the previous *NEC* editions, informational notes cannot contain any requirements or mandatory text. If an informational note is needed to provide additional explanation or guidance for users, consideration should be given to incorporating it into the requirements. Section 3.1.3 of the revised *NEC Style Manual* is new and requires informational notes to immediately follow the rule to which apply. Each technical committee was directed by the *NEC* Correlating Committee to include this editorial work as part of their work on the 2014 *NEC*. As a result, many informational notes were relocated to follow the rule they applied to. It was apparent that over the years, some informational notes had shifted and were no longer immediately following the provision to which they applied. Many technical committees either deleted informational notes completely because they were no longer necessary, or incorporated them into *Code* text.

Comment: 2-5
Proposal: 2-17a

## Grouping

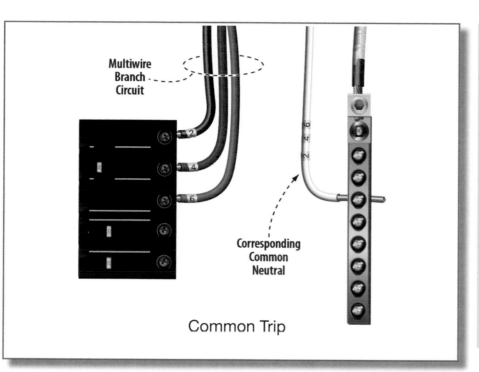

Multiwire Branch Circuit

Corresponding Common Neutral

Common Trip

### Code Language

**210.4 Multiwire Branch Circuits.**

**(A) through (C)** (See *NEC* Text)

**(D) Grouping.** The ungrounded and grounded circuit conductors of each multiwire branch circuit shall be grouped by cable ties or similar means in at least one location within the panelboard or other point of origination.

*Exception: The requirement for grouping shall not apply if the circuit enters from a cable or raceway unique to the circuit that makes the grouping obvious or if the conductors are identified at their terminations with numbered wire markers corresponding to the appropriate circuit number.*

*(See NEC for actual text)*

## Significance of the Change

The revision to this exception provides another practical means to qualify for relief from the general multi-wire branch circuit grouping requirements of 210.4(D). Information in the substantiation indicated that multi-wire branch circuit conductors in commercial and industrial occupancies are often installed and identified with numeric wire markers on each individual conductor (typically adjacent to the circuit breaker and neutral bar). Although the existing code requirement is adequate to accomplish grouping, this additional method is superior to the use of tape or cable tie bundling since those methods are often obscured by other conductors in a crowded panelboard gutter space. By installing the wire marker near the termination point, its corresponding multi-wire branch circuit numbers will be readily evident. It should be noted that the *Code* currently does not require that branch circuits be identified by circuit number. The various identification means for branch circuits is provided in 210.5(C)(2). The exception previously only relaxed this rule where the grouping of a multi-wire branch circuit was obvious. The new text added to the exception provides another practical example of where the grouping can be easily achieved by installers and readily compliance can be more readily determined by electrical inspectors.

### Change Summary

- The revision provides additional relief from the grouping requirements in 210.4(D).
- The words "or if the conductors are identified at their terminations with numbered wire markers corresponding to the appropriate circuit number" have been added to this exception.
- Circuit numbers must be marked on corresponding common neutral conductor of a multi-wire branch circuit at their terminations.

Comment: None
Proposal: 2-19

# Bathtubs or Shower Stalls

## Code Language

**(A) Dwelling Units.** All 125-volt, single-phase, 15- and 20-ampere receptacles installed in the locations specified in 210.8(A)(1) through (10) shall have ground-fault circuit-interrupter protection for personnel.

(9) Bathtubs or shower stalls – Where receptacles are installed within 1.8 m (6 ft) of the outside edge of the bathtub or shower stall.

*(See NEC for actual text)*

## Change Summary

- GFCI protection requirements for dwelling units have been expanded.
- A new list item (9) dealing with bathtubs and shower stalls has been added to 210.8(A).
- GFCI protection is required for receptacles installed within 1.8 m (6 ft) of the outside edge of a bathtub or shower stall in residential occupancies.

## Significance of the Change    *Courtesy of Pass and Seymour Legrand*

Favorable action by CMP-2 results in a new requirement for GFCI protection for receptacles located within 6 feet of the outside edge of a bathtub or shower stall. Information in the substantiation indicated that this new requirement would mirror that found in 680.71 for hydromassage tubs. This is a logical provision since sometimes bathtubs or shower stalls are not always located in an area that meets the *NEC* definition of a bathroom. Consequently under previous *NEC* rules, any 125-volt, 15- or 20-ampere, single-phase receptacles installed in those areas would not require GFCI protection. Many of these areas may have tile or other conductive and possibly other floors that are considered grounded surfaces. This presents a serious danger to a person getting out of the tub or shower, who is soaking wet and is likely to use a non-GFCI protected receptacle. This new list item (9) closes this gap in the GFCI protection requirements within 6 feet of tubs and showers that are not in bathrooms or bathroom areas. This new requirement will provide a better level of safety for residential occupants and improve enforcement capabilities for inspectors requiring GFCI protection for such receptacles when no *Code* text previously existed.

Comment: None
Proposal: 2-46

## Laundry Areas

### Code Language

**(A) Dwelling Units.** All 125-volt, single-phase, 15- and 20-ampere receptacles installed in the locations specified in 210.8(A)(1) through (10) shall have ground-fault circuit-interrupter protection for personnel.

(10) Laundry Areas

*(See NEC for actual text)*

### Significance of the Change

Action by CMP-2 results in a ground-fault circuit-interrupter protection (GFCI) requirement for receptacles installed in laundry areas. This change incorporates a new list item (10) in this section that requires GFCI protection for 125 volt, 15- and 20-ampere, single-phase receptacles installed in laundry areas. It should be noted that the word "area" is used in list item (10) rather than "room" which necessitates judgment by the authority having jurisdiction as to what constitutes a laundry area. If the laundry equipment is installed in a designated laundry room, all 125-volt, 15- and 20-ampere, single-phase receptacles installed in that room would not require GFCI protection, just those located in the laundry area. Obviously if the room is small enough all receptacles would require the GFCI protection. In the panel statement to Comment 2-23 CMP-2 indicated that laundry areas involve electrical appliances and water with a resulting increased risk of electric shock. The panel's action to require GFCI protection of receptacles in laundry areas addresses this increased risk and is consistent with the GFCI protection of other receptacles in areas near water. It should also be understood that this GFCI protection is required for receptacles in the laundry area, not for appliance(s) for laundry use.

### Change Summary

- GFCI protection requirements for dwelling units have been expanded.
- A new list item (10) dealing with laundry areas has been added to 210.8(A).
- GFCI protection is required for receptacles installed in laundry areas of dwelling units.

Comment: 2-23
Proposal: 2-47

# Rooftops

## Code Language

### (3) Rooftops

*Exception No. 1 to (3): Receptacles on rooftops shall not be required to be readily accessible other than from the rooftop.*

*Exception No. 2 to (3) and (4): Receptacles that are not readily accessible and are supplied by a branch circuit dedicated to electric snow-melting, deicing, or pipeline...(See 2011 NEC text).*

*Exception No. 3 to (4): In industrial establishments only, where the conditions of maintenance and supervision ensure that only qualified personnel are involved,.... (See 2011 NEC text).*

**(See NEC for actual text)**

## Significance of the Change

In the 2011 *NEC* development process, Section 210.8 was revised to require the GFCI receptacles required by 210.8(A) through (C) be readily accessible. GFCI receptacles installed on rooftops in accordance with 210.8(B)(3) and 210.63 could be considered as not readily accessible by definition, subject to interpretation. Information in the substantiation indicated that unless rooftop(s) on a building, other than a dwelling unit(s), is provided with a permanent ladder for rooftop access, a GFCI receptacle(s) installed on the rooftop do not necessarily meet the readily accessible requirement as written. The exception provides practical relief from the readily accessible requirement while maintaining the ready access to the GFCI device from rooftop locations where it is most likely necessary, such as for rooftop service personnel. If a portable ladder is needed to access the rooftop, the readily accessible requirement is not met, unless the GFCI protection for rooftop receptacles is installed at the circuit breaker. The proposed exception fixes a problem in relation to the defined term *Accessible, Readily* while providing a practical exception to list item (3) that narrows the readily accessible requirement for roof to GFCI receptacles to ready access from the rooftop.

## Change Summary

- A new Exception No. 1 to list item (3) has been added to this section.
- Previous exceptions Nos. 1 and 2 have been renumbered accordingly as Exception No. 2 to list items (3) and (4) and Exception No. 3 to list item (4).
- GFCI receptacles for rooftops only have to be readily accessible from the rooftop.

Comment: None

Proposals: 2-51, 2-52

# Garages, Service Bays, and Similar Areas

## Code Language

**(B) Other Than Dwelling Units.** All 125-volt, single-phase, 15- and 20-ampere receptacles installed in the locations specified in 210.8(B)(1) through (8) shall have ground-fault circuit-interrupter protection for personnel.

(8) Garages, service bays, and similar areas other than vehicle exhibition halls and showrooms.

*(See NEC for actual text)*

## Significance of the Change

List item (8) has been revised to become more enforceable and provide more complete GFCI protection requirements for all 125-volt, single-phase, 15- and 20-ampere receptacles installed in garages, service bays, and similar areas in other than dwelling units. Information provided with the substantiation indicated that many commercial garages have receptacles installed for purposes other than the use of hand tools. In geographical areas that experience winter, many garages for cars, trucks and busses have 125-volt, 15- or 20-ampere, single-phase receptacles installed at each stall for electric engine block heaters or even for level 1 electric vehicle chargers. Cord-and-plug connected engine block heaters may not be listed and therefore not subject to the maximum leakage current requirement of the standard for appliances when these receptacles are not GFCI protected. The frame of the vehicle can posibly become energized during a ground fault condition, posing an electric shock hazard to personnel. Action on Comment 2-27 provides the necessary relief for vehicle exhibition halls and showrooms of automobile dealers. This revision provides needed clarification for designers, installers and inspectors relative to the applicability of GFCI requirements in this rule.

## Change Summary

- List item (8) has been revised by removing the list of items for which receptacles could be used since it was not inclusive.
- The words "other than vehicle exhibition halls and showrooms" have been added.
- The revision expands the GFCI requirements of this section to all garages, service bays, and similar areas except for vehicle exhibition halls and showrooms.

Comments: 2-27, 2-28
Proposals: 2-49, 2-50

# 210.8(D)

Article 210 Branch Circuits

Part I General Provisions

NEW

## Kitchen Dishwasher Branch Circuit

### Code Language

**210.8(D) Kitchen Dishwasher Branch Circuit.** GFCI protection shall be provided for outlets that supply dishwashers installed in dwelling unit locations.

*(See NEC for actual text)*

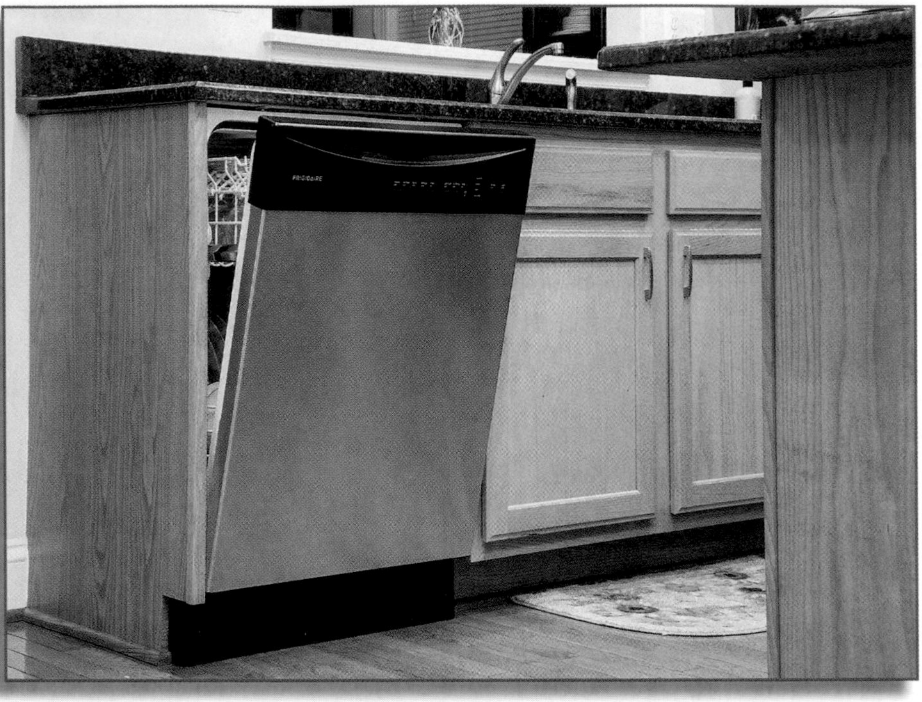


Courtesy of Rob Colgan (NECA)

### Change Summary

- Requirements for GFCI protection in dwelling unit kitchens have been expanded.
- A new subdivision (D) titled Kitchen Dishwasher Branch Circuit has been added to 210.8.
- Outlets supplying dishwashers are required to be GFCI protected.

### Significance of the Change

This new requirement expands the ground-fault circuit interrupter protection that must be installed in dwelling units. Although the original proposal was rejected due to the lack of two-thirds of the vote, the submitter's presentation to the panel appeared to have an impact on its acceptance in the comment stages of the process. Information in the negative ballot statements alluded to the appliances of today having different end-of-life failure modes and and behavior than the electromechanical dishwashers of the past. As such, CMP-2 acted favorably to Comment 2-29 reversing the original panel action on this proposal (2-58). The result is a new requirement for GFCI protection for outlets supply dishwashers in dwelling units. An interesting issue with this change is that the title of the subdivision (D) is Kitchen Dishwasher Branch Circuits, which would indicate that entire branch circuit should be protected, but the text indicates that the outlets supplying dishwashers shall be GFCI protected.

Comment: 2-29
Proposal: 2-58

# Arc-Fault Circuit-Interrupter Protection

IStock Photo Courtesy of NECA

## Code Language

**210.12 Arc-Fault Circuit-Interrupter Protection.** Arc-fault circuit-interrupter protection shall be provided as required in 210.12(A), (B) and (C). The arc-fault circuit interrupter shall be installed in a readily accessible location.

**(A) Dwelling Units.** All 120-volt, single phase, 15- and 20-ampere branch circuits supplying outlets or devices installed in dwelling unit kitchens, family rooms... laundry areas...(see *NEC* text)...shall be protected by any of the means described in 210.12(A)(1) through (6): ...(See *NEC* text for list items 1 through 6 and the Exception)...

*(See NEC for actual text)*

## Significance of the Change

This revision incorporates the changes in Proposals 2-80, 2-82a and 2-116. Arc-fault circuit interrupters whether of the outlet device types or circuit breakers shall be installed in readily accessible locations. The reasons mirror the readily accessible requirements for ground-fault circuit interrupters (GFCIs) accepted in the 2011 *NEC* development process. Ready access is required for occupants and service personnel to test periodically as required by the manufacturer and to determine that a trip has occurred and initiate troubleshooting procedures prior to resetting. Proposal 2-82a sought to expand the AFCI protection requirements throughout the dwelling unit, but action on Proposals 2-80 and 2-82a continues to expand AFCI protection only incrementally to include kitchens and laundry areas in the 2014 edition. The rooms and areas where AFCI protection is required are intended to mirror the rooms and areas provided in 210.52(A). Subdivision (A) has also been revised by adding list items (1) through (6) that provide various methods of providing arc-fault circuit interrupter protection specified in this section. These revisions are covered in the significant changes under 210.12(A) of this textbook. List item (2) is revised requiring the first outlet box to be marked to indicate it is the first outlet of the branch circuit.

## Change Summary

- This section has been revised to require arc-fault circuit interrupters to be installed in readily accessible locations.

- Subdivision (A) now recognizes arc-fault circuit interrupter protection requirements have been expanded to kitchens and laundry areas.

- List items (1) through (6) provide the acceptable methods of accomplishing the branch circuit arc-fault protection requirements and associated conditions.

Comment: 2-59

Proposals: 2-80, 2-82a, 2-116, 2-122, 2-124

# Arc-Fault Circuit Interrupter Protection

## Code Language

**(A) Dwelling Units.** All 120-volt, single phase, 15- and 20-ampere branch circuits supplying outlets...(See NEC text)... shall be protected by any of the means described in 210.12(A)(1) through (6):

(1) A listed combination-type arc-fault circuit...(see *NEC* text)

(2) A listed branch/feeder-type AFCI installed...(see *NEC* text)

(3) A listed supplemental arc protection circuit breaker...(see *NEC* text)

(4) A listed outlet branch-circuit type arc-fault circuit interrupter...(see *NEC* text)

(5) If RMC, IMC, EMT, Type MC, or steel-armored Type AC cables meeting the requirements of 250.118...(see *NEC* text)

(6) Where a listed metal or nonmetallic conduit or tubing...(see *NEC* text)

*Exception: Where an individual branch circuit to a fire alarm...(see NEC text)*

*(See NEC for actual text)*

## Change Summary

- Section 210.12(A) has been revised and expanded to provide multiple methods of providing AFCI protection for branch circuits in dwelling units.

- This revision results from information in a UL Fact Finding Report.

- The revision expands the permitted uses of device-type AFCI protection under specific conditions provided in list items (1) through (6) of this section.

Comments: 2-46, 2-52

Proposals: 2-80, 2-82a, 2-85, 2-92

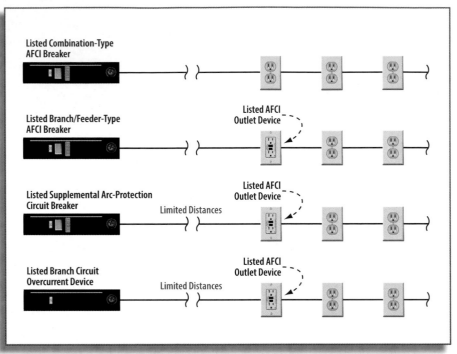

## Significance of the Change

CMP-2 continued its work on Proposal 2-153 that was held in the 2011 cycle. The proposal sought to permit the use of outlet device-type AFCI protection at the first outlet in a branch circuit, under restrictive conditions. Favorable action by CMP-2 on Proposal 2-92 and others, in addition to actions on Comments 2-46 and 2-52, and others, results in acceptance of this concept in the 2014 *NEC*. This revision expands the types of arc-fault circuit interrupter protective devices and specific conditions associated with each application. The expansion results from information obtained in UL Fact Finding Study titled *Evaluation of Run Length and Available Current on Breaker Ability to Mitigate Parallel Arcing Faults*. List items (1) through (3) provide the acceptable methods of using arc-fault circuit interrupters in circuit breaker configurations. List items (4) through (6) provide specific allowances for using arc-fault circuit interrupter protection in device-type configurations and under specific conditions stated within each list item. List items (3) and (4) have specific conditions including a length limitation based wire size used, aligning with the fact finding study. The information contained in former exceptions 1 and 2 have been incorporated into list items (5) and (6) in this section.

# Branch Circuit Extensions or Modifications

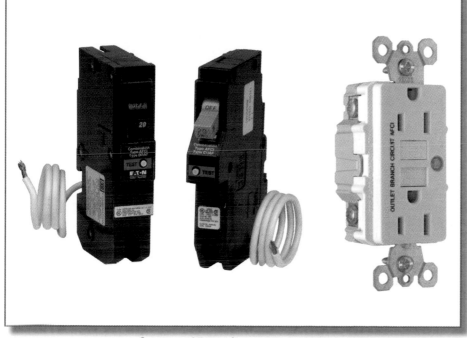

*Courtesy of Eaton Corporation and Pass and Seymour Legrand*

## Code Language

**(B) Branch Circuit Extensions or Modifications — Dwelling Units.** In any of the areas specified in 210.12(A), where branch-circuit wiring is modified, replaced, or extended, the branch circuit shall be protected by one of the following:

(1) A listed combination-type AFCI located at the origin of the branch circuit

(2) A listed outlet branch-circuit type AFCI located at the first receptacle outlet of the existing branch circuit

*Exception: AFCI protection shall not be required where the extension of the existing conductors is not more than 1.8 m (6 ft.) and does not include any additional outlets or devices.*

*(See NEC for actual text)*

## Significance of the Change

The new exception to 210.12(B) provides a reasonable level of relief from having to provide AFCI protection for the entire branch circuit even if no additional outlets or devices are added. Information in the substantiation addressed service changes or relocating a panelboard and the branch circuit has to be moved or slightly lengthened to accomplish the work. Having to apply the AFCI requirements specified in (B) in these scenarios can create undue hardship for owners and electrical contractors in that such requirements can cause the entire branch circuit to have to be replaced. The reason is that some existing branch circuits were installed as 3-wire home runs with a shared neutral. Some AFCI protective devices require a branch circuit without a shared neutral. The exception provides the needed relief for installers and inspectors, but is restrictive in that the modification cannot include adding any outlets or devices and must be accomplished within a 6 foot length. As indicated in affirmative ballot statements to this proposal, this new exception will promote a more uniform interpretations and application of AFCI requirements to branch circuit modifications or extensions.

## Change Summary

- A new exception has been added to subdivision (B).
- AFCI protection is not required if the extension is not longer than 6 feet and does not include any devices or outlets.
- The new exception provides reasonable relaxation of AFCI protection for existing branch circuits that are moved or lengthened but no additional outlets are installed.

Comment: None
Proposal: 2-115

# 210.12(C)

## AFCI Protection – Dormitory Units

### Code Language

**(C) Dormitory Units.** All 120-Volt, single phase, 15- and 20-ampere branch circuits supplying outlets installed in dormitory unit bedrooms, living rooms, hallways, closets, and similar rooms shall be protected by a listed arc-fault circuit interrupter meeting the requirements of 210.12(A)(1) through (6) as appropriate.

*(See NEC for actual text)*

### Change Summary

- A new subdivision (C) titled Dormitory Units has been added to 210.12.
- The AFCI protection requirements are expanded to outlets installed in dormitory unit bedrooms, living rooms, hallways, closets, and similar rooms.
- This new subdivision continues the incremental expansion of AFCI protection for dwelling units.

### Significance of the Change

This new subdivision (C) in 210.12 extends the AFCI protection requirements to branch circuits supplying outlets installed in dormitory unit bedrooms, living rooms, hallways, closets, and similar room. Information included in the proposal drew the comparison between occupants dwelling units and habitants living in dormitories. The same conditions that warrant AFCI protection in dwelling units also exist in these types of living quarters for students. Substantiation with Comment 2-37 provided references to statistical comparisons between fires in dwelling units and dormitories provided the justification needed to require AFCI protection in dormitories. Additionally, the submitter emphasized the changes and evolution taking place in dormitory properties themselves. In the past, dormitories typically did not have kitchens in the individual units. Today, dormitories often closely resemble apartment buildings with suite style apartments that include kitchens and most, if not all, of the same features are included in dwelling units as defined. The result is a requirement for AFCI protection by a listed arc-fault circuit interrupter meeting the requirements of 210.12(A)(1) through (6) as appropriate.

Comment: 2-37
Proposal: 2-78

# Ground-Fault Protection of Equipment – Branch Circuits

## Code Language

**210.13 Ground-Fault Protection of Equipment.** Each branch circuit disconnect rated 1000 amperes or more and installed on solidly grounded wye electrical systems of more than 150 volts to ground, but not exceeding 600 volts phase-to-phase, shall be provided with ground-fault protection of equipment in accordance with the provisions of 230.95.

Informational Note: For buildings that contain health care occupancies, see the requirements of 517.17.

*Exception No. 1: The provisions of this section shall not apply to a disconnecting means for a continuous industrial…(See 2014 NEC text).*

*Exception No. 2: The provisions of this section shall not apply if ground-fault protection of equipment is provided…(See 2014 NEC text).*

*(See NEC for actual text)*

## Significance of the Change

Each branch circuit disconnect rated at 1000 amperes or greater and having a phase-to-ground voltage exceeding 150, must be protected by ground-fault protection of equipment as defined in Article 100. This requirement essentially parallels the requirements in 215.10 and 230.95, because the arcing hazards for equipment are the same at that voltage and current level. Information in the substantiation identified the gap in the *NEC* relative to this type of protection for branch circuits in these voltage and ampere ranges. As provided in the substantiation, there are many installations where a separate transformer with a 480Y/277 secondary is developed to supply an industrial machine or other single load. These are branch circuits by definition, not feeders. Such machines typically have a 1000-ampere, or larger, disconnecting means, overcurrent protective devices, controllers, and so forth that warrant the ground fault protection. Even though previous editions of the *NEC* did not require ground-fault protection of equipment (GFPE) for branch circuits, many designers specified it. These large branch circuits typically terminate in enclosures containing large disconnects, overcurrent devices, breakers, and so forth that should be afforded protection against arcing ground faults. The revision brings consistency in the requirements for ground-fault protection of equipment.

## Change Summary

- A new Section 210.13 titled Ground-Fault Protection of Equipment has been added to Article 210.

- The ground-fault protection for equipment requirements in 230.95 for services and 215.10 for feeders now apply to qualifying branch circuits.

- Applies to branch circuits that exceed 150-volts phase-to-ground and the branch circuit disconnect is rated 1000 amperes or greater.

Comment: None

Proposal: 2-125

# Electric Vehicle Branch Circuit

## Code Language

**210.17 Electric Vehicle Branch Circuit.** An outlet(s) installed for the purpose of charging electric vehicles shall be supplied by a separate branch circuit. This circuit shall have no other outlets.

Informational Note. See 625.2 for the definition of *Electric Vehicle*.

*(See NEC for actual text)*

## Significance of the Change    *Courtesy of Pass and Seymour Legrand*

This new requirement builds on the concepts presented in Proposals 2-61 and 2-64, which were rejected, as they were overly restrictive for electric vehicle charging loads, which are optional. The new section does provide clear requirements for installing separate (individual) branch circuits for electric vehicle supply equipment (EVSE) where necessary for vehicle charging. Charging loads associated with electric vehicle supply equipment are continuous duty loads. Generally, these loads shall not exceed 80 percent or the conductor capacity or 80percent of the rating of the branch circuit overcurrent device. The current load profiles of levels 1 and 2 electric vehicle supply equipment are such that in order to comply with 210.19(A)(1), 210.20(A)(1) and 625.40, individual branch circuits must be installed. This rule applies even to branch circuits used for cord- and plug-connected types of EVSE. As required in 625.5, electric vehicle supply equipment is required to be listed. The installation instructions with this equipment typically require connection to an individual branch circuit. This new section in Article 210 provides users with more specific individual branch circuit requirements that apply to occupancies where electric vehicle supply equipment is installed and used.

## Change Summary

- A new Section 210.17 titled Electric Vehicle Branch Circuit has been added to Article 210.

- Requires an outlet installed for electric vehicle charging loads be provided with a separate branch circuit.

- The revision aligns with the load profile requirements for electric vehicle supply equipment (EVSE) and correlates with Sections 210.19(A)(1) and 210.23.

Comment: None
Proposal: 2-128a

# Branch-Circuit Ratings – Ampacity and Size

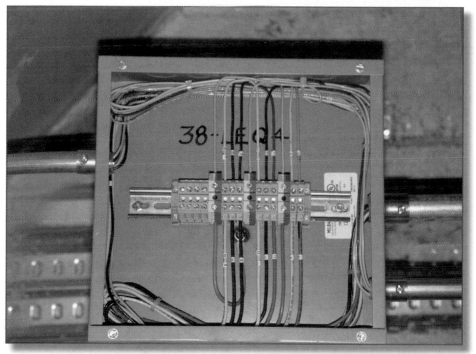

*Courtesy of Rick Maddox, Clark County, NV*

## Code Language

**(1) General.** Branch-circuit conductors shall have an ampacity not less than the maximum load to be served. Conductors shall be sized to carry not less than the larger of 210.19(A)(1)(a) or (b).

(a) Where a branch circuit supplies continuous loads or any combination of continuous and noncontinuous loads, the minimum branch-circuit conductor size shall have an allowable ampacity not less than the noncontinuous load plus 125 percent of the continuous load.

(b) The minimum branch-circuit conductor size shall have an allowable ampacity not less than the maximum load to be served after the application of any adjustment or correction factors.

*(See NEC for actual text)*

## Significance of the Change

This section has been revised editorially and to clarify that the minimum ampacity required for the conductors has to be the larger of two required calculations. Information in the substantiation indicated that as currently written, the text "before the application of any adjustment or correction factors" is misleading, and can create confusion. As written in the 2011 *NEC*, the last sentence in 210.19(A)(1) is specifying to multiply continuous loads by 125 percent and then apply additional correction factors based on conditions of use. The revised wording and arrangement makes it clear that two separate calculations are necessary. By separating the two calculation requirements of this rule, a condition is created where the conductor must be the larger of (a) or (b). Condition (a) requires that the conductors have an allowable ampacity of 125 percent of the continuous load plus the non-continuous load. Condition (b) requires that the conductors also have an allowable ampacity to carry the maximum load served after the conductor ampacity has had any correction or adjustment factors applied. Once the two calculations are performed, the larger of the two must be used.

## Change Summary

- Section 210.19(A)(1) has been revised and arranged into a list format for clarity.
- The minimum ampacity for branch circuit conductors must carry the load served and be the larger of either calculation required in (a) or (b).
- The informational notes have been relocated before the requirement and the existing exception has not changed.

Comment: 2-70
Proposals: 2-130a, 2-131

# 210.22

## Permissible Loads, Individual Branch Circuits

### Code Language

**210.22 Permissible Loads, Individual Branch Circuits.** An individual branch circuit shall be permitted to supply any load for which it is rated, but in no case shall the load exceed the branch-circuit ampere rating.

*(See NEC for actual text)*

*Courtesy of Tom Garvey*

### Change Summary

- A new section 210.22 titled Permissible Loads, Individual Branch Circuits has been added to Article 210.
- The words "an individual branch circuit shall be permitted to supply any load for which it is rated" have been removed from 210.23 and incorporated into 210.22.
- The revision separates the capacity requirements for individual branch circuits and multiple outlet branch circuits.

### Significance of the Change

This editorial revision improves usability and clarity in the application of 210.23. As written in the 2011 *NEC*, 210.23 contained the requirements for two different types of circuits, individual branch circuits and multiple outlet branch circuits. This new section 210.22 now provides the capacity requirements for just individual branch circuits. Separating this into two sections serves to point out these differences between the two requirements and clears up confusion as to the application of each section. The companion Proposal 2-141 editorially revised 210.23 by removing the text that referred to individual branch circuits. Splitting these two separate capacity requirements serves to clarify the different capacity requirements for each type of circuit. As part of this revision, the title of 210.23 has been revised to Permissible Loads, Multiple-Outlet Branch Circuits. As a result of this revision, no technical changes have been made to either of the requirements in new 210.22 and existing 210.23.

Comment: None
Proposals: 2-139, 2-140

# ADA Accessibility Design Requirements

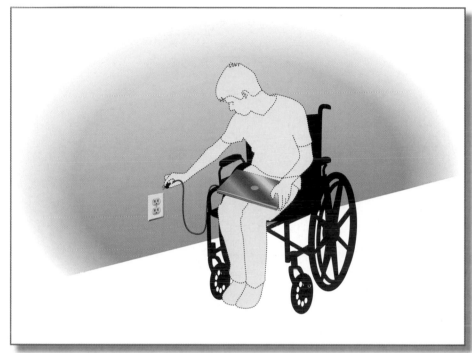

## Code Language

**210.50 General.** Receptacle outlets shall be installed as specified in 210.52 through 210.64.

Informational Note: See Informative Annex J for information regarding ADA accessibility design.

*(See NEC for actual text)*

## Significance of the Change

This new informational note provides a useful correlation and reference to new Annex J that contains additional information that may be necessary for installation of receptacles, switches and other electrical devices that must also comply with the accessibility requirements in ANSI 117.1 Accessible and Usable Buildings and Facilities. Informative Annex J is new resulting from favorable action on Proposal 1-191a. The new annex is titled ADA Standards for Accessible Design. This annex is not a part of the requirements of the *NEC*, but is included for informational purposes only. The provisions cited in this Informative Annex will assist users of the Code in properly considering various electrical design constraints of other building systems and are part of the 2010 ADA Standards for Accessible Design and are the same as those found in ANSI/ICC A117.1-2009, Accessible and Usable Buildings and Facilities. Although located following 210.50, the new informational note would be applicable to the subdivisions of 210.60 and 210.70 that address other than dwelling units.

## Change Summary

- A new informational note has been added following 210.50 to correlate with new Annex J.
- Reference is made to a new Annex J that provides specific guidelines on ADA accessibility design.
- Outlet and switch box locations in other than dwelling units are often impacted by requirements in ANSI 117.1 Accessible and Usable Buildings and Facilities.

Comment: None
Proposal: 2-143a

# Balconies, Decks and Porches

## Code Language

**(3) Balconies, Decks, and Porches.** Balconies, decks, and porches that are attached to the dwelling unit and are accessible from inside the dwelling unit shall have at least one receptacle outlet accessible from the balcony, deck, or porch. The receptacle outlet shall not be located more than 2.0 m (6 1/2 ft) above the balcony, deck, or porch walking surface.

*(See NEC for actual text)*

## Change Summary

- List item (3) in 210.52(E) has been revised for clarity and more uniform application.

- The revision clarifies that the balcony, deck, or porch must be attached to the dwelling unit.

- As revised the required receptacle outlet must be accessible from the balcony, deck, or porch walking surface.

## Significance of the Change

This revision incorporates the changes suggested by Proposals 2-169, 2-170, and 2-176 as modified by Comment 2-80. This section deals with the requirements for a receptacle outlet installation at balconies, porches, and decks to discourage misuse of cords, such as running them through windows and doors to supply loads on the porch, deck, or balcony. While the revision seems editorial in nature, installation location requirements have been added. The first significant change is that the balcony, porch, or deck must be attached to the dwelling unit it serves. The second change is that the receptacle outlet must be accessible from the walking surface of the balcony, porch or deck. By adding the term *walking surface* to this section, it becomes clear where the 2.0 m (6-1/2 ft) measurement must be taken from. The revision should improve application resulting in more consistency for installers and inspectors.

Comments: 2-80, 2-81

Proposals: 2-169, 2-170, 2-176

# Basement, Garages, and Accessory Buildings

## Significance of the Change

This section as revised, improves usability and clarity of the receptacle outlet requirements for attached and detached garages for dwelling units. The requirements for receptacle outlets in attached and detached garages of dwelling units have been expanded and become more restrictive. The branch circuit supplying garage receptacle(s) is not permitted to supply any outlets outside the garage. Another new requirement is that at least one receptacle must be provided for each vehicle space of the attached or detached garage. In other words, a one-car garage requires at least one receptacle installed in that single vehicle space. For a two-car garage, at least two receptacles must be installed, one in each vehicle space. The exact location for the receptacle outlets in these vehicle spaces is not specified. This section continues to exclude any outlets that are installed for special equipment such as welders, central vacuum equipment, electric vehicle supply equipment, and so forth. As required in 210.8(A)(2), ground-fault circuit interrupter protection is required for these receptacle outlets.

## Code Language

**(G) Basement, Garages, and Accessory Buildings.** For a one-family dwelling, at least one receptacle outlet shall be installed in the areas specified in 210.52(G)(1) through (3). These receptacles shall be in addition to receptacles required for specific equipment.

**(1) Garages.** In each attached garage and in each detached garage with electric power. The branch circuit supplying this receptacle(s) shall not supply outlets outside of the garage. At least one receptacle outlet shall be installed for each car space.

**(2) Accessory Buildings.** In each accessory building with electric power.

**(3) Basements.** In each separate unfinished portion of a basement.

*(See NEC for actual text)*

## Change Summary

- This section has been renumbered into a three list items addressing (1) garages, (2) accessory buildings, and (3) basements

- List item (1) has been revised with more specific requirements for receptacle outlets in garages.

- The branch circuit can supply no outlet outside of the garage and at least one receptacle outlet is required in each car space.

Comments: 2-82, 2-83
Proposals: 2-178a, 2-179, 2-180

# Receptacle Required at Service Equipment

## Code Language

**210.64 Electrical Service Areas.** At least one 125-volt, single-phase 15- or 20-ampere-rated receptacle outlet shall be installed within 15 m (50 ft) of the electrical service equipment.

*Exception: The receptacle outlet shall not be required to be installed in one- and two-family dwellings.*

**(See NEC for actual text)**

## Significance of the Change

This new section requires at least one 125-volt, single-phase 15- or 20-ampere rated receptacle outlet to be installed within 50 feet of service equipment. Although many engineered designs often specified a receptacle outlet in these locations, it was never a requirement of the *NEC*. Information provided in the substantiation indicated that this change was proposed for the same reason that a receptacle is required for servicing HVAC equipment as provided in 210.63. These receptacles are often needed for connecting portable electrical data acquisition equipment for the essential and qualitative analysis of the electrical system along with testing and servicing the electrical equipment. Presently, to accomplish the connection of such instruments and other tools, extension cords are run through doors, windows, or other openings throughout the building and often connected to non-GFCI-protected receptacles creating other hazards for personnel. This new section is an improvement in the *NEC* and an enhancement in safety for personnel. It should be noted that this general requirement does not specify that these required receptacles be protected by ground-fault circuit interrupter (GFCI) protection. The GFCI requirements in 210.8 would apply to receptacles required by this section if they are installed in locations specified in 210.8.

## Change Summary

- A new 210.64 titled Electrical Service Areas has been added to Article 210.
- At least one 125-volt, single-phase, 15- or 20-ampere rated receptacle outlet shall be installed within 50 ft of service equipment.
- By exception, one- and two-family dwelling units are exempt from the rule.

Comment: 2-86
Proposal: 2-191

## Feeder Ampacity

### Code Language

**(1) General.** Feeder conductors shall have an ampacity not less than required to supply the load as calculated in Parts III, IV, and V of Article 220. Conductors shall be sized to carry not less than the larger of 215.2(A)(1)(a) or (b).

(a) Where a feeder supplies continuous loads or any combination of continuous and noncontinuous loads, the minimum feeder conductor size shall have an allowable ampacity not less than the noncontinuous load plus 125 percent of the continuous load.

(b) The minimum feeder conductor size shall have an allowable ampacity not less than the maximum load to be served after the application of any adjustment or correction factors.

*(See NEC for actual text)*

### Significance of the Change

Section 215.2(A)(1) has been revised to clarify the minimum ampacity for the feeders has to be the larger of two required calculations. Feeders must be sized to carry the load calculated in accordance with Parts III, IV, and V of Article 220. The substantiation indicated that as currently written, the text "before the application of any adjustment or correction factors" is misleading. As written in the 2011 *NEC*, the last sentence in 215.2(A)(1) is specifying to multiply continuous loads by 125 percent and then apply additional correction factors based on conditions of use. The revised wording and arrangement clarifies that two separate calculations are necessary. By separating the two calculation requirements of this rule, a condition is created where the conductors must be the larger of (a) or (b). Condition (a) requires that the conductors have an allowable ampacity of 125 percent of the continuous load plus the non-continuous load. Condition (b) requires that the conductors also have to carry the maximum load served after the conductor ampacity has had any correction or adjustment factors applied. Once the two calculations are performed, the larger of the two must be used.

### Change Summary

- Section 215.2(A)(1) has been revised and arranged into a list format for clarity.
- The minimum ampacity for feeder conductors must carry the calculated load and be the larger of either calculation required in (a) or (b).
- The informational notes have been relocated directly following the requirement and the existing exception has not changed.

Comments: None
Proposals: 2-201

**REVISION**

# Identification for Feeders – DC Systems

## Code Language

**(C) Identification of Ungrounded Conductors.** Ungrounded conductors shall be identified in accordance with 215.12(C)(1) or (C)(2), as applicable.

**(1) Feeders Supplied from More Than One Nominal Voltage System.** (See *NEC* text)...and splice points in compliance with 215.12(C)(1)(a) and (b).

(a) *Means of Identification.* (See *NEC* text)

(b) *Posting of Identification Means* (See *NEC* text)

**(2) Feeders Supplied from Direct Current Systems** (See *NEC* text)

(a) *Positive Polarity, Sizes 6 AWG or Smaller* (See *NEC* text)

(b) *Negative Polarity, Sizes 6 AWG or Smaller* (See *NEC* text)

*(See NEC for actual text)*

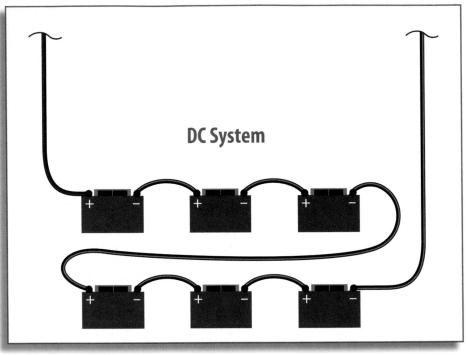

**DC System**

## Significance of the Change

This revision is the work of the *NEC* DC Task Force assigned by the *NEC* Correlating Committee in the 2014 cycle. The substantiation indicated direct current applications are experiencing a re-emergence because electric vehicle charging, solar photovoltaic systems, micro-grids, small wind electric systems, etc. can achieve greater efficiencies and energy savings. The industry continues to install these different applications using dc wiring, however, there are prevalent inconsistencies in conductor identification methods and various polarity identification schemes. Another concern is that the grounded conductors of negatively-grounded or positively-grounded two-wire direct current systems are actually identified in accordance with 200.6. Such conductor identification inconsistencies result in risk and confusion to installers and service personnel. The new identification requirements in this section ensure that consistent identification means for dc feeders are required and grounded feeder conductors of dc systems follow the identification rules in 200.6. It can be seen in list item (2) that the size break point for identification is consistent with that of 200.6. Sizes 4 AWG and larger dc conductors follow one set of requirements while (2)(a) and (b) address sizes 6 AWG and smaller have other identification methods specified including red as positive and black as negative.

## Change Summary

- Subdivision (C) of this section has been rearranged in a list format conforming to the *NEC Style Manual*.

- This section has also been expanded to specify identification for feeders supplied by dc systems.

- The color red has been designated for positive conductors and the color black is designated for negative conductors.

Comment: 2-100
Proposal: 2-217

## Lighting Load for Specified Occupancies

### Code Language

*Exception: Where the building is designed and constructed to comply with an energy code adopted by the local authority, the lighting load shall be permitted to be calculated at the values specified in the energy code where the following conditions are met:*

*(1) A power monitoring system is installed that will provide continuous information regarding the total general lighting load of the building.*

*(2) The power monitoring system will be set with alarm values to alert the building owner or manager if the lighting load exceeds the values set by the energy code.*

*(3) The demand factors specified in 220.42 are not applied to the general lighting load.*

**(See NEC for actual text)**

### Significance of the Change

Proposal 2-320 (Log # 3751) from the 2011 development cycle was resubmitted as Proposal 2-228 for the 2014 *NEC*. Additional substantiation and support from several major universities across the country justified the new exception that provides relief from the standard load calculation requirements provided in 220.12. CMP-2 acted favorable to the additional information provided and supported the proposed exception. The change recognizes that there are calculations required by Article 220 that can be adjusted to align with energy codes where so adopted by the enforcing jurisdiction. The new exception recognizes that where a jurisdiction adopts an energy code, lighting load calculation values need to be consistent between the *NEC* and the adopted energy *Code*. Without this exception, a conflict is often created. The basic conditions of the exception are that an energy code is adopted by the jurisdiction, the power system is monitored and equipped with appropriate alarms, and the demand factors of 220.42 are not applied to the general lighting load. This is new ground for the *NEC*, but necessary as energy management incentives and mandates increase. The *NEC* continues a progressive approach to this concept and is also equipped with a new Article 750 covering energy management systems.

### Change Summary

- A new exception has been added to 220.12.
- Lighting loads are permitted to be calculated at the values specified in an applicable energy code where it is adopted by the jurisdiction.
- Three conditions of the exception include monitoring, alarms and not applying demand factors to the general lighting load as provided in 220.42.

Comments: 2-102, 2-104, 2-106, 2-107, 2-110, 2-111, 2-119a

Proposal: 2-228

# Wiring on Buildings or Other Structures

## Code Language

**225.10 Wiring on Buildings (or Other Structures).** The installation of outside wiring on surfaces of buildings (or other structures) shall be permitted for circuits of not over 1000 volts, nominal, as open wiring on insulators, as multiconductor cable, as Type MC cable...(See *NEC* text)...

*(See NEC for actual text)*

*Courtesy of General Cable*

## Change Summary

- The words "or other structures" have been added to the title of this section and in the first sentence.
- As revised, this section applies to other structures in addition to just buildings; both are defined in Article 100.
- The wiring methods referenced in this section have been changed to the appropriate acronym.

Comment: None

Proposals: 4-20, 4-21, 4-22, 4-23, 4-24, 4-25, 4-26

## Significance of the Change

The revision in this section is to add the words "or other structures" which expands these recognized wiring methods to other structures in addition to just buildings. Both terms *building* and *structure* are defined in Article 100 as follows:

*Building.* A structure that stands alone or that is cut off from adjoining structures by fire walls with all openings therein protected by approved fire doors.

*Structure.* That which is built or constructed.

While a building is always a structure, a structure is not always a building. Buildings typically have occupants and are intended for habitation, while structures typically are not. As an example, a single-family dwelling is a building, but a carport, water tower, flag pole, antenna mast, and so forth, are structures. The revision to this section clarifies that the types of wiring methods listed in this section are permitted for use as outside feeder or branch circuit wiring whether installed on a building or structure. The revision should improve clarity and usability for installers and inspectors applying these provisions. The other revisions in this section changed each written wiring method to the recognized acronym, for example: the words "electrical metallic tubing" are changed to EMT.

# Entering, Exiting, or Attached to Buildings or Structures

## Code Language

**225.11 Feeder and Branch-Circuit Conductors Entering, Exiting, or Attached to Buildings or Structures.** Feeder and branch-circuit conductors entering or exiting buildings or structures shall be installed in accordance with the requirements of 230.52. Overhead branch circuits and feeders attached to buildings or structures shall be installed in accordance with the requirements of 230.54.

*(See NEC for actual text)*

## Significance of the Change

The previous title of this section was Circuit Exits and Entrances. The title has been revised to clarify that the circuits addressed in this requirement are both feeders and branch circuits. The other revision in this section is to add the words "or structures" to the title and in the rule. Information in the substantiation indicated that many structures are not buildings by definition. The requirements for outside wiring should be the same for walls, towers, tanks, poles, signs, and other structures that may not be a building such as a house, store, office building. In all cases the branch circuit and feeder wiring is outside and as such, the requirements of this section should apply to buildings and other structures. Both terms *building* and *structure* are defined in Article 100 to clarify the distinct differences between them. It should be noted that while a building is always a structure, a structure is not always a building. As revised it is clear that the requirements in 230.52 and 230.54 apply to outside branch circuits and feeders attached to buildings and structures. The revision should improve clarity and usability for installers and inspectors applying these provisions.

## Change Summary

- The section title has been changed to Feeder and Branch Circuit Conductors, Entering, Exiting, or Attached to Buildings or Structures.
- The words "or structures" have been included in both the title and the rule.
- The revision clarifies what was meant by "circuit exits.." and includes "structures" in addition to just buildings.

Comment: None
Proposals: 4-27, 4-28

# Masts as Support

## Code Language

**225.17 Masts as Supports.** Only feeder or branch-circuit conductors specified within this section shall be permitted to be attached to the feeder and/or branch-circuit mast. Masts... (See *NEC* text)...shall be installed in accordance with 225.17(A) and (B).

**(A) Strength.** The mast shall be of adequate strength...(See *NEC* text)... Hubs intended for use with a conduit that serves as a mast for support of feeder or branch-circuit conductors shall be identified for use with a mast.

**(B) Attachment.** Feeder and/or branch-circuit conductors shall not be attached to a mast between a weatherhead...(See *NEC* text)...located above the building or other structure.

*(See NEC for actual text)*

## Change Summary

- This section has been revised and rearranged into a list format in accordance with the *NEC Style Manual*.
- The revision clarifies that only the hubs are required to be identified for use with service masts.
- The revision clarifies the suitable point of attaching branch circuits or feeders in relationship to the weatherhead.

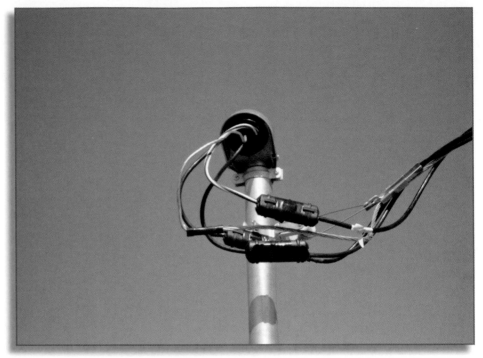

## Significance of the Change

The previous text was revised and subdivided into titled subsections for usability and clarity. The text relative to "all raceway fittings being identified for use with a mast" was removed as not all fittings, such as a rigid conduit coupling, are specifically identified for use with a mast. The added text addressing hubs parallels the language in the UL Guide Information for Electrical Equipment (*White Book*) under the Category of "Conduit Fittings (DWTT)" which specifies hubs intended for use with conduit that serves as a service mast, in accordance with the *NEC*, are marked on the fitting or carton to indicate suitability for use with service entrance equipment. Finally, language in (B) has been added to prohibit feeder and/or branch circuit conductors from being attached between a coupling and the weatherhead or between a coupling and the end of the conduit where the coupling is located above the last point of secure attachment of the raceway to the building or other structure or where the coupling is located above the building or other structure. The revisions to this section should promote more uniform application of mast support requirements for outside branch circuits and feeders.

Comment: None
Proposal: 4-30

# Feeder and Branch Circuit Raceway Seals

Basement

Feeder

Seal

## Code Language

**225.27 Raceway Seal.** Where a raceway enters a building or structure from an underground distribution system, it shall be sealed in accordance with 300.5(G). Spare or unused raceways shall also be sealed. Sealants shall be identified for use with the cable insulation, conductor insulation, bare conductor, shield, or other components.

*(See NEC for actual text)*

## Significance of the Change

The general purpose of sections 225.7 and 230.8 is to minimize the migration of moisture and wetness from entering wiring enclosures through raceways and cables that enter buildings or structures. Sealant material is required to be installed within the raceway to fill in all gaps between the inside of the raceway and the contained conductors. This process forces the sealing material or compound into contact with the individual conductors contained in the raceway. This revision clarifies that the sealant used to meet the requirements in 225.27 must be identified for use with the cable, individual conductor insulation, and bare conductor material. Single conductors in raceways are a very common type of wiring entering buildings and need to be included in this provision in addition to just cables. Sealants used with bare conductors are likely to have deleterious effects on the conductor type and should also be included. While no companion proposal was submitted to revise 230.8, the same problem exists in that section. The change in this section should alert installers and inspectors that the sealant material selected and installed to meet the requirements of 225.27 and 230.8 must be identified for use with cable, conductor insulation, and bare conductor material in the raceway.

## Change Summary

- The words "conductor insulation, bare conductor" have been added to this section.
- The revision clarifies that this requirement applies to cable sheaths, individual conductor insulation, and the bare conductor material itself.
- Sealant must be identified for this specific use with individual insulated conductors, bare conductors and cables.

Comment: None
Proposal: 4-38

## Disconnect Type

### Code Language

**225.36 Type.** The disconnecting means specified in 225.31 shall be comprised of a circuit breaker, molded case switch, general-use switch, snap switch, or other approved means. Where applied in accordance with 250.32(B) Exception, the disconnecting means shall be suitable for use as service equipment.

*(See NEC for actual text)*

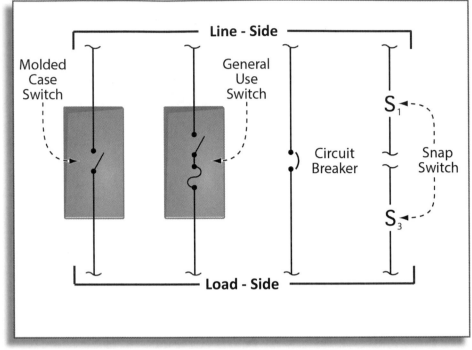

### Change Summary

- The title of this section has been changed from Suitable for Service Equipment to Types.
- The types of acceptable disconnects are provided in addition to other disconnecting means that are approved.
- Generally, the disconnecting means no longer has to be suitable for use as service equipment unless installed to meet the provisions in 250.32(B) Exception.

Comment: None

Proposals: 4-55, 4-51, 4-52, 4-54, 4-56, 4-57, 4-59, 4-63

### Significance of the Change

Action on Proposal 4-55 continues the work of CMP-4 started in the comment stages of the 2011 *NEC* development cycle. Comment 4-19 (Log # 1437) in the 2011 cycle was held because of introducing new material. The revision in 225.36 this cycle removes the exception that allowed 3-way and 4-way switches for residential disconnects on outbuildings and garages. This revision also expands the provisions to all occupancies, not just residential occupancies. The substantiation indicated the intention of disallowing three-way switch loops is clear because they do not disconnect all ungrounded conductors. This revision also removes the suitable for use as service equipment (SUSE) requirement, which involves greater internal spacing, grounding provisions, and so forth. These are only justified in instances where there is a true service exposure, with no overcurrent protection ahead of the equipment. The principal wiring difference for SUSE ratings is that identified in the original 2011 *NEC* proposal 4-46, namely, that a re-grounding provision must be incorporated. The requirements in 225.38 can be satisfied using a snap switch equipped with the requisite poles provided on the device. Therefore, the exception to 225.38 has also been deleted because its only purpose was to allow 3-way and 4-way switch loops.

# Disconnecting Means Location and Type

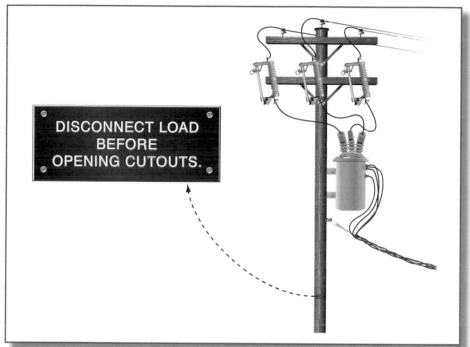

## Code Language

**(A) Location.** A building or structure disconnecting means shall be located in accordance with 225.32, or, if not readily accessible, it shall be operable by mechanical linkage from a readily accessible point. For multibuilding industrial installations under single management, it shall be permitted to be electrically operated by a readily accessible, remote-control device in a separate building or structure.

**(B) Type.** Each building...(See *NEC* text)... available at its supply terminals.

*Exception: Where the individual disconnecting means...(See NEC text)... to the fused cutouts and shall read DIS-CONNECT LOAD BEFORE OPEN-ING CUTOUTS.*

*(See NEC for actual text)*

## Significance of the Change

Section 225.52(A) has been revised editorially to clarify the requirements and to correlate with the provisions in 230.205(A) as the two sections relate to the same requirements. Information in Comment 4-32 indicated that for campus-style installation, pole-mounted disconnects are often provided in outdoor feeders not supplied by the utility. As revised, the correlation between articles 225 and 230 continues to establish more consistency between similar requirements. The words "similarly located" have been removed since they can lead to confusion. The revised text in (A) provides the specific allowances of this section. The exception relaxes the requirements for simultaneous disconnecting of all ungrounded conductors when conforming to the provisions in the exception. The exception has been revised to specify exact language that must be provided on the sign. As previously written, the exception was not as clear as to the message that must be conveyed. It is important to disconnect the load before opening cutouts individually. The specific text mandated for the sign addressed in the exception will promote consistency in field applications and enhance safety for operators of disconnecting means that are comprised of individual cutouts. As revised, the sign must read "DISCONNECT LOAD BEFORE OPENING CUTOUTS."

## Change Summary

- This revision incorporates changes suggested in Proposals 4-69 and 4-72 and Comment 4-32.
- The disconnecting means location provisions in (A) have been expanded to correlate with 230.205(A).
- The words "DISCONNECT LOAD BEFORE OPENING CUTOUTS" have been added to the exception.

Comment: 4-32
Proposals: 4-69, 4-72

# Pre-energization and Operational Tests

## Code Language

**(A) Pre-Energization and Operating Tests.** The complete electrical system design, including settings for protective, switching, and control circuits, shall be prepared in advance and made available on request to the authority having jurisdiction and shall be performance tested when first installed on-site. Each protective, switching, and control circuit shall be adjusted in accordance with the system design and tested by actual operation using current injection or equivalent methods as necessary to ensure that each and every such circuit operates correctly to the satisfaction of the authority having jurisdiction.

*(See NEC for actual text)*

## Change Summary

- This section has been revised to require specific settings and testing requirements.
- The words "including settings for protective, switching, and control circuits, shall be prepared in advance and made available on request to the authority having jurisdiction" have been added.
- The requirement clarifies what settings are actually required to be available for the AHJ.

*Courtesy of Shermco Industries*

## Significance of the Change

This requirement was introduced in the 2011 *NEC* but it was not clear that information about the complete system design had to be available to the authority having jurisdiction in advance or energizing the system, which is what was always intended. As revised, this section is clear that information about the complete system design must be provided in advance and all test reports and operational testing be performed prior to energizing the system. Previously, this section was open-ended and not specific enough to be applied consistently to meet the intended objectives. The words "system design" is more specific and is inclusive of protective switching and control circuits. Adding the words "including settings for protective, switching, and control circuits" make it clear what specific information must be prepared in advance and made available to the authority having jurisdiction. The revisions to this section promote more uniform application of these provisions for system over 1000 volts. The informational note following this section provides users with a reference to an excellent standard that deals with acceptance testing of these types of systems. Users are encouraged to refer to NETA ATS-2007 *Acceptance Testing Specifications for Electrical Power Distribution Equipment and Systems* for additional information.

Comment: None

Proposal: 4-81

# Conductors Considered Outside the Building

## Code Language

**230.6 Conductors Considered Outside the Building.**

Conductors shall be considered outside of a building or other structure under any of the following conditions:

(1) through (4) ...(See *NEC* Text)...

(5) Where installed within rigid metal conduit (Type RMC) or intermediate metal conduit (Type IMC) used to accommodate the clearance requirements in 230.24 and routed directly through an eave but not a wall of a building.

*(See NEC for actual text)*

## Significance of the Change

This revision limits application of this provision to heavy wall steel conduits passing directly through an eave cavity. As revised, rigid metal conduit (RMC) and intermediate metal conduit (IMC) are the only metal raceways recognized by this section for passing through an eave of a building. It is important to note that masts are not necessarily always made up of steel pipe. For example, a heavy timber with service-entrance cable (Type SE) fastened to it could qualify as a mast within the provisions of 230.28. Heavy wall conduit masts have historically been used for this purpose without objections or any known problems. The revision further qualifies the acceptable use to only a direct pass-through to limit the amount routed through the building eave cavity. CMP-4 was presented with examples of installations such as one with a PVC conduit routed up outside a building, then horizontally through an eave cavity some ten feet, and then up to the weatherhead. This type of installation was never intended, as the length of unprotected service conductors was not limited within the hollow portions of a building or structure. This revision provides clear direction for installers and inspectors that apply this provision.

## Change Summary

- This section applies to IMC and RMC used to route service conductors directly through a building eave.

- The revision excludes masts constructed of material other than RMC or IMC.

- The revision clarifies that a conduit mast can be routed directly through, but not routed excessively within the eave or run through a building wall.

Comment: None
Proposal: 4-103

# Service Masts as Support

## Code Language

**230.28 Service Masts as Supports.** Only power service-drop or overhead service conductors shall be permitted to be attached to a service mast. Service masts...(See *NEC* text)...shall be installed in accordance with 230.28(A) and (B).

**(A) Strength.** The service mast shall be of adequate strength...(See *NEC* text)...Hubs intended for use with a conduit that serves as a service mast shall be identified for use with service-entrance equipment.

**(B) Attachment.** Service-drop or overhead service conductors shall not be attached to a service mast between a weatherhead...(See *NEC* text)... located above the building or other structure.

*(See NEC for actual text)*

## Change Summary

- This section has been revised and rearranged into a list format in accordance with the *NEC Style Manual*.
- The revision clarifies that only the hubs are required to be identified for use with service masts.
- The revision clarifies the suitable point of attaching service drops or overhead service conductors in relationship to the weatherhead.

## Significance of the Change

The previous text was revised and subdivided into titled subsections for usability and clarity. The text relative to "all raceway fittings being identified for use with a mast" was removed as not all fittings, such as a rigid conduit coupling, are specifically identified for use with a mast. The added text addressing hubs, parallels the language in the UL Guide Information for Electrical Equipment (*White Book*) under the Category of "Conduit Fittings (DWTT)" which specifies hubs intended for use with conduit that serves as a service mast, in accordance with the *NEC*, are marked on the fitting or carton to indicate suitability for use with service entrance equipment. Finally, language in (B) has been added to prohibit the service drop or overhead service conductors from being attached between a coupling and the weather-head or between a coupling and the end of the conduit where the coupling is located above the last point of secure attachment of the raceway to the building or other structure or where the coupling is located above the building or other structure. The revisions to this section should promote more uniform application of mast support requirements for service drops and overhead service conductors.

Comment: None
Proposal: 4-114

# Underground Service Conductors

## Significance of the Change

Comment 4-30 to Proposal 4-93 in the 2011 *NEC* development cycle was held based on 4.4.6.2.2 of the NFPA Regulations Governing Committee Projects. The concerns related to incorporating the term *listed direct buried cable* in this section creating correlation issues that could not be resolved during the 2011 *NEC* process, and as such returns to the 2014 *NEC* process as Proposal 4-115. The problem was that not all direct buried cables are suitable for use as underground service conductors, such as Type UF. Favorable action on Proposal 4-115 and Comment 4-45 results in the expansion of this section to include a list of underground wiring methods that are suitable for installation as underground service conductors. The list is inclusive with no exceptions. As revised, this section is numbered into a list format conforming to the *NEC Style Manual*. The term *service-lateral* has been changed to *underground service conductors* and the existing exception relating to bare grounded conductor use has remained unchanged. The revisions to this section should enhance usability and clarity for installers and inspectors relative to which underground wiring can be used for underground service conductors.

## Code Language

**(A) Insulation.** Underground service… (See *NEC* text)…

**(B) Wiring Methods.** Underground service conductors shall be installed in accordance with the applicable requirements of this *Code* covering the type of wiring method used and shall be limited to the following methods:

(1) Type RMC conduit

(2) Type IMC conduit

(3) Type NUCC conduit

(4) Type HDPE conduit

(5) Type PVC conduit

(6) Type RTRC conduit

(7) Type IGS cable

(8) Type USE conductors or cables

(9) Type MV or MC cable identified for direct burial applications

(10) Type MI cable, where suitably protected against physical damage and corrosive conditions

*(See NEC for actual text)*

## Change Summary

- This section has been renumbered in a list format and expanded to include acceptable wiring methods.

- New subdivision (B) provides a list of wiring methods suitable for use as underground service conductors.

- The previous exception related to use of bare grounded conductors remains the same in 230.30(A).

Comment: 4-45

Proposals: 4-115, 4-116

## Service-Entrance Conductors – Minimum Size and Rating

### Code Language

**(A) General.** The ampacity of service-entrance conductors shall not be less than either 230.42(A)(1), (A)(2) or (A)(3). Loads...(See *NEC* text)...shall be that value for which the busway has been listed or labeled.

(1) The sum of the noncontinuous loads plus 125 percent of continuous loads

*Exception: Grounded conductors that are not connected to an overcurrent device shall be permitted to be sized at 100 percent of the continuous and noncontinuous load.*

(2) The sum of the noncontinuous load plus the continuous load after the application of any adjustment or correction factors.

(3) The sum of the noncontinuous load...(See *NEC* text)...rating.

*(See NEC for actual text)*

### Change Summary

- In list item (2) the words "conditions of use have been applied" have been replaced with the words "the application of any adjustment or correction factors."
- The revision clarifies both calculations in list items (1) and (2) must be performed and the service conductors size cannot be smaller than the larger of the two calculations.

### Significance of the Change

Action on Comment 4-48 clarifies the provisions in list item (2) and that two calculations must be performed. Information in the substantiation indicated that the 2011 current text of this section is not clear. Section 230.42(A) is specifying to multiply continuous loads by 125 percent and then apply the correction and/or adjustment factors. This is inconsistent with the way example D(3)(a) is calculated in Informative Annex D. There are two different and separate calculations necessary when applying this section and the larger of the two must be used for sizing the service conductors. One calculation considers continuous loads without considering the correction and/or adjustment factors. The other calculation considers correction and/or adjustment factors with all loads (continuous and non-continuous) calculated at 100 percent. Similar revisions were made to 210.19(A)(1) and 215.2(A)(1) to improve clarity and provide users with more specific method of determining the minimum size service conductors required. The revision promotes a more consistent method of determining minimum conductor ampacities as required by 210.19(A)(1), 215.2(A) and 230.42(A).

Comment: 4-48

Proposal: 4-120

# Cable Tray – Labeling

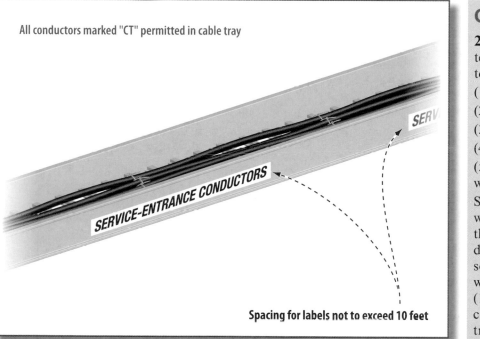

All conductors marked "CT" permitted in cable tray

SERVICE-ENTRANCE CONDUCTORS

SERV

Spacing for labels not to exceed 10 feet

## Code Language

**230.44 Cable Trays.** Cable tray systems shall…(See *NEC* text)…limited to the following methods:

(1) Type SE Cable

(2) Type MC Cable

(3) Type MI Cable

(4) Type IGS Cable

(5) Single conductors 1/0 and larger with CT rating.

Such cable trays shall be identified with permanently affixed labels with the wording "Service-Entrance Conductors." The labels shall be located so as to be visible after installation with a spacing not to exceed 3 m (10 ft) so that the service-entrance conductors are able to be readily traced through the entire length of the cable tray.

*(See NEC for actual text)*

## Significance of the Change

This section has been revised to delete the words "thermoplastic-insulated" expanding this provision to all conductors that have a cable tray (CT) use marking. List item (5) is not intended to limit the single-conductor use to only conductors with thermoplastic insulation. The other revision to this section is to incorporate the words "with a spacing not to exceed 3 m (10 ft)" into the second paragraph. As revised a maximum spacing interval is now provided for the labels required in this section. These changes are similar to the spacing intervals for the labeling required in 392.18(H) for cable trays that contain medium- and high-voltage conductors. A 10-foot spacing is reasonable given the importance of the service conductors relative to the entire electrical system from a service continuity standpoint and from a worker safety perspective. The 10-foot spacing intervals of the required of labels will readily allow determination of cable trays that contain service conductors, which are typically not provided with overcurrent protection other than what might be provided on the supply side of the utility transformer. The markings help ensure that conductors other than service conductors are not installed in the tray as prohibited by this rule.

## Change Summary

- The words "thermoplastic-insulated" have been removed from this section.
- The words "with a spacing not to exceed 3 m (10 ft)" have been added to this section.
- This section now provides a maximum distance interval that the required labels must be provided to ensure the cable tray use is readily evident.

Comment: None
Proposals: 4-133, 4-134, 4-135

# Meter Disconnect Switches – Marking

## Code Language

(3) Meter disconnect switches nominally rated not in excess of 1000 V that have a short-circuit current rating equal to or greater than the available short-circuit current, provided that all metal housings and service enclosures are grounded in accordance with Part VII and bonded in accordance with Part V of Article 250. A meter disconnect switch shall be capable of interrupting the load served. A meter disconnect shall be legibly field marked on its exterior in a manner suitable for the environment as follows:

METER DISCONNECT
NOT SERVICE EQUIPMENT

*(See NEC for actual text)*

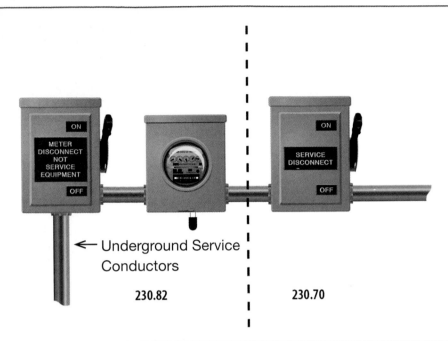

Underground Service Conductors

230.82          230.70

## Change Summary

- A new last sentence has been added to list item (3) in this section.
- A legible field marking must be applied to the exterior of the disconnect indicating its purpose.
- The marking must be suitable for the environment and include the exact words "Meter Disconnect Not Service Equipment."

## Significance of the Change

This revision is actually a resubmittal of Comment 4-52 in the 2011 *NEC* development process. The requirement to identify a meter disconnect switch provides a clear differentiation from the service disconnecting means and equipment. The meter disconnecting means is a safety switch for those servicing, replacing, or reinserting an electric meter. The main purpose served by meter disconnects is that they provide the ability to remove the load from the service before extracting or inserting an across-the-line meter. This is typically a utility company regulation and is usually required on services with a 480Y/277-volt supply, although it is not limited to that voltage level alone. The challenge when these meter disconnects are installed is that users can confuse them with the required service disconnecting means for the occupancy. Service disconnects must be identified as such, no change there. As revised, the marking requirement will allow operators of service and meter disconnects to readily identify the purpose served by each disconnect. Often the two disconnects are located adjacent to the meter installation, but not in all cases. Comment 4-64 emphasized that with the new marking requirement, operators will know to look elsewhere for service disconnecting means that may not be located adjacent to the meter.

Comment: 4-64
Proposal: 4-156

# Taps Not Over 10 Feet Long

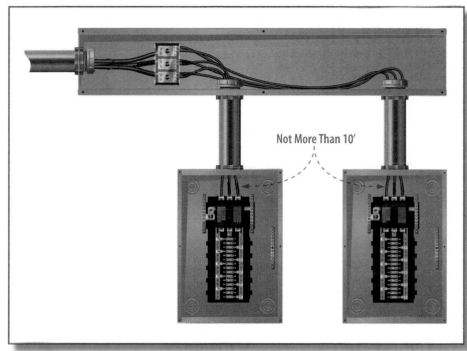

Not More Than 10'

## Code Language

**(1) Taps Not over 3 m (10 ft) Long.**
…(See *NEC* text)…

(1) The ampacity of the tap conductors is

**a.** Not less than …(See *NEC* text)…

**b.** Not less than the rating of the equipment containing an overcurrent device(s) supplied by the tap conductors or not less than the rating of the overcurrent protective device at the termination of the tap conductors.

*Exception to b: Where listed equipment, such as surge protective device(s) (SPDs), is provided with specific instructions on minimum conductor sizing, the ampacity of the tap conductors supplying that equipment shall be permitted to be determined based on the manufacturer's instructions.*

**(See *NEC* for actual text)**

## Significance of the Change

These revisions are a continuation of the work started by CMP-10 on Proposal 10-46 and Comment 10-17 in the 2011 *NEC* development cycle. As revised, this section now clarifies what was meant by the word "device" as previously used in b. Information provided in the substantiation indicated that The word "device" should be replaced with more descriptive terms since the definition of *device* is, "A unit of an electrical system that carries or controls electric energy as its principal function." Though obviously not intended by 240.24(B)(1)(1) b, the broad definition of device includes wire and other conductors such as busway. Revising the section to reference equipment containing overcurrent device(s) narrows the application of the section beyond what the previous wording literally meant. Action by CMP-10 on Comment 10-14 also refines the exception and expands it slightly to apply to surge protective devices (SPDs) and other similar equipment that may be connected by a tap in accordance with the provisions of this section. The revision and new exception improve clarity and promote more consistent application of the 10-foot tap rules. Similar revisions have also been incorporated into 240.21(C)(2) which addresses transformer secondary conductors.

## Change Summary

- The words "equipment containing an overcurrent" have been added in front of the word "device(s)" in b.

- A new exception has been added covering SPDs and other similar devices only if in accordance with manufacturer's instructions.

- The revision clarifies what type of equipment the tap conductors must terminate in.

Comment: 10-14
Proposal: 10-32

# Outside Taps of Unlimited Length

## Code Language

**(5) Outside Taps of Unlimited Length.**...(See *NEC* text)...

(1) The tap conductors are protected from...(See *NEC* text)...

(2) The tap conductors terminate at a single ...(See *NEC* text)...

ampacity of the tap conductors. This single ...(See *NEC* text)...

(3) The overcurrent device for the tap conductors is an integral part ...(See *NEC* text)...

(4) The disconnecting means for the tap conductors ...(See *NEC* text)... the following:

a. Outside of a building or structure

b. Inside, nearest the point of entrance of the tap conductors

c. Where installed in accordance with 230.6, nearest the point of entrance of the tap conductors

*(See NEC for actual text)*

## Change Summary

- This editorial revision adds the word "tap" in front of the word "conductors" in each of the section list items.

- The revision clarifies that the conductor referred to in each list item is the "tap" conductor(s).

- Improves application of this section addressing outside tap conductors of unlimited length.

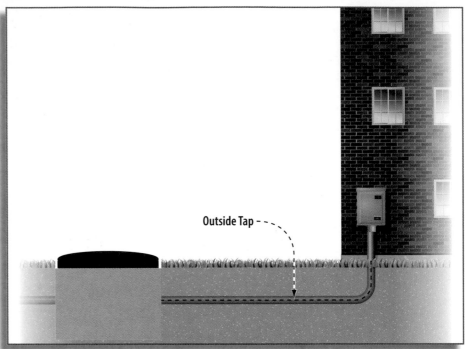

Outside Tap - - - -

## Significance of the Change

Section 240.21(B)(5) clearly indicates that tap conductors installed outside do not have a general length limitation. *Code*-making Panel 10 acted favorably to this proposed editorial revision in the interest of enhancing usability and clarity of this provision. Although the word "tap" was included in the title of list item (5) to 240.21(B), all of the list items that followed under (5) previously only referred to "conductors." Even though it was probably understood by many users that tap conductors are what is implied by each list items (1) through (4), the incorporation of the word "tap" should make it clear and remove any second guessing in applying this provision. Section 240.21(B)(5)(4) c. continues to provide and important reference to 230.6 to assist users in determining what is considered "outside" a building or structure, which is essential in proper application of this section. As an example, if a conduit penetrates a building foundation and is routed under the building slab until it is turned up through the slab, the conduit and conductors are considered outside the building until they emerge from the slab, which is the point of entrance mentioned in this provision.

Comment: None
Proposal: 10-36

# Transformer Secondary Conductors

## Code Language

**(2) Transformer Secondary Conductors Not Over 3 m (10 ft) Long.**
…(See *NEC* text)…

(1) The ampacity …(See *NEC* text)…

a. Not less than …(See *NEC* text)…

b. Not less than the rating of the equipment containing an overcurrent device(s) supplied by the secondary conductors or not less than the rating of the overcurrent protective device at the termination of the secondary conductors.

*Exception: Where listed equipment, such as surge protective device(s) (SPDs), is provided with specific instructions on minimum conductor sizing, the ampacity of the tap conductors supplying that equipment shall be permitted to be determined based on the manufacturer's instructions.*

*(See NEC for actual text)*

## Change Summary

- The words "equipment containing an overcurrent" have been added in front of the word "device(s)" in b.
- A new exception has been added covering SPDs and other similar devices only if in accordance with manufacturer's instructions.
- The revision clarifies what type of equipment the transformer secondary conductors must terminate in.

## Significance of the

## Change

These revisions are a continuation of the work started by CMP-10 on Proposal 10-52 and Comment 10-19 in the 2011 *NEC* development cycle. As revised, this section now clarifies what was meant by the word "device(s)" as previously used in b. Information provided in the substantiation indicated that the word "device" should be replaced with more descriptive terms since the definition of *device* is, "A unit of an electrical system that carries or controls electric energy as its principal function." Revising this section to reference equipment containing overcurrent device(s) narrows the application of the section beyond what the previous wording literally meant or could have implied. Action by CMP-10 on Comment 10-16 also refines the exception and expands it slightly to apply to surge protective devices (SPDs) and other similar equipment that may be connected by a tap in accordance with the provisions of this section. The revision and new exception improve clarity and promote more consistent application of the 10-foot tap rules. Similar revisions have also been incorporated into 240.21(B)(1) which addresses 10-foot feeder tap conductors.

Comment: 10-16

Proposals: 10-39, 10-40, 10-41

# Arc-Energy Reduction

## Code Language

**240.87 Arc Energy Reduction.** Where the highest continuous current trip setting for which the actual overcurrent device installed in a circuit breaker is rated or can be adjusted is 1200 A or higher, 240.87(A) and (B) shall apply.

**(A) Documentation.** ...(see *NEC* text)...

**(B) Method to Reduce Clearing Time.** One of the following or approved equivalent means shall be provided:

(1) Zone-selective interlocking

(2) Differential relaying

(3) Energy-reducing maintenance switching with local status indicator

(4) Energy-reducing active arc flash mitigation system

(5) An approved equivalent means

Informational Note No. 1: (no change)

Informational Note No. 2: ...(see *NEC* text)...

*(See NEC for actual text)*

## Change Summary

- This section is now titled Arc Energy Reduction and arranged in a list format.
- Applies to circuit breakers with a trip rating of 1200 amperes or greater.
- Subdivision (B) includes new list items (4) and (5) recognizing other methods of arc energy reduction by a specific system/equipment other approved means.

Comment: 10-24

Proposals: 10-53a, 10-56

*GE Arc Vault™ Protection System photography courtesy of GE's Industrial Solutions business*

## Significance of the Change

Section 240.87 in 2011 *NEC* provided a great start for "safety through design" installation requirements. The revisions in the 2014 cycle refine these requirements further by expanding methods to reduce clearing times and recognizing additional systems or methods of reducing arc-flash incident energy levels. As revised, the section title Arc Energy Reduction is more reflective of the requirements covered in this section. Favorable action on Comment 10-24 added a current range of 1200 amperes where this requirement would apply. In other words where the highest continuous current trip setting for which the circuit breaker is rated or can be adjusted is 1200 amperes or higher, the provisions in (A) and (B) apply. The result is to increase the number of larger circuit breakers that must meet the requirement, the ones that are associated with higher arc-flash incident energy levels. And it also reduces the number of smaller breakers that must meet these arc-flash incident energy reduction requirements, because, in general, smaller breakers are associated with much lower levels of incident energy. There are various effective arc mitigation and arc-energy reduction methods. The authority having jurisdiction can also approve other energy reduction methods. New Informational note No. 2 provides information about the equipment in new list item (4).

# Connection of Grounding and Bonding Equipment

## Code Language

**250.8 Connection of Grounding and Bonding Equipment**

**(A) Permitted Methods.** Equipment grounding conductors, grounding electrode conductors, and bonding jumpers shall be connected by one or more of the following means:

List items (1) through (8) remain as in 2011 *NEC*.

*(See NEC for actual text)*

## Significance of the Change

Connections of grounding electrode conductors, bonding jumpers, and equipment grounding conductors are covered by the general provisions in 250.8. Sheet metal screws are generally unacceptable for connecting grounding and bonding conductors. Often a grounding or bonding conductor connection is established by using a lug (pressure connector) that is fastened to an enclosure by used of a machine screw into a threaded hole, or by using a lug that it fastened to the enclosure by a machine screw and a nut. This involves the use of the methods listed in (1) and (5) which is more than just one of the items listed in this section. The revision to the driving text in (A) is now clear that any of these connections can be accomplished using only one or a combination of the methods listed in list items (1) through (8). The revision corrects an inadvertent oversight that could have limited the connection options of this section if applied and enforced literally. The revision aligns this section with how *NEC Code-*Making Panel 5 intended it to be applied.

## Change Summary

- The words "or more" have been added to Subdivision (A).
- This revision clarifies that one or more of the means provided in list items (1) through (8) could be used to make grounding and bonding connections.
- As previously written in 2011 *NEC*, only one of the means in (1) through (8) were permitted.

Comment: None

Proposal: 5-53

# Protection of Ground Clamps and Fittings

## Code Language

**250.10 Protection of Ground Clamps and Fittings**

Ground clamps or other fittings exposed to physical damage shall be enclosed in metal, wood, or equivalent protective covering.

*(See NEC for actual text)*

## Change Summary

- This section has been reduced from a list format into a single sentence.
- As revised, the protection requirements for ground clamps and fittings are simplified and consistent with 250.10 in the 2011 *NEC*.
- The requirement applies where the clamp or fitting is exposed to physical damage.

## Significance of the Change

This editorial revision is an improvement in clarity of this requirement. Information in the substantiation indicated that generally the use of a list format in the *NEC* improves clarity however this section was unclear even in a list format. As revised, the list format is removed and words "where they are not likely to be damaged" have been removed improving consistency with *NEC Style Manual* by eliminating words that are vague or unenforceable. The requirements of this section have not changed in the 2014 edition of the *NEC*. The difference is that the concept of the clamp or fitting being approved for general use with or without protection has been removed. The only judgment necessary is whether or not the location of the clamp or fitting renders it vulnerable or exposed to physical damage. If the ground clamp or fitting is exposed to physical damage, then protection by metal, wood, or equivalent protective covering must be provided.

Comment: None
Proposal: 5-55

For additional information, visit qr.njatcdb.org Item #1209

# Ungrounded System Marking

Caution marking warns of an ungrounded system and the operating voltage and aligns with 408.3(F)(2).

Caution marking required in 250.21(C) must meet the requirements in 110.21(B).

Applies where the signal words "danger", "warning", or "caution" are used in NEC rules.

⚠ **CAUTION**

**UNGROUNDED SYSTEM OPERATING _____ VOLTS BETWEEN CONDUCTORS**

Note: The signal word communicates the degree of hazard. The other label components provide the specific hazard, instructions, and could also include a graphic (See ANSI Z535.4-2011).

## Code Language

**(C) Marking.** Ungrounded systems shall be legibly marked "Caution: Ungrounded System Operating — _____ Volts Between Conductors" at the source or first disconnecting means of the system. The marking shall be of sufficient durability to withstand the environment involved.

*(See NEC for actual text)*

## Significance of the Change

The revision provides more complete and consistent direction for users regarding the exact language to be used for the markings or labels required by this section. The revised text effectively correlates with Section 408.3(F)(2) which requires switchboard or panelboard containing an ungrounded electrical system as permitted in 250.21 be legibly and permanently field marked as follows:

Caution Ungrounded System Operating—
_____ Volts Between Conductors

Information provided in the substantiation indicated that if the system disconnect is in a panelboard or switchboard, two different labels are required on the panelboard or switchboard, one for Section 250.21 that says "Ungrounded System" and one for Section 408.3(F)(2) that says "Caution Ungrounded System Operating — _____ Volts Between Conductors." The label required in Section 408.3(F)(2) includes the words "caution" and "voltage" is more complete from a safety standpoint than just using the words "Ungrounded System." This revision will prevent redundant requirements for two labels that say almost the same thing on panelboards and switchboards for this type of system in cases where the first disconnect is located in the panelboard or switchboard. There are new requirements in 110.21(B) that apply where a marking provision using a signal word danger, warning, or caution appears in a code rule.

## Change Summary

- This section has been revised to correlate with 408.3(F)(2).
- The words "Ungrounded System" have been replaced by the words "Caution Ungrounded System Operating — _____Volts Between Conductors."
- Section 110.21(B) provides requirements for markings and signs that use the signal words danger, caution, or warning.

Comment: None
Proposals: 5-64, 5-65, 5-66

# 250.24(A) & (E)

Article 250 Grounding and Bonding

Part II System Grounding

*REVISION*

## Grounding Service-Supplied Alternating-Current Systems

### Code Language

**250.24(A) System Grounding Connections.** ...(See *NEC* text)...

**(1) General.** The grounding electrode ...(See *NEC* text)...the overhead service conductors, service drop, underground service conductors, or service lateral to, including ...(See *NEC* text)...disconnecting means.

Informational Note: See definitions of *Service Conductors, Overhead; Service Conductors, Underground; Service Drop;* and *Service Lateral* in Article 100.

**(E) Ungrounded System Grounding Connections.** A premises wiring... (See *NEC* text)...at any accessible point from the load end of the overhead service conductors, service drop, underground service conductors, or service lateral to the service disconnecting means.

*(See NEC for actual text)*

### Change Summary

- The terms *overhead service conductors* and *underground service conductors* have been added to 250.24(A)(1) and 250.24(E).
- The revision correlates with the definitions of these terms in Article 100.
- The definitions of the terms *service drop* and *service lateral* as revised in the 2011 NEC are on the supply side of the service point.

Comment: None

Proposals: 5-68, 5-69, 5-70a, 5-75, 5-76

### Significance of the Change

The definitions of the terms *service drop* and *service lateral* were revised during the 2011 *NEC* development process. This revision resulted in these terms applying to overhead drops or underground laterals that are on the supply side of the service point, meaning the *NEC* did not apply to them, but utility regulations did. The definitions of the terms *service conductors*, *overhead* and *service conductors*, *underground* were added during the 2011 *NEC* development process. Additional work was done in the *NEC*, specifically in Article 230 to incorporate the newly defined terms. Basically where an *NEC* rule uses the terms *overhead service conductors* or *underground service conductors*, the *NEC* applies. If the *NEC* uses the term *service drop* or *service lateral*, the *NEC* does not apply to that portion of the run. The changes in Section 250.24(A)(1) and 250.24(E) combine the new terms with the existing terms and present both in each section. The result is that the requirements of 250.24 apply whether the service conductors (underground or overhead) are on the supply side of the service point or the load side of the service point. The revision corrects an inadvertent oversight that carried over from the 2011 *NEC* development process.

# System Bonding Jumper at Two Locations

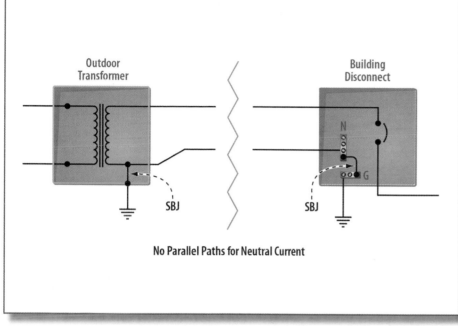

Outdoor Transformer

Building Disconnect

N

G

SBJ

SBJ

**No Parallel Paths for Neutral Current**

## Code Language

*Exception No. 2: If a building or structure is supplied by a feeder from an outdoor transformer, a system bonding jumper at both the source and the first disconnecting means shall be permitted if doing so does not establish a parallel path for the grounded conductor. If a grounded conductor is used in this manner, it shall not be smaller than the size specified for the system bonding jumper but shall not be required to be larger than the un-grounded conductor(s). For the purposes of this exception, connection through the earth shall not be considered as providing a parallel path.*

*(See NEC for actual text)*

## Significance of the Change

Exception No. 2 has been revised to apply specifically to installations of feeders that supply buildings or structures fed from outdoor transformers. The revised text provides for the limited case(s) where the grounded conductor, usually a neutral, can be bonded at the source of a separately derived system and at the required disconnecting means for a building or structure served and continues to prohibit parallel paths. Panel action on proposal 5-88 also allows the elimination of the supply-side bonding jumper where the grounded conductor must serve as the ground fault return path, which would required a system bonding jumper in both locations. Action on Proposal 5-244c adds a new exception to 250.32(B) to require the grounded conductor to be connected to the equipment grounding conductors, grounding electrode conductor and the first disconnecting mean enclosure when this exception is applied. While there are few installations where this now exception could be used, adding it following 250.30(A)(1) removes the previous conflict and provides an alternative for installations that could effectively satisfy the requirements for no parallel paths for neutral current. As revised the exception now is limited in application only to installations of transformers outdoors.

## Change Summary

- The first sentence of Exception No. 2 to 250.30(A)(1) has been revised.
- The revised exception now specifically addresses buildings or structures supplied by feeder(s) from outdoor transformers.
- A system bonding jumper is permitted to be installed at both locations if doing so does not create a parallel path for system grounded conductor current.

Comment: None

Proposal: 5-85

## Supply-Side Bonding Jumper

### Code Language

*Exception: A supply-side bonding jumper shall not be required between enclosures for installations made in compliance with 250.30(A)(1), Exception No. 2.*

**(See NEC for actual text)**

### Change Summary

- A new exception has been added following 250.30(A)(2).
- A supply-side bonding jumper is not required between enclosures where a system bonding jumper installed at both locations and a parallel path is not created for the system grounded conductor current.
- The new exception is necessary after requirements for supply-side bonding jumper(s) were added in the 2011 *NEC*.

### Significance of the Change

This revision aligns with the same allowances for installing two system bonding jumpers as provided in 250.30(A)(1) Exception No. 2. The 2011 *NEC* did not allow relief from having to install a supply-side bonding jumper, even if there were no parallel paths established by installing a system bonding jumper at both ends. Information in the substantiation with Proposal 5-87 clearly identified a conflict between these two sections and subsequent need for the exception. Action by CMP-5 results in a new exception that provides the needed correlation and relief. It should be noted that the new exception relaxes the requirement to provide the supply-side bonding jumper, but requires compliance with the restrictions of Exception No. 2 to 250.30(A)(1). In other words, the supply-side bonding jumper does not have to be installed between enclosures, where a system bonding jumper is installed at both ends, and doing so does not create any parallel path for neutral or grounded system conductor current. While there are few installations where this new exception could be used, adding it following 250.30(A)(2) removes the conflict and provides an alternative for installations that could effectively satisfy the requirements for no parallel paths for neutral current.

Comment: None
Proposals: 5-88, 5-87

# Grounding Electrode Conductor – Single and Multiple Systems

*Courtesy of Schneider Electric*

## Code Language

**250.30(A)(5) Grounding Electrode Conductor, Single Separately Derived System.** A grounding...(See 2011 *NEC* text )...

*Exception No. 2: If the source of a separately derived system is located within equipment listed and identified as suitable for use as service equipment, the grounding electrode conductor from the service or feeder equipment...(See 2011 NEC text)...*

**250.30(A)(6) (b)** *Tap Conductor Size.* Each tap conductor...(See 2011 *NEC* text)...

*Exception: If the source of a separately derived system is located within equipment listed and identified as suitable for use as service equipment, the grounding electrode conductor from the service or feeder equipment...(See 2011 NEC text)...*

*(See NEC for actual text)*

## Significance of the Change

This exception has been revised to clarify how it was intended to be applied and eliminate some contended confusion in the field. Information in the substantiation indicated that this exception has been widely misinterpreted and applied to conflict with the purpose of the grounding electrode conductor as described in an informational note under 250.4(A)(1) and 250.30(A)(4) because it allows a grounding electrode conductor of unlimited length to be used in lieu of an electrode located as near as practical and preferably in the same area as the transformer. The second sentence of 250.30(A)(4) is clear, that the nearest of either a water pipe electrode or metal building frame electrode must be used, yet some were using this exception to circumvent the general rule. The proposed change makes clear that this exception is intended to apply to separately derived systems that are an integral component of listed equipment and not installed in separate enclosures. The other key to applying this exception is that the grounding electrode conductor installed for the service or feeder on the primary side of the transformer must be large enough to serve as the grounding electrode conductor required for the secondary of the derived system.

## Change Summary

- The words "is located within equipment listed and identified as Suitable for Use as Service Equipment" have been incorporated into the same exception appearing in two locations within this section.

- The revision clarifies that the source of a separately derived system must be an integral component of the equipment and not located in a separate enclosure.

Comment: None

Proposals: 5-90, 5-91

## Supplied by a Feeder(s) or Branch Circuit(s)

### Code Language

*Exception No. 2: If system bonding jumpers are installed in accordance with 250.30(A)(1), Exception No. 2, the feeder grounded circuit conductor at the building or structure served shall be connected to the equipment grounding conductors, grounding electrode conductor, and the enclosure for the first disconnecting means.*

*(See NEC for actual text)*

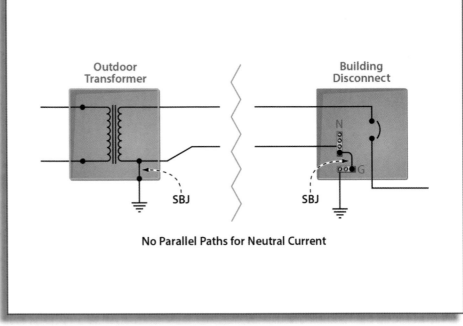

Outdoor Transformer

Building Disconnect

SBJ            SBJ

**No Parallel Paths for Neutral Current**

### Change Summary

- A new exception No. 2 has been added to 250.32(B)(1).
- The exception applies if two system bonding jumpers are installed in accordance with 250.30(A)(1) Exception No. 2.
- A system bonding jumper is permitted to be installed at both locations if doing so does not create a parallel path for system grounded conductor current.

### Significance of the Change

This new exception is necessary to provide the needed correlation between exceptions to 250.32(B)(1) and 250.30(A)(1) Exception No. 2. The new exception provides installation requirements for connecting the grounded conductors at the building or structure disconnecting means if a system bonding jumper is installed at both the source and the building disconnect as permitted by 250.30(A)(1) Exception No. 2. The general requirement of 250.32(B)(1) is to keep the grounded conductor separate and isolated from ground, grounding electrode conductors, equipment grounding conductors and so forth, as the feeder or branch circuit arrives at the building disconnecting means. If the building or structure is supplied from an outdoor separately derived system such as a transformer, there was previously no relief to the requirements in 250.32(B)(1) and provision for alignment with the exceptions in 250.30(A)(1) and (A)(2). Action by CMP-5 results in development of this new exception providing the needed correlation for consistency and uniform application in the few instances where more than a single system bonding jumper is permitted by exception. Once again, the installation of two system bonding jumpers is only permitted at both locations if doing so does not create a parallel path for system grounded conductor current.

Comment: None
Proposal: 5-244c

# Buried Grounding Electrode Conductors

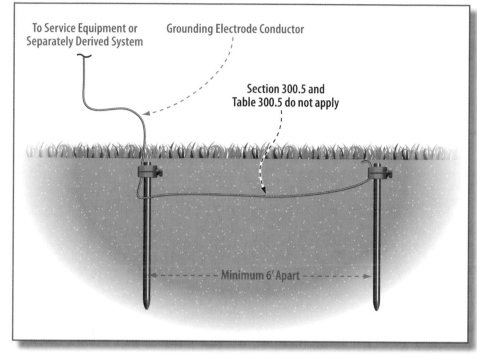

To Service Equipment or Separately Derived System

Grounding Electrode Conductor

Section 300.5 and Table 300.5 do not apply

Minimum 6' Apart

## Significance of the Change

There continues to be confusion as to whether or not 300.5 and Table 300.5 apply to grounding electrode conductors and bonding jumpers that are installed to form a grounding electrode system. The revision to this section provides clear direction for installers. Article 300 covers wiring methods to all wiring installations unless modified by the other articles in Chapter 3. Article 300 and Table 300.5 would not apply to grounding electrode conductors and bonding conductors installed from the grounding electrodes to the grounding electrode, unless a wiring method provides physical protection as required by 250.64(E). During the 2014 *NEC* development process CMP-3 and CMP-5 worked together and agreed that Table 300.5 should not be used because it introduces various requirements that may not be appropriate for grounding electrode conductors. For example, installing the grounding electrode conductor routed down the exterior wall of a building, offset to the burial depth, and then turned back up to connect to an electrode that is close to the foundation wall would usually required sharp bends that could decrease its effectiveness. This revision incorporates new text in 250.64(B) where the other requirements for the installation of grounding electrode conductors and associated enclosures are located.

## Code Language

**250.64(B) Securing and Protection Against Physical Damage.** Where exposed, a grounding electrode conductor or its enclosure shall be securely fastened to the surface on which it is carried. Grounding electrode conductors shall be permitted to be installed on or through framing members. A 4 AWG or larger copper or aluminum grounding electrode conductor shall be protected if... (See *NEC* Text)... or cable armor. Grounding electrode conductors smaller than 6 AWG shall be protected in (RMC), IMC, PVC, RTRC, (EMT), or cable armor. Grounding electrode conductors and grounding electrode bonding jumpers shall not be required to comply with 300.5.

*(See NEC for actual text)*

## Change Summary

- A new last sentence has been added to 250.64(B).
- The new text clarifies that the requirements in 300.5 for underground installations do not apply to buried grounding electrode conductors or bonding jumpers of the grounding electrode system.
- Chapter 3 wiring methods that contain grounding electrode conductors must comply with 300.5.

Comment: 3-13
Proposal: 3-39

## Tap Connections at Busbars

### Code Language

(3) Connections to an aluminum or copper busbar not less than 6 mm thick × 50 mm wide (1/4 in. thick × 2 in. wide) and of sufficient length to accommodate the number of terminations necessary for the installation. The busbar shall be securely fastened and shall be installed in an accessible location. Connections shall be made by a listed connector or by the exothermic welding process. If aluminum busbars are used, the installation shall comply with 250.64(A).

*(See NEC for actual text)*

### Change Summary

- The first sentence of list item (3) has been revised by adding the words "and of sufficient length to accommodate the number of terminations necessary for the installation."

- A length dimension has been added and is variable (no minimum or maximum).

- The busbar must be long enough to accomplish all necessary GEC tap conductors.

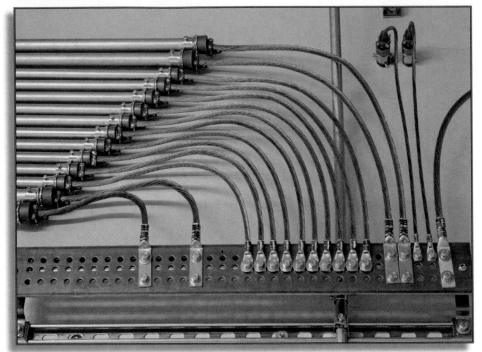

*IStock Photo Courtesy of NECA*

### Significance of the Change

Section 250.64(D)(1) provides three methods of connecting grounding electrode conductor taps to a common grounding electrode conductor. The methods are exothermic welding, connectors listed as grounding and bonding equipment, and connections to a busbar. List item (3) previously included the allowance for connecting to an aluminum or copper busbar not less than 1/4 in. thick and not less than 2 in. wide. The length dimension was not previously included which simply implied that if this method were used, the bar needed to be long enough for all GEC tap conductors intended to be connected to the bar. List item (3) has been revised by simply including information about the required length, but no dimension is given. The bar must be long enough for terminating all tap conductors that must be connected to it. Some manufacturers of grounding and bonding equipment have produced grounding busbars specifically for this purpose and are available in different lengths such as 12 inches or 24 inches long. It should be noted that one could field construct a copper or aluminum busbar to meet the provisions of this section. The additional language included in this section clarifies the length dimension requirements in this section.

Comment: None
Proposal: 5-120

# Sole Connection to Rod, Pipe, or Plate Electrode(s)

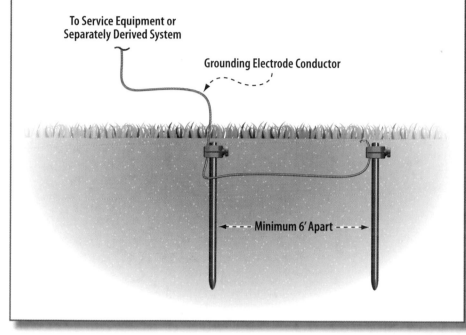

To Service Equipment or Separately Derived System

Grounding Electrode Conductor

Minimum 6' Apart

## Code Language

**(A) Connections to a Rod, Pipe, or Plate Electrode(s).** Where the grounding electrode conductor is connected to a single or multiple rod, pipe, or plate electrode(s), or any combination thereof, as permitted in 250.52(A)(5) or (A)(7), that portion of the conductor that is the sole connection to the grounding electrode(s) shall not be required to be larger than 6 AWG copper wire or 4 AWG aluminum wire.

*(See NEC for actual text)*

## Significance of the Change

This section has been revised to clarify its application relative to what is meant by the term sole connection. There continues to be confusion that exists for installations of two ground rods and whether this section could be applied for the maximum sized grounding electrode conductor installed to the first ground rod and to the jumper between ground rods. The revision clarifies that the sole connection provisions of this section deal with the types of electrodes in this section and not just the issue of only one electrode involved in the connection. For example, if a rod, pipe, and plate electrode were all installed, one could misapply the section thinking the rules for grounding electrode system now apply. The change makes it clear that if a grounding electrode conductor is installed to two ground rods connected together with a bonding jumper as required in 250.53(A)(2), the maximum size grounding electrode conductor to the first rod does not have to be larger than a 6 AWG copper wire or 4 AWG aluminum wire.

## Change Summary

- This revision clarifies that the provisions in this section relate to the type of electrode and the sole connection.
- This section applies to a grounding electrode conductor(s) connecting solely to a single rod, pipe, or plate electrode(s) or to any combination of those types.
- The largest size required by this section has not been changed.

Comment: None
Proposals: 5-131, 5-132

# Sole Connection to Concrete-Encased Electrode(s)

## Code Language

**(B) Connections to Concrete-Encased Electrodes.** Where the grounding electrode conductor is connected to a single or multiple concrete-encased electrode(s) as permitted in 250.52(A)(3), that portion of the conductor that is the sole connection to the grounding electrode(s) shall not be required to be larger than 4 AWG copper wire.

*(See NEC for actual text)*

*Courtesy of Cogburn Brothers, Inc.*

## Change Summary

- This revision clarifies that the provisions in this section relate to the type of electrode and the sole connection.
- This section applies to a grounding electrode conductor(s) connecting solely to a concrete electrode(s) or to any number of those types.
- The largest size required by this section has not been changed.

## Significance of the Change

This section has been revised to clarify its application relative to what is meant by the term *sole connection*. The revision clarifies that the sole connection provisions of this section deal with both the type of electrodes in this section and the issue of only one electrode involved in the sole connection. As revised, the sole connection provisions of this section deal with the types of electrodes addressed in this section in addition to the number of these types of electrode(s) involved in the connection. The changes should help clarify that if a grounding electrode conductor is installed to multiple concrete-encased electrodes connected together with a bonding jumper(s), the maximum size grounding electrode conductor to the first concrete-encased electrode or any bonding jumper(s) between multiple concrete-encased electrodes does not have to be larger than a 4 AWG copper wire. If concrete-encased electrode(s) are installed in a grounding electrode system, the grounding electrode conductor size is dependent on the location in the grounding electrode system relative to the connection(s) or sole connection to it.

Comment: None
Proposal: 5-135

# Table 250.66 Note 1

## Size of Grounding Electrode Conductor

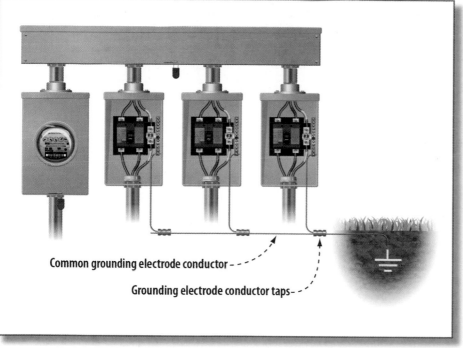

Common grounding electrode conductor ----

Grounding electrode conductor taps----

## Code Language

Notes

1. If multiple sets of service-entrance conductors connect directly to a service drop, set of overhead service conductors, set of underground service conductors, or service lateral, the equivalent size of the largest service-entrance conductor shall be determined by the largest sum of the areas of the corresponding conductors of each set.

*(See NEC for actual text)*

## Significance of the Change

Notes to tables in the *NEC* are enforceable as requirements. Informational notes in the *Code* are not enforceable. Table 250.66 includes two such table notes. Note 1 is intended to provide information about determining minimum size grounding electrode conductors for installations of multiple sets of service-entrance conductors. Information in the substantiation for Proposals 5-128 and 5-129 indicated that there is confusion that exists as to determining the minimum size GEC in these types of installations. Action by CMP-5 removes the reference to 230.40 Exception No. 2. As revised this note more closely aligns with the language in 250.64(D)(1) which provides specific requirements for sizing the common grounding electrode conductor and the grounding electrode conductor taps for services. The revised note clarifies that the method for calculating the size of a grounding electrode conductor when multiple sets of service conductors are installed, applies for installations other than those described in 230.40, Exception No. 2. Where a set of service-entrance conductors is tapped to feed multiple service disconnects, the minimum size grounding electrode conductor will be based on the table without the use of note one.

## Change Summary

- The reference to 230.40 Exception No. 2 has been removed from this note.

- The revision clarifies determining the grounding electrode conductor size if multiple sets of service-entrance conductors are present.

- The size grounding electrode conductor is determined using the largest sum of the areas of the corresponding conductors of each set and applying Table 250.66.

Comment: None
Proposals: 5-128, 5-129

# Grounding Electrode Connections

## Code Language

**250.68(C) Grounding Electrode Connections.** Grounding electrode conductors and bonding jumpers shall be permitted to be connected at the following locations and used to extend the connection to an electrode(s):

**(1)**…(See *NEC* text)…

**(2)** The metal structural frame of a building shall be permitted to be used as a conductor to interconnect electrodes that are part of the grounding electrode system, or as a grounding electrode conductor.

**(3)** A concrete-encased electrode of either the conductor type, reinforcing rod or bar installed in accordance with 250.52(A)(3) extended from its location within the concrete to an accessible location above the concrete shall be permitted.

*(See NEC for actual text)*

## Change Summary

- The section title has been change to Grounding Electrode Connections reflecting what is covered.

- List item (2) has been revised to clarify the use of structural metal frames for interconnecting electrodes or serving as a conductive path to the grounding electrode system.

- New list item (3) addresses conductive paths installed from concrete-encased electrodes to accessible connection locations.

## Significance of the Change

This section covers grounding electrode conductors and conductive paths to grounding electrodes. The title of this section has been revised to reflect that grounding electrode connections are covered. The revised text clarifies that structural metal is treated the same as metallic water systems relative to what constitutes a grounding electrode, by definition. The charging text in 250.68(C) makes it clear that structural metal can be used to interconnect wire-type bonding jumpers or grounding electrode conductors or extensions of the wire-type bonding conductor or grounding electrode conductors to a grounding electrode system. The conductive path to grounding electrodes can be other than wire-type conductors that interconnect grounding electrodes of a grounding electrode system. Action by CMP-5 on Comment 5-49 also removes list items a. through c. as these provided no value and only added to confusion and misapplication of this section. A new list item (3) has been added to reflect a common practice of establishing a conductive path extended to a concrete-encased electrode. This addition clarifies that rebar installed in this fashion is obviously not a conductor of the wire type, but is a conductive path extended for connection of grounding electrode conductors and bonding jumpers.

Comment: 5-49
Proposals: 5-138, 5-141

# Bonding in Hazardous (Classified) Locations

*Courtesy of Donald Cook/IAEI*

## Code Language

**250.100 Bonding in Hazardous (Classified) Locations.** Regardless of the voltage of the electrical system, the electrical continuity of non–current-carrying metal parts of equipment, raceways, and other enclosures in any hazardous (classified) location, as defined in 500.5, 505.5, and 506.5, shall be ensured by any of the bonding methods specified in 250.92(B)(2) through (B)(4). One or more of these bonding methods shall be used whether or not equipment grounding conductors of the wire type are installed.

Informational Note. See 501.30, 502.30, 503.30, 505.25, or 506.25 for specific bonding requirements.

*(See NEC for actual text)*

## Significance of the Change

This section has been revised to effectively correlate with the specific restrictive bonding requirements for hazardous (classified) locations addressed within Chapter 5. Efforts by CMP-14 to delete this section were rejected by CMP-5 to retain the general bonding requirements and information in this section. The language requiring bonding "regardless of the voltage" is an essential provision necessary for installers and enforcement. It makes clear that even low voltage installations must conform to these bonding requirements. The panel statement to Comment 5-52 clarified that 250.100 provides the initial bonding requirements in hazardous locations, regardless of the voltage, be accomplished and that it be completed by one of the specific methods in 250.92(B)(2) through (4). The hazardous location articles amend the base requirement with additional requirements. For example, Section 501.30 requires wiring and equipment be grounded. Section 501.30(A) then goes on to further modify the installation specified in 250.92(B)(2) but does not establish the initial requirement for bonding to start with. Other initial base bonding requirements are missing from the other referenced hazardous location sections. Action by CMP-5 on Proposal 5-160 and Comment 5-52 retains 250.100 and results in effective correlation with the specific bonding requirements contained in the chapter 5 articles.

## Change Summary

- Section 250.100 contains the general restriction of bonding, regardless of the voltage applied.

- Section 250.100 has been revised by adding references to 500.5, 505.5, and 506.5 in the first sentence.

- A new Informational Note has been added to correlate provisions in the Chapter 5 articles that contain specific and more restrictive bonding requirements.

Comment: 5-52
Proposal: 5-160

## New Table for Supply-Side Sizing

### Code Language

Table 250.102(C)(1), Notes

Informational Note: See Chapter 9, Table 8, for the circular mil area of conductors 18 AWG through 4/0 AWG.

**250.102(C)(1) Size for Supply Conductors in a Single Raceway or Cable.** The supply-side bonding jumper shall not be smaller than specified in Table 250.102(C)(1).

**250.102(C)(2) Size for Parallel Conductor Installations in Two or More Raceways.** Where...(See *NEC* text) ...selected from Table 250.102(C)(1)...(See *NEC* text)...

Informational Note: The term *supply conductors* includes ungrounded conductors that do not have overcurrent protection on their supply side and terminate at service equipment or the first disconnecting means of a separately derived system.

*(See NEC for actual text)*

### Change Summary

- Table 250.102(C)(1), Notes, and Informational Notes have been added to Part V of Article 250.
- The new table provides sizes for grounded conductors, main bonding jumpers, supply-side bonding jumpers, system bonding jumpers, and requires using 12.5 percent rule if exceeding the table values.
- References in Article 250 have been changed from 250.66 to 250.102(C)(1) and Table 250.102(C)(1).

Comment: 5-56

Proposal: 5-42

**Table 250.102(C)(1) Grounded Conductor, Main Bonding Jumper, System Bonding Jumper, and Supply-Side Bonding Jumper for Alternating Current Systems (in part without notes)**

| Size of Largest Ungrounded Service-Entrance Conductor or Equivalent Area for Parallel Conductors (AWG/kcmil) | | Size of Grounded Conductor or Bonding Jumper[a] (AWG/kcmil) | |
|---|---|---|---|
| Copper | Aluminum or Copper-Clad Aluminum | Copper | Aluminum or Copper-Clad Aluminum |
| 2 or smaller | 1/0 or smaller | 8 | 6 |
| 1 or 1/0 | 2/0 or 3/0 | 6 | 4 |
| 2/0 or 3/0 | 4/0 or 250 | 4 | 2 |
| Over 3/0 through 350 | Over 250 through 500 | 2 | 1/0 |
| Over 350 through 600 | Over 500 through 900 | 1/0 | 3/0 |
| Over 600 through 1100 | Over 900 through 1750 | 2/0 | 4/0 |
| Over 1100 | Over 1750 | | |
| | | See Notes | |

a For the purpose of this table, the term bonding jumper refers to main bonding jumpers, system bonding jumpers, and supply-side bonding jumpers.

### Significance of the Change

This new table and corresponding changes to related sections simplify the sizing requirements for fault carrying conductors that are not sized using Table 250.122. In previous *NEC* editions, multiple sections such as for main bonding jumpers, system bonding jumpers, supply side bonding jumpers and grounded conductors referred to Table 250.66 for sizing the conductor or jumper and required application of the 12.5 percent rule for larger sizes. Table 250.66 is titled Grounding Electrode Conductor for Alternating-Current Systems and has a maximum required conductor size of 3/0 AWG copper or 250 kcmil aluminum or copper-clad aluminum. The new table and revised text leaves Table 250.66 for sizing only grounding electrode conductors and bonding conductors for connections of electrodes in grounding electrode systems. The new Table 250.102(C)(1) and including 12.5 percent note applies to all other fault carrying conductors not addressed by Table 250.66 or Table 250.122. Corresponding references to the new table have been provided in Sections 250.24(C)(1), 250.28(D)(1) (1), 250.30(A)(2)(a), 250.102(C)(1) and 250.102(C)(2). This new table and revised references should improve usability, clarity, and result in more accurate sizing of system bonding jumpers, supply-side bonding jumpers, main bonding jumpers and grounded conductors.

# Ungrounded Conductors of Traffic Signal Circuits

## Code Language

*Exception No. 3: Conductors with green insulation shall be permitted to be used as ungrounded signal conductors where installed between the output terminations of traffic signal control and traffic signal indicating heads. Signaling circuits installed in accordance with this exception shall include an equipment grounding conductor in accordance with 250.118. Wire-type equipment grounding conductors shall be bare or have insulation or covering that is green with one or more yellow stripes.*

*(See NEC for actual text)*

## Significance of the Change

This new exception provides for use of the color green in ungrounded conductors for the signaling circuits between the controller and the signal heads above the roadway. Information provided in the substantiation indicated that proper operation of traffic signal equipment is an important part of public safety. This equipment and wiring should only be installed and/or maintained by qualified persons. It is and has been a long-standing practice to use a conductor with green insulation as the signal conductor installed between the controller and the green indicating light located in the traffic signal head, and persons qualified to work on this equipment are aware of this long-standing practice. Although this type of equipment and wiring system is often installed in right-of-way locations and sometimes exempt from permits, the *NEC* rules are typically applied to these electrical designs and installations. Enforcement and application of this section without this exception can lead to confusion and a possible increase in the hazards associated with malfunctioning traffic signals, in addition to safety concerns for workers that service and troubleshoot such systems. The new exception provides a needed relaxation of the general requirement and aligns with current traffic signal industry wiring practices.

## Change Summary

- A new Exception No. 3 has been added to 250.119.
- The exception relaxes general equipment-grounding conductor identification requirements for ungrounded signal conductors to traffic signal heads.
- The signal circuits to the heads must include an equipment-grounding conductor that is bare or have insulation or covering that is green with yellow stripes.

Comment: None
Proposal: 5-41a

# Use of EGC Grounding Electrode Conductor

## Code Language

**250.121 Use of Equipment Grounding Conductors.** An equipment grounding conductor shall not be used as a grounding electrode conductor.

*Exception. A wire-type equipment grounding conductor installed in compliance with 250.6(A) and the applicable requirements for both the equipment grounding conductor and the grounding electrode conductor in Parts II, III and VI of this article shall be permitted to serve as both an equipment grounding conductor and a grounding electrode conductor.*

*(See NEC for actual text)*

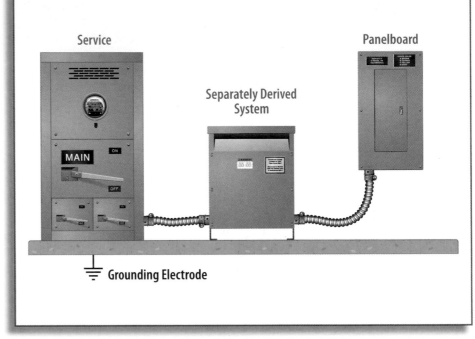

Grounding Electrode

## Change Summary

- A new exception has been added to 250.121.
- The new exception recognizes only wire-type equipment grounding conductors for simultaneous use as both a grounding electrode conductor and an equipment-grounding conductor, simultaneously.
- The single conductor must meet all installation and sizing requirements for both conductors and satisfy the requirements in 250.6(A) relating to objectionable current.

## Significance of the Change

Section 250.121 was new for 2011 *NEC* and restricted all equipment grounding conductors in 250.118 from being used as a grounding electrode conductor. The *NEC* was previously silent on this issue and therefore did not place any restriction on it. The restriction in 250.121 is appropriate for all grounding electrodes identified in that 250.118, with the exception of a wire type in 250.118(1). If a wire type satisfies all applicable requirements for both the equipment grounding conductor and the grounding electrode conductor simultaneously, there should be an allowance. Action by CMP-5 on Comment 5-66a introduces an exception to this general restriction providing an opportunity to install a single conductor to serve both functions simultaneously, but only in strict conformance with this exception. It was made known to the panel that there are some installations that could accomplish what is conveyed in the exception, but these installations are very few. Equipment grounding conductors installed in accordance with this restrictive exception that do not carry current during normal operating conditions must also comply with 250.6(A).

Comment: 5-66a
Proposal: 5-190

# Increases in Size of Equipment Grounding Conductors

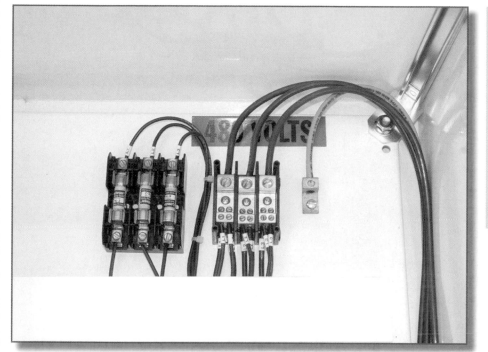

## Code Language

**(B) Increased in Size.** Where ungrounded conductors are increased in size from the minimum size that has sufficient ampacity for the intended installation, wire-type equipment grounding conductors, where installed, shall be increased in size proportionately according to the circular mil area of the ungrounded conductors.

*(See NEC for actual text)*

## Significance of the Change

This revision relates to concepts introduced by Proposal 5-290 and Comment 5-18 held in the 2011 *NEC* development process. Information provided with the substantiation indicated that it is not necessary to impose a proportional increase in size of a wire-type equipment-grounding conductor in all cases where the ungrounded conductors of the circuit are increased in size. The inserted language makes the requirement simple and clear. It was also emphasized that, as written, this section is overly restrictive and technically incorrect in some cases to require an increase in the minimum size of an equipment-grounding conductor. During a ground fault event the equipment-grounding conductor functions only for a short time and can be insulated, covered, or bare. Equipment grounding conductors must have the capacity to safely conduct any fault that could occur in the circuit. The revision should assist installers and inspectors in making accurate determinations when increases in size of the equipment grounding conductor are essential to maintain the minimum effective ground-fault current path as described in 250.4(A)(5) and (B)(4).

## Change Summary

- The words "from the minimum size that has sufficient ampacity for the intended installation" have been added to this section.
- The adjustment in size applies to wire-type equipment grounding conductor(s) if increasing the size of the ungrounded conductors relates to sufficient ampacity.
- If ungrounded conductors sized larger than the required minimum are installed, no proportional adjustment in EGC is required.

Comment: None
Proposals: 5-199, 5-198

# Maximum Size DC Grounding Electrode Conductor

## Code Language

**250.166 Size of the Direct-Current Grounding Electrode Conductor.** The size of the grounding electrode conductor for a dc system shall be as specified in 250.166(A) and (B), except as permitted by 250.166(C) through (E). The grounding electrode conductor for a dc system shall meet the sizing requirements in this section but shall not be required to be larger than 3/0 copper or 250 kcmil aluminum.

*(See NEC for actual text)*

## Change Summary

- A new last sentence has been added to Section 250.166.
- The revision provides maximum sizes for dc system grounding electrode conductor(s).
- The GEC must meet the requirements of 250.166 but does not have to be sized larger than 3/0 copper or 250 kcmil aluminum.

## Significance of the Change

No maximum size grounding electrode conductor was previously provided in this section except for grounding electrode conductors that are a sole connection to grounding electrodes as covered in 250.166(C), (D), or (E). This revision incorporates maximum sizes for dc system grounding electrode conductors that are consistent with those provided in Table 250.66 for ac grounding electrode conductors. The result is more practical sizing requirements for larger dc systems with large neutral and system conductors. Where larger dc systems are installed, the grounding electrode conductor is typically not permitted to be smaller than the neutral conductor of the system, which in some cases could be overly restrictive. As an example, if a dc system neutral, other than covered in 250.166(A) for 3-wire balancer sets, is (3) 500 kcmil copper paralleled, the GEC must be 1500 kcmil copper minimum. This is far more restrictive than necessary given the purpose of grounding electrode conductors. Other examples include sizing grounding electrode conductors for the dc output of large-scale photovoltaic installations. Action by CMP-5 clarifies that grounding electrode conductors for dc systems must meet the sizing requirements in 250.166, and the maximum size required is either 3/0 copper or 250 kcmil aluminum or copper-clad aluminum.

Comment: None
Proposal: 5-222

# Direct-Current Ground Fault Detection

*Courtesy of PDE Total Energy Solutions*

## Code Language

**250.167 Direct-Current Ground Fault Detection.**

**(A) Ungrounded Systems.** Ground-fault detection systems shall be required for ungrounded systems.

**(B) Grounded Systems.** Ground-fault detection shall be permitted for grounded systems.

**(C) Marking.** Direct-current systems shall be legibly marked to indicate the grounding type at the dc source or the first disconnecting means of the system. The marking shall be of sufficient durability to withstand the environment involved.

Informational Note: *NFPA 70E*-2012 identifies four dc grounding types in detail.

*(See NEC for actual text)*

## Significance of the Change

This new provision is the result of a joint effort by the *NEC* Correlating Committee assigned DC Task Group and the IEEE Stationary Battery Codes Working Group. Ground-fault detection for ungrounded dc systems was not a requirement in previous *NEC* editions. Some dc applications cannot utilize a grounded system, thereby making it necessary to have floating or an ungrounded dc power system. An unintentional ground fault on this type of system can result in fires or a shock hazard. Grounded dc systems are not all grounded in the same manner. Ground-fault detection would not be appropriate for all four types grounding methods. The new mandatory requirement for ground-fault detection ensures that a method to monitor such systems for ground faults is provided. Subdivision (B) is permissive in that ground-fault detection is not required, but is permitted for grounded dc systems. A new informational note in this section references NFPA 70E *Standard for Electrical Safety In the Workplace* providing some detail on four different dc grounding methods. This new provision also includes requirements for legibly marking dc systems indicating the type of grounding method used. The marking has to be suitable for the environment where it is installed.

## Change Summary

- Section 250.167 has been added to Part VIII of Article 250 covering direct-current systems.

- Ground-fault detection systems are now required for ungrounded dc systems and shall be permitted for grounded dc systems.

- The dc system shall be marked at the source or first disconnect to identity the type of dc grounding system applied.

Comment: None
Proposals: 5-223

# Ground-Fault Current Path Required

## Code Language

**250.186 Ground-Fault Circuit Conductor Brought to Service Equipment.**

**(A) Systems with a Grounded Conductor at the Service Point.** Where an ac system operating at over 1000 volts is grounded...(See *NEC* text)... The grounded conductor(s) shall be installed in accordance with 250.186(A)(1) through (A)(4). The size of the solidly grounded circuit conductor(s) shall be the larger of that determined by 250.184 or 250.186(A)(1) or (A)(2).

*Exception: Where two or more service ...(See NEC Text)...*

**(1)** through **(4)** ...(See *NEC* text)...

**(B) Systems Without a Grounded Conductor at the Service Point.**

**(1)** through **(3)** ...(See *NEC* text)...

*(See NEC for actual text)*

## Change Summary

- This new section requires a fault current path installed from the source to the service equipment.
- For grounded systems, a grounded conductor must be installed and routed with the ungrounded conductors to each service disconnecting means.
- For ungrounded systems, a supply-side bonding jumper must be installed and routed with the ungrounded conductors to each service disconnecting means.

*Courtesy of Schneider Electric*

## Significance of the Change

This new section compliments the work of the High Voltage Task Group work in the 2014 *NEC* cycle. Presently 250.24(C) requires a grounded conductor to be brought to the service for grounded systems 1000 volts or below. The main purpose for this conductor is to ensure a low-impedance path be provided for ground fault current to return to the utility supply transformer or source and facilitate overcurrent device operation during a ground fault event. The same need exists for systems over 1000 volts but there were no requirements. Some jurisdictions relied on the performance requirements of 250.4(A) to ensure a suitable ground fault return path was provided. This new section establishes the requirement to ensure a suitable, effective ground-fault current path is provided for services and systems over 1000 volts and also accounts for instances where the serving utility may or may not provide a neutral (grounded conductor) with their distribution system. Where a utility does not provide a neutral conductor there is generally a static line or other ground fault return path where the supply side bonding jumper can be connected to completing the return circuit. This new provision enhances consistency with essential performance requirements in 250.4.

Comments: 5-101, 5-103
Proposal: 5-234

# Grounding and Bonding of Fences and Structures

*Courtesy of Donald Cook/IAEI*

## Code Language

**250.194 Grounding and Bonding of Fences and Other Metal Structures.** Metallic fences enclosing, and other metal structures in or surrounding, a substation with exposed electrical conductors and equipment shall be grounded and bonded to limit step, touch, and transfer voltages.

**(A) Metal Fences.** Where metal fences are located within 5 m (16 ft) of the exposed electrical conductors or equipment, the fence shall be bonded to the grounding electrode system with wire-type bonding jumpers as follows:

(1) – (6)…(See *NEC* text)…

**(B) Metal Structures.** All exposed conductive metal structures, including guy wires within 2.5 m (8 ft) …(See *NEC* text)…

*(See NEC for actual text)*

## Significance of the Change

This new section continues expanding the provisions for medium and high voltage installations in the *NEC* and compliments the work of the High Voltage Task Group in the 2014 *NEC* cycle. For multiple reasons including ordinances, safety, security, economics, and so forth, metal fences are often installed around substations. At the medium and high voltage level, many live parts are exposed in substations. Since fences will be accessible to the general public and other personnel, they must be grounded and bonded to limit the rise of hazardous potential on the fence. This revision establishes basic prescriptive requirements for grounding and bonding of metal fences built in and around electrical substations. For situations where step and touch potential considerations indicate additional grounding and bonding design is required, alternate designs performed under engineering supervision are allowed. Designers are also referred to the industry standard on the grounding of fences in and around substations, which is IEEE 80 *Guide for Safety In AC Substation Grounding*. Although many substation fences are required by and typically covered by utility regulations and the National Electrical Safety Code (NESC), these new provisions in Part X of Article 250 provide a basis for installations covered by the *NEC*.

## Change Summary

- Section 250.194 has been added to cover grounding and bonding of metal fences and other equipment for substations.
- Subdivision (B) covers grounding and bonding of metal structures and guy wires associated with substations.
- A reference to IEEE 80 *Guide for Safety In AC Substation Grounding* for design and installation of fence grounding.

Comment: None
Proposal: 5-241

# Chapter 3

## Articles 300–393
## Wiring Methods and Materials

# Significant Changes
## TO THE *NEC*® 2014

## Title and Scope of Article 300

### Code Language

**Chapter 3 Wiring Methods and Materials**

**Article 300 General Requirements for Wiring Methods and Materials**

**I. General Requirements**

**300.1 Scope.**

**(A) All Wiring Installations.** This article covers general requirements for wiring methods and materials for all wiring installations unless modified by other articles in Chapter 3.

*(See NEC for actual text)*

*Courtesy of Bill McGovern, City of Plano, TX*

### Change Summary

- The title of Chapter 3 remains as Wiring Methods and Materials.
- The title of Article 300 has been revised to General Requirements for Wiring Methods and Materials.
- The scope of Article 300 has been revised to clarify its application to, and inclusion of general requirements for wiring methods and materials for all installations.

### Significance of the Change

These changes are editorial only and improve the accuracy in the title of Article 300. As revised, the title now more effectively reflects what is covered. Information in the substantiation indicated that wiring methods are generally recognized as cable assemblies, conduits, and raceways covered in Chapter 3 of the *NEC*. Revising the title of Article 300 to General Requirements for Wiring Methods and Materials clarifies what is covered in that article and that the specific types of materials used for wiring installations are provided in the balance of the Chapter 3 articles. General rules for wiring installations are included in Article 300 and specific rules for electrical wiring such as cables, raceways, cable trays, and so forth are specifically covered and described in Articles 310 through 399. These subsequent articles typically provide the general information about each type or wiring including but not limited to installation requirements, uses permitted, uses not permitted, and construction specifications. Article 300 is more general in nature and provides base rules applicable to various wiring methods and materials installed in various general applications and locations. These revisions provide an editorial enhancement and do not change any technical requirements.

Comment: None

Proposals: 3-8, 3-9

# Conductors of Different Systems Over 1000 Volts

*Courtesy of Schneider Electric*

## Code Language

**(C) Conductors of Different Systems.**...(see *NEC* text)...

**(2) Over 1000 Volts, Nominal.**...(see *NEC* text)...

(c) In motors, transformers, switchgear, switchboards, control assemblies, and similar equipment, conductors of different voltage ratings shall be permitted.

(d) In manholes, if the conductors of each system are permanently and effectively separated from the conductors of the other systems and securely fastened to racks...(see *NEC* text)...

*(See NEC for actual text)*

## Significance of the Change

This section has been revised to apply to systems and installations over 1000 volts, while Section 300.3(C)(1) has been revised to apply to systems 1000 volts or less. This revision results from work of the High Voltage Task Group appointed by the *NEC* Correlating Committee prior to the 2014 *NEC* development cycle. The Task Group identified the demand for increasing voltage output levels of wind generation and photovoltaic systems as an area of concern and that existing *NEC* requirements be revised globally to address these new voltage output levels. Section 300.3(C)(2) could have been previously misinterpreted as an inclusive list so the second revision in this section is to include the terms *transformers* and *switchboards* in (C)(2)(c). A transformer has no operational similarity in an electrical installation as compared to a motor, switchgear, or control assembly. Many misapplied the phrase *similar equipment* as not covering transformers. Switchgear can have an over 1000-volt primary and contain a transformer integral within the switchgear assembly, which would require application of this section. The revision clarifies that the conductor separation requirements in this section are applicable in switchgear and switchgear with integral transformers in addition to the other equipment referenced in this section.

## Change Summary

- List item (2) has been changed to address over 1000 volt applications.
- List item (2)(c) has been expanded to include transformers and switchboards.
- The revision clarifies that transformers and switchboards are also included in the conductor separation requirements where voltages exceed 1000.

Comment: None
Proposals: 3-12,
3-15, 3-15a

# 300.5(D)(4)

**REVISION**

# Protection from Enclosure or Raceway Damage

## Code Language

**300.5(D)(4) Enclosure or Raceway Damage.** Where the enclosure or raceway is subject to physical damage, the conductors shall be installed in rigid metal conduit, intermediate metal conduit, RTRC-XW, Schedule 80 PVC conduit, or equivalent.

*(See NEC for actual text)*

*Courtesy of FRE Composites*

## Change Summary

- List item (4) has been revised by adding Type RTRC-XW as an acceptable wiring method.

- Reinforced Thermosetting Resin Conduit-XW provides similar physical protection characteristics to those of Schedule 80 PVC.

- The revision clarifies use of RTRC-XW for use in locations where the raceway or enclosure would be subject to physical damage.

## Significance of the Change

This revision incorporates reinforced thermosetting resin conduit, Type RTRC-XW into 300.5(D)(4). Where the enclosure or raceway is subject to physical damage, the contained conductors must be protected by installation in rigid metal conduit (RMC), intermediate metal conduit (IMC), Schedule 80 PVC or equivalent, and now reinforced thermosetting resin conduit, Type RTRC-XW. The original Proposal 3-106 in the 2011 *NEC* development cycle was accepted to add reinforced-thermosetting resin conduit Type RTRC-XW to 300.50(C) while Comment 3-44 only addressed 300.5(D)(4) for the 2011 *NEC*. Since there wasn't a proposal to add RTRC-XW to 300.5(D)(4), the comment was held for the 2014 revision cycle because it was considered as new material that did not have full public review. As such, Comment 3-106 returned to the 2014 *NEC* development cycle as Proposal 3-97. Action by CMP-3 incorporates RTRC-XW in this section as an acceptable form of protection against physical damage that is equivalent to Schedule 80 PVC. It should be noted that the informational note to 355.10(F) indicates that RTRC-XW is identified for areas of physical damage. The incorporation of RTRC-XW in this section correlates with both 355.10(F) and 355.100 where more detail is provided in the construction specifications for this type of conduit.

Comment: None

Proposal: 3-97

# Protection Against Corrosion and Deterioration

## Code Language

**300.6 Protection Against Corrosion and Deterioration**....(see *NEC* text)...

**(A) Ferrous Metal Equipment....** (see *NEC* text)...

Informational Note: Field-cut threads are those threads that are cut in conduit, elbows, or nipples anywhere other than at the factory where the product is listed.

*(See NEC for actual text)*

## Significance of the Change

This new informational note clarifies the corrosion requirements and applicability of this section. It describes what is meant by protection for threads that are "cut in the field." The substantiation indicated there was still confusion in the field regarding protection of threads against corrosion. The misunderstanding appears to be that only straight lengths of rigid steel conduit and intermediate metal conduit are provided with corrosion protection. However, elbows, couplings and nipples associated with rigid steel conduit and intermediate metal conduit are listed to the same product standard (UL 6 and UL 1242 respectively) for the applicable material type. Section 5.4.2 of UL 6 and 7.2 of UL 1242 entitled *Protection of Threads* requires that threads that are cut after the protective coatings are applied shall be treated to keep corrosion from taking place before the conduit is installed. Cutting oils are not permitted as corrosion protection and are removed during the process of applying the corrosion protection coatings. All threads are required to be corrosion protected, after cutting, as part of the product listing. Including the terms *elbows* and *nipples* in the note clarifies that the corrosion protection applies to these fittings, but is handled by the manufacturer before the product leaves the factory.

## Change Summary

- A new informational note has been added following 300.6(A).
- The informational note clarifies which *field-cut* threads have to be protected by an approved electrically conductive, corrosion resistant compound.
- Where threads are cut and coated by the manufacturer and the product is manufactured and listed at the factory, additional corrosion protection is not necessary.

Comment: 3-17
Proposal: 3-51

# Wiring in Fabricated Ducts

## Code Language

**(B) Ducts Specifically Fabricated for Environmental Air.** Equipment, devices, and the wiring methods specified in this section shall be permitted within such ducts only if necessary for the direct action upon, or sensing of, the contained air. Where equipment or devices are installed and illumination is necessary to facilitate maintenance and repair, enclosed gasketed-type luminaires shall be permitted.

Only wiring methods consisting of Type MI cable without an overall nonmetallic covering, Type MC cable employing a smooth or corrugated impervious metal sheath without an...(see *NEC* text)...

*(See NEC for actual text)*

Note: **Subsequent NFPA Standards Council Action Pending**

## Change Summary

- The last sentence of (B) has become the first sentence and is the driving requirement of this section.
- The revised first sentence clarifies that only the wiring methods specified in (B) are permitted in these spaces.
- The words "without an overall nonmetallic covering" have been added following Type MI cable to clarify its permitted use.

Air Duct

In-duct electrical equipment

MI Cable

## Significance of the Change

This revision is technical for clarification in applicability. Note that metal raceways and metal-sheathed cables are permitted in air ducts only if they are without an overall nonmetallic covering. Section 300.22(B) in the 2011 *NEC* was only in partial correlation with this requirement. This requirement has been revised to bring about complete correlation with NFPA 90A-2012 that contains specific requirements for cables in air ducts. Section 4.3.4.4 of NFPA 90A requires electrical wires and cables and optical fiber cables shall consist of wires or cables listed as having a maximum peak optical density of 0.50 or less, an average optical density of 0.15 or less, and a maximum flame spread distance of 1.5 m (5 ft) or less when tested in accordance with NFPA 262, *Standard Method of Test for Flame Travel and Smoke of Wires and Cables for Use in Air-Handling Spaces,* or shall be installed in metal raceways without an overall nonmetallic covering or metal sheathed cable without an overall nonmetallic covering. This revision makes it clear that type MI cable and other cables installed in an application covered by 300.22(B) must not have an overall nonmetallic covering.

Comment: None
Proposal: 3-81

For additional information, visit qr.njatcdb.org Item #1210

# Raceways in Wet Locations Above Grade

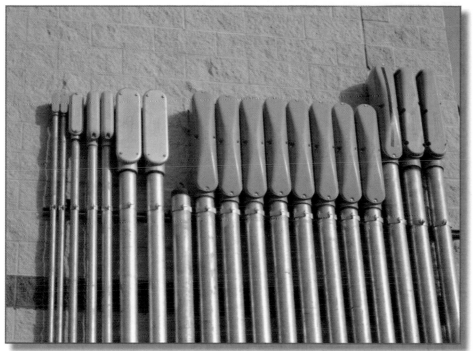

## Code Language

**300.38 Raceways in Wet Locations Above Grade.** Where raceways are installed in wet locations above grade, the interior of these raceways shall be considered to be a wet location. Insulated conductors and cables installed in raceways in wet locations above grade shall comply with 310.10(C).

*(See NEC for actual text)*

## Significance of the Change

This new Section 300.38 aligns the above-ground raceway installation requirements for over 1000 volts applications consistent with the requirements in Section 300.9 for those above-ground raceway installations in applications of 1000 volts or less. The problem is the same, so the requirements must be the same. Raceways installed in wet locations must contain conductors that are suitable for use in wet locations. Information provided in the substantiation indicated that some interpret 300.2(A) to limit Part I of Article 300 to less than 1000-volt installations only. In some cases, the limitations are for 1000 volts or less, and that Part II only gives specific permission for over 1000 volts. Action by CMP-3 on Comment 3-30 results in this new provision in Part II of Article 300. Including this consistent requirement in both Parts I and II should remove any doubts that conductors and cables installed in above-ground raceways in wet locations must be suitable for use in wet locations, whether the conductors are rated for 1000 volts or less, or over 1000 volts. This new section references 310.10(C) requiring such installed conductors and cables to be suitable for use in wet locations and so marked, or listed for use in wet locations.

## Change Summary

- A new Section 300.38 has been added to Part II of Article 300.
- This section addresses the interior of raceways in wet locations above ground for installations over 1000 volts.
- Consistent with the provisions in 300.9, the interior of raceways in wet locations for installations over 1000 volts are considered wet; suitable conductors are required.

Comment: 3-30
Proposal: 3-92

# Underground Installations in Industrial Establishments

## Code Language

**(2) Industrial Establishments.** In industrial establishments, where conditions of maintenance and supervision ensure that only qualified persons service the installed cable, nonshielded single-conductor cables with insulations types up to 2000 volts that are listed for direct burial shall be permitted to be directly buried.

*(See NEC for actual text)*

## Change Summary

- A new list item (2) has been added to 300.50(A) and the existing list items renumbered accordingly.
- This provision applies only to industrial establishments that provide controlled and supervised conditions and service by only qualified persons.
- Direct-buried, nonshielded single-conductor cables with insulations types up to 2000 volts and listed for direct burial shall be permitted.

## Significance of the Change

This new provision in list item (2) applies only to industrial establishments that provide controlled and supervised conditions and service by only qualified persons. Direct-buried, non-shielded single-conductor cables with insulations types up to 2000 volts that are listed for direct burial are now permitted under the controlled conditions indicated in (2). Information in the substantiation that common practices in large utility-scale solar installations are to install 2000-volt rated conductors in direct burial applications to carry power from combiner boxes to the inverter(s). Since these installations are typically controlled and not accessible to the public and maintenance is controlled by the facility owner, direct-buried single conductor, non-shielded conductor installations are appropriate. There are listed photovoltaic conductors rated at 2000 volts that are also listed for direct burial applications. Including this provision in 300.50 ensures that the *NEC* is ready for not only higher voltage photovoltaic installations but other higher voltage installations and similarly listed cable types that may be developed in the future. Incorporating this new provision in 300.50 makes it easy for the code user to reference and apply the appropriate installation requirements, such as burial depth and placement of warning tape for direct burial conductors.

Comment: None

Proposal: 3-96

# Grouping of Paralleled Conductors

*Courtesy of Cogburn Bros. Inc.*

## Code Language

(6) Where paralleled in ferrous metal enclosures or raceways, conductors shall be grouped with all conductors of the same circuit to prevent heating effects from imbalances of current.

> Informational Note: Where conductors are paralleled in ferrous metal enclosures or raceways, failure to group one conductor from each phase in each raceway or grouping within a wiring method may result in overheating and current imbalance.

*(See NEC for actual text)*

Note: **Subsequent NFPA Standards Council Action Pending**

## Significance of the Change

This new requirement is to group conductors of paralleled conductor arrangements in a manner that minimizes the effects of imbalance and heat. The requirement a~~pplies to para~~lleled conductors in ferrous metal enclosures and raceways. I~~~~ ~~the substantia~~tion stated that there have b~~~~ ~~ failures of para~~lleled conductors installed in wire~~~~ ~~ts and enclosure~~s due to minimize induction a~~~~ ~~ the require-~~ment for each paralleled ph~~~~ ~~onductor. The~~ proper grouping of the phas~~~~ ~~utral conductors~~ reduces inductive overheati~~~~ ~~ s current~~ division between each cond~~~~ ~~ This was~~ introduced in the comment ~~~~ ~~ stated that the~~ problem of induction and g~~~~ ~~est with~~ conductor sets installed in magnetic (ferrous) enclosures, but could also be present in nonferrous enclosures, and CMP-6 added nonferrous enclosures and raceway to the requirement. During the technical session, action on amending motions 6-4 through 6-7 reversed the inclusion of nonferrous raceways and enclosures in the new requirement. This action removed the potential conflicts with Section 300.5(I) Exception No. 2.

> The information reported here was accurate as of July 26, 2013. Subsequent action in the NFPA standards development process after this date overturned the reported information. Accordingly, this change to the *Code* did not occur.

## Change Summary

~~A n~~ew list item (6) has been ~~add~~ed to 310.10(H)(2).

~~Th~~e new requirement is to ~~gro~~up conductors of paralleled ~~con~~ductor arrangements in a ~~man~~ner that minimizes the ef~~fect~~s of imbalance and heat.

~~The~~ requirement applies to ~~para~~lleled conductors in fer~~rou~~s metal enclosures and raceways.

Comments: 6-4, 6-5, 6-6, 6-7

Proposals: 6-15, 6-17

# Paralleled Equipment Bonding Jumpers

## Code Language

**(6) Bonding Jumpers.** Where parallel equipment bonding jumpers or supply-side bonding jumpers are installed in raceways, they shall be sized and installed in accordance with 250.102.

*(See NEC for actual text)*

*Courtesy of Bill McGovern, City of Plano, TX*

## Change Summary

- The title of list item (6) has been revised to Bonding Jumpers to expand its application.
- The term *supply-side bonding jumpers* has been added to this provision.
- Paralleled equipment bonding jumpers and supply-side bonding jumpers must meet the sizing requirements in 250.102.

Comment: None
Proposal: 6-17

## Significance of the Change

This section has been revised to incorporate the term *supply-side bonding jumpers*. Installations using paralleled conductor arrangements conforming to 310.10(H) typically also include either equipment grounding conductors or equipment bonding jumpers as applicable. Where equipment grounding conductors are installed with paralleled arrangements, they must be sized in accordance with 250.122 and the minimum sizes provided in Table 250.122. Where equipment bonding jumpers are installed with paralleled circuits, they are required to be sized according to 250.102. In the 2011 *NEC*, the term *supply-side bonding jumper(s)* was introduced as a definition in 250.2 and various sections within Article 250 were revised to incorporate the use of this term. Supply-side bonding jumper(s) are those installed on the line or supply side of service or separately derived system overcurrent devices. Section 250.102 includes installation and sizing requirements for supply-side bonding jumpers and equipment bonding jumpers on the load side of an overcurrent device, as provided in 250.102(D). The revision clarifies that these bonding jumpers installed in parallel arrangements, whether supply side or load side, must meet the applicable sizing rules in 250.102. Sizing requirements for supply-side bonding jumpers are provided in 250.102(C) which references Table 250.102(C) and associated notes.

## Adjustment Factors for Current-Carrying Conductors

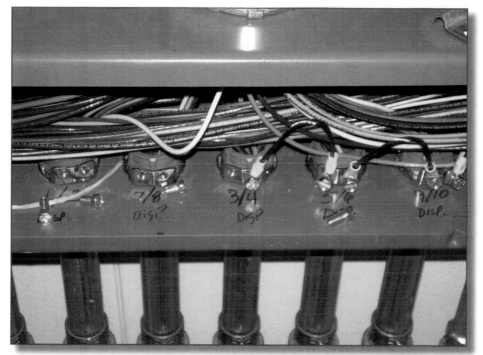

### Significance of the Change

This note has been revised to clarify that spare conductors must be included in the application of adjustment factors. The substantiation indicated concerns from enforcement relative to problems with spare conductors being installed without benefit of inspection and application of mutual conductor heating derating factors, and subsequently connected to loads. The change to this note has also clarified that conductors, other than spare conductors, that handle non-coincidental loads, are not carrying current simultaneously. In these cases, the correction factors do not have to include those conductors in the application of the correction table factors. The substantiation identified a clear example of such condition being one of the travelers in a three-way or four-way switch loop. Another example provided in the substantiation was of two large, identical three-phase motors fed through a common raceway and wired to a single VFD through an interlocking contactor assembly that precluded simultaneous operation. Other common conditions occur often in industrial applications where this type of installation should qualify for the relief this revised note provides. Prior to this revision the literal enforcement of the factors in this table would have unnecessarily caused increases in wire sizes that in turn could have required an increases in raceway sizes.

### Change Summary

- The note to Table 310.15(B)(3)(a) has been revised.
- The total number of conductors that are included in the adjustment factor includes spare conductors.
- Conductors that cannot be energized simultaneously are not required to be included in the quantity of conductors used in the adjustment factor.

Comment: None
Proposal: 6-40

# Raceways and Cables on Rooftops in Sunlight

## Code Language

(c) *Raceways and Cables Exposed to Sunlight on Rooftops.* Where raceways or cables are exposed to direct sunlight on or above rooftops, the adjustments shown in Table 310.15(B)(3)(c) shall be added to the outdoor temperature to determine the applicable ambient temperature for application of the correction factors in Table 310.15(B)(2)(a) or Table 310.15(B)(2)(b).

**Table 310.15(B)(3)(c) Ambient Temperature Adjustment for Raceways or Cables Exposed to Sunlight on or Above Rooftops...** (see *NEC* table)...

*(See NEC for actual text)*

*IStock Photo Courtesy of NECA*

## Change Summary

- The word "circular" has been removed from this section and the title of the table.

- The words "or cables" have been added to this section and in the title of the table.

- Ambient temperature correction factors in Table 310.15(B)(2)(a) or Table 310.15(B)(2)(b) apply to conductors in raceways and cables on or above rooftops and exposed to direct sunlight.

## Significance of the Change

This section in previous editions of the *NEC* only applied to circular raceways installed on or above rooftops and exposed to direct sunlight. Other noncircular raceways and cables were not included as part of the original research that caused the change in the 2008 *NEC*. The word "circular" has been removed from this section and title of the table, no longer limiting these correction factors to just circular raceways. The word "cables" has been added both in the title of the table and in the text. The substantiation referred to subsequent research on rooftop temperature adjustment that included MC cable, tray cable and other cable types and included all wiring methods currently permitted for rooftop installations. This research revealed that conductors in all wiring methods experienced significant ambient temperature increases above outdoor temperature when exposed to direct sunlight. The Fact-Finding Report (File IN16969) by Underwriters Laboratories (UL) addresses and substantiates these concerns and thus validates the revisions incorporated in this section and table. As revised, the correction factors in 310.15(B)(3)(c) apply to all raceways and cables installed on or above rooftops where exposed to direct sunlight.

Comment: None

Proposals: 6-26, 6-31

## New Exception for XHHW-2 Conductors

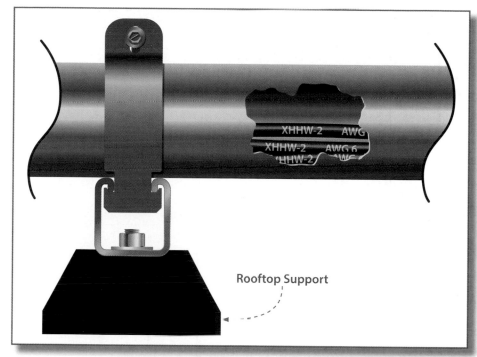

Rooftop Support

### Code Language

(c) *Raceways and Cables Exposed to Sunlight on Rooftops.* Where raceways or cables are exposed to direct sunlight on or above rooftops, the adjustments shown in Table 310.15(B) (3)(c) shall be added to the outdoor temperature to determine the applicable ambient temperature for application of the correction factors in Table 310.15(B)(2)(a) or Table 310.15(B)(2)(b).

*Exception: Type XHHW-2 insulated conductors shall not be subject to this ampacity adjustment.*

*(See NEC for actual text)*

### Significance of the Change

Technical substantiation confirmed that thermoset insulation is superior to thermoplastic insulation in high heat applications. Industry standards from IEEE, ICEA and NEMA indicate that thermoset insulation is adequate for much higher temperatures than those experienced on rooftops for the period of time indicated. Two rounds of testing were performed to validate that thermoset insulated conductors are more resistant to high heat conditions than thermoplastic. First, General Cable performed comparative testing of thermoplastic and thermoset insulated wires at high temperature under physical stress. The test is normally run for one hour during wire certification testing, but this test ran for 60 days to better emulate the expected lifetime exposure of conductors to high heat over time. The results indicated that thermoset insulation is more resistant to high heat than thermoplastic. The thermoplastic conductors showed significant signs of stress and aging. Underwriters Laboratories performed the same testing and achieved similar results. UL also performed tensile and elongation, flexibility, and dielectric voltage withstand and breakdown tests. Published industry standards and testing submitted with Comment 6-37 demonstrated that thermoset insulation is clearly more resistant to high heat applications than thermoplastic insulation. The new exception exempts XHHW-2 conductors from the correction factors in Table 310.15(B)(3)(c).

### Change Summary

- A new exception has been added following 310.15(B)(3)(c).
- Ambient temperature correction factors in Table 310.15(B)(2)(a) or Table 310.15(B)(2)(b) do not apply to XHHW-2 insulated conductors in raceways and cables on or above rooftops and exposed to direct sunlight.
- The new exception is the result of performance testing by both General Cable and Underwriters Laboratories.

Comment: 6-37
Proposal: 6-41

# Conductor Size for Dwelling Services and Feeders

## Code Language

**(7) 120/240-Volt, Single-Phase Dwelling Services and Feeders.** For one-family dwellings and the individual dwelling units of two-family and multifamily dwellings, service and feeder conductors supplied by a single-phase, 120/240-volt system shall be permitted be sized in accordance with 310.15(B)(7)(1) through (4).

(1) For a service rated 100 through 400 A...(see *NEC* text)...not less than 83% of the service rating.

(2) For a feeder rated 100 through 400 A...(see *NEC* text)...not less than 83% of the feeder rating.

(3) In no case shall a feeder for an individual dwelling unit be required to have an ampacity greater than that specified in 310.15(B)(7)(1) or (2).

(4) Grounded conductors...(see *NEC* text)...

*(See NEC for actual text)*

## Change Summary

- Table 310.15(B)(7) has been deleted and Section 310.15(B)(7) has been revised and re-structured into a list format.

- An 83 percent multiplier is provided for calculating ampacity for feeders and service conductors supplying dwelling units, if the conditions of this section are met.

- A new informational note references a new Annex (D7) where an example calculation is provided.

Comment: 6-52
Proposal: 6-49a

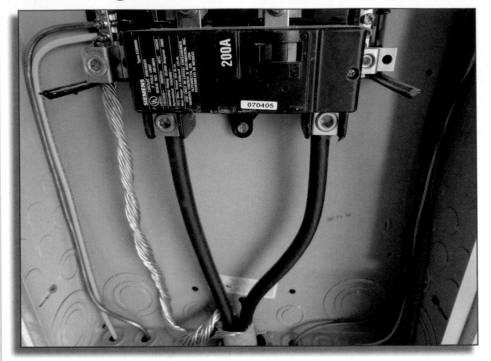

## Significance of the Change

This section has been restructured into a list format and an 83 percent multiplier has replaced Table 310.15(B)(7). It was determined during the Sixteenth NFPA Annual Meeting that 84 percent was used to establish the aluminum residential service conductor size. However, the 84 percent factor resulted in larger sizes for some conductors compared to the sizes in the 2011 *NEC*. Therefore an 83 percent multiplier was selected to maintain consistency with the sizes in the 2011 *NEC* Table 310.15(B)(7). CMP-6 also analyzed the existing Table 310.15(B)(7) values and determined that the conductor sizes provided were equivalent to those if a 0.83 multiplier was applied to each service ampere rating. The resulting conductor size ends up the same as existing values in Table 310.15(B)(7), if the same conductor types and installation conditions are applied. Informational Note No. 1 clarifies that adjustment and correction factors apply depending on conditions of use. Informational Note No. 2 references a useful Annex (D7) that provides an example of applying the 83 percent factor. This revision eliminates the need for defining the term "main power feeder" in 310.15(B)(7), which reduces confusion considerably. These revisions enhance usability and clarity of this section and provide for more consistent application for qualifying dwelling service and feeder conductors.

# Conductor Shields Grounded at One Point

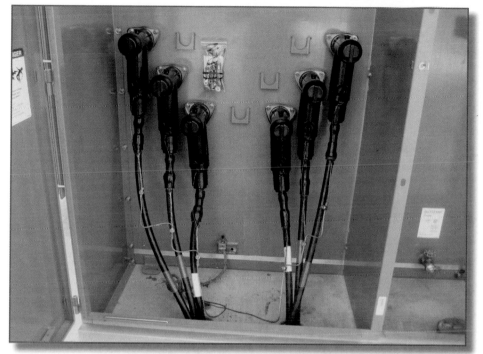

*Courtesy of Cogburn Bros. Inc.*

## Code Language

**(1) Grounded Shields.** Ampacities shown in Table 310.60(C)(69), Table 310.60(C)(70), Table 310.60(C)(81), and Table 310.60(C)(82) shall apply for cables with shields grounded at one point only. Where shields for these cables are grounded at more than one point, ampacities shall be adjusted to take into consideration the heating due to shield currents.

Informational Note: Tables other than those listed contain the ampacity of cables with shields grounded at multiple points.

*(See NEC for actual text)*

## Significance of the Change

This section has been revised to clarify its application to cables that have shields grounded at only one point. Current version of the *NEC* leaves the reader to infer or guess that tables are based on connection of grounded shields at both ends of the conductor installation. The revised text in list item (1) makes it clear that the majority of the tables (those not listed as exceptions) already show reduced ampacity to account for the losses due to shield currents. Tables 310.60(C)(69), 310.60(C)(70), 310.60(C)(81), and 310.60(C)(82) shall apply for cables with shields grounded connected at one point only. The new informational note provides users with information that prompts use of other table ampacities where the cable shields are connected at multiple points and thus subjecting those to additional cable stresses at those grounding connection points.

## Change Summary

- List item (1) has been revised and a new informational note was added.
- As revised, the tables identified in this section provide ampacities for cables that have shields connected at only one point.
- Tables other than those included in list item (1) must be used for cable ampacities if the shields are grounded at multiple points.

Comment: 6-62
Proposal: 6-68

# Warning Marking for Feed Through Conductors

## Code Language

(3) A warning label complying with 110.21(B) is applied to the enclosure that identifies the closest disconnecting means for any feed-through conductors.

*(See NEC for actual text)*

Feed Through Conductors

Panelboard Supply

⚠ WARNING ⚠
FEED-THROUGH CONDUCTORS
IN PANELBOARD SUPPLIED
FROM SWITCHBOARD MDB

PANEL A

⚠ **WARNING** ⚠

**FEED-THROUGH CONDUCTORS
IN PANELBOARD SUPPLIED
FROM SWITCHBOARD MDB**

## Change Summary

- The words "complying with 110.21(B)" have been added to list item (3).
- The warning label required by this section must identify the closest disconnect for any conductors feeding through the equipment.
- The warning label must also meet the requirements for labels and markings that use the signal words warning, caution, or danger.

## Significance of the Change

This revision is one of several coordinated changes to provide consistency of danger, caution, and warning sign or markings required throughout the *NEC*. The added text in (3) correlates this warning marking requirement with 110.21(B) and the marking requirements in ANSI Z535.4. Section 110.21(B) is titled *Field-Applied Hazard Markings.* The new rules for field-applied markings require effective and consistent hazard warnings using appropriate colors, words, or symbols. These markings are generally not permitted to be hand written, with an exception for portions of the markings or labels that are variable or subject to change such as those required by 110.24 or 110.16. Hand-written portions must be legible and must also be durable for the environment where they are installed. Important aspects of this revision are the references, from informational notes, to the ANSI Z535.4-2011 standard titled *Product Safety Signs and Labels.* Many existing *NEC* rules specify the signal words danger, warning, or caution in marking and label requirements, yet they are inconsistently applied in the field. This is one of several *NEC* rules that have been revised to reference 110.21(B) promoting a more consistent approach in developing and application of the hazard markings, labels, and signs for wiring methods and equipment.

Comment: None
Proposal: 9-26

# Installation in Wet or Damp Locations

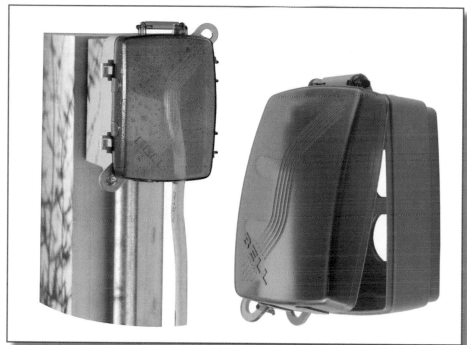

*Courtesy of Hubbell Incorporated*

## Code Language

**314.15 Damp or Wet Locations.** In damp or wet locations, boxes, conduit bodies, outlet box hoods, and fittings shall be placed or equipped so as to prevent moisture from entering or accumulating within the box, conduit body, outlet box hoods, or fitting. Boxes, conduit bodies, and fittings installed in wet locations shall be listed for use in wet locations. Approved drainage openings not larger than 6 mm (1/4 in.) shall be permitted to be installed in the field in boxes or conduit bodies listed for use in damp or wet locations. For installation of listed drain fittings, larger openings are permitted to be installed in the field in accordance with manufacturer's instructions.

*(See NEC for actual text)*

## Significance of the Change

This section includes outlet box hoods in the requirements for boxes, conduit bodies, and fittings installed in wet or damp locations. Information in the substantiation stated that 406.9(B)(1) requires "extra duty" outlet box hoods installed in a wet locations to be listed. All outlet box hoods must be listed when installed in wet locations as they are relied upon to provide protection for enclosed devices. The revision in this section incorporates provisions for listed drainage fittings and those provided in the field. The substantiation to Proposal 9-35 indicated that electricians have added weep holes in the field since electrical enclosures were first used in wet locations, and will continue doing so. Properly provided drainage improves the safety and durability of electrical installations. Since the field orientation of installed cast aluminum or other such enclosures cannot be known at the time of manufacture, it would be impossible for such openings to be provided in advance by the manufacturer. This rule has been revised to recognize drainage openings that are provided in the field if approved by the authority having jurisdiction. Listed drainage fittings may be larger than 1/4 inch where installed in accordance with the manufacturer's instructions.

## Change Summary

- Two new last sentences have been added to this section.
- Approved drainage openings not larger than 6 mm (1/4 in.) shall be permitted to be installed in the field.
- Listed drainage fittings with opening larger than 1/4 inch are permitted to be installed in accordance with the manufacturer's instructions.

Comment: 9-26
Proposals: 9-33, 9-35

# Box Mounting Screws for Devices

## Code Language

**314.25 Covers and Canopies.** In completed installations, each box shall have a cover, faceplate, lampholder, or luminaire canopy, except where the installation complies with 410.24(B). Screws used for the purpose of attaching covers, or other equipment, to the box, shall be either machine screws matching the thread gauge or size that is integral to the box or shall be in accordance with the manufacturer's instructions.

*(See NEC for actual text)*

## Change Summary

- A new last sentence has been added to 314.25.
- Screws for covers or attaching equipment to boxes shall be compatible and have matching machine threads or be in accordance with the manufacturer's instructions.
- Drywall screws and other screws are not permitted to be used with boxes unless otherwise listed for use with those types.

## Significance of the Change

This section requires that each box have a cover, faceplate, lampholder, or luminaire canopy, except where the installation complies with 410.24(B). A new second sentence specifies that screws used for attaching covers, or other equipment to the box, shall be either machine screws matching the thread gage or size integral to the box or be in accordance with the manufacturer's instructions. Use of drywall screws and other screws that are not intended for fastening luminaires or other equipment to boxes is not acceptable and can result in damage to the box and inadequate support of the equipment. Manufacturer's installation instructions cover this in most cases for listed boxes and equipment, but having the additional text will help clarify this requirement. CMP-9 incorporated the concepts into the additional sentence but also accounted for nonmetallic outlet boxes and product standards that allow the use of thread forming screws for the attachment of covers provided they meet the performance requirements cited in the applicable standard. This type of screw is typically used with nonmetallic junction boxes and provided with the box. The revision clarifies that drywall screws and other inappropriate screws are not permitted for use with boxes unless otherwise listed for that use.

Comment: None
Proposal: 9-55

# Vertical Surface Outlets for Luminaires

## Code Language

**(1) Vertical Surface Outlets.** Boxes used at luminaire or lampholder outlets in or on a vertical surface shall be identified and marked on the interior of the box to indicate the maximum weight of the luminaire that is permitted to be supported by the box if other than 23 kg (50 lb).

*Exception: A vertically mounted luminaire or lampholder weighing not more than 3 kg (6 lb) shall be permitted to be…(See* NEC *text)…*

**(See NEC for actual text)**

## Significance of the Change

This section has been revised to address all luminaire outlets installed in walls and other vertical surfaces. Information in the substantiation indicated that previously, this requirement only applied to luminaire outlet boxes installed in walls. The revision clarifies that regardless of the vertical surface where the luminaire outlet is installed, the marking requirements in this section apply. Outlet boxes used to support luminaires and lampholders are often mounted on vertical surfaces other than walls, such as on posts of columns. The text "for the purposes" proposed by the submitter was not incorporated to be consistent with other actions taken by the Panel. Action by CMP-9 also results in this section applying to outlets mounted "in or on" the vertical surface to include flush and surface mounted wiring installations in the requirement. The key is that these boxes be identified for the weight of the luminaire they are intended to support, if other than 23 kg (50 lbs). The exception still addresses boxes that are intended to support luminaires weighing not more than 3 kg (6 lbs.) and permits support of such luminaires with no less than two size No. 6 or larger screws.

## Change Summary

- The title of list item (1) has been changed from Wall Outlets to Vertical Surface Outlets.

- The section text and the exception have been revised to reference vertical surface outlets.

- The revision expands requirements for identifying and marking maximum luminaire weight on outlets installed in or on walls and other vertical surfaces.

Comment: None
Proposal: 9-58

# Ceiling Outlets for Luminaires

## Code Language

**(2) Ceiling Outlets.** At every outlet used exclusively for lighting, the box shall be designed or installed so that a luminaire or lampholder may be attached. Boxes shall be required to support a luminaire weighing a minimum of 23 kg (50 lb). A luminaire that weighs more than 23 kg (50 lb) shall be supported independently of the outlet box, unless the outlet box is listed and marked on the interior of the box to indicate the maximum weight the box shall be permitted to support.

*(See NEC for actual text)*

## Change Summary

- The last sentence of list item (2) has been revised.
- The interior of a listed box must be marked to indicate the maximum weight the box shall be permitted to support.
- The revision results in a required marking that would be accessible to installers and inspectors with or without building finish surface materials installed.

## Significance of the Change

This section has been revised to require the markings specified in this section be located on interior of the outlet box. The interior of a box designed to support a luminaire that weighs more than 23 kg (50 lb) should be required to be marked on the interior of the box with the maximum weight of the luminaire that can be supported from the box, so the installer and inspector of the luminaire installation will have access to the maximum weight value. The revision provides direction for box manufacturers relative to placement of markings related to appropriate and intended use of such ceiling boxes as means of support for luminaires. A luminaire that weighs more than 23 kg (50 lb) must generally be supported independently of the outlet box, unless the outlet box is listed and marked on the interior of the box.

Comment: None
Proposal: 9-62

# Boxes for Ceiling-Suspended Fans

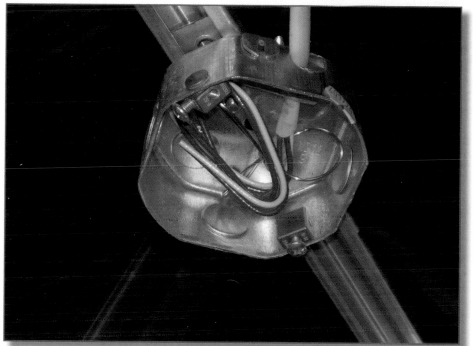

## Significance of the Change

This section deals specifically with the box requirements for ceiling-suspended paddle fans. This rule is one of a few in the *NEC* that anticipates an action later after the initial wiring installation is completed. In dwelling units, where spare, separately switched, ungrounded conductors are roughed in to ceiling-mounted outlet box, in a location acceptable for a ceiling-suspended paddle fan, the outlet box or outlet box system must be listed for sole support of a ceiling-suspended paddle fan. Adding *two-family* into this section will ensure the requirement for a ceiling fan outlet box applies to all dwellings, not just single- and multi-family. Article 100 provides definitions for the terms single-family dwelling, a two-family dwelling and multifamily dwellings. As written in the previous *NEC* editions, ceiling boxes installed in a two-family dwelling where spare separately switched ungrounded conductors are supplied would literally not require a listed ceiling fan box being installed. This revision corrects this and promotes consistency for wiring installations in dwelling units and will ensure that listed ceiling-suspended paddle fan outlet boxes are installed. The requirements for installing the listed ceiling fan box apply whether the fan is installed initially or at a later date.

## Code Language

**(C) Boxes at Ceiling-Suspended (Paddle) Fan Outlets.** Outlet boxes or outlet box systems…(See *NEC* text)…

Where spare, separately switched, ungrounded conductors are provided to a ceiling-mounted outlet box, in a location acceptable for a ceiling-suspended (paddle) fan in single-family, two-family or multi-family dwellings, the outlet box or outlet box system shall be listed for sole support of a ceiling-suspended (paddle) fan.

*(See NEC for actual text)*

## Change Summary

- The term *two-family dwellings* has been added to the second paragraph.
- The change expands the requirement to single-family, two-family, and multifamily dwelling units.
- The revision provides for a more uniform and consistent requirement for anticipated support provisions for ceiling-suspended paddle fan installations.

Comment: None
Proposal: 9-63

# Conductor Fill at Smaller Conduit Bodies

## Code Language

**(3) Smaller Dimensions.** Listed boxes or listed conduit bodies...(See *NEC* text)...

Listed conduit bodies of dimensions less than those required in 314.28(A)(2), and having a radius of the curve to the centerline not less than that indicated in Table 2 of Chapter 9 for one-shot and full-shoe benders, shall be permitted for installations of combinations of conductors permitted by Table 1 of Chapter 9. These conduit bodies shall be marked to show they have been specifically evaluated in accordance with this provision. Where the permitted combinations of conductors for which the box or conduit body has been listed...(See *NEC* text)...

*(See NEC for actual text)*

*Courtesy of Thomas and Betts*

## Change Summary

- A new paragraph has been added to list item (3) addressing conduit body sizes in relation to conductor fill.

- The new text allows use of conduit bodies smaller than those required in 314.28(A)(2) with conditions.

- The revision provides a practical allowance for conductor combinations in conduit bodies where marked to indicate suitability for such use.

## Significance of the Change

This section now permits the use of conduit bodies smaller than those required in 314.28(A)(2) with conditions. The revision provides a practical allowance for conductor combinations in conduit bodies where marked to indicate suitability for such use. Section 314.28(A)(3) in the 2011 *NEC* was restrictive and technically did not permit the number of conductors allowed by Table 1, Chapter 9 for the conduit or tubing used with smaller conduit bodies. The substantiation indicated that smaller designs of conduit bodies effectively negate wire jamming concerns addressed in Table 1, Chapter 9, Informational Note No. 2. Also, listed conduit bodies having a radius of curve to the centerline not less than as indicated in Table 2, Chapter 9 are available on the market. This new text allows reduced size conduit bodies but includes both listing and marking requirements so their use will be readily apparent to installers and inspectors. The term *combinations of conductors* as used in (3) is appropriate in this new text so as to avoid confusion with, or misapplication of 314.16(B)(1). The new text added to this section provides for use of smaller listed conduit bodies for combinations of conductors where the combinations are marked on the product.

Comment: 9-32
Proposal: 9-67

# Floor Coverings – Size of Carpet Squares

Courtesy of TE Connectivity Enterprises Network

## Code Language

**324.41 Floor Coverings.** Floor-mounted Type FCC cable, cable connectors, and insulating ends shall be covered with carpet squares not larger than 1.0 m (39.37 in.) square. Carpet squares that are adhered to the floor shall be attached with release-type adhesives.

*(See NEC for actual text)*

## Significance of the Change

Article 324 provides requirements for installing flat conductor cable, Type FCC. One of the requirements for this wiring method deals with accessibility because this wiring is subject to modification or relocation to accommodate its use. This change increases the permitted size for carpet squares laid on top of flat conductor cable installations. The 2011 *NEC* and previous editions required that flat conductor cable be installed under carpet squares that did not exceed 914 mm (36 in.) square. This language required standardization of modular carpet square size to U.S. units of measure, which automatically precluded the use of modular carpet products and manufacturers that standardize on SI units of measure. The intent of this section is to permit a maximum size requirement that maintains practical accessibility to the flat conductor cable installation. Such access is easily achievable even with the slight adjustment in size to allow for carpet squares to be sized using SI units. CMP-7 acted favorably to the adjustment in carpet square sizes since the SI Unit standard 1.0 m carpet square is similarly equivalent in application to the current U.S. customary standard 914 mm (36 in.) carpet square requirement. This revision continues the long progression in the *NEC* of incorporating metric units of measure.

## Change Summary

- The size carpet square permitted has been increased from 914 mm (36 in.) square to 1.0 m (39.37 in.) square.
- The revision allows use of modular carpet products that would have previously been restricted due to size.
- This change continues the progression in the *NEC* to globally incorporate the use of SI units of measure.

Comment: None
Proposal: 7-23

# 330.10(A)(11)b & c

## Article 330 Metal-Clad Cable: Type MC

### Part II Installation

# MC Cable – Uses Permitted

## Code Language

(11) In wet locations where a corrosion-resistant jacket is provided over the metallic covering and any of the following conditions are met:

a. The metallic covering is impervious to moisture.

b. A jacket resistant to moisture is provided under the metal covering.

c. The insulated conductors under the metallic covering are listed for use in wet locations.

*(See NEC for actual text)*

*Courtesy of General Cable*

## Change Summary

- List item 11 has been revised to clarify that a corrosion resistant jacket is required over the metallic covering.
- The revision aligns this section with UL Standard 1569 *Metal Clad Cables.*
- MC cable in wet locations must have a corrosion-resistant jacket as the outer layer of the cable assembly and meet one of a, b, or c.

## Significance of the Change

This section has been revised to clarify that metal-clad cable, Type MC, is permitted for use in wet locations if it has a corrosion-resistant jacket over the metallic covering and the metallic covering is either impervious to moisture, or a jacket resistant to moisture is provided under the metal covering, or the insulated conductors under the metallic covering are listed for use in wet locations. The revised wording in the driving text of list item (11) is now consistent with that in the product standard requirements for cable jackets in UL 1569 *Metal Clad Cables* that contains the performance requirements that define what constitutes resistance to moisture. As the substantiation in Proposal 7-27 indicated, the corrosion resistant jacket provides protection for the metal covering of the cable. The protection should be provided for all metal coverings, not only for metallic coverings over conductors in the assembly that are suitable for wet locations. The revision provides clear direction for installers and inspectors relative to metal clad cable permitted for use in wet locations, and the conditions that it must meet to qualify for installation in such locations.

Comment: None

Proposals: 7-26a, 7-27

# MC Cable in Vertical Installations

*Courtesy of General Cable*

## Code Language

**(B) Securing.** Unless otherwise provided, cables shall be secured at intervals not exceeding 1.8 m (6 ft). Cables containing four or fewer conductors sized no larger than 10 AWG shall be secured within 300 mm (12 in.) of every box, cabinet, fitting, or other cable termination. In vertical installations, listed cables with ungrounded conductors 250 kcmil and larger shall be permitted to be secured at intervals not exceeding 3 m (10 ft).

*(See NEC for actual text)*

## Significance of the Change

This section has been revised to specifically permit securing intervals for listed MC cables in vertical installations to not exceed a distance of 3 m (10 ft). MC Cables with integral conductor support have been commonly used for high-rise installations without offsets or directly securing the conductors under the armor. This revision requires the cable to be listed. The original proposal action on Comment 7-5 is related to substantiation provided in the UL Fact-Finding Report, Project 12ME07391, dated November 30, 2012. Evaluation and testing revealed no slipping with internal integral conductor support. In vertical installations, listed cables with ungrounded conductors in sizes of 250 kcmil and larger are now allowed to be secured at intervals not exceeding 3 m (10 ft). This change somewhat relaxes the general securing requirements from 6 ft and now permits a maximum of 10 feet, but only for listed MC cables in sizes 250 kcmil and larger used in vertical installations.

## Change Summary

- A new last sentence has been added to 330.30(B).
- Vertical installations of listed MC cables in sizes 250 kcmil and larger are permitted to be secured at intervals not exceeding 3 m (10 ft).
- Some MC cables are listed and identified for vertical installation where supported at intervals not exceeding 10 feet.

Comment: 7-5
Proposal: 7-29

# MC Cable – Securing and Supporting

## Code Language

**330.30 Securing and Supporting**
…(See *NEC* text)…

**(A)** through **(C)**…(See *NEC* text)…

**(D) Unsupported Cables.** Type MC cable shall be permitted to be unsupported where the cable:

(1) and (2) …(See *NEC* text)…

(3) Is Type MC of the interlocked armor type in lengths not exceeding 900 mm (3 ft) from the last point where it is securely fastened and is used to connect equipment where flexibility is necessary to minimize the transmission of vibration from equipment or to provide flexibility for equipment that requires movement after installation.

*(See NEC for actual text)*

*Courtesy of YESCO*

## Change Summary

- A new list item (3) has been added to 330.30(D).

- Unsupported interlocking armor-type MC cable is permitted in lengths not exceeding 3 ft from the last point where it is securely fastened.

- The relief applies where flexibility is necessary to minimize the transmission of vibration from equipment or to provide flexibility after installation.

## Significance of the Change

Metal-clad cable is an inherently flexible wiring method that naturally provides for some degree of movement and flexing during normal operation. This new provision in 330.30(D) provides a relaxation from the previous required support means prescribed for this wiring method. The substantiation from the National Electrical Manufacturers Association (NEMA) indicated that the construction of MC cable that includes interlocked armor and twisted conductors under the armor makes it suitable for use where flexibility is needed at terminations. This new allowance applies only to the interlocking metal tape style of metal-clad cable. The smooth tube, and corrugated tube types are more rigid in construction and do not afford the same level of flexibility. The change also aligns with current industry field-wiring installation practices for connecting equipment where flexibility is necessary after installation because of anticipated movement, or for connections to equipment that may produce vibration in normal operation. New list item (3) provides clear direction for installers and inspectors and allows for practical relief from securing and supporting MC cable as normally required by subdivisions (B) and (C) of this section.

Comment: None
Proposal: 7-31

# Devices of Insulating Material – Without Boxes

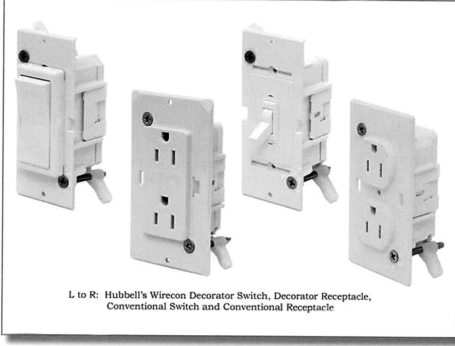

L to R: Hubbell's Wirecon Decorator Switch, Decorator Receptacle, Conventional Switch and Conventional Receptacle

*Courtesy of Wirecon Division of Hubbell Incorporated*

## Code Language

**(B) Devices of Insulating Material.** Self-contained switches, self-contained receptacles, and nonmetallic-sheathed cable interconnector devices of insulating material that are listed shall be permitted to be used without boxes in exposed cable wiring and for repair wiring in existing buildings where the cable is concealed. Openings in such devices shall form a close fit around the outer covering of the cable, and the device shall fully enclose the part of the cable from which any part of the covering has been removed. Where connections to conductors are by binding-screw terminals, there shall be available as many terminals as conductors.

*(See NEC for actual text)*

## Significance of the Change

This section has been revised to specifically require only listed devices that are permitted without using boxes. Information in the substantiation explained that *rewiring* constitutes providing new wire. New wiring installations can meet the general requirements in the *NEC* that specify where outlet boxes are required. Justification for a concealed splice when rewiring occurs seems to be difficult and the concealed splice seems to be unwarranted and not without some risk. However, rewiring in some cases is a burden to owners because of damage to finished surfaces. A safe repair would be a practical solution for an existing unsafe condition. A concealed splice should always be a last resort and this change would limit the application to those situations. As revised, this section now specifies listed self-contained switches, listed self-contained receptacles, and listed nonmetallic sheathed cable interconnector devices for use without boxes in repair and exposed wiring installations. Requiring listed self-contained switches, receptacles, and interconnectors ensures that these products addressed in 334.40(B) have been tested and evaluated to the product standard for such devices. There is no additional restriction for these types of listed devices when installed exposed.

## Change Summary

- This section has been revised to specifically address self-contained switches, self-contained receptacles, and nonmetallic sheathed cable interconnectors without boxes.
- These types of wiring devices and splices must be listed.
- As revised, these devices are permitted for repair and exposed wiring, not rewiring applications.

Comments: 7-8, 7-9, 7-10
Proposals: 7-49, 7-50, 7-51

## USE Cable Ampacity – Exterior

### Code Language

(b) *Exterior Installations.* In addition to the provisions of this article, service entrance cable used for feeders or branch circuits, where installed as exterior wiring, shall be installed in accordance with Part I of Article 225. The cable shall be supported in accordance with 334.30. Type USE cable installed as underground feeder and branch circuit cable shall comply with Part II of Article 340.

*Exception: Single conductor Type USE and multi-rated USE conductors shall not be subject to the ampacity limitations of Part II of Article 340.*

**(See NEC for actual text)**

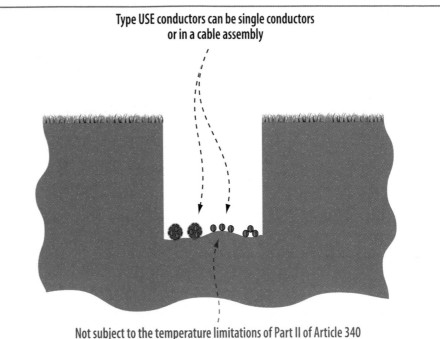

Type USE conductors can be single conductors or in a cable assembly

Not subject to the temperature limitations of Part II of Article 340

### Change Summary

- A new exception has been added following 338.10(B)(4)(b).
- Underground service-entrance cable is defined in 338.2 and can be a single conductor or it can be an assembly of multiple conductors.
- Type USE cable installed as feeders or branch circuits is not subject to the ampacity limitations provided in 340.80.

### Significance of the Change

Underground service-entrance cable is covered by the requirements in Article 338 with references to requirements in parts of other articles. Type USE cable can be triplex cable, quad cable assemblies, or single-conductor cable. Proposal 7-65 identified a possible source of confusion as it relates to the permitted ampacities of single conductor and multiple conductor underground service-entrance cable, Type USE. The last sentence of 338.10(B)(4)(b) indicates that USE cable installed as branch circuits or feeders in underground applications must comply with Part II of Article 340. This places an ampacity limitation to that of 60-degree conductors in accordance with 310.15. Action on Comment 7-12 by CMP-7 resulted in a new exception following this section. Where USE cable installed underground it is rated 75°C but because of the text in (b) it is required to be limited to 60°C when used as a underground feeder or branch circuit. The exception clarifies that single conductor Type USE and multiple conductor USE cables are not subject to the ampacity limitations of Part II of Article 340, but still must meet the other installation requirements in Part II of Article 340.

Comment: 7-12

Proposal: 7-59

# Definition of Rigid Metal Conduit (RMC)

*Courtesy of Tim Arendt*

## Code Language

**Rigid Metal Conduit (RMC).** A threadable raceway of circular cross section designed for the physical protection and routing of conductors and cables and for use as an equipment grounding conductor when installed with its integral or associated coupling and appropriate fittings.

*(See NEC for actual text)*

## Significance of the Change

While this revision is more editorial in nature, it simplifies the definition for clarity. Proposal 8-48 indicated that the last two sentences were more informative in nature and were not needed in the definition. As revised, the definition continues to provide information about what constitutes rigid metal conduit (RMC) and that this type of conduit is suitable for use as an equipment grounding conductor if installed with appropriate fittings. In the future, this definition can even be simplified further, because rigid metal conduit is already recognized by 250.118(2) as a suitable equipment grounding conductor. The last two sentences in the 2011 definition were repetitive and describe types of metals used to manufacture rigid metal conduit (RMC) including any protective coatings. Section 344.6 requires rigid metal conduit, factory elbows, couplings, and associated fittings to be listed. Section 344.10(A) provides the applications for various types of rigid metal conduit. The information in 344.10(B) provides specifics about the permitted uses in corrosive environments while (C) covers installations in cinder fill and (D) covers wet locations. Action by CMP-8 on Proposal 8-52a relocates the last sentences addressing permitted construction materials from the definition to a new Section 344.100 which covers construction specifications.

## Change Summary

- The definition of rigid metal conduit (RMC) has been revised and simplified.
- The last two sentences have been removed and the information has been relocated to 344.100.
- The revision leaves a definition of rigid metal conduit without inclusion of the material it is made from or conductive coatings that may be applied during manufacturing processes.

Comment: None
Proposals: 8-47, 8-48

# Securing and Supporting Type FMC

## Code Language

*Exception No. 4: Lengths not exceeding 1.8 m (6 ft) from the last point where the raceway is securely fastened for connections within an accessible ceiling to a luminaire(s) or other equipment. For the purposes of this exception, listed flexible metal conduit fittings shall be permitted as a means of support.*

**(See NEC for actual text)**

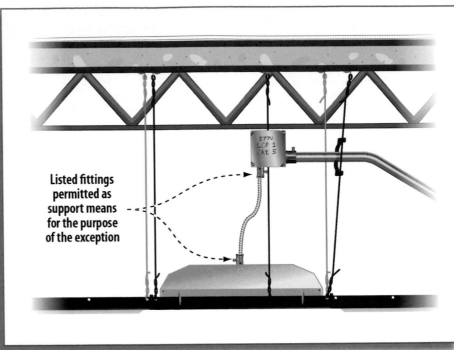

Listed fittings permitted as support means for the purpose of the exception

## Change Summary

- A new last sentence has been added to Exception No. 4.
- Listed flexible metal conduit fittings shall be permitted as a means of support for lengths up to 1.8 m (6 ft).
- This revision clarifies that for the purpose of this exception, additional support for flexible metal conduit is not a requirement.

## Significance of the Change

This exception has been revised to align with industry practices and similar exceptions for Type AC and MC cables that are installed to luminaires in accessible ceilings. Information in the substantiation pointed out that the requirements for supporting and securing flexible metal conduit in accessible ceilings to luminaries should be the same as those provided in 320.30(D)(3) for armored-clad (Type AC) cable, and in 330.30(D)(2) for metal-clad (Type MC) cable. The product standard UL 514B includes performance requirements for flexible metal conduit fittings (assembly, resistance, and pull), which are the same as the performance requirements for AC and MC fittings that are permitted as a means of support for type this application. This revision also aligns with current industry practices for wiring lay-in style luminaires installed in accessible ceiling spaces. It is common to install a 6-foot flexible conduit whip from a junction box in a ceiling and then connect it directly to a lay-in luminaire in a suspended ceiling frame without the use of support other than by the flexible metal conduit fittings. This revised exception should clarify these installations as acceptable for installers and inspectors and promote a more uniform and practical applications of this wiring method.

Comment: 8-11
Proposal: 8-54

## Securing and Supporting Type LFMC

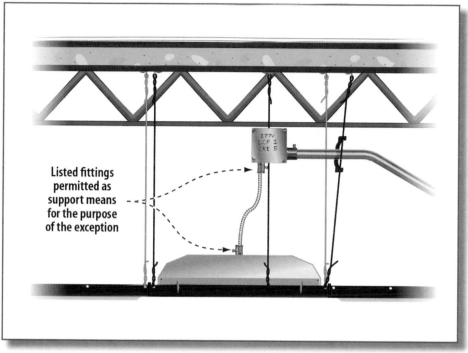

**Listed fittings permitted as support means for the purpose of the exception**

### Code Language

*Exception No. 4: Lengths not exceeding 1.8 m (6 ft) from the last point where the raceway is securely fastened for connections within an accessible ceiling to luminaire(s) or other equipment. For the purposes of 350.30, listed LFMC fittings shall be permitted as a means of support.*

*(See NEC for actual text)*

## Significance of the Change

This exception has been revised to align with industry practices and similar exceptions for Type AC and MC cables that are installed to luminaires in accessible ceilings. Information in the substantiation pointed out that the requirements for supporting and securing liquidtight flexible metal conduit in accessible ceilings to luminaries should be the same as those provided in 320.30(D)(3) for armored-clad (Type AC) cable, and in 330.30(D)(2) for metal-clad (Type MC) cable. The product standard UL 514B includes performance requirements for flexible metal conduit fittings (assembly, resistance, and pull), which are the same as the performance requirements for AC and MC fittings that are permitted as a means of support for type this application. This revision also aligns with current industry practices for wiring lay-in style luminaires installed in accessible ceiling spaces. An example is a 6-foot liquidtight flexible metal conduit whip from a junction box in a ceiling that connects it directly to a lay-in luminaire in a suspended ceiling frame without the use of support other than by the liquidtight flexible metal conduit fittings. This revised exception should clarify these installations as acceptable for installers and inspectors and promote a more uniform and practical applications of this wiring method.

### Change Summary

- A new last sentence has been added to Exception No. 4.
- Listed liquidtight flexible metal conduit fittings shall be permitted as a means of support for lengths up to 1.8 m (6 ft).
- This revision clarifies that for the purpose of this exception, additional support for liquidtight flexible metal conduit is not a requirement.

Comment: None
Proposal: 8-57

# Straight Fittings for Direct Burial Applications

## Code Language

**350.42 Couplings and Connectors.** Only fittings listed for use with LFMC shall be used. Angle connectors shall not be concealed. Straight LFMC fittings shall be permitted for direct burial where marked.

*(See NEC for actual text)*

*Courtesy of Thomas and Betts*

## Change Summary

- A new first and last sentence has been added to 350.42.

- Straight liquidtight flexible metal conduit fittings are suitable for direct burial applications where marked for this use.

- This revision aligns with similar allowances provided for straight fittings used in direct burial installations for liquidtight flexible nonmetallic conduit (LFNC).

## Significance of the Change

Liquidtight flexible metal conduit (LFMC) is suitable for use in direct burial applications as indicated in 350.10(3). Section 350.6 indicates that all LFMC and associated fittings are required to be listed. The new first sentence clarifies that only listed fittings are to be used with LFMC. This revision recognizes listed LFMC fittings for use in direct burial applications were the fittings are marked for that use. Similar provisions already exist for straight liquidtight flexible nonmetallic conduit (LFNC) fittings as provided in 356.42. Like LFNC fittings, LFMC fittings are evaluated for the use with LFMC. Information in the substantiation indicated that misuse of PVC conduit fittings has been prominent and included using solvent cement and PVC conduit fittings to LFMC, since this product has similar outside diameters of PVC conduit. This type of installation is unacceptable as LFMC fittings are required to be listed and the listing and installation requirements are specific. Including the language in this section to recognize straight LFMC fittings for use in direct burial applications enhances consistency and should clarify permitted uses for inspectors and installers. Only straight fittings are acceptable for direct buried applications since 350.42 prohibits angle connectors from being installed concealed.

Comment: 8-13
Proposals: 8-58, 8-59

For additional information, visit qr.njatcdb.org Item #1214

## LFNC Use Over 600 Volts

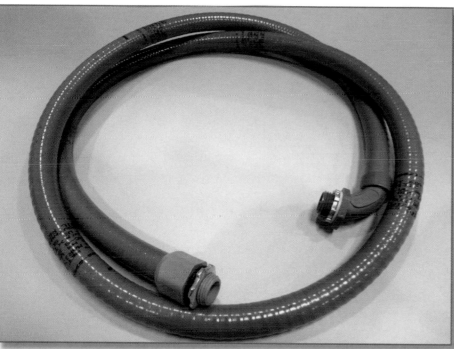

### Code Language

**356.12 Uses Not Permitted**...(See *NEC* text)...

(3) In lengths longer than 1.8 m (6 ft), except as permitted by 356.10(5) or where a longer length is approved as essential for a required degree of flexibility

(4) In any hazardous (classified) location, except as permitted by other articles in this *Code*

*(See NEC for actual text)*

### Significance of the Change

Former list item (4) in 356.12 generally restricted liquidtight flexible nonmetallic conduit (LFNC) to applications in voltages of 600 and less. Action on Proposal 8-81a removed list item (4) and broadened the use of LFNC to applications up to and over 600 volts. CMP-8 recognized that it is a common practice to utilize LFNC for conductors for voltages over 1000 volts. As an example, 600.32(A) permits conductors rated over 1000 volts often installed for secondary circuits of neon signs or cold cathode lighting systems. Information in the substantiation also indicated that LFNC is required to be listed and is required to meet or exceed the very rigorous physical requirements such as impact and crush resistivity evaluations as provided in the product standard UL1660, *Liquid-Tight Flexible Nonmetallic Conduit*. In addition, The Underwriters Laboratories (UL) Guide Information for Electrical Equipment (*White Book*) category DXOQ does not limit LFNC to 600 volts. This change clarifies that LFNC is no longer limited to installations where the voltage is 600 or less. Note that CMP-8 did not accept raising the voltage thresholds from 600 volts to 1000 volts as suggested in Proposal 8-82.

### Change Summary

- Former list item (4) has been deleted from this section and the remaining list items have been renumbered accordingly.

- The restriction of liquidtight flexible nonmetallic conduit (LFNC) to applications 600 volts and less has been removed.

- LFNC is now recognized by the *NEC* for use in applications over 600 volts.

Comment: 8-18
Proposal: 8-81a

# Grounding Requirements

## Code Language

**356.60 Grounding.** Where equipment grounding is required, a separate equipment grounding conductor shall be installed in the conduit.

*Exception No. 1: As permitted in 250.134(B), Exception No. 2, for dc circuits and 250.134(B), Exception No. 1, for separately run equipment grounding conductors.*

*Exception No. 2: Where the grounded conductor is used to ground equipment as permitted in 250.142.*

**(See NEC for actual text)**

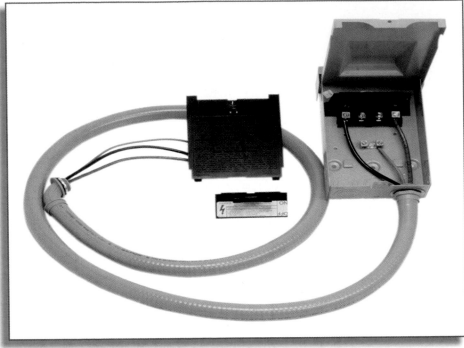

*Courtesy of Eaton Corporation*

## Change Summary

- This section has been revised into a single requirement and two exceptions that follow.

- The revision promotes consistency between other articles for flexible wiring methods that contain grounding requirements and related exceptions.

- As revised, equipment grounding conductors are always required in LFNC unless otherwise indicated in the exceptions or as modified in Chapter 6.

## Significance of the Change

Article 356 provides requirements for listed liquidtight flexible nonmetallic conduit (LFNC) and associated fittings. This type of conduit wiring method is nonmetallic, and as such never qualifies as an equipment grounding conductor; a separate equipment grounding conductor must generally always be provided for grounding equipment, bonding, and providing an effective path for ground fault current. This revision harmonizes 356.60 with 348.60 and 350.60, which contains grounding and bonding requirements for flexible metal conduit and liquidtight flexible metal conduit. Sections 348.60 and 350.60 were revised in the 2011 *NEC* to clarify the requirements for installing an equipment grounding conductor for vibration or where flexibility is necessary after installation. As revised, the general rule continues to specify installation of a wire-type equipment grounding conductor in LFNC installations. Exception No. 1 recognizes separately installed EGC for dc circuits and Exception No. 2 recognizes limited installations where the grounded conductor performs the equipment grounding and serves as an effective ground-fault current path. Action by CMP-8 also removed the term *Bonding* from the title of this section. Informational Note No. 1 following the definition of *Grounding Conductor, Equipment* clarifies that equipment grounding conductors also perform bonding functions.

Comment: 8-21

Proposal: 8-84

# Adjustment Factors – Application

## Code Language

**(B) Adjustment Factors.** The adjustment factors in 310.15(B)(3)(a) shall be applied only where the number of current-carrying conductors, including neutral conductors classified as current-carrying under the provisions of 310.15(B)(5), exceeds 30 at any cross section of the wireway. Conductors for signaling circuits or controller conductors between a motor and its starter and used only for starting duty shall not be considered as current-carrying conductors.

*(See NEC for actual text)*

## Significance of the Change

The revised language helps users clearly understand when correction factors must be applied to multiple current-carrying conductors installed in the same wireway. The previous text could have been interpreted to require application of correction factors if the total number of conductors installed anywhere within a wireway exceeded 30. As revised, this section is clear that the adjustment factors of 310.15(B)(3)(a) only applies where the number of current carrying conductors exceeds 30 at a cross section of the wireway, as opposed to the total number of conductors in the wireway. Information provided in the substantiation indicated that in the 2011 cycle, similar proposals to clarify the requirements of this section, but these were rejected. The inspiration for this revision was simply to restore the text as it appeared prior the 2002 edition. In the 2002 and 2005 *NEC* revision cycles, changes made to this section result in an inadvertent separation of the concept of "current-carrying conductors exceeding 30 at any cross section." In the 2008 *NEC* development cycle this separation became even further exacerbated when the section was sub-divided into 376.22(A) & (B). As revised, it is clear that adjustment factors of 310.15(B)(3)(a) apply where more than 30 conductors total are at a cross section.

## Change Summary

- This section has been revised by adding the words "at any cross section of the wireway."
- The revised text clarifies that correction factors are not based on the total number of current-carrying conductors in the wireway exceeding 30.
- Adjustment factors apply where the total of current-carrying conductors at any cross section exceeds 30.

Comment: None
Proposal: 8-137

# Installation of Power Distribution Blocks

## Code Language

**(1) Installation.** Power distribution blocks installed in metal wireways shall be listed. Power distribution blocks installed on the line side of the service equipment shall be listed for the purpose.

*(See NEC for actual text)*

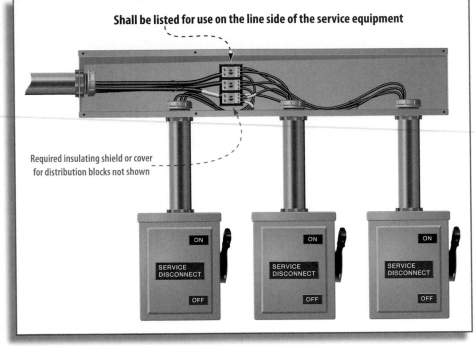

**Shall be listed for use on the line side of the service equipment**

Required insulating shield or cover for distribution blocks not shown

ON
SERVICE DISCONNECT
OFF

ON
SERVICE DISCONNECT
OFF

ON
SERVICE DISCONNECT
OFF

## Change Summary

- List item (1) was revised by adding a second sentence.
- Power distribution blocks are permitted to be installed on the line side of the service disconnect or the load side.
- Power distribution blocks installed on the line side of the service equipment shall be listed.

## Significance of the Change

The revision to list item (1) clarifies that power distribution blocks are permitted to be installed on either the load side of service disconnecting means overcurrent protection, or the line side if it is so listed. Information provided in the substantiation with Proposal 8-140 indicated that category QPQS of the UL Guide *Information for Electrical Equipment* currently only recognizes use of power distribution blocks on the load side of service equipment. Although it is not uncommon to see power distribution blocks installed in that position, it is apparent that industry practices do incorporate their use in some applications. Action by CMP-8 on Comment 8-43 results in an allowance for power distribution blocks on the supply side of service equipment, but only where listed for that application. This change provides an opportunity for power distribution block manufacturers to have this type of product evaluated and listed for use on the supply side of service equipment. Installers and inspectors should take note of the UL *White Book* category QPQS where additional information about acceptable use of power distribution blocks is provided. Listed products should be installed and used in accordance with any installation instructions included in the listing or labeling.

Comment: 8-43

Proposal: 8-140

# Installation of Power Distribution Blocks

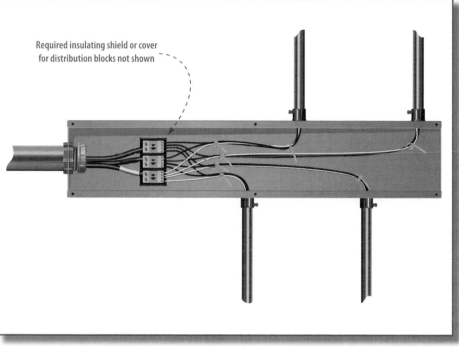

Required insulating shield or cover for distribution blocks not shown

## Code Language

**376.56(B) Power Distribution Blocks**...(See *NEC* text)...

**(5) Conductors.** Conductors shall be arranged so the power distribution block terminals are unobstructed following installation.

*(See NEC for actual text)*

## Significance of the Change

Requirements for power distribution blocks were added to Section 314.28(E) during the 2011 *NEC* development process. Much of that text being derived from the existing language in 376.56(B) for power distribution blocks installed in wireways. During the 2011 *NEC* development cycle, action by CMP-9 also added list item (5) which indicated that if conductors passing through the pull or junction box containing power distribution blocks, access to the distribution blocks should be maintained so terminals can be torqued or tested safely and without relocating or damaging the through conductors. This was a positive addition in regards to safety of individuals that may maintain and service the installation. As revised, this section now aligns with 314.28(E) and contains the same installation requirements for power distribution blocks, whether installed in a box or in wireway. Where power distribution blocks are installed, they must meet all the requirements in list items (1) through (5). A revision has also been made to list item (1) in 376.55(B) and recognizes power distribution blocks for use on the line side of service equipment where so listed.

## Change Summary

- A new list item (5) has been added to 376.56(B).
- This new requirement prohibits conductors from being installed in a manner that obstructs access to the power distribution blocks.
- This new list item (5) is now consistent with 314.28(E)(5) that contains the same requirement applicable to boxes containing power distribution blocks.

Comment: 8-42

Proposals: 8-142, 8-141

# Industrial Exception to Marking Requirements

## Code Language

**(H) Marking...**(See *NEC* text)...

..."DANGER— HIGH VOLT-AGE—KEEP AWAY" placed in a readily visible position on all cable trays, with the spacing of warning notices not to exceed 3 m (10 ft). The danger marking(s) or labels shall comply with 110.21(B).

*Exception: Where not accessible (as applied to equipment), in industrial establishments where the conditions of maintenance and supervision ensure that only qualified persons service the installation, cable tray system warning notices shall be located where necessary for the installation to ensure safe maintenance and operation.*

**(See NEC for actual text)**

*Courtesy of Bill McGovern, City of Plano, TX*

## Change Summary

- The words "the danger marking(s) or labels shall comply with 110.21(B)" have been added to 392.18(H).
- A new industrial exception relaxes the general ten-foot marking interval requirement.
- The marking must be appropriately located for the conditions of use and must comply with the provisions in 110.21(B).

Comment: None

Proposals: 8-180, 8-179, 8-180, 8-182

## Significance of the Change

A new last sentence has been added to this section and references 110.21(B) for requirements that apply to the danger labels. The new exception to this section relaxes the general danger marking requirements in industrial installations. Information provided in the substantiation pointed out that the requirement to placard all cable tray installations with danger notices every 3 m (10 ft) is not practical in all types of occupancies, especially under controlled conditions and the marking should address the readability and potential hazards. Some cable tray installations are at elevated locations where it would not be practical to install and see such danger notices. It was also pointed out that in most supervised industrial establishments, it isn't necessary to mark the cable trays that have cables rated over 600 volts. Personnel in refineries and petrochemical plants for example, are trained and qualified to recognize different voltage levels in cable tray systems, and they are trained not disturb them by walking on them or moving them while energized. There have been no reports indicating the absence of signage resulted in unsafe working conditions or accidents. Some cable tray installations may extend thousands of feet and this marking every ten feet is not reasonable or practical.

# Low-Voltage Suspended Ceiling Power Systems

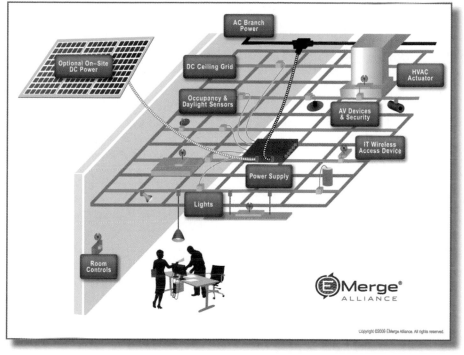

*Courtesy of EMerge Alliance*

## Code Language

**Article 393 Low-Voltage Suspended Ceiling Power Distribution Systems**

**I. General** …(See *NEC* text)…

**393.1 Scope.**

**393.2 Definitions.**

**393.6 Listing Requirements.**

**II. Installation**…(See *NEC* text)…

**393.10 Uses Permitted.**

**393.12 Uses Not Permitted.**

**393.14 Installation.**

**393.21 Disconnecting Means.**

**393.30 Securing and Supporting.**

**393.40 Connectors and Enclosures.**

**393.45 Overcurrent and Reverse Polarity (Backfeed) Protection.**

**393.56 Splices.**

**393.57 Connections.**

**393.60 Grounding.**

**III. Construction Specifications**…(See *NEC* text)…

*(See NEC for actual text)*

## Significance of the Change

This new article provides the *NEC* with requirements applicable to new technologies that incorporate low-voltage power systems and equipment, beyond just lighting. Information in the substantiation indicated that growing interest in alternative energy sources such as photovoltaics, wind turbines, batteries, fuel cells, and so forth and the proliferation of low voltage, low-power devices such as sensors, LV lighting, IT equipment, AV equipment, has created a significant need for *NEC* rules supporting the practical safeguarding of circuits and electrical equipment operating at 30 volts ac or 60 volts dc or less. The previous *NEC* included specific requirements for lighting systems operating at 30 volts in Article 411, but there were no similar requirements for power distribution operating at 30 volts or less for listed non-lighting systems and their associated listed components. Derived primarily from concepts and requirements in Articles 411 and 725, this new article slightly expands the scope of these systems with the addition of low voltage and Class 2, power-limited non-lighting loads while maintaining the clear requirements necessary for safe installation. This new article includes a requirement that these systems are specifically listed as a system and associated fittings and components be identified as part of the complete system.

## Change Summary

- A new Article 393 titled Low-Voltage Suspended Ceiling Power Distribution Systems has been added to Chapter 3.

- This new article readies the *NEC* with requirements for new technology dc wiring systems and equipment.

- This type of equipment and associated fittings are required to be listed which drives the requirement for installation instructions.

Comment: None
Proposal: 18-10a

# Chapter 4

## Articles 400–490
## Equipment for General Use

# Table 400.5(A)(1)

**Article 400 Flexible Cords and Cables**

**Part I General**

REVISION

## New Types and Sizes of Cords and Cables

### Code Language

See the graphic reproduction of Table 400.5(A)(1)...(in part)

*(See NEC for actual text)*

Table 400.5(A)(1) Allowable Ampacity for Flexible Cords and Cables [Based on Ambient Temperature of 30°C (86°F). See 400.13 and Table 400.4.]

| Copper Conductor Size (AWG) | Thermoplastic Types TPT, TST | Thermoset Types C, E, EO, PD, S, SJ, SJO, SJOW, SJOO, SJOOW, SO, SOW, SOO, SOOW, SP-1, SP-2, SP-3, SRD, SV, SVO, SVOO, NISP-1, NISP-2 / Thermoplastic Types ETP, ETT, SE, SEW, SEO, SEOO, SEOW, SEOOW, SJE, SJEW, SJEO, SJEOO, SJEOW, SJEOOW, SJT, SJTW, SJTO, SJTOW, SJTOO, SJTOOW, SPE-2, SPE-3, SPT-1, SPT-1W, SPT-2, SPT-2W, SPT-3, NISPE-1, NISPE-2, NISPT-1, NISPT-2, ST, STW, SRDE, SRDT, STO, STOW, STOO, STOOW, SVE, SVEO, SVEOO, SVT, SVTO, SVTOO | | Types HPD, HPN, HSJ, HSJO, HSJOW, HSJOO, HSJOOW |
|---|---|---|---|---|
| | | Column A[1] | Column B[2] | |
| 27[a] | 0.5 | — | — | — |
| 20 | — | 5[b] | [c] | — |
| 18 | — | 7 | 10 | 10 |
| 17 | — | 9 | 12 | 13 |
| 16 | — | 10 | 13 | 15 |
| 15 | — | 12 | 16 | 17 |
| 14 | — | 15 | 18 | 20 |
| 13 | — | 17 | 21 | — |
| 12 | — | 20 | 25 | 30 |
| 11 | — | 23 | 27 | — |
| 10 | — | 25 | 30 | 35 |
| 9 | — | 29 | 34 | — |
| 8 | — | 35 | 40 | — |
| 6 | — | 45 | 55 | — |
| 4 | — | 60 | 70 | — |
| 2 | — | 80 | 95 | — |

[a] Tinsel cord.
[b] Elevator cables only
[c] 7 amperes for elevator cables only; 2 amperes for other types.
[1] The allowable currents under column A apply to 3-conductor cords and other multiconductor cords connected to utilization equipment so that only 3 conductors are current carrying.
[2] The allowable currents under column B apply to 2-conductor cords and other multiconductor cords connected to utilization equipment so that only 2 conductors are current carrying.

### Change Summary

- Table 400.5(A)(1) has been revised by incorporating additional cord and cable types in the table heading.
- Sizes 9, 11, and 13 AWG conductors and corresponding ampacities have been incorporated into the table.
- The notes to Table 400.5(A)(1) have been re-identified using superscript letters.

### Significance of the Change

Revisions to Table 400.5(A)(1) expand the table in types and sizes; and address usability issues regarding the notes to the table. The table heading has been expanded to include HSJOW and HSJOOW in the right column. Types NISP-1, NISP-2, SEOO, NISPE-1, NISPE-2, NISPT-1, NISPT-2, STW and SVEOO have been added to the third column from the left. This table has also been expanded to include sizes 9, 11, and 13 AWG and their corresponding ampacities. Column A provides ampacities of 9 AWG (29 amperes), 11 AWG (23 amperes), and 13 AWG (17 amperes). Column B provides ampacities of 9 AWG (34 amperes), 11 AWG (27 amperes), and 13 AWG (21 amperes). Information in the substantiation indicated that including the additional cord types in this table would align with types already included in Table 400.4. Conductor sizes 9, 11 and 13 AWG are used in flex cords in both North America and Europe (AWG equivalents to standard metric mm²); these sizes and ampacities are needed in Table 400.5(A)(1). The allowable ampacities are based on ratios of existing values in table 400.5(A)(1). CANENA Technical Harmonization Subcommittee 20: Flexible Cords, which is responsible for development of the tri-national UL/CSA/ANCE standard for flexible cords.

Comment: None
Proposals: 6-85, 6-94a, 6-95, 6-96

# Equipment Grounding Conductor Identification – Cords

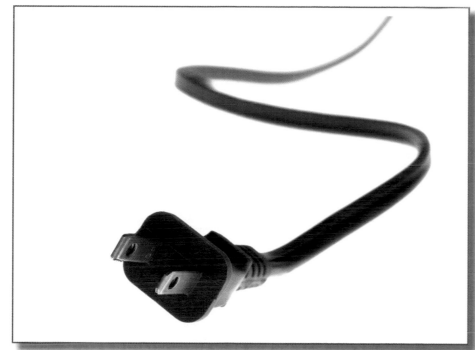

iStock Photo Courtesy of NECA

## Code Language

**400.23 Equipment Grounding Conductor Identification.** A conductor intended to be used as an equipment grounding conductor shall have a continuous identifying marker readily distinguishing it from the other conductor or conductors. Conductors having a continuous green color or a continuous green color with one or more yellow stripes shall not be used for other than equipment grounding conductors. Cords or cables consisting of integral insulation and jacket without a nonintegral grounding conductor shall be permitted to be green. The identifying marker shall consist of one of the methods in 400.23(A) or (B).

*(See NEC for actual text)*

## Significance of the Change

The revision clarifies the identification requirements for the integral insulation and jackets of cords and cables that do not contain an equipment grounding conductor. Prior to this revision, the color green would have been prohibited from this use. Cords and cables are produced with an integral insulation and jacket combination that is green in color. This section as revised now makes it clear that this is not a violation of the *NEC*. Information in the substantiation indicated that the use of green insulation for grounding is understood, however cords or cables consisting of integral insulation and jacket without a non-integral grounding conductor where connected to equipment not required to be grounded should not be considered a hazard or misuse of the cords or cables. Action by CMP-5 on Proposal 5-188 also incorporates a new Exception No. 2 to 250.119 that provides the needed correlation with the general equipment grounding conductor identification rules in Article 250. The revision allows cord and cable manufacturers to produce products without restricting the use of the color green for a combined integral insulation and jacket of the cord or cable assembly. This type of identification is common for cords or cables for holiday use.

## Change Summary

- A new third sentence has been added to this section.
- The revision permits cords or cables with integral insulation and jacket and without an equipment grounding conductor to be green in color.
- The change clarifies identification for cords and cables without an equipment grounding conductor to align with a similar exception to 250.119.

Comment: 6-75
Proposal: 6-105

REVISION | REORGANIZE | NEW

# Grounded Conductor at Switch Locations

## Code Language

**(C) Switches Controlling Lighting Loads...**(See *NEC* text)...

1. Where conductors enter the box enclosing the switch through a raceway...(See *NEC* text)...

2. Where the box enclosing the switch is accessible...(See *NEC* text)...without removing finish materials

3. Where snap switches with integral enclosures complying with 300.15(E)

4. Where a switch does not serve a habitable room or bathroom

5. Where multiple switch locations control the same lighting load such that the entire floor area of the room or space is visible from the single or combined switch locations

6. Where lighting in the area is controlled by automatic means

7. Where a switch controls a receptacle load

*(See NEC for actual text)*

## Change Summary

- This section has been restructured into a list format and the former exception has been incorporated into positive text.

- New list item (3) relaxes the grounded conductor requirement at switches with integral enclosures.

- New list item (5) relaxes the grounded conductor requirement in locations where multiple switches control the same lighting load.

Comments: 9-44, 9-45, 9-46

Proposals: 9-87, 9-88, 9-89, 9-90, 9-91

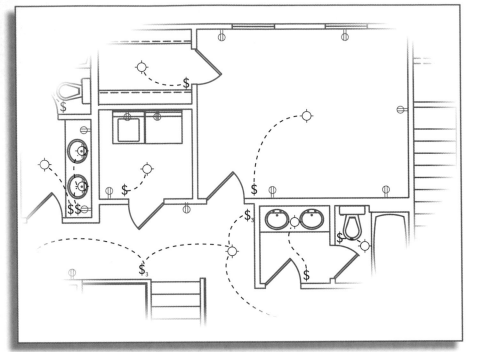

## Significance of the Change

This section generally requires a grounded conductor at lighting load switch locations. There are now seven conditions allowing relief from installing a grounded conductor at the switch box. List items (1) and (2) reflect the provisions of previous Exception and conditions (1) and (2) to 404.2(C). List item (3) reflects the concept provided in Proposal 9-87 to exempt switches with integral enclosures that comply with 300.15(E). List items (4), (5), (6), and (7) reflect concepts provided in Proposal 9-89. Grounded conductors are no longer required at locations in non-habitable rooms or bathrooms, in common locations where multiple switches control the same lighting load, such as where 3-way and 4-way switches are installed, in locations where the lighting is controlled by automatic means, and at switches that control receptacles. In cases where 3-way or 4-way switches are installed, the grounded conductor is required at only one of the switch boxes locations as long as entire space is visible from all switch locations. CMP-9 acted favorable to not requiring a grounded conductor in bathrooms or rooms that are not habitable, such as a closet, as these are overly restrictive. The revision clarifies the requirements while providing practical relief consistent with the substantiation.

# Warning Signs for Switches

## Code Language

*Exception: The blades and terminals supplying the load of a switch shall be permitted to be energized when the switch is in the open position where the switch is connected to circuits or equipment inherently capable of providing a backfeed source of power. For such installations, a permanent sign shall be installed on the switch enclosure or immediately adjacent to open switches with the following words or equivalent: WARNING — LOAD SIDE TERMINALS MAY BE ENERGIZED BY BACKFEED. The warning sign or label shall comply with 110.21(B).*

**(See NEC for actual text)**

## Significance of the Change

The additional sentence in this exception places specific requirements for the warning sign required in this exception. The reference to new 110.21(B) is being incorporated *Code*-wide in multiple *NEC* provisions that use the words danger, caution, or warning. These are signal words that according to ANSI Z535.4 *Product Safety Signs and Labels,* include specific criteria that must be followed in developing signs or markings. Examples of criteria that must be met are content of the label of marking, size of the font, colors to be used based on the signal word used. As an example the markings required by this exception uses the signal word "WARNING" which requires the color orange to be used. In addition to the sign required by this exception, there are many other labeling and marking requirements throughout the *NEC* that use of a signal word such as danger, caution, and warning. For consistency and improved clarity throughout the *NEC*, the markings, labels, and signs are required to meet 110.21(B) and are generally not permitted to be hand written. The informational notes provided in 110.21(B) provide effective guidance and assist users by reference to the appropriate guidelines for developing such labels and markings.

## Change Summary

- A new last sentence has been added to the exception for 404.6(C).
- Referencing 110.21(B) places additional requirements for warning signage required by this exception.
- Section 110.21(B) includes specific requirements for caution, danger, and warning markings or signs, and provides a reference to ANSI Z535.4 *Product Safety Signs and Labels.*

Comment: None

Proposal: 9-94

# Fastening Means For Snap Switches

## Code Language

**404.10 Mounting of Snap Switches.**

**(A) Surfce Type.** ...(See *NEC* text)...

**(B) Box Mounted.** Flush-type snap switches mounted in boxes that are set back of the finished surface as permitted in 314.20 shall be installed so that the extension plaster ears are seated against the surface. Flush-type ...(see *NEC* text)... the box. Screws used for the purpose of attaching a snap switch to a box shall be of the type provided with a listed snap switch, or shall be machine screws having 32 threads per inch or part of listed assemblies or systems, in accordance with the manufacturer's instructions.

*(See NEC for actual text)*

## Change Summary

- A new last sentence has been added to this section to address snap switch fastener screws.
- Screws for snap switches must be either machine screws matching the thread gage or size that is integral to the box.
- Fastening means that are in accordance with the manufacturer's installation instructions are acceptable.

## Significance of the Change

This section addresses switches in flush box installations and requires the mounting yoke or strap of the switch to be seated against the box or plaster ring. A new last sentence specifies that screws used for attaching snap switches to the box, shall be either machine screws matching the thread gage or size integral to the box or be in accordance with the manufacturer's instructions. Use of drywall screws and other screws that are not intended for fastening snap switches or other equipment to boxes is not acceptable and can result in damage to the box and inadequate fastening of the device. Manufacturer's installation instructions cover this in most cases for listed boxes and equipment, but the additional text helps clarify this requirement. CMP-9 incorporated the proposed concepts into the additional sentence and accounted for nonmetallic outlet boxes and product standards that might recognize use thread forming screws for attachment of snap switches provided they meet the performance requirements in the applicable standard. This type of screw is typically used with nonmetallic boxes and is often supplied with the box. Drywall screws and other inappropriate screws are not permitted for use in fastening snap switches to boxes or plaster rings.

Comment: 9-52

Proposal: 9-98

**NEW**

# Marking for Controlled Receptacles

**Energy Management Panel**

## Code Language

**406.3 Receptacle Rating and Type.**

**(A) Through (D).** ...(See *NEC* text)...

**(E) Controlled Receptacle Marking.** All nonlocking-type, 125-volt, 15- and 20-ampere receptacles that are controlled by an automatic control device, or that incorporate control features that remove power from the outlet for the purpose of energy management or building automation, shall be marked with the symbol shown in Figure 406.3(E) and located on the controlled receptacle outlet where visible after installation.

*Exception: The marking is not required for receptacles controlled by a wall switch that provide the required room lighting outlets as permitted by 210.70.*

*(See NEC for actual text)*

## Significance of the Change

Multiple performance requirements included in the energy codes can drive installation requirements in the *NEC*. Building automation systems and energy management systems can automatically control loads connected through receptacles. This provision places a specific marking requirement for controlled receptacle outlets, except switch-controlled receptacle outlets in accordance with 210.70. Although the exact location of the marking is not provided, however a specific universal power symbol must be provided at the receptacle outlet. This can be interpreted to mean marking the receptacle face or the faceplate for the receptacle outlet, which would both meet the intent as currently written. A new figure 406.3(E) is provided in this section to promote consistent identification for these receptacle outlets. The substantiation indicated energy management codes that are currently being widely adopted such as ASHRAE 90.1 and could require that up to 50 percent of 125-volt, 15- and 20-ampere receptacles be automatically controlled. The automatic control could be by an energy management system, timer, or sensor. Occupants should know which receptacle outlets are automatically controlled to avoid cord- and plug-connected loads from being unintentionally turned on or off which raises safety concerns as well as inconvenience. It is important to readily identify receptacle outlets that are automatically energized.

## Change Summary

- A new subdivision (E) titled Controlled Receptacle Marking, Exception, and associated figure have been added to 406.3.
- This requirement applies to receptacles controlled by building automation or energy management systems.
- A specific power symbol marking must be applied to non-locking type, all 125-volt, 15- and 20-ampere automatically controlled receptacle outlets and be visible after installation.

Comment: 18-13 Hold
Proposal: 18-15

**REVISION**

# AFCI and GFCI Replacement Receptacles

## Code Language

**(D) Replacements.** Replacement of receptacles shall comply with 406.4(D) (1) through (D)(6), as applicable. Arc-fault circuit-interrupter type and ground-fault circuit-interrupter type receptacles shall be installed in a readily accessible location.

*(See NEC for actual text)*

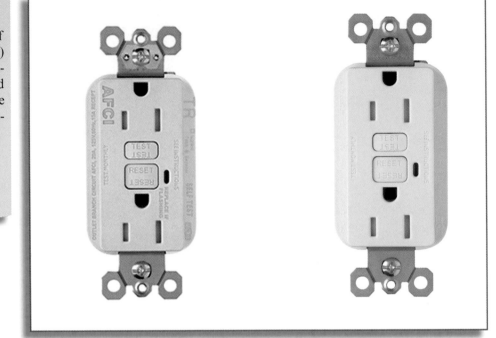

*Courtesy of Pass and Seymour Legrand*

## Change Summary

- A new last sentence has been added to 406.4(D) addressing receptacle replacements.

- All AFCI and GFCI outlet devices installed as replacements are required to be readily accessible.

- The revision clarifies that ready access is required to perform required periodic testing and response to tripped conditions.

## Significance of the Change

Favorable action by CMP-2 on Proposal 2-77 and Comment 2-29 in the 2011 *NEC* development process resulted in new readily accessible requirements for ground-fault circuit-interrupter (GFCI) devices. Ground-fault circuit-interrupter (GFCI) devices and now arc-fault circuit interrupter (AFCI) devices are both required to be readily accessible as provided in Article 210. This revision aligns the readily accessible requirement for AFCI and GFCI devices covered in 210.8(A) and (B) with the rules for replacement AFCI and GFCI devices required by 406.4(D). While it is clear that ready access is required for AFCI and GFCI installations, there were no such provisions for replacements, but the same needs exist. Justification for the ready access is primarily related to occupant or user accessibility to exercise the monthly testing and reset features of the device. Arc-fault circuit-interrupter protection and GFCI protection can be accomplished by circuit breaker types or device types which have the same test and reset features and requirements for monthly testing. Accessibility to these replacement protective devices should not be different than the ready access required for newly installed GFCI and AFCI devices. This revision also promotes consistency with the listing requirements for these devices that specify monthly testing and resetting operations which facilitates ready access.

Comment: None
Proposal: 18-18

*REVISION*

# Fastening Means for Receptacles

## Code Language

**406.5 Receptacle Mounting.** Receptacles shall be mounted in identified boxes or assemblies. The boxes or assemblies shall be securely fastened in place unless otherwise permitted elsewhere in this *Code*. Screws used for the purpose of attaching receptacles to a box shall be of the type provided with a listed receptacle, or shall be machine screws having 32 threads per inch or part of listed assemblies or systems, in accordance with the manufacturer's instructions.

*(See NEC for actual text)*

## Significance of the Change

The first sentence of this section has been revised to require receptacles be fastened to identified boxes or assemblies. A new last sentence specifies that screws used for attaching receptacles to the box be machine screws of 32 threads per inch, or part of a listed assembly or system. Use of drywall screws and other screws that are not intended for fastening receptacles or other equipment to boxes is unacceptable and can result in damage to boxes and inadequate fastening of devices. Manufacturer's installation instructions usually cover this in most cases for listed boxes and equipment, but the additional text helps clarify this requirement. Listed boxes or assemblies could specify use of thread-forming screws in nonmetallic outlet boxes and applicable product standards might recognize use thread forming screws for attachment of receptacles provided they meet the performance requirements in the applicable standard. This type of screw is typically used with nonmetallic boxes and is supplied with the box. Section 110.3(B) covers this in the requirement to install devices in accordance with any instructions provided in the listing or labeling. Drywall screws and other inappropriate screws are not permitted for use in fastening snap receptacles to boxes or plaster rings.

## Change Summary

- The first sentence has been revised and a new last sentence has been added to this section.
- Screws for receptacles must be either 6-32 machine screws matching the thread gage or size that is integral to the box or part of a listed assembly or system.
- Fastening means in accordance with manufacturer's installation instructions are acceptable.

Comments: 18-19 18-20
Proposals: 18-28, 18-30, 18-31

# 406.5(E) & (F)

Article 406 Receptacles, Cord Connectors, and Attachment Plugs

## Receptacles in the Face-Up Position

### Code Language

**(E) Receptacles in Countertop and Similar Work Surfaces.** Receptacles...(See *NEC* text)...shall not be installed in a face-up position in countertops or similar work surfaces. Where receptacle assemblies for countertop applications are required to provide ground-fault circuit-interrupter protection...(See *NEC* text)...

**(F) Receptacles in Seating Areas and Other Similar Surfaces.** In seating areas or similar surfaces, receptacles shall not be installed in a face-up position unless the receptacle is any of the following:

(1) Part of an assembly listed as a furniture...(See *NEC* text)...

(2) Part of an assembly listed either as household furnishings...(See *NEC* text)...

(3) Listed either as a receptacle assembly for countertop...(See *NEC* text)...

(4) Installed in a listed floor box

*(See NEC for actual text)*

### Change Summary

- Subdivision (E) has been revised and expanded to all occupancies and 210.8 GFCI protection applies.
- Subdivision (F) is new and titled Receptacles in Seating Areas or Similar Surfaces.
- Receptacles installed in seating areas or similar surfaces are not permitted in the face-up position unless the installation meets one of list items (1) through (4).

Comment: 18-23
Proposals: 18-32, 18-33, 18-34

### Significance of the Change

The restriction of receptacles from being installed in the face-up position has been expanded to apply to all occupancies, not just dwelling units. The problems related to receptacles installed in the face-up position are the same regardless of occupancy type. There are receptacle assemblies that are manufactured and listed specifically for these types of applications and those assemblies should be used for receptacles in countertop and other work surfaces. A new provision is has been incorporated as subdivision (F) and existing (F) and (G) have been renumbered. This new text restricts receptacles installed in seating areas and similar surfaces from being installed in the face-up position unless they are part of an assembly listed for that application. Information provided in the substantiation referred to benches in public areas with receptacles installed as part of the assembly. These products address receptacle use for laptop computers, device charging, and powering other portable loads. Receptacles installed in the face-up position in these types of situations also present similar hazards. Where installing receptacles in floors or other similar surfaces, it is required be accomplished with an assembly listed for the application to minimize damage and potential exposure to energized conductors or circuit parts.

# Receptacle Outlet Hood Covers

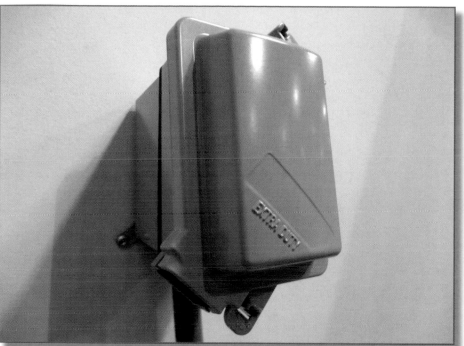

## Significance of the Change

This section has been revised and expanded in application to all occupancies and is no longer limited to just one- and two-family dwellings. The extra duty required strength and performance of in-use covers are not unique to just dwelling units. The substantiation in Proposal 18-37 clearly and simply emphasized that the support of receptacle outlets in wet locations had nothing to do with the requirements for extra duty receptacle outlet box hoods. As revised, this requirement now applies to all receptacle outlet boxes installed in wet locations, no longer limited to just those installed and supported at grade locations. Prior to this revision, the extra duty in-use cover was only required at locations of receptacles mounted on posts or other structures installed from grade and remote from buildings. The revision promotes consistency in the requirement for listed in-use receptacle outlet hoods that are identified as extra duty. Multiple types of extra duty in-use covers are produced that can meet this requirement. The revised *Code* text does not specify that these hood covers be metallic types, only that they be listed and identified as extra duty.

## Code Language

**(1) Receptacles of 15 and 20 Amperes in a Wet Location.** Receptacles of 15 and 20 amperes installed in a wet location shall have an enclosure that is weatherproof whether or not the attachment plug cap is inserted. An outlet box hood installed for this purpose shall be listed and shall be identified as "extra-duty." All 15- and 20- ampere, 125- and 250-volt non-locking-type receptacles shall be listed weather-resistant type.

*(See NEC for actual text)*

## Change Summary

- The words "other than one- and two-family dwellings" have been removed from this section.
- The text related to how the receptacle outlet is supported has also been removed from this section.
- Listed and identified extra duty receptacle covers (hoods) are required for all 15- and 20-ampere, 125- and 250-volt receptacles installed in a wet location.

Comment: None
Proposals: 18-37, 18-38

**REVISION** **REORGANIZE**

## Tamper-Resistant Receptacle Exemptions

### Code Language

**406.12 Tamper-Resistant Receptacles.** Tamper-resistant receptacles shall be installed as specified in 406.12(A) through (C).

**(A) Dwelling Units.** In all areas specified in 210.52, all nonlocking-type 125-volt, 15- and 20-ampere receptacles shall be listed tamper-resistant receptacles.

**(B) Guest Rooms and Guest Suites of Hotels and Motels.** All nonlocking-type 125-volt, 15- and 20-ampere receptacles located in guest rooms and guest suites of hotels and motels shall be listed tamper-resistant receptacles.

**(C) Child Care Facilities.** In all child care facilities, all nonlocking-type 125-volt, 15- and 20-ampere receptacles shall be listed tamper-resistant receptacles.

*Exception to (A), (B), and (C): Receptacles in the following locations shall not be... (See NEC text)...*

**(See NEC for actual text)**

### Change Summary

- Sections 406.13 and 406.14 have been incorporated as subdivisions (B) and (C) in 406.12.

- The previous exception to 406.12 now applies to dwelling units, guest rooms of hotels and motels, and child care facilities.

- These revisions improve consistency in the requirements and exceptions for tamper resistant receptacles.

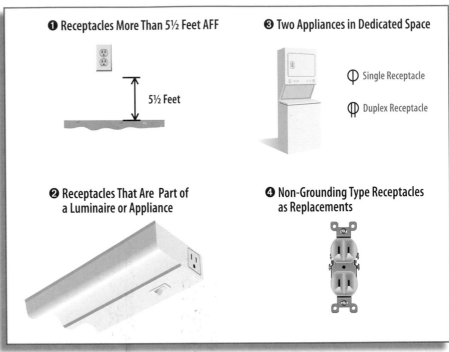

❶ Receptacles More Than 5½ Feet AFF

5½ Feet

❷ Receptacles That Are Part of a Luminaire or Appliance

❸ Two Appliances in Dedicated Space

Ⓟ Single Receptacle

Ⓟ Duplex Receptacle

❹ Non-Grounding Type Receptacles as Replacements

### Significance of the Change

In the 2011 *NEC*, new requirements for added to Article 406 that specified installing tamper-resistant receptacles in child care facilities and in the guest rooms and guest suites of hotels and motels. Action by CMP-18 on Proposal 18-41a is primarily editorial in nature and results in enhanced clarity and usability. Since 406.12, 406.13, and 406.14 all dealt with requirements for tamper-resistant receptacles, it was logical to combine the rules into a single section. As a result, 406.13 and 406.14 have been incorporated into 406.12 and subdivided accordingly. The other significant change addressing consistency is the placement and applicability of the former exception to 406.12. This exception exempts receptacles from having to be tamper resistant if the receptacles meet any of four conditions. As revised, this exception now applies to subdivisions (A), (B), and (C). As revised, the requirements for tamper-resistant receptacles for various occupancies are now all addressed in one section with the same receptacle exceptions for all occupancies. No technical revisions have been added to this section.

Comment: 18-25
Proposal: 18-41a

# Receptacles Controlled by Dimmers

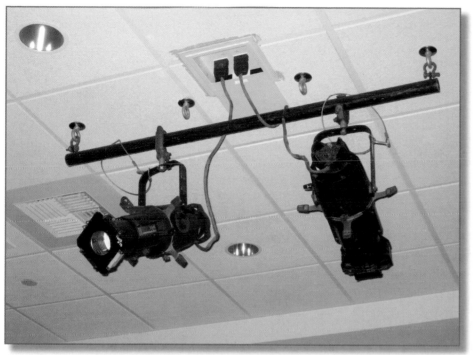

## Code Language

**406.15 Dimmer-Controlled Receptacles.** A receptacle supplying lighting loads shall not be connected to a dimmer unless the plug/receptacle combination is a nonstandard configuration type that is specifically listed and identified for each such unique combination.

*(See NEC for actual text)*

## Significance of the Change

Dimmers are generally not permitted to be connected to or control receptacles. Section 404.14 requires that general-use dimmers be used only with permanently installed incandescent luminaires unless listed for the control of other loads. A new 406.15 effectively correlates with 404.14 and also provides a similar restriction of receptacles being controlled by dimmers. Information in the substantiation indicated that there is a belief among some installers that it is permitted to dim a receptacle for such items as 125-volt cord-and-plug connected luminaires, low-voltage lighting, or rope lights. These types of lighting are often installed under shelving or cabinets and the amount of lighting effect is said to be too bright. The manufacturers of such lighting sometimes have a dimming accessory feature that is listed with their product where the consumer may demand it. The added language in this new section will ensure standard grade 125-volt, 15- and 20-ampere receptacles are generally not permitted to be controlled from dimming devices. Lighting is permitted to be dimmed through a nonstandard receptacle and plug combination that is listed and identified for the unique combination.

## Change Summary

- A new 406.15 titled Dimmer Controlled Receptacles has been added to Article 406 and aligns with 404.14(E).
- The new provision generally restricts receptacles from being connected to or controlled by dimmers.
- Non-standard configuration receptacles that are listed and identified for dimming applications and combined use with dimmers are permitted.

Comment: None
Proposal: 18-53

# 408.2, 408.3, & Others

Article 408 Switchboards and Panelboards

Part I General, II Switchboards, IV Construction Specifications

## Panelboards, Switchboards, and Switchgear

### Code Language

**408.2 Other Articles.** Switches, circuit breakers, and overcurrent devices used on switchboards, switchgear, and panelboards and their enclosures shall comply with this article and also with the requirements of Articles 240, 250, 312, 404, and other articles that apply. Switchboards, switchgear, and panelboards in hazardous (classified) locations shall comply with the applicable provisions of Articles 500 through 517.

**408.3 Support and Arrangement of Busbars and Conductors.**

**(A) Conductors and Busbars on a Switchboard, Switchgear, or Panelboard.** Conductors and busbars on a switchboard, switchgear, or panelboard shall comply with 408.3(A)(1), (A)(2), and (A)(3) as applicable.

*(See NEC for actual text)*

### Change Summary

- The word "switchgear" has been incorporated into 408.2, 408.3 and other sections with Article 408.
- The reference to Article 314 has been removed from 408.2.
- The requirements in Parts I, II and IV of Article 408 apply to panelboards, switchboards and switchgear operating at 1000 volts and less.

*Courtesy of Donald Cook/IAEI*

### Significance of the Change

The revised definition of the term *Switchgear* provides the basis for incorporating this type of equipment within applicable requirements in Article 408. Parts I, II and IV have requirements that apply to switchgear as well as switchboards and panelboards. Part III applies specifically to panelboards so the term *switchgear* was not incorporated in any rules in Part III. This revision clarifies that various rules in Article 408 do apply to switchgear although previous *NEC* editions did not mention this type of equipment within Article 408. These changes in Article 408 are a sampling of multiple *Code*-wide revisions to add the term switchgear where the requirements applied. Action by CMP-9 on Proposal 9-103a aligns these revisions with the revised definition of the term *switchgear.* The reference to Article 314 within 408.2 has been removed as the requirements for boxes differ and really don't relate to the rules in Article 408. The other revision to this article was to change the voltage threshold from 600 volts to 1000 volts. These revisions clarify that the rules in Article 408 apply to switchgear as well as panelboards and switchboards. The title of the article remains as Switchboards and Panelboards in the 2014 edition.

Comment: 9-55
Proposal: 9-103a

## DC Bus Arrangements

*iStock Photo Courtesy of NECA*

### Code Language

**(E) Bus Arrangement.**

**(1) AC Phase Arrangement.** Alternating-current phase arrangement on 3-phase buses shall be A, B, C from front to back, top to bottom, or left to right, as viewed from the front of the switchboard, switchgear, or panelboard. The B phase shall be that phase having the higher voltage to ground on 3-phase, 4-wire, delta-connected systems. ...(See *NEC* text)...

> *Exception:* ...(*See* NEC *text*)...
>
> Informational Note: ...(See *NEC* text)...

**(2) DC Bus Arrangement.** Direct-current ungrounded buses shall be permitted to be in any order. Arrangement of dc buses shall be field marked as to polarity, grounding system, and nominal voltage.

*(See NEC for actual text)*

### Significance of the Change

This section has been revised to include the term *switchgear* in the bus arrangement requirements and exception. The informational note was not impacted by the revisions to this section, other than for placement. A significant revision to this section includes incorporating a new list item (2) that addresses requirements for dc bus arrangements in switchboards, switchgear, and panelboards. There is no specific sequence or order for the dc busses in these types of equipment. The arrangement of dc buses must include labeling related to polarity, the grounding system and nominal voltage. It should be noted that identification for equipment grounding conductors and grounded conductors in this equipment still apply. This revision is a continuation of the work of an assigned *NEC* DC Task Force that worked in the 2014 development cycle to populate the *Code* with dc requirements as determined necessary. Use of dc systems, wiring, and equipment is growing and the *NEC* must be equipped with rules that can apply. This revision was just part of a *Code*-wide effort that resulted in identifying several revisions and gaps where new dc requirements were incorporated.

### Change Summary

- The title of 408.3(E) has been changed to Bus Arrangement.
- This section has been rearranged into a list format and incorporated the word "switchgear" in list item (1) and the existing exception and the existing informational note remains unchanged.
- New list item (2) incorporates requirements for dc ungrounded buses in equipment.

Comments: 9-55, 9-58
Proposals: 9-110, 9-103a

# 408.3(F)(3), (4), & (5)

**Article 408 Switchboards and Panelboards**

**Part I General Provisions**

## Panelboards, Switchboards, and Switchgear Identification

### Code Language

**(3) High-Impedance Grounded Neutral AC System.** A switchboard, switchgear, or panelboard containing a high-impedance grounded neutral ac system in accordance with 250.36 shall be legibly and permanently field marked as follows: CAUTION …(See *NEC* text)…

**(4) Ungrounded DC Systems.** A switchboard, switchgear, or panelboard containing an ungrounded dc electrical system in accordance with 250.169 shall be legibly and permanently field marked as follows: CAUTION …(See *NEC* text)…

**(5) Resistively Grounded DC Systems.** A switchboard, switchgear, or panelboard containing a resistive connection between current-carrying conductors and the grounding system to stabilize voltage to ground shall be legibly and permanently field marked as follows: CAUTION …(See *NEC* text)…

*(See NEC for actual text)*

### Change Summary

- Three list items have been added to 408.3(F) and the word "switchgear" has been added.
- Additional Caution markings are now required for switchboards, switchgear, and panelboards used with high-impedance grounded neutral systems, ungrounded dc systems, and resistance grounded dc systems.
- The "Caution" markings in list items (1) through (5) must comply with 110.21(B).

Comments: 9-55, 9-58, 9-63

Proposals: 9-111, 9-103a

Additional caution markings are required in 408.3(F)(3), (4), and (5).

All caution markings required in 408.(3)(F) must meet the new requirements in 110.21(B).

Applies where the signal words "danger", "warning", or "caution" are used in NEC rules.

Signal words communicate the degree of hazard. The other label components provide the specific hazard, instructions, and could also include a graphic (See ANSI Z535.4-2011).

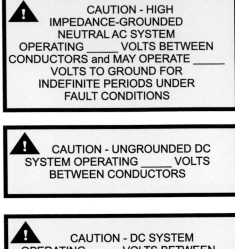

CAUTION - HIGH IMPEDANCE-GROUNDED NEUTRAL AC SYSTEM OPERATING _____ VOLTS BETWEEN CONDUCTORS and MAY OPERATE _____ VOLTS TO GROUND FOR INDEFINITE PERIODS UNDER FAULT CONDITIONS

CAUTION - UNGROUNDED DC SYSTEM OPERATING _____ VOLTS BETWEEN CONDUCTORS

CAUTION - DC SYSTEM OPERATING _____ VOLTS BETWEEN CONDUCTORS and MAY OPERATE _____ VOLTS TO GROUND FOR INDEFINITE PERIODS UNDER FAULT CONDITIONS

### Significance of the Change

CMP 9 acted favorably to the concepts introduced in the proposal and has broadened the coverage to include high-impedance grounded neutral ac systems for completeness. For usability, this section was arranged into a list sequence in accordance with the *NEC Style Manual*. The term *switchgear* has been included to correlate with other *Code*-wide changes regarding the use of this term introduced in this cycle. The caution label requirement has been added for list items (1) through (5) and has been modified to indicate the potential voltage to ground during worst-case conditions, thereby correctly stating the hazard. The same concept was extended to the resistively grounded dc system for the same reason. The point of inserting impedance (or resistance) into these systems is to allow continuity of operation under conditions where one phase (or polarity) has become grounded. The dc system refers to a ground connection and not an equipment grounding connection because the connection will often be made to a supply-side bonding jumper and not to an equipment grounding conductor.

## Wire-Bending Space Within Enclosures

*Courtesy of Schneider Electric*

### Code Language

**(A) Top and Bottom Wire-Bending Space.** (Note *Exceptions No. 1-4.*) The enclosure for a panelboard shall have the top and bottom wire-bending space sized in accordance with Table 312.6(B) for the largest conductor entering or leaving the enclosure.

**(B) Side Wire-Bending Space.** Side wire-bending space shall be in accordance with Table 312.6(A) for the largest conductor to be terminated in that space.

**(C) Back Wire-Bending Space.** Where...(See *NEC* text)...in Table 312.6(A). The distance between the center of the rear entry and the nearest termination for the entering conductors shall not be less than the distance given in Table 312.6(B).

*(See NEC for actual text)*

### Significance of the Change

Section 408.55 provides minimum wire-bending space requirements for enclosures containing panelboards. Top, bottom, and side wire-bending space were adequately addressed in previous NEC editions. Information provided in the substantiation indicated that when conductors entering the back of a panelboard enclosure it is silent. This new language would ensure a minimum required bending space similar to that required by section 314.28(A)(2). There are also requirements for conductor deflection within wireways that reference the dimensions corresponding to one wire per terminal in Table 312.6(A) shall apply. Action by CMP-9 results in specific requirements for wire-bending space for conductors that enter the rear of a panelboard enclosure. New subdivision (C) clarifies the minimum space required for conductors entering enclosures opposite a removable cover and the minimum distance required from the center of the rear-entry raceway to the terminal(s). Appropriate references to 312.6(A) and (B) accordingly. CMP-9 also included provisions similar to those in Exception No. 1 to 312.6(B)(2) in order to prevent insulation damage for a conductor bent 90 degrees and then pushed directly into a terminal or immediately bent another 90 degrees in order to accommodate the terminal orientation.

### Change Summary

- The section has been restructured into three subdivisions and expanded to address rear wire-bending space in enclosures.
- The four exceptions following (A) remain as in the 2011 *NEC* and the last sentence of former 408.55 was located into (B) dealing with side wire-bending space.
- New Subdivision (C) includes new requirements for rear wire-bending spaces.

Comment: None
Proposals: 9-130, 9-131

# Listed Luminaires, Lampholders, and Retrofit Kits

## Code Language

**410.6 Listing Required.** All luminaires, lampholders, and retrofit kits shall be listed.

*(See NEC for actual text)*

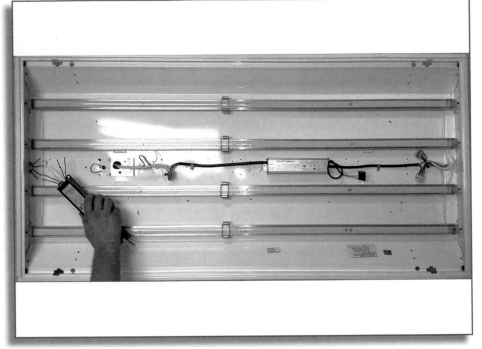

*Courtesy of Independence LED Lighting, LLC*

## Change Summary

- The words "and retrofit kits" have been added to 410.6.
- Retrofit kits used in listed luminaires are required to be listed.
- Installation, use, and application of retrofit kits will have to conform to applicable standards and installation instructions included in the listing.

## Significance of the Change

Many existing electrical systems in building structures are being evaluated to identify areas where reducing energy consumption is possible. Lighting is typically the first part of the electrical system that is likely to be able to be converted to more energy saving technology. It is very common these days to see conventional core and coil ballast being replaced with electronic types and many luminaires are also being equipped with LED technology. For example, converting fluorescent or incandescent luminaires to LED technology typically involves incorporating a power supply, LEDs, ands wiring as required. Information provided in the substantiation indicated that he changing of illumination systems in luminaires presents hazards for electricians doing maintenance after the conversion. LEDs and LED power sources must be replaced like with like to ensure electrical safety and avoid compromising the listing profile of the luminaire and creating a hazard to property or persons servicing the installation. Retrofit kits are covered in the Guide Information for Electrical Equipment (*White Book*) under category IEUQ. Listed retrofit kits will provide information about compatibility with types of luminaires and installation instructions that will be helpful for installers, maintainers, and inspectors.

Comment: None

Proposal: 18-59

# Protection for Luminaires

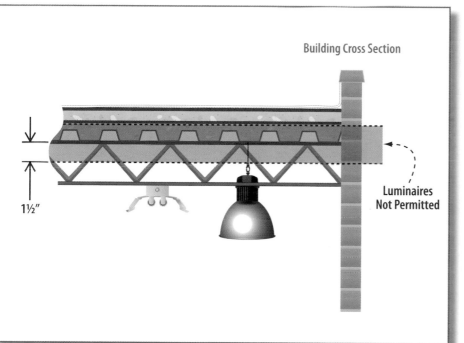

Building Cross Section

1½″

Luminaires
Not Permitted

## Code Language

**410.10(F) Luminaires Installed in or Under Roof Decking.** Luminaires installed in exposed or concealed locations under metal-corrugated sheet roof decking shall be installed and supported so there is not less than 38 mm (1½ in.) measured from the lowest surface of the roof decking to the top of the luminaire.

*(See NEC for actual text)*

## Significance of the Change

Roofing and reroofing operations can result in damage to electrical equipment located closer than 1 ½ inches from the under side of roof decking. The roof material fasteners are capable of penetrating raceways boxes and now luminaires. Information in the substantiation indicated that physical damage is not limited to only cables, raceways and boxes installed within these locations. The luminaire itself, conductors and its associated equipment such as the ballast(s) and transformer within the equipment could also be subject to physical damage by penetrating roof fasteners. Section 300.4(E) does not permit the cables, raceways, or boxes to be installed within this area, therefore the addition of this new section would serve to help prevent the same type of damage from happening to luminaires. Action by CMP-18 incorporates the new provisions that restrict luminaires from being installed closer than 1 ½ inches from the lowest surface of roof decking. Installers and inspectors now benefit by having specific language that applies to protection of luminaires, where previous *NEC* editions were silent on the issue.

## Change Summary

- A new subdivision (F) titled Luminaires Installed in or Under Roof Decking has been added to 410.10.
- The requirement is consistent with the provisions in 300.4(E).
- This new requirement restricts luminaires from being installed closer than 1½ inches from the lowest surface of roof decking.

Comment: None
Proposal: 18-66

# Covering Combustible Material at Outlet Boxes

## Code Language

**410.23 Covering of Combustible Material at Outlet Boxes.** Any combustible wall or ceiling finish exposed between the edge of a luminaire canopy or pan and an outlet box having a surface area of 1160 mm² (180 in.²) or more shall be covered with noncombustible material.

*(See NEC for actual text)*

## Change Summary

- The words "having a surface area of 1160 mm² (180 in²) or more" have been added to this section.

- Covering combustible material applies only if 180 in² or more of combustible material is exposed between the box and canopy or pan.

- This revision aligns with requirements in UL 1598 *Standard for Luminaires.*

## Significance of the Change

This revision incorporates as specific dimension into this section to prescribe specifically where covering combustible material between the box and canopy or pan is required. Underwriters Laboratories proposed this revision in an effort to align the *NEC* with UL 1598 *Standard for Luminaires*. Information in the substantiation indicated that listed luminaires are evaluated to the requirements of the Standard for Luminaires, ANSI/ UL1598. Based on requirements in the ANSI/UL 1598 standard, listed canopy-style surface or ceiling-mounted luminaires do not require a back-plate or back-cover provided the total area of the surface being covered by the canopy is less than 1160 mm² (180 in²). In addition, these listed canopy style luminaires are evaluated based on requirements in the product standard to ensure that temperatures on wall or ceiling surfaces on which the luminaire is mounted do not exceed 90 degrees centigrade. The requirements for "listed" luminaires fulfills the requirement of Section 410.23 and therefore, does not warrant the need for additional protection of a combustible mounting surface beyond what the listed luminaire provides. This revision to 410.23 provides the needed clarification. The image provides for a comparison between a noncombustible surface such as sheet rock and a combustible surface such as wood.

Comment: None

Proposal: 18-69

## Lighting Connected to Class-2 Power Supplies

### Code Language

**Article 411—Lighting Systems Operating at 30 Volts or Less and Lighting Equipment Connected to Class-2 Power Sources**

**411.1 Scope.** This article covers lighting systems operating at 30 volts or less and their associated components. This article also covers lighting equipment connected to a Class 2 power source.

**411.2 Definition.** ...(not in *NEC* text)...

**411.3 Low-Voltage Lighting Systems.**

**(A) General.** Lighting systems operating at 30 volts or less shall consist of an isolating power supply, low-voltage luminaires, and associated equipment that are all identified for the use ...(See *NEC* text)...

**(B) Class 2.** ...(See *NEC* text)...

*(See NEC for actual text)*

### Significance of the Change

This revision to the title and scope expands the coverage of Article 411 from just low-voltage lighting systems to equipment connected to Class 2 power supplies. By deleting 411.2, the requirements for listing as a complete system have been removed, however, all the components used to build a system must be identified for that use. Information in the substantiation indicated that with the advent of new lighting technologies such as solid state lighting and direct current distribution systems, there is need to better correlate Articles 411 and 725 and chapter 9 tables 11(A) & 11(B) to more accurately address ac and dc Class-2 lighting equipment rated at 30 volts or less. Nationally recognized lighting equipment standards including UL1598 and UL 2108, allow lighting equipment to be listed and identified for connection to Class-2 power supplies without the need for the equipment to be evaluated as complete system. This revision results in a more consistent correlation between the *NEC* and product standards while at the same time providing effective coverage of new technologies that provide both ac and dc power for systems and equipment that are already manufactured and evaluated for these applications.

### Change Summary

- Article 411 has been expanded to include equipment connected to Class-2 Power Supplies.
- Section 411.3 has been simplified to describe the components of a low-voltage lighting system, maximum output, and include a reference to Chapter 9, Table 11(A) or 11(B).
- Section 411.2 has been deleted, as complete listed systems are no longer required.

Comments: 18-39, 18-41
Proposal: 18-85

# Ground-Fault Circuit-Interrupter Protection

## Code Language

**422.5 Ground-Fault Circuit-Interrupter (GFCI) Protection.** The device providing GFCI protection required in this article shall be readily accessible.

*(See NEC for actual text)*

*Courtesy of Eaton Corporation*

## Significance of the Change

This new section provides a general requirement that ground-fault circuit-interrupter (GFCI) protection installed for appliances is required to be readily accessible. The substantiation indicated manufacturers of GFCI protective devices routinely require that the GFCI device be tested not less often than monthly to ensure it is providing the life-safety protection intended. The GFCI device must be located in a readily accessible location to facilitate this periodic testing and also any troubleshooting process that may be required to determine why a device has tripped. An identical requirement that the GFCI devices be located in a readily accessible location was incorporated into 210.8 for the 2011 *NEC*. Identical accessibility must also be provided for the appliances requiring GFCI protection in Article 422 because the problem is the same. Previously it was contended that unless the GFCI protection was provided to meet the requirements in 210.8, that ready access was not required. Ready access is required for GFCI protection installed for appliances as required in Article 422. The added section will clarify for installers and Code enforcers that the readily accessible rule for GFCIs installed for appliances is intended to be the same as for any GFCI installed in accordance with 210.8.

## Change Summary

- A new section 422.5 titled Ground-Fault Circuit-Interrupter (GFCI) Protection has been added to Part I of Article 422.
- GFCI protective devices installed for appliances covered by Article 422 must be readily accessible.
- The new requirement aligns with the readily accessible requirements for GFCI devices in 210.8.

Comment: None
Proposals: 17-19, 17-42

# Tire Inflation and Vacuum Machines – GFCI Protection

## Code Language

**422.23 Tire Inflation and Automotive Vacuum Machines.** Tire inflation machines and automotive vacuum machines provided for public use shall be protected by a ground-fault circuit-interrupter.

*(See NEC for actual text)*

## Significance of the Change

Public vacuums and tire inflation stations are installed in multiple locations such as at motor fuel dispensing facilities, service centers, and car wash facilities, and so forth. Ground-fault circuit-interrupter (GFCI) protection provides effective shock and electrocution protection for persons. The substantiation for this new requirement included a report of an electrical shock incident that occurred while a person was using a tire inflation machine. The substantiation also indicated that tire inflation and vacuum machines are located in commercial establishments and are heavily used by the public. The equipment is often exposed to rain, snow, and puddles of accumulated standing water and is usually misused to the point of deterioration and failure. Abused, deteriorated electrical equipment combined with a wet environment is a condition that contributes to the increased risk of an electrical shock and electrocution hazards. Over the years, GFCI's have demonstrated their value in preventing electrocution in exactly these conditions. Action by CMP-17 results in this new GFCI requirement enhancing protection for the public from shock and electrocution. The GFCI devices required by this section must be readily accessible.

## Change Summary

- A new 422.23 titled Tire Inflation and Automotive Vacuum Machines has been added to Article 422.
- Any tire inflation equipment or vacuum machine for public use must be protected by ground-fault circuit-interrupter (GFCI) protection for personnel.
- The GFCI protection (circuit breaker or outlet device) is required to be readily accessible.

Comment: None
Proposal: 17-31

# 424.66(B)

## Working Space Required at Duct Heaters

### Code Language

**424.66 Installation.** ...(See *NEC* text)...

**(A) General.** Working space...(See *NEC* text)...comply with 424.66(B).

**(B) Limited Access.** Where the enclosure is located in a space above a ceiling, all of the following shall apply:

(1) The enclosure shall be accessible through a lay-in type ceiling or an access panel(s).

(2) The width of the working space shall be the width of the enclosure or a minimum of 762 mm (30 in.) whichever is greater.

(3) All doors or hinged panels shall open to at least 90 degrees.

(4) The space in front of the enclosure shall comply with the depth requirements of Table 110.26(A)(1). A horizontal ceiling T-bar shall be permitted in this space.

Informational Note: For additional information...*Systems.*

*(See NEC for actual text)*

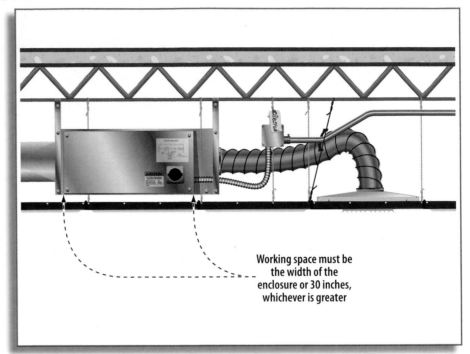

Working space must be the width of the enclosure or 30 inches, whichever is greater

### Change Summary

- A new subdivision (B) titled Limited Access has been added to 424.66.

- The width and depth of working space in 110.26 is required in front of duct heater enclosures containing equipment that requires servicing while energized.

- The revision requires duct heater equipment enclosures to be located so as to provide the minimum clearances.

### Significance of the Change

Section 424.66 previously only provided a general reference to 110.26, but did not provide any specific minimum requirements for working space. This revision incorporates working space for enclosures that have limited access, specifically, those located above suspended ceiling grids and other ceilings with access panels. Information provided in the substantiation identified the need for improvement in this section to clarify what many considered a "gray area" in the *NEC*. Minimum working space at this type of equipment is of significant importance for the safety of service personnel. Performing service operations or maintenance on this type of equipment often requires work from elevated platforms or ladders. Without the minimum working space, the task is further complicated and the risk of shock and injury is greatly increased. As revised, the minimum width of the working space must be the width of the enclosure or a minimum of 762 mm (30 in.) whichever is greater and the minimum depth of space in front of the enclosure shall comply with Table 110.26(A)(1). Any equipment doors or hinged panels must open to at least 90 degrees. This revision will require coordination between the builder and mechanical contractor during initial installation to achieve the minimum space required.

Comment: 17-19
Proposal: 17-75

# 430.52(C)(5)

## Article 430 Motors, Motor Circuits, and Controllers
### Part IV Motor Branch-Circuit Short-Circuit and Ground-Fault Protection

*REVISION*

# Fuse Protection for Power Electronic Devices

## Code Language

**(5) Power Electronic Devices.** Semiconductor fuses intended for the protection of electronic devices shall be permitted in lieu of devices listed in Table 430.52 for power electronic devices, associated electromechanical devices (such as bypass contactors and isolation contactors), and conductors in a solid-state motor controller system, provided that the marking for replacement fuses is provided adjacent to the fuses.

*(See NEC for actual text)*

## Significance of the Change

Information provided in the substantiation indicated that the term *Suitable* is vague and unenforceable and is recommended by the *NEC Style Manual* that its use be avoided. This section was revised by adding the words "semiconductor fuses" to clarify the specific type of fuse intended by this provision. The semiconductor fuses are also permitted to protect associated electromechanical devices and conductors in a solid-state motor control system. The revised wording clarifies the type of fuses that are permitted in this application and clarifies that these fuses are also permitted in systems that also contain non-electronic power devices. These types of fuses are typically recognized to UL 248-13, the *Standard for Semiconductor Fuses.* This type of fuse has a much faster reaction time at lower fault levels to ensure appropriate protection for delicate electronics that are used in many of today's modern electronic frequency controllers and starters.

## Change Summary

- The words "Semiconductor fuses intended for the protection of electronic devices" have been added to this section.
- The revision clarifies that semiconductor fuses can also protect associated electromechanical devices and conductors in a solid-state motor control system.
- As revised the specific type of fuse is included in the rule.

Comment: None
Proposal: 11-35a

# Motor Circuit and Adjustable-Speed Drive Protection

## Code Language

**430.130 Branch-Circuit Short-Circuit and Ground-Fault Protection for Single Motor Circuits Containing Power Conversion Equipment.**

**(A) Circuits Containing Power Conversion Equipment.** Circuits containing power conversion equipment shall be protected by a branch-circuit short-circuit and ground-fault protective device in accordance with the following:

(1) The rating and type ...(See *NEC* text)...

(2) Where maximum ...(See *NEC* text)...

(3) A self-protected ...(See *NEC* text)...

**(B) Bypass Circuit/Device.** Branch-circuit short-circuit and ground-fault protection shall also be provided for a bypass circuit/device(s)...(See *NEC* text)...

**430.131 Several Motors or Loads on One Branch Circuit Including Power Conversion Equipment.** For installations meeting all the requirements of 430.53 that include one or more power converters... (See *NEC* text)...

*(See NEC for actual text)*

## Change Summary

- Sections 430.130 and 430.131 have been added to Part X of Article 430.

- The new provisions include methods of providing branch circuit short-circuit and ground-fault protection for power conversion equipment applications.

- Section 430.130 addresses single motor applications and 430.131 addresses several motors on one branch circuit that includes power conversion equipment.

Comment: 11-21
Proposal: 11-60a

## Significance of the Change

These two new sections in Part X of Article 430 describe how branch circuit short-circuit and ground-fault protection can be provided for motors and branch circuits that supply either a single motor on a circuit, or multiple motors on a circuit. This protection can be provided using 430.52(C)(1), (3), (5), or (6) based on the motor FLA as determined using 430.6. It can also be provided by properly equipped power conversion equipment and associated manufacturer's instructions. Self-contained power conversion equipment can also provide the necessary protection for the motor and branch circuit as long as the equipment is so identified for providing that protection. The new informational note indicates that many types of power conversion equipment have branch circuit, short-circuit and ground-fault protection ratings marked on the equipment. The revision provides users with needed branch circuit short circuit and ground-fault protection methods for adjustable speed drive equipment.

# Generator Nameplate Information

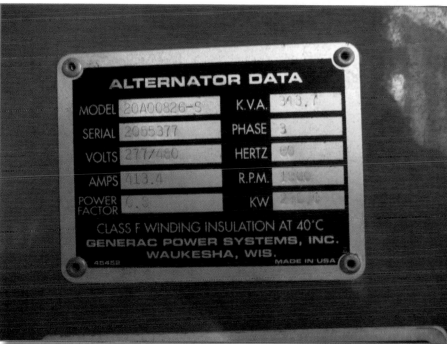

*Courtesy of John E. Kelly and Sons, Inc.*

## Code Language

**445.11 Marking.** Each generator shall be provided with a nameplate giving the manufacturer's name, the rated frequency, the number of phases if of ac, the rating in kilowatts or kilovolt-amperes, the normal volts and amperes corresponding to the rating, the rated revolutions per minute, and the rated ambient temperature or rated temperature rise.

Nameplates for all stationary generators and portable generators rated more than 15 kW shall also give the power factor, the subtransient and transient impedances, the insulation class, and the time rating.

Marking shall be provided by the manufacturer to indicate whether or not the generator neutral is bonded to the generator frame. Where the bonding of a generator is modified in the field, additional marking shall be required to indicate whether the generator neutral is bonded to the generator frame.

*(See NEC for actual text)*

## Significance of the Change

This section has been restructured and revised to clarify the information required to be included on generator nameplates. Generally, all generators must be marked with manufacturer's name, number of phases if AC, and following ratings: frequency, kW or kVA, voltage, amperes, RPM, and ambient temperature or temperature rise. Generators 15 kA and smaller are typically used to power temporary loads and the information that is permitted to be omitted from the nameplate for these smaller generators is not relevant to their proper application as with larger generators. Generators rated more than 15 kW must provide additional information such as power factor, sub-transient and transient impedances, insulation system class, and time rating. Larger generators can produce higher levels of available fault current. Including sub-transient reactance on the nameplates can help determine the short-circuit current a generator can develop. However, 15 kW and smaller generators do not produce significant levels of fault current, so the information is very seldom utilized and thus unnecessary for inclusion on the nameplate. The revision provides the needed demarcation between general nameplate information for all generators and the additional information required on nameplates of generators larger than 15 kW. Generators must also be marked to indicate if the neutral is or is not bonded to the frame of the generator.

## Change Summary

- Section 445.11 has been expanded into three paragraphs and revised.
- Nameplates must generally include manufacturer's name, number of phases if ac, frequency, kW or kVA, voltage, amperes, RPM, and ambient temperature or temperature rise.
- Generators rated greater than 15 kW must be marked with power factor, subtransient and transient impedances, insulation system class, and time rating.

Comment: 13-2
Proposal: 13-11

# 445.17 Exception

**NEW**

## Generator Terminal Housing Exception

### Code Language

**445.17 Generator Terminal Housings.** Generator terminal housings shall comply with 430.12. Where a horsepower rating is required to determine the required minimum size of the generator terminal housing, the full-load current of the generator shall be compared with comparable motors in Table 430.247 through Table 430.250. The higher horsepower ratings of Table 430.247 and Table 430.250 shall be used whenever the generator selection is between two ratings.

*Exception: This section shall not apply to generators rated over 600 volts.*

*(See NEC for actual text)*

*Courtesy of Cogburn Bros, Inc*

### Change Summary

- A new exception has been added to 445.17, Generator Terminal Housings.
- The size of generator terminal housing must generally comply with 430.12 for motors.
- These requirements do not apply to generators rated over 600 volts, but information is provided in Part XI of Article 430.

### Significance of the Change

Section 445.17 address a very important problem related to insufficient wire-bending and wire termination space in generator housings. Generators can have an overcurrent device to terminate output conductors, or be equipped with landing pads if the overcurrent protection device is remote. Wire-bending space and space for making connections at generator terminal housings have presented significant challenges for installers. In some cases, the generator housings had to be modified to accommodate all conductors connected to the generator. This is especially problematic if a generator is used in an application where conductors have been increased in size to deal with voltage drop concerns. Where a horsepower rating is required to determine the required minimum size of the generator terminal housing, the full-load current of the generator shall be compared with comparable motors specified in Tables 430.247 through Table 430.250. The higher horsepower ratings in Tables 430.247 through Table 430.250 must be used if the generator selection is between two ratings. This new exception allows the generator manufacturer to determine proper the terminal housing size for over 1000 volt circuits, while maintaining the requirements of 430.12 to provide reasonable size minimum size generator terminal housing for 1000 volts.

Comment: None
Proposals: 13-14, 13-15

# GFCI Protection for Portable Generators

## Code Language

**445.20 Ground-Fault Circuit-Interrupter Protection for Receptacles on 15-kW or Smaller Portable Generators.** All 125-volt, single-phase, 15- and 20-ampere receptacle outlets that are a part of a 15-kW or smaller portable generator either shall have ground-fault circuit-interrupter protection for personnel integral to the generator or receptacle, or shall not be available for use when the 125/250-volt locking-type receptacle is in use. If the generator does not have a 125/250-volt locking-type receptacle, this requirement shall not apply.

*(See NEC for actual text)*

## Significance of the Change

This change increases the electrical safety for small portable generators that have both a 125/250 locking receptacle and 15- or 20-ampere receptacles. The 125-volt, single-phase, 15- and 20-ampere receptacles on the generator must have ground-fault circuit-interrupter (GFCI) protection, or not be usable when the 125/250 V locking receptacle is in use. Portable generators are typically listed to UL 2200. If a portable generator case is not grounded and the generator is not connected to another electrical system there is no ground fault current path back to the generator and no shock hazard; therefore, in this case, GFCI protection for generator receptacles serves no appreciable benefit. However, this situation changes if a portable generator is interconnected to a premise wiring system that is grounded and, in addition, the generator has 15- and 20-ampere receptacles. When a generator has an isolated or bonded neutral, and is connected to a grounded premises wiring system, the generator becomes part of a grounded system. In this instance, the 15- and 20-ampere receptacle circuits are part of a grounded circuit, and can present a line-to-ground fault shock hazard unless the receptacles are GFCI protected. The revision clarifies the GFCI receptacle protection requirements for portable generators.

## Change Summary

- New 445.20 titled Ground-Fault Circuit-Interrupter Protection for Receptacles on 15 kW or Smaller, Portable Generators has been added to Article 445.

- If 15 kW or smaller portable generator has a 125/250-volt locking receptacle, then all 125-volt, single-phase, 15- and 20-ampere receptacles must have ground-fault circuit-interrupter (GFCI) protection, or not be usable when the 125/250 V locking receptacle is in use.

Comment: 13-16
Proposal: 13-19

# Transformer Grounding and Bonding Connections

## Code Language

**(A) Dry-Type Transformer Enclosures.** Where separate equipment grounding conductors and supply-side bonding jumpers are installed, a terminal bar for all grounding and bonding conductor connections shall be secured inside the transformer enclosure. The terminal bar shall be bonded to the enclosure in accordance with 250.12 and shall not be installed on or over any vented portion of the enclosure.

*Exception: Where a dry-type transformers is equipped with wire-type connections (leads), the grounding and bonding connections shall be permitted to be connected together using any of the methods in 250.8 and shall be bonded to the enclosure if of metal.*

**(B) Other Metal Parts.** ...(See *NEC* text)...

*(See NEC for actual text)*

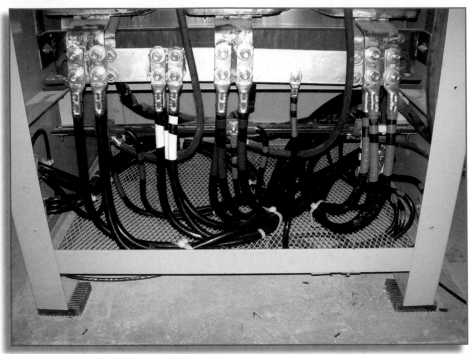

## Change Summary

- A new subdivision (A) and exception have been added to 450.10 and the existing text has been identified as (B) Other Metal Parts.

- This new provision provides specific requirements for grounding and bonding connections in transformer enclosures.

- A separate grounding terminal bar must be installed, but not over vented portions of the enclosure.

Comment: None
Proposal: 9-144

## Significance of the Change

This new provision incorporates specific requirements for grounding and bonding connections in transformer enclosures. Information in the substantiation indicated that the connections of grounding and bonding conductors in dry type transformer enclosures continue to be problematic and inconsistently made without clear requirements in the *NEC*. It is very common to see grounding and bonding conductors connected to the enclosure at or over the venting openings in the bottom of the transformer enclosure, often resulting in less than effective connections. Grounding and bonding connections must be effective to accomplish the required grounding and bonding and provide an effective ground fault current path. Dry type transformer enclosures, specifically the vented portions have not been evaluated as grounding and bonding equipment and should not be depended upon to serve as effective ground fault current paths. The new requirement for a terminal bar eliminates the inconsistencies and provides needed direction for installers. The new requirement also restricts the grounding terminal bar from being installed over a vented portion of the dry type enclosure. A new exception has also been incorporated to relax this requirement for transformers with pigtail leads where there may be only one connection to the enclosure and the rest accomplished using wire connectors.

# New Informational Notes and Definitions in Article 480

## Significance of the Change

Section 480.2 has been expanded to include defined words and terms related to storage battery installations and equipment. The new definitions are associated with current words or terms used within Article 480, but were not defined in previous editions. Including definitions of these terms assists users in understanding and applying relevant storage battery requirements. These new definitions were developed as a joint effort of the *NEC* DC Task Group of the Correlating Committee and the IEEE Stationary Battery Codes Working Group. The responsibilities of this working group were to identify gaps in the *NEC* where dc wiring rules either needed to be revised, expanded, or added. Article 480 has a long history in the *Code* and has gone through few revisions in previous editions. An important revision within the article is the addition of an informational note following 480.1 that references relevant IEEE standards. The informational notes also provide references covering battery technologies other than lead-acid, monitoring, spill containment. Words and terms mean what they imply by definition. The new and revised definitions in 480.2 assist designers, installers and *Code* enforcers in proper application of the requirements.

## Code Language

**Cell.** The basic electrochemical unit, characterized by an anode and a cathode, used to receive, store, and deliver electrical energy.

**Container.** A vessel that holds the plates, electrolyte, and other elements of a single unit in a battery.

Informational Note: A container may be single-cell or multi-cell and is sometimes referred to in the industry as a "jar."

**Electrolyte.** The medium that provides the ion transport mechanism between the positive and negative electrodes of a cell.

**Intercell Connector.** An electrically conductive ...(See *NEC* text)...

**Intertier Connector.** An electrical conductor used ...(See *NEC* text)...

**Terminal.** That part of a cell, container, or battery ...(See *NEC* text)...

*(See NEC for actual text)*

## Change Summary

- The definition of *Nominal Battery Voltage* has been revised and six new definitions have been added to 480.2.

- The new definitions relate to storage batteries and interconnection components of battery systems.

- These new definitions are related to expanded requirements for dc systems being incorporated in multiple articles throughout the *NEC*.

Comment: None
Proposals: 13-24, 13-26, 13-27, 13-28, 13-29, 13-30, 13-32

**NEW**

# Accessible Battery Terminals

## Code Language

**480.8(C) Accessibility.** The terminals of all cells or multi-cell units shall be readily accessible for readings, inspection, and cleaning where required by the equipment design. One side of transparent battery containers shall be readily accessible for inspection of the internal components.

*(See NEC for actual text)*

*Courtesy of PDE Total Energy Solutions*

## Change Summary

- A new subdivision (C) titled Accessibility has been added to 480.8.
- Where required by the design, the terminals of all cells or multi-cell units are required to be readily accessible for cleaning, taking readings and inspection.
- All transparent battery containers must also be readily accessible for visual inspection of the internal components.

## Significance of the Change

This new requirement resulted from a joint effort of the *NEC* DC Task Group of the Correlating Committee and the IEEE Stationary Battery Codes Working Group. This new text is derived from text deleted from NFPA 70E-2009, 320.5(A)(2), because it is an installation requirement that is outside the scope of NFPA 70E. Most battery systems require visual inspection to determine maintenance, servicing, or replacement needs. All require periodic or regular monitoring of voltage, resistance, etc. Where measurements taken manually, the measurement points (such as where to put test instrument probes) must be readily accessible so as not to create a hazard to service or maintenance personnel. Some equipment designs encapsulate the batteries into modules with embedded monitoring where standard maintenance practices are neither required nor possible. Some battery types are made of transparent containers, thereby allowing visual inspection of internal components; however some are not transparent. This new text makes it clear that one side of transparent battery containers must be readily accessible for inspection of internal components, and where necessary because of the installation or equipment design, the terminals of cells or multi-cell units are required to be readily accessible.

Comment: None
Proposal: 13-38

# Workspace and Egress Requirements for Battery Rooms

*Courtesy of Bill McGovern, City of Plano, TX*

## Code Language

**(D) Top Terminal Batteries.** Where top terminal batteries are installed on tiered racks, working space in accordance with the battery manufacturer's instructions shall be provided between the highest point on a cell and the row or ceiling above that point.

**(E) Egress.** A personnel door's intended for entrance to, and egress from, rooms designated as battery rooms shall open in the direction of egress and shall be equipped with listed panic hardware.

*(See NEC for actual text)*

## Significance of the Change

Section 480.9 has been modernized and expanded for the 2014 NEC. These changes address present day battery technology while at the same time provide the most up to date safety requirements for electrical battery rooms. One updated requirement now specifically address sufficient diffusion and ventilation of hazardous gases and vapors (if present) from battery rooms according to provisions appropriate to the battery technology used. For enforcement of this requirement, a new informational note refers the user to NFPA 1, Fire Code, Chapter 52 for specific regulations regarding ventilation of battery rooms. Another new requirements in Section 480.9(C) require battery room spaces to comply with the present working clearances of 110.26. New requirements in Section 480.9(D) address minimum clearance spaces above tiered battery racks or above the top rack of batteries and the ceiling. Manufacturers recommended instructions and dimensions must be followed to ensure the final installation provides sufficient space and clearance to properly maintain, service or remove any top tier batteries safely. And finally, egress doors for battery rooms, according to Section 480.9(D), are now required to open in the direction of egress and in addition, these egress doors must be equipped with listed panic hardware.

## Change Summary

- Two subdivisions were added to 480.9 titled (D) Top Terminal Batteries and (E) Egress.
- For top terminal batteries installed on tiered racks, the battery manufacturer provides minimum clearance distances between top battery terminal and the ceiling.
- Personnel doors for battery rooms must swing in the direction of egress and be equipped with listed panic hardware.

Comments: 13-26, 13-27
Proposals: 13-44, 13-45

## NEW

# No Gas Piping in Battery Rooms

## Code Language

**480.9(F) Piping in Battery Rooms.** Gas piping shall not be permitted in dedicated battery rooms.

*(See NEC for actual text)*

*Courtesy of Bill McGovern, City of Plano, TX*

## Change Summary

- A new subdivision (F) titled Piping in Battery Rooms has been added to 480.9.
- This new provision restricts gas piping from being installed in any dedicated battery room as formerly provided in NFPA 70E.
- The new restriction eliminates possibilities of corrosion and leakage from escalating into extreme hazards of explosion and fire.

## Significance of the Change

Gas piping must not be installed in any dedicated battery room. Information provided in Proposal 13-46 indicated that this new provision is text removed from NFPA 70E because that document is not an installation code. Additional substantiation provided in Comment 13-28 which reemphasized that gas piping present the following possible hazards if located in a battery room:

(1) The gas itself, if accidentally released into the room, could have a damaging effect on the battery containers and/or connections; or

(2) The gas (which is presumed to be flammable), could be ignited by the battery system, which is always energized (although we acknowledge that a battery will not spontaneously spark); or

(3) In the event of overcharging and/or thermal runaway on a battery system, atomized electrolyte could corrode or otherwise impair the integrity of metallic gas piping over time.

Battery systems, by their very nature, are used for essential standby power or even emergency system applications. Therefore, battery rooms should be designed to a somewhat higher standard than other occupancies to ensure the highest level of safety. This new requirement resulted from a joint effort of the *NEC* DC Task Force of the Correlating Committee and the IEEE Stationary Battery Codes Working Group.

Comment: 13-28
Proposal: 13-46

## Equipment Over 1000 Volts, Nominal

iStock Photo Courtesy of NECA

### Code Language

**Article 490 Equipment Over 1000 Volts, Nominal**

**490.21(B)(7) High-Voltage Fuses.** Switchgear and substations…(See *NEC* text)…

**490.22 Isolating Means.** Means shall be provided to…switchgear units…(See *NEC* text)…

**Article 490 Part III.** Equipment – Switchgear and Industrial Control Assemblies

**490.30 General.** Part III covers assemblies of switchgear and industrial control equipment…(See *NEC* text)…

**490.47 Switchgear Used as Service Equipment.** Switchgear installed as high-voltage service equipment…(See *NEC* text)…

*(See NEC for actual text)*

### Significance of the Change

These revisions correlate Article 490 with actions taken by CMP 9 to place a revised definition of what used to be *Metal- Enclosed Power Switchgear* in Article 100. The change will renames that defined term as simply *Switchgear* and incorporates several editorial changes to the content accordingly, including adding an informational note. The revisions to the definition expand its application to all switchgear types such as metal-clad switchgear, metal-enclosed switchgear, and low-voltage power circuit breaker switchgear as covered in Article 490. It should be noted that while the definition of *switchgear* is located in Article 100, CMP-9 maintains technical responsibility for this definition. *Code*-wide revisions have been made to remove the term *metal-enclosed* from the term *metal-enclosed switchgear*. CMP-9 also acted favorably to increasing the voltage threshold from 600 volts to 1000 volts throughout Article 490. This revision is also part of a global effort throughout the *NEC* to provide applicable requirements for systems and sources that have outputs greater than 600 volts. Those proposals were submitted by an assigned high-voltage task group and the work is incremental and expected to continue in the 2017 *NEC* development process.

### Change Summary

- The title and sections within Article 490 have been revised to increase the voltage from 600 to 1000.
- The term *metal-enclosed switchgear* has been replaced with the term *switchgear*.
- The definition of *Metal-Enclosed Switchgear* in Article 100 has been revised to no longer include the term *metal-enclosed* as all switchgear covered by the *NEC* is metal enclosed.

Comment: 9-77
Proposals: 9-152a, 9-153

# Warning Signs for Equipment Subject to Backfeed

## Code Language

**490.25 Backfeed.** Installations where the possibility of backfeed exists shall comply with (a) and (b), which follow....DANGER — CONTACTS ON EITHER SIDE OF THIS DEVICE MAY BE ENERGIZED BY BACKFEED.

(a) A permanent sign in accordance with 110.21(B) shall be installed on the disconnecting means enclosure or immediately adjacent to open disconnecting means with the following words or equivalent:

> DANGER — CONTACTS
> ON EITHER SIDE OF THIS
> DEVICE MAY BE ENERGIZED
> BY BACKFEED

(b) A permanent and legible single-line diagram of the local switching arrangement, clearly identifying each point of connection to the high-voltage section, shall be provided within sight of each point of connection.

*(See NEC for actual text)*

## Change Summary

- A new 490.25 titled Backfeed has been added to Part II of Article 490.
- The new requirement warns qualified persons of the possibilities of contacts within the equipment being energized by backfeed.
- A reference to 110.21(B) has been provided for additional requirements related to danger signs installed on equipment.

Comment: None
Proposal: 9-165

Danger sign required warning of possible energized contacts on either side of the device due to backfeed.

Danger signs required in 490.25 must meet the requirements in 110.21(B).

Applies where the signal words "danger", "warning", or "caution" are used in NEC rules.

Note: The signal word communicates the degree of hazard. The other label components provide the specific hazard, instructions, and could also include a graphic (See ANSI Z535.4-2011).

## Significance of the Change

This new section provides a significant safety enhancement through required signage on equipment that could be subject to backfeed. Medium and high-voltage installations are often installed double-ended or supplied from two sources and interconnected through suitable tie or interlocking switching arrangements. Equipment that is paralleled could also be subject to backfeed. These types of installations can have contacts and energized parts on both sides of disconnecting means in the equipment. This new requirement gives qualified persons an immediate and deliberate danger warning about the possible hazard from contacts energized by backfeed. The danger sign must include the text "DANGER — CONTACTS ON EITHER SIDE OF THIS DEVICE MAY BE ENERGIZED BY BACKFEED." This new section also incorporates a reference to 110.21(B) for additional and specific requirements for signs and markings that include a signal word such as danger, caution, or warning. This section also includes a requirement to provide a permanent and legible single-line diagram of the local switching arrangement that identifies each point of connection to the high-voltage section. These new requirements not only improve the installation, but also enhance the process of implementing safety-related work practices.

# Substations, Warning Signs, and Diagrams

## Significance of the Change

This change resulted from work of the High-Voltage Task Group for the 2014 *NEC* development cycle. Section 225.70 titled *Substations* has been appropriately relocated to 490.48 and expanded into three subdivisions titled *Documentation*, *Warning Signs*, and *Diagrams*. Subdivision (A) is new and requires the engineering design of substations be provided and available to the authority having jurisdiction. List items (1) through (9) provide the specific elements of the substation installation that must be detailed in the design. Subdivision (B) titled *Warning Signs* is essentially what formerly existed in 225.70. Subdivision (C) titled *Diagram* is new and requires a readily visible and permanent single-line diagram to illustrate the circuits and equipment in the substation design. The diagram must be located within the same room or area as the substation switchgear and must clearly identify interlocks, isolation means, and all possible sources of energy under normal and emergency operating conditions. The equipment must cross-reference the single-line diagram. The new requirements for single-line drawings are also a safety enhancement. The relocation of substation requirements and markings, new requirements addressing engineering design requirements, and single-line diagrams for substations are much better suited in Article 490 covering equipment over 1000 volts.

## Code Language

**490.48 Substations.**

**(A) Documentation.** Documentation of the engineered design by a qualified licensed professional engineer engaged primarily in the design of substations shall be available upon the request of the authority having jurisdiction and shall include consideration of the items in 490.48(A)(1) through (9):

**(1) General.**

**(2) Protective Grounding.**

**(3) Guarding Live Parts**...(See *NEC* text)

**(B) Warning Signs.**

**(1) General.** A permanent, legible warning notice complying with 110.21(B) and reading DANGER – HIGH VOLTAGE ...(See *NEC* text)

**(C) Diagram.** A permanent single-line diagram of the switchgear shall be provided in a readily visible location within the same room...(See *NEC* text)

*(See NEC for actual text)*

## Change Summary

- Section 225.70 titled *Substations* has been relocated to new 490.48 and expanded to three subdivisions.

- Documentation of the engineered substation design must be provided by a qualified professional engineer and made available to the AHJ.

- Warning signs must meet the requirements in 110.21(B) and permanent single-line diagrams must be provided in a readily visible location.

Comments: 9-10, 9-17, 9-79
Proposals: 4-86, 4-87, 4-89, 4-91, 4-93, 4-94, 9-153, 9-179

# Chapter 5

## Articles 500–590
## Special Occupancies

**REVISION**

# Definition of Combustible Dust

## Code Language

**500.2 Definitions. …Combustible Dust.** Dust particles that are 500 microns or smaller (material passing a U.S. No. 35 Standard Sieve as defined in ASTM E 11-09, *Standard Specification for Wire Cloth and Sieves for Testing Purposes*) and present a fire or explosion hazard when dispersed and ignited in air.

Informational Note: See ASTM E 1226–12a, *Standard Test Method for Explosibility of Dust Clouds, or ISO 6184-1, Explosion protection systems — Part 1: Determination of explosion indices of combustible dusts in air,* for procedures for determining the explosibility of dusts.

*(See NEC for actual text)*

## Change Summary

- The definition of *combustible dust* in 500.2 has been revised and a new informational note has been added.

- This revision responds to both NFPA Annual Meeting action and Standards Council action.

- The revised definition is more specific and contains both national and international standard references and is suitable for use within enforceable codes and standards.

Comments: 14-6,14-1
Proposal: 14-11a

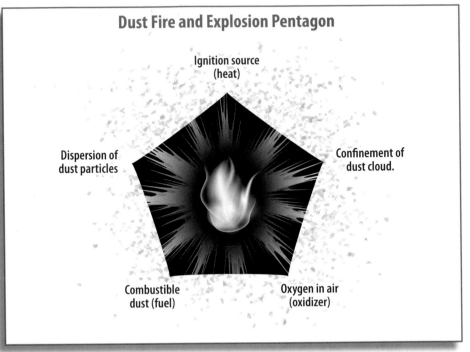

**Dust Fire and Explosion Pentagon**

Ignition source (heat)

Dispersion of dust particles

Confinement of dust cloud.

Combustible dust (fuel)

Oxygen in air (oxidizer)

## Significance of the Change

Many fires and explosions from dust explosions occurred from 2002 through 2004 resulting in more than 175 worker deaths and injuries. In 2008, another dust explosion and fire resulted in the 14 deaths and 38 injuries in a Georgia plant. This accident, together with past dust events generated public outcry of suspected unsafe working practices and working conditions. Congressional hearings were held, experts testified, promises were made, and safety experts responded. Now the *NEC* development process responds. Action by CMP-14 on Proposal 14-11a and Comments 14-6 and 14-1 results in a revised definition for combustible dust. Other dust definitions published by NFPA were not considered suitable for an enforceable code. The particle size used in the revised definition is specified as 500 microns to harmonize with national and international area classification standards and their annexes. A new informational note has been added following the revised definition and references ASTM E 1226, *Standard Test Method for Explosibility of Dust Clouds*, or ISO 6184-1, Explosion protection systems - Part 1: Determination of explosion indices of combustible dusts in air, for procedures for determining the explosibility of dusts. The revision affirms that particle size is necessary to properly classify and not over-classify a location where combustible dust is present.

## Pyrophoric Materials

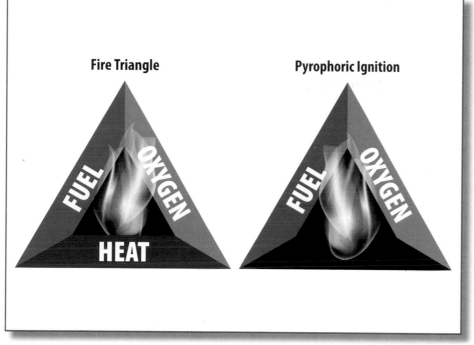

**Fire Triangle**

**Pyrophoric Ignition**

### Code Language

**500.5 Classifications of Locations.**
**(A) Classifications of Locations.**
Locations shall be classified depending on the properties of the flammable gas, flammable liquid–produced vapor, combustible liquid–produced vapors, combustible dusts, or fibers/flyings that may be present, and the likelihood that a flammable or combustible concentration or quantity is present. Each room, section, or area shall be considered individually in determining its classification. Where pyrophoric materials are the only materials used or handled, these locations are outside the scope of this article.

*(See NEC for actual text)*

### Significance of the Change

The fundamental electrical safety documents used as a basis for hazardous (classified) location requirements within the *NEC* are NFPA 497, *Recommended Practice for the Classification of Flammable Liquids, Gases, or Vapors and of Hazardous (Classified) Locations for Electrical Installations in Chemical Process Areas*, and NFPA 499, *Recommended Practice for the Classification of Combustible Dusts and of Hazardous (Classified) Locations for Electrical Installations in Chemical Process Areas*.

Understanding that pyrophoric materials are substances that ignite quickly upon exposure to oxygen, both of these NFPA documents specifically exclude pyrophoric materials in their statement of scope. The reason for the exclusion is that fire and explosion can instantly occur in areas without any wiring or any electricity present. Therefore, the safety requirements of *NEC* could never prevent a fire or explosion due to the presence or the handling of pyrophoric material.

As a result the committee removed the existing second sentence and added a new last sentence to 500.5(a) and 505.5(a). Both sections relate to area classification and state "Where pyrophoric materials are the only material used or handled, these locations are outside the scope of this article."

### Change Summary

- The existing second sentence concerning pyrophoric material was removed, rewritten and added back in to the paragraph as a new last sentence.
- Pyrophoric materials are extremely hazardous materials that spontaneously ignite in air.
- The electrical safety requirements of hazardous (classified) locations cannot protect against pyrophoric ignition.

Comment: 14-38
Proposals: 14-15a, 14-136a

## Autoignition Temperature

### Code Language

**500.6 Material Groups.**

**(A) Class I Group Classifications.**

Informational Note No. 3: ...(See *NEC* text)... Carbon disulfide is one of those chemicals because of its low autoignition temperature (90°C) ...(see *NEC* text).

**500.8 Equipment.**

**(B) Approval for Class and Properties**

**(1) ...(See *NEC* text).** In addition, Class I equipment shall not have any exposed surface that operates at a temperature in excess of the autoignition temperature of the specific gas or vapor.

**500.8 Equipment.**

**(D) Temperature.**

**(1) Class I Temperature.** The temperature marking ...(See *NEC* text)... shall not exceed the autoignition temperature of the specific gas ...(See *NEC* text)....

*(See NEC for actual text)*

### Change Summary

- The term *ignition temperature* was replaced with *autoignition temperature* in some cases.
- The term *ignition temperature* applies to combustible dusts and fibers whereas *autoignition temperature* more correctly applies to volatile flammable liquids, gases and vapors.
- For Articles 500, 501 and 505, using the term *autoignition temperature* promotes consistency with other industry standards.

Comment: None
Proposals: 14-18, 14-23, 14-25, 14-26, 14-60, 14-63, 14-64, 14-67, 14-68, 14-71, 14-73, 14-74, 14-146, 14-153

### Significance of the Change

American Petroleum Institute (API) publications such as Recommended Practices RP 500 and RP 505 as well as NFPA 497 and NFPA 499 define the term *Autoignition Temperature* or (AIT) as the minimum temperature required to ignite or cause self-sustained combustion of a solid, liquid, or gas independently of the heated or the heating element. The term *ignition temperature* is often used synonymously with autoignition temperature, but sometimes incorrectly.

In order to promote consistency of terms between standards, the term *autoignition temperature* is used when referring to material properties of flammable liquids, gases and vapors, and is consistent with how the term is used in NFPA 497. The term *ignition temperature* is used when referring to the material properties of combustible dusts, and is consistent with how the term is used in NFPA 499.

Carrying this consistency into the *NEC*, the term *autoignition temperature* will now be used within Articles 501, 505 and the applicable sections of Article 500. Whereas the previous term *ignition temperature* will continue to be used in Articles 502, 506, and the applicable sections of Article 500.

This clarifying change repeats in 500.8(B)(1), 500.8(D)(1), 501.105(B)(2), 501.115(B)(1)(4), 501.120(B)(3), 501.125(A), 501.130(B)(1), 501.135(B)(1)(1) Exception No. 2, 505.9, and 505. 9(D).

# Listed Conduit and Cable Fittings

*Courtesy of Donald Cook/IAEI*

## Significance of the Change

Class I locations are those hazardous (classified) locations in which flammable liquids, flammable gases or flammable vapors are or maybe present. Using electrical equipment in Class I locations requires electrical equipment be surrounded or enclosed within suitable enclosures that prevents electrical equipment from being a source of ignition or explosion in the hazardous classified area. These listed enclosures actually prevent any ignition or explosion within the enclosure from spreading hot gases or vapors to outside the enclosure into the hazardous location area itself. Therefore, the manufacturer accurately machines threaded openings into the wall(s) of these enclosures to accept only listed fittings. In order to further ensure the integrity of the listed enclosure, the *NEC* requires that only listed conduit, listed conduit fittings and listed cable fittings are an acceptable connection method for wiring methods to a listed hazardous (classified) location enclosure.

## Code Language

**500.8 Equipment**

**(E) Threading.** ...(See *NEC* text)...

**(1) Equipment Provided with Threaded Entries for NPT-Threaded Conduit or Fittings.** For equipment provided with threaded entries for NPT-threaded conduit or fittings, listed conduit, listed conduit fittings, or listed cable fittings shall be used. All NPT-threaded conduit and fittings shall be threaded with a National (American) Standard Pipe Taper (NPT) thread.

NPT-threaded entries into explosion-proof equipment shall be made up with at least five threads fully engaged.

*Exception: For listed explosionproof equipment, joints with factory-threaded NPT entries shall be made up with at least four and one-half threads fully engaged. ...(See NEC text )...*

*(See NEC for actual text)*

## Change Summary

- Only listed conduit, listed conduit fittings and listed cable fittings are allowed to connect to hazardous location equipment provided with threaded entries for NPT connections.
- NPT threaded conduit and fittings are threaded with standard pipe thread taper.
- These requirements help to maintain and ensure the required integrity of the hazardous location equipment enclosure.

## Fiber Optic Cables in Hazardous (Classified) Locations

### Code Language

**501.10 Wiring Methods.**

**(A) Class I, Division 1.**

**(1) General**

(e) *Optical fiber cable types OFNP, OFCP, OFNR, OFCR, OFNG, OFCG, OFN, and OFC* shall be permitted to be installed in raceways in accordance with 501.10(A). These optical fiber cables shall be sealed in accordance with 501.15.

(and)

**(B) Class I, Division 2.**

**(1) General**

(7) Optical fiber cable Types...shall be permitted to be installed in cable trays or any other raceway in accordance with 501.10(B). Optical fiber cables...(See *NEC* text)...

**502.10 Wiring Methods.**

**(A) Class II, Division 1.**

**(1) General.** (5). ...(See *NEC* text)...
(and)

**(B) Class I, Division 2**

**(1) General (8).** ...(See *NEC* text)...

*(See NEC for actual text)*

### Change Summary

- Optical fiber cables are now permitted in raceways and cable trays within hazardous (classified) locations in Class I and Class II, Division 1 and 2 locations.
- Optical fiber cable must be sealed according to 501.15 or 502.15.
- Section 770.3(A) currently permits these cables be installed in these locations where sealed.

Comments: 14-10, 14-12, 14-25, 14-26, 14-42, 14-45, 14-59, 14-60

Proposals: 4-32, 4-37, 14-83, 14-88, 14-163, 14-169, 14-219, 14-223

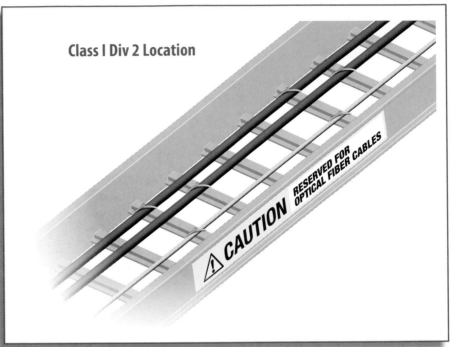

**Class I Div 2 Location**

CAUTION RESERVED FOR OPTICAL FIBER CABLES

### Significance of the Change

Articles 501, 502, 505 and 506 now include installation requirements for optical fiber cables within hazardous (classified) locations. Section 770.3(A) previously contained permission to use of optical fiber cables in hazardous (classified) locations provided the optical fiber cables are sealed in accordance with 501.15 and 502.15. This revision is necessary for correlation because, according to 90.3, the requirements in Chapter 7 are not allowed to modify the requirements of Chapter 5. These installation requirements are now correlated between Articles 501, 502 and 770. These new requirements make it clear that specific types of optical fiber cables are permitted only in recognized raceway installations within Class I, Division 1 and Class II, Division 1 locations. However, for Class I, Division 2 and Class II, Division 2 locations, optical fiber cables are permitted to be installed in both permitted raceways and cable trays installations. In addition, the sealing requirements must be met according to the applicable article, class and division for the particular installation. Companion revisions regarding optical fiber cables were also added to 501.10(B)(1)(7), 502.10(A)(1)(5), 502.10(B)(1)(8), 505.15(B)(1)(g), 505.15(C)(1)(h), 506.15(A)(7), and 506.15(C)(9).

# Flexible Connection Wiring Method for Class I, Division 2

*Courtesy of Thomas and Betts*

## Code Language

**501.10 Wiring Methods**

**(A) Class I, Division 1.** …(See *NEC* text)…

**(B) Class I, Division 2.** …(See *NEC* text)…

**(1) General.** …(See *NEC* text)…

**(2) Flexible Connections.** …(See *NEC* text)…

(1) Listed flexible metal fittings.

(2) Flexible metal conduit with listed fittings.

(3) Interlocked armor Type MC cable with listed fittings.

(4) Liquidtight flexible metal conduit with listed fittings.

(5), (6), and (7) …(See *NEC* text)…

*(See NEC for actual text)*

## Significance of the Change

Type MC cable is permitted to be used in hazardous (classified) locations as stated in 330.10(9) "… where specifically permitted by other articles in this *Code*." Section 501.10(B)(1)(5) specifically permits Type MC cables to be used within Class I, Division 2 locations. Prior to 2014 *NEC*, MC cable was not specifically mentioned within Section 501.10(B)(3) for use with flexible connections. New for this edition, iterlocked armor Type MC cable used with listed fittings, is now permitted to make flexible connections where the provisions of limited flexibility are required. The substantiation notes the construction of interlocked armor Type MC cable is comparable to the flexible metal conduit constructions and the twisted conductors under the armor making it suitable for use where flexibility is needed. In addition, interlocked armor Type MC cable with listed fittings is equal to the other permitted wiring methods that are currently used to provide for flexible connections where flexibility is necessary.

## Change Summary

- New list item (3) Interlocked armor Type MC cable was added to 501.10(B)(2) allowing up to six different flexible types of connections.
- Interlocked armor Type MC cable requires listed fittings identified for such use.
- Interlocked armor Type MC cable continues to be a Class I, Division 2 wiring method.

Comments: 14-13, 14-14
Proposal: 14-38

# 501.15(C)(6) & Others

Articles 501, 505

Part II Wiring

## Optical Fiber Tubes Within a Seal

### Code Language

**501.15 Sealing and Drainage**

**(C) Class I, Divisions 1 and 2.**

**(6) Conductor or Optical Fiber Fill.** The cross-sectional area of the conductors or optical fiber tubes (metallic or nonmetallic) permitted in a seal shall not exceed 25 percent of the cross-sectional area of a rigid metal conduit ...(See *NEC* text)...of fill.

(and)

**(D) Cable Seals, Class I, Division 1.**

**(2) Cables Capable of Transmitting Gases or Vapors.** Cables with a gas/vaportight continuous sheath capable of transmitting gases or vapors through the cable core, installed in conduit, shall be sealed ...(See *NEC* text)... so that the sealing compound can surround each individual insulated conductor or optical fiber tube and the outer jacket.

*(See NEC for actual text)*

### Change Summary

- Optical fiber tubes (metallic or nonmetallic) installed in a seal must not exceed 25 percent of the cross-sectional area of a rigid metal conduit unless specifically marked otherwise.

- The cross-sectional area of the optical fiber tube(s) must be used, not that area of the optical fibers themselves.

- Expanded cross-sectional area seals are readily available.

Comment: None

Proposals: 14-48, 14-49, 14-172, 14-173, 14-174, 14-176

*Courtesy of Thomas and Betts*

### Significance of the Change

This change applies to Class I, Divisions 1 and 2 locations, as well as Zone 1 locations. This change adds metallic or nonmetallic fiber tubes to the standard 25 percent fill language for conductors as they pass through hazardous (classified) location seal fittings. Standard seal fittings are manufactured with a smaller inside diameter than the matching conduit for a seal fitting. This smaller "conductor area" decidedly limits the entire conduit fill to 25 percent area of the cross-sectional area of available conduit fill as opposed to the most common fill area of 40 percent fill. Conduit seal manufacturers also produce listed seal fittings that have "increased" cross sectional area. The listing requirements for all hazardous (classified) location sealing fittings require that the manufacturer lists the maximum number and size of conductors that may be installed within the sealing fitting in the manufactures installation instructions provided with each fitting. This change requires limited fill for the standard sealing fittings, but clearly recognizes the "expanded cross-sectional area" of the modern seals by using the language "unless specifically marked otherwise." These proposals are a result of an assigned Task Group consisting of members of CMP3, CMP14, and CMP16, and additional industry representatives. This change repeats in 501.15(D)(2), 505.16(B)(5), 505.16(B)(6), 505.16(C)(2)(a), and 505.16(D)(5).

## Add-On Secondary Seal For Process Sealing

### Significance of the Change

A process seal is a device used to prevent the migration of process fluids outside their containment vessels and into an external electrical system. Accidents have occurred where combustible gases or vapors are compressed and/or monitored by electrical motors or devices. When the process seal at an electrical interfacing device fails, compressed products of combustion, driven by high pressure, enter electrical conduits and raceways, passing through ordinary conduit seals (unable to withstand high pressure), and use those raceways to enter control and electrical rooms. This migration often ends in catastrophic explosions and fires far from the point of origin. The requirements of Section 501.17 were developed as a result of such explosions and fires. A single primary process seal used to prevent process fluid migration is not considered to be sufficient, and Section 501.70 includes a few additional means to mitigate the high-pressure products of combustion. This change provides the necessary language to select a new option of safety by using an add-on secondary seal with the same pressure and temperature criteria as the primary seal. According to the substantiation, requirements for an add-on secondary seal will be included in the next edition of ANSI/ISA-12.27.01.

### Code Language

**501.17 Process Sealing.** This section shall apply to process-connected equipment …(See *NEC* text)…

(1) A suitable barrier …(See *NEC* text)…

(2) A Listed Type MI …(See *NEC* text)…

(3) A drain or vent …(See *NEC* text)…

(4) An add-on secondary seal marked "secondary seal" and rated for the pressure and temperature conditions to which it will be subjected upon failure of the single process seal.

Process-connected electrical equipment that does not rely on a single process seal or is listed and marked "single seal" or "dual seal" shall not be required to be provided with an additional means of sealing.

Informational Note: For construction and testing requirements for process sealing for listed and marked single seal, dual seal, or secondary seal equipment, requirements refer to ANSI/ISA-12.27.01-2011, *Requirements for Process Sealing Between Electrical Systems and Flammable or Combustible Process Fluids.*

*(See NEC for actual text)*

### Change Summary

- A new list item (4) has been added to 501.17 and addresses add-on secondary seals.

- The add-on secondary seal has the same pressure and temperature construction and test rating requirements as those of the primary seal.

- These requirements originate from ANSI/ISA-12.27.01-2011 *Requirements for Process Sealing Between Electrical Systems and Flammable or Combustible Process Fluids.*

Comment: None

Proposal: 14-54

**DELETION** | **REVISION**

# Grounding and Bonding in Hazardous Locations

## Code Language

**501.30 Grounding and Bonding, Class I, Divisions 1 and 2.** Regardless of the voltage of the electrical system, wiring and equipment in Class I, Division 1 and 2 locations shall be grounded as specified in Article 250 and in accordance with the requirements of 501.30(A) and (B).

**(A) Bonding.** (see *NEC* text)

*(See NEC for actual text)*

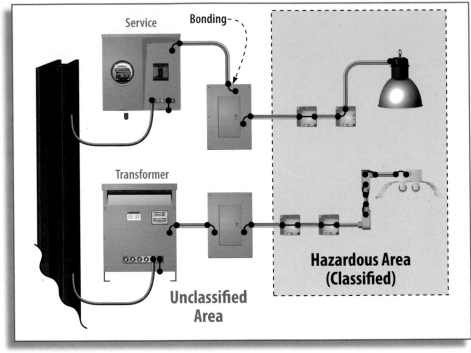

## Change Summary

- The informational notes, referencing general bonding requirements, have been deleted from Articles 501, 502, 503, 505.
- The words "Regardless of the voltage of the electrical system" have been added to 501.30, 502.30, 503.30, 505.25 and 506.25.
- The general bonding requirements for wiring in hazardous locations are effectively covered in 250.100.

Comments: 14-19, 14-28, 14-30, 14-48, 14-62
Proposal: 14-56a

## Significance of the Change

Bonding in hazardous (classified) locations is already covered in Article 250, Part V, Section 250.100. According to Section 90.3, Chapters 1 through 4 apply generally, except as amended by Chapters 5, 6 and 7. The electrical continuity of non–current-carrying metal parts of all equipment in any hazardous (classified) location must be ensured by using any of the bonding methods specified in 250.92(B)(2) through (B)(4). But most importantly, one or more of these bonding methods are required to be used whether or not equipment grounding conductors of the wire type are installed. CMP-14 revised 501.30, 502.30, 505.25 and 506.30 by incorporating the words "regardless of the voltage of the electrical system" to establish consistency with 250.100. These words clarify that these bonding requirements apply to all circuits of all voltages. Bonding requirements for intrinsically safe circuits and systems are covered in 504.60. Action by CMP-5 on Comment 5-52 to Proposal 5-160 retains 250.100 because it contains the general provisions for bonding in all hazardous locations and refers to the appropriate bonding methods. Section 250.100 provides the initial requirement that bonding in hazardous locations be completed and that it be completed by one of the specific methods in 250.92(B)(2) through (B)(4).

# Multiwire Branch-Circuit Provisions

## Code Language

Code text deleted from four articles:

**501.40 Multiwire Branch Circuits.** In a Class I, Division 1 location, a multiwire branch circuit shall not be permitted.

*Exception: Where the disconnect device(s) for the circuit opens all ungrounded conductors of the multiwire circuit simultaneously.*

**(See NEC for actual text)**

## Significance of the Change

In the past, four separate *NEC* sections were necessary to ensure that when a circuit in a hazardous location was disconnected, all circuits and possible arc sources were removed. Multiwire branch circuits present challenges in that while one conductor may be disconnected, there could still be current present in the other ungrounded conductors and associated grounded (neutral) conductor of the same multiwire branch circuit. In a hazardous location, these hazards increase because the current on the neutral presents a potential arc-producing point in the circuit if the neutral were opened while carrying the normal current. The revision removes unnecessary requirements from 501.40, 502.40, 505.21, and 506.21 because the requirements are already addressed in 210.4(B). The previous language in these sections provided a general restriction that prohibited installation of multiwire branch circuits in these hazardous (classified) locations. The exceptions to each of these sections then proceeded to allow the multiwire branch circuit if a disconnecting device opened all ungrounded conductors of the multiwire branch circuit. These revisions to these four articles result in the allowance of multiwire branch circuits in hazardous locations because they have to comply with 210.4(B) anyway. These sections are now redundant and no longer necessary.

## Change Summary

- Multiwire branch circuit provisions in Articles 501, 502, 505 and 506 have been deleted.
- Requirements for disconnecting ungrounded conductors of multiwire branch circuits are covered in 210.4(B).
- Multiwire branch circuits are permitted in hazardous (classified) locations where all ungrounded conductors can be disconnected simultaneously from the branch circuit at their point of origin.

Comment: None
Proposals: 14-59, 14-92, 14-184, 14-225a

# Informational Note Warns Risk of Ignition

## Code Language

**501.125 Motors and Generators.**

**(A) Class I,** ....(See *NEC* text)...

**(B) Class I,** ....(See *NEC* text)...

Informational Note No. 1, 2, and 3...(See *NEC* text)...

Informational Note No. 4: Reciprocating engine-driven generators, compressors, and other equipment installed in Class I Division 2 locations, may present a risk of ignition of flammable materials associated with fuel, starting, compression, and so forth, due to inadvertent release or equipment malfunction by the engine ignition system and controls. ...(See *NEC* text)... see ANSI/ISA-12.20.01-2009, *General Requirements for Electrical Ignition Systems for Internal Combustion Engines in Class I, Division 2 or Zone 2, Hazardous (Classified) Locations.*

*(See NEC for actual text)*

## Change Summary

- New Informational Note No. 4 warns of possible area ignition due to inadvertent release or equipment malfunction by an associated engine ignition system and controls.

- Informational Note No. 1 urges consideration of equipment surface temperatures located within in these locations.

- Informational Note No. 2 suggests possible equipotential bonding between the parts of motors and generators.

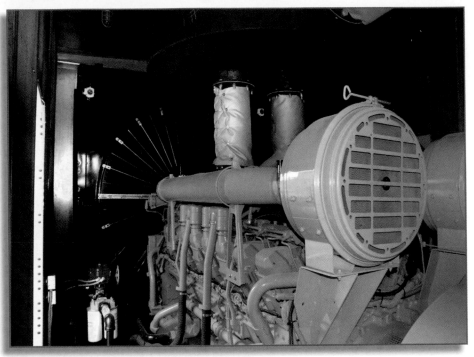

## Significance of the Change

For most motor and generator applications within hazardous (classified) locations, only listed and labeled products are usually considered. Because the *NEC* does not specifically require listed or identified equipment for Class I, Division 2 locations, choosing specialty equipment can present challenges. Therefore, informational notes provide additional guidance to assist the user in selecting, wiring and naming product standard titles where specific and additional information is available. One requirement within Class I, Division 2 locations is to specifically exclude all motors and generators that contain internal arcing and sparking switches, unless the entire assembly is identified or listed for the specific class and division required for the application. Another common practice within Class I, Division 2 locations is to ensure surface temperatures within or on any equipment selected never exceed 80 percent of the autoignition temperature of the specific vapor or gas present at the location. New Informational Note No. 4 warns the users about the need to investigate and verify that engine driven generators, compressors and alike, located within Class I areas, cannot become a source of ignition. Common risks include inadvertent release of product, liquid, or vapor, or an equipment malfunction by the engine ignition system and controls.

Comment: 14-22
Proposal: 14-66

## Power Cords Match Explosion Protection Technique

*Courtesy of Donald Cook/IAEI*

### Significance of the Change

Section 501.140(A)(1) was revised to clarify this section covers power cords that attach to the utilization equipment with a cord connector and have an attachment plug for connection to premises wiring. In the past, there has been some confusion regarding these Code requirements. This section covers the flexible cord connections between Class I or II hazardous location portable lighting equipment and the fixed portion of the supply circuit. The new second sentence requires a flexible cord be attached to the lighting unit using a cord connector listed for use in hazardous (classified) locations and matching the explosion protection technique used for the portable lighting equipment connection compartment. This change ensures that all cord connectors used must be listed for hazardous (classified) locations, match the class, division and other protection techniques of the wiring compartment of the portable lighting equipment. ANSI UL 2225 is the suitable product standard for judging cord fittings and cord connectors for use in hazardous (classified) locations. Section 502.140(A) and (B) was rewritten using similar format and structure from Section 501.140(A) and (B), while incorporating suitable Class II protection techniques and installation methods.

### Code Language:

**501.140 Flexible Cords, Class I, Divisions 1 and 2.**

**(A) Permitted Uses.** Flexible cords shall be permitted.

(1) For connection between portable lighting equipment or other portable utilization equipment and the fixed portion of its supply circuit. The flexible cord shall be attached to the utilization equipment with a cord connector listed for the protection technique of the equipment wiring compartment. An attachment plug in accordance with 501.140(B)(4) shall be employed.

**502.140 Flexible Cords — Class II, Divisions 1 and 2.**

**(A) Permitted Uses.** ...(See *NEC* text)...

**(B) Installation.** ...(See *NEC* text)...

*(See NEC for actual text)*

### Change Summary

- A new second sentence was added to list item (1) requires flexible cord to be attached with a cord connector listed for the protection technique of the equipment wiring compartment.
- An attachment plug for flexible cord must meet the requirements of 501.140(B)(4).
- Protection techniques covered in this section include Class I, Division 1 and 2 enclosures.

Comment: None
Proposals: 14-75, 14-96

**NEW**

# Material Group

## Code Language

**506.6 Material Groups.**

For the purposes of testing, approval, and area classification, various air mixtures (not oxygen enriched) shall be grouped as required in 506.6(A), (B), and (C).

**(A) Group IIIC.** Combustible metal dust.

Informational Note ...(See *NEC* text)...

**(B) Group IIIB.** Combustible dust other than combustible metal dust.

Informational Note ...(See *NEC* text)...

**(C) Group IIIA.** Solid particles, including fibers, greater than 500 µm in nominal size which may be suspended in air...

*(See NEC for actual text)*

Note: **Subsequent NFPA Standards Council Action Pending**

## Change Summary

- A new 506.6 titled Material Groups has been added and includes three first level subdivisions for metallic dusts, combustible dusts and fibers and flyings
- Group IIIC is equivalent to Class II, Group E; Group IIIB is equivalent to Class II, Groups F and G.
- Groups IIIA is for Fibers and Flyings, equivalent to Class III.

Class II, Zone 20
Group III B
-20°C and +40°C

Class II, Division 1
Group G
-20°C and +40°C

## Significance of the Change

In order to properly select and apply electrical equipment for use in specific hazardous locations, it is first necessary to divide hazardous materials into specific material groups having similar ignition characteristics. A new section, 506.6 titled Material Groups is now included in Article 506, Zone 20, 21, and 22, Locations for Combustible Dusts or Ignitable Fibers/Flyings. This new section is divided into three major material groups. The first group is (A) Group IIIC, Combustible metal dust, which is similar to Class II, Group E dust (electrically conductive such as aluminum and magnesium). The second group is (B) Group IIIB, Combustible dust other than metal dust, similar to Class II, Group F dust (combustible carbonaceous dust) and Group G (flour and grain dust). Finally, the third group is (C) Group IIIA, Solid particles, including fibers, which may be suspended in air, similar to materials presently described with Class III ignitable fibers/flyings. Within each level, there is an accompanying informational note or two describing how each Group III(A), (B) or (C) item directly relates to each Class II or Class III item. Since this new Materials Group section is numbered as 506.6, the 2011 former 506.6 titled Special Permission was renumbered as 500.7.

Comment: None
Proposal: 14-200a

# Classified Area Adjacent to Dispensers

*iStock Photo courtesy of NECA*

## Significance of the Change

Figure 514.3(a), Classified Areas Adjacent to Dispensers [30A: Figure 8.3.2(a)] has been slightly revised, and an additional Figure 514.3(b) Classified Areas Adjacent to Dispenser Mounted on Aboveground Storage Tank has been added. NFPA 30A Figure 8.3.2(a) and Figure 8.3.2(b) are extracted material from NFPA 30A-2012, *Motor Fuel Dispensing Facilities and Repair Garages*. Generally, Class I, Division 2 classified areas extend a 20 ft. horizontal distance out from the dispenser up to a height of 18 in. above grade in all lateral open areas. Generally, for aboveground tanks above 18 in., the Class I, Division 2 classified area extends to envelop the tank in all directions and extend upward to envelop the horizontal area of the dispenser a top of the tank. Although not shown, for common automobile-type ground mounted fuel dispenser(s) where the elevated area is above 18 in., generally, the Class I, Division 2 classified area extends upward and surrounds the dispenser(s) and the top of the tank to a height somewhat close to the actual point of dispensing. The revised Figure 514.3(a) and new Figure 514.3(b) provide a clear delineation of the classified locations at aboveground storage tanks where motor fuel dispensers are installed, eliminating the need to refer to NFPA 30A for such determinations.

## Code Language

**514.3 Classification of Locations.**

**(A) Unclassified Locations.**

**(B) Classified Locations.**

(1) Class I Locations.

Table 514.3(B)(1) Class I Locations — Motor Fuel Dispensing Facilities (Table) Note 2. Refer to Figure 514.3(a) and 514.3(b) for an illustration of classified location around dispensing devices.

...(See Figure 514.3(a)...

**Figure 514.3(a) Classified Areas Adjacent to Dispensers [30A: Figure 8.3.2(a)]**

...(See Figure 514.3(b)...

**Figure 514.3(b) Classified Areas Adjacent to Dispenser Mounted on Aboveground Storage Tank [30A: Figure 8.3.2(b)]**

*(See NEC for actual text)*

## Change Summary

- Existing Figure 514.3(a) has been revised to show a new below-grade sump classified area as Class I, Division 1.

- A new Figure 514.3(b) was added to show the classified area adjacent to a dispenser mounted on aboveground storage tanks.

- Both figures and associated text are extracted material from NFPA 30A-2012.

Comment: None
Proposal: 14-237

**RELOCATE**

# Motor Fuel Dispensing in Marinas and Boatyards

## Code Language

**514.3 Classifications of Locations.**

**(A) Unclassified Locations.** ...(See *NEC* text)...

**(B) Classified Locations.** ...(See *NEC* text)...

**(C) Motor Fuel Dispensing Stations in Boatyards and Marinas.**

**(1) General.** Electrical wiring and equipment located at or serving motor fuel dispensing locations shall be installed on the side of the wharf, pier, or dock opposite from the liquid piping system.

Informational Note: For additional information, see NFPA 303-2011, *Fire Protection Standard for Marinas and Boatyards*, and NFPA 30A-2012, *Motor Fuel Dispensing Facilities and Repair Garages*.

**(2) Classification of Class I, Division 1 and 2 Areas.** ...(See *NEC* text)...

*(See NEC for actual text)*

## Change Summary

- All motor fuel dispensing station requirements were relocated from Article 555, Marinas and Boatyards to 514.3(C) in Article 514, Motor Fuel Dispensing Stations.

- No new requirements were added to Section 514.3(C) Motor Fuel Dispensing Stations in Boatyards and Marinas.

- All requirements for motor fuel dispensing facilities are under the purview of CMP 14.

## Significance of the Change

New for the 2014 *NEC*, electrical requirements for motor fuel dispensing stations previously located in Marinas and Boatyards have been relocated to Article 514, Motor Fuel Dispensing Facilities. The *NEC* Correlating Committee noted that motor fuel dispensing stations are under the purview of *Code* Making Panel 14. The jurisdiction of CMP 14 includes area classification and electrical equipment and wiring requirements for hazardous (classified) locations found in Articles 500 through 516. Section 555.21 in the 2011 *NEC* provided requirements for marina fuel dispensing facilities which have not changed, but are now positioned in 514.3(C), Motor Fuel Dispensing Stations in Boatyards and Marinas. As a result, Article 514 now contains all motor fuel dispensing station requirements related to hazardous (classified) locations. Relocating these requirements from Article 555 to Article 514 improves the usability, clarity and facilitates accurate correlation. Since CMP-14 has the responsibility for requirements at all motor fuel dispensing facilities, the relocation allows for closer monitoring and review all proposed changes dealing with area classification and their related issues.

Comment: None
Proposal: 14-237

# Essential Electrical Systems in Health Care Facilities

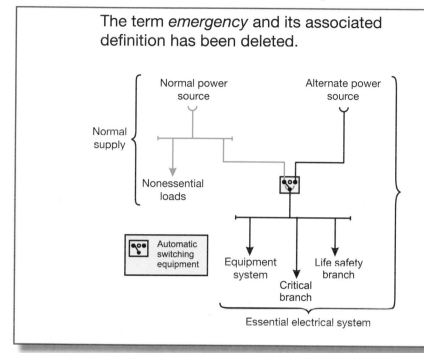

The term *emergency* and its associated definition has been deleted.

Normal power source

Alternate power source

Normal supply

Nonessential loads

Automatic switching equipment

Equipment system

Critical branch

Life safety branch

Essential electrical system

## Code Language

...Deleted Definition...

**517.2 ~~Emergency System.~~**
~~Emergency System. A system of circuits and equipment intended to supply alternate power to a limited number of prescribed functions vital to the protection of life and safety. [99:3.3.41]~~

*(See NEC for actual text)*

## Significance of the Change

NFPA 99 *Health Care Facilities Code* includes performance requirements that predicate the installation requirements in the *NEC*. The term *emergency system* where used throughout the *NEC* typically mandates application of requirements in Article 700. The performance requirements for the critical branch of a health care facility essential electrical system are covered in Chapter 6 of NFPA 99, many of which are not consistent with the prescription requirements in Article 700. NFPA Standards Council determinations in 2010 assisted the technical committees of NFPA 99 and NFPA 70 in establishing that the performance requirements in NFPA 99 would be required to harmonize the *NEC*. Removing the term *emergency system* from Article 517 should promote consistency between NFPA 99 and Article 517 rules pertaining to the essential electrical system. This revision is related to a history of standards development work and coordination between the NFPA 99 HEA-ELS and *NEC Code*-Making Panel 15, which required a few development cycles. The life safety branch of health care facilities is still an emergency system that requires application of requirements in both Article 517 and Article 700 and accordingly, 517.26 has been revised to reference Article 700 for requirements that must be applied to the life safety branch of a health care facility.

## Change Summary

- The definition of the term *Emergency System* was deleted from 517.2 and from multiple provisions within Article 517.
- The term used in NFPA 99 and Article 517 is *Essential Electrical System*.
- The deletion clarifies the applicability of Article 700 to the essential electrical system.

Comment: None
Proposal: 15-13

# 517.2

**REVISION** | **NEW**

# Definitions of Article 517.2

## Code Language

**517.2 Definitions.**

**Equipment Branch.** A system of …(See *NEC* text)…

**Life Safety Branch.** A system of …(See *NEC* text)…

**Patient Care Space** …(See *NEC* text)…

*Basic Care Space* …(See *NEC* text)…

*General Care Space* …(See *NEC* text)…

*Critical Care Space* …(See *NEC* text)…

*Support Space*

Informational Note No 1: The governing body…(See NEC text)…

Informational Note No. 2: Basic care space is typically a location where basic medical or dental care, treatment, or examinations are performed. Examples include, but are not limited to, examination or treatment rooms in clinics, medical and dental offices, nursing homes, and limited care facilities.

*(See NEC for actual text)*

## Change Summary

- Multiple defined terms in 517.2 have been revised to align with NFPA 99 *Health Care Facilities Code*.

- The word "space" replaces the words "room or area" in multiple definitions.

- A new definition of the term *Basic Care Space* and associated informational note have been added to 517.2.

Comments: 15-5, 15-10, 15-11, 15-12,15-14
Proposals: 15-14, 15-16, 15-19, 15-20, 15-21

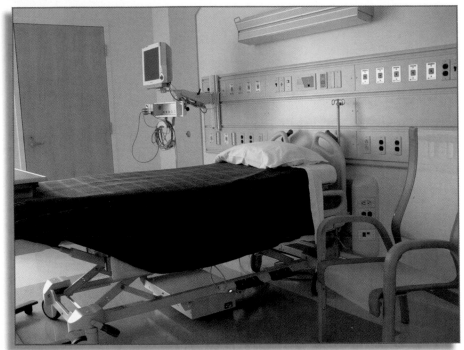

*Courtesy of Rick Maddox Clark County, NV*

## Significance of the Change

The revisions to defined terms in 517.2 are necessary to align these definitions with the same defined terms in NFPA 99 *Health Care Facilities Code*. Material extracted from another standard and included in the *NEC* will normally be followed by brackets containing the section number from which the extracted material was derived. A change to each of these definitions occurred between the proposal and comment stages of the process resulted in the word "room" being replaced by the word "space." Action by CMP-15 on Comment 15-12 incorporates the word "space" which was determined to be more appropriate and consistent with such locations in health care facilities. While extracted material is supposed to duplicate the information from one standard to another, in this case, there will be a required transition and additional revisions needed for currently defined terms contained in NFPA 99. The statements by CMP-15 indicate that coordination of the defined terms will be accomplished during the development process of NFPA 99-2015 edition. Basic care space has been added to describe a space where basic medical or dental care, treatment, or examinations are performed such as in clinics, medical offices, nursing homes and limited care facilities.

# Definition of Wet Procedure Location

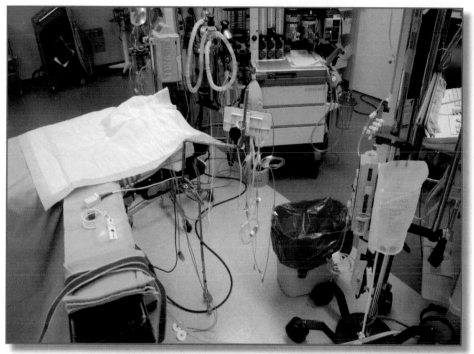

*Courtesy of Thomas Garvey/IAEI*

## Code Language

**517.2 Definitions**

**Wet Procedure Location.** The area in a patient care space where a procedure is performed that is normally subject to wet conditions while patients are present, including standing fluids on the floor or drenching of the work area, where either such condition is intimate to the patient or staff.

Informational Note: Routine housekeeping procedures and incidental spillage of liquids do not define a wet procedure location.

*(See NEC for actual text)*

## Significance of the Change

Many requirements and defined terms in NFPA 99 *Health Care Facilities Code* are duplicated in *NEC* Article 517. The revisions to defined terms in 517.2 are necessary to align these definitions with the same defined terms in NFPA 99 *Health Care Facilities Code*. Action by *NEC* CMP-15 on Proposal 15-24 results in a new definition of the term *Wet Procedure Location* in 517.2. Information provided in the substantiation indicated that wet procedure areas are addressed directly in Section 517.20 and in 517.60 and may also be associated with 517.160. In NFPA 99 3.3.138 and new subsections as recently revised, the defined term *wet procedure* area is no longer included. Revisions to the definitions included under the term *Patient Care Space* have also removed this definition. This revision retains the defined term in the *NEC* to allow users to identify wet procedure locations and apply safety-related requirements that address dangerous shock hazards to patients and staff. There is no bracketed reference following this definition as it is no longer included in NFPA 99. The new definition includes an informational note that further assists in appropriate application of the requirements.

## Change Summary

- The definition of *wet procedure location* formerly in the group of definitions under Patient Care Space has been deleted.
- A separate definition of *Wet Procedure Location* and associated informational note, have been added to 517.2.
- This *NEC* definition allows application of a term no longer defined in NFPA 99 *Health Care Facilities Code*.

Comment: 15-17
Proposal: 15-24

# Number of Receptacles – General Care Locations

## Code Language

**(B) Patient Bed Location Receptacles.** Each patient bed location shall be provided with a minimum of eight receptacles. They shall be permitted to be of the single, duplex, or quadruplex type or any combination of the three. All receptacles shall be listed "hospital grade" and shall be so identified. The grounding terminal of each receptacle shall be connected to an insulated copper equipment grounding conductor sized in accordance with Table 250.122.

*(See NEC for actual text)*

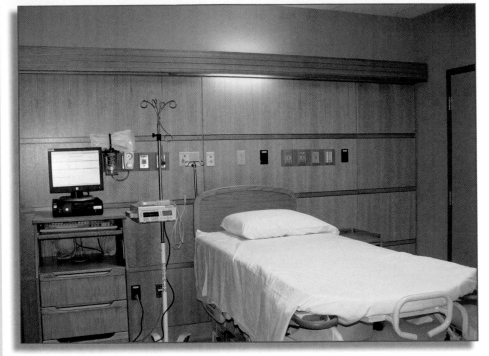

## Change Summary

- The first sentence in 517.18(B) has been revised by changing the word "four" to "eight."
- The minimum number of receptacles required in a general care patient bed location has increased to eight.
- These receptacles are required to be listed and identified as "hospital grade" and connected to an insulated copper equipment grounding conductor.

## Significance of the Change

The minimum number of receptacles required in a general care patient bed location has been four for several years. This revision increases the minimum number required to align with the NFPA 99 standard. Advances in medical technology have resulted in more medial appliances and equipment being utilized in general care patient bed locations to provide necessary care. The NFPA 99-2012 *Health Care Facilities Code* has been revised by increasing the number of receptacles in general patient care bed locations. This revision in 517.18(B) aligns with Section 6.3.2.2.6.2 (A) of NFPA 99. A minimum of eight receptacles must now be installed in general care patient bed locations and they must be listed "hospital grade" and so identified. The equipment grounding conductor connected to the grounding terminal of these receptacles is required to be insulated, copper and sized in accordance with Table 250.122. Each general care patient bed location must be provided with a minimum of two branch circuits, one from the normal system and one from the critical branch. All normal system branch circuits must originate from the same panelboard. This revision brings the 2014 *NEC* current with NFPA 99-2012 relative to the minimum number of receptacles required at general care patient bed location.

Comment: None

Proposals: 15-35 and 15-36

# Receptacles in General Care Pediatric Locations

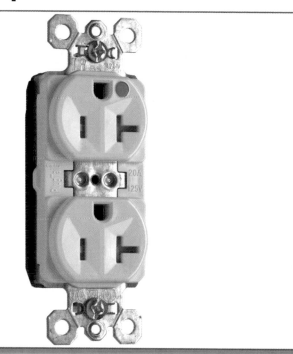

## Code Language

**517.18(C) Designated General Care Pediatric Locations.** Receptacles that are located within the patient rooms, bathrooms, playrooms, and activity rooms of pediatric units, other than nurseries, shall be listed tamper-resistant or shall employ a listed tamper-resistant cover. [**99:** 6.3.2.2.6.2(F)]

*(See NEC for actual text)*

*Courtesy of Pass and Seymour Legrand*

## Significance of the Change

The heath care requirements in Article 517 must correlate and not conflict with the provisions in NFPA 99, the *Health Care Facilities Code*. This revision in 517.18(C) is required as the new text is now extracted directly from NFPA 99 and is followed with the NFPA 99 Section in brackets. Receptacles covered by this requirement are those installed in patient rooms, bathrooms, playrooms, and activity rooms of pediatric units, other than nurseries of designated general care locations. The revisions, as compared to the previous requirement, are that the tamper-resistant receptacles are only required in designated general care pediatric locations and not specifically in the patient care areas. It should be noted that the term *patient room* is still included in this requirement, and patient care could be administered within a patient room. As in the previous edition, these requirements can be accomplished by installing either a listed tamper-resistant receptacle(s), or a listed tamper-resistant cover. The governing body of the health care facility is typically responsible for designation of patient care rooms, spaces, or areas in health care facilities. This revision aligns the *NEC* with NFPA 99 relative to locations where receptacles must be tamper-resistant because of the normal presence of children.

## Change Summary

- Section 517.18(C) has been revised to align with the requirement in NFPA 99, Section 6.3.2.2.6.2(F).
- The revision results in correlation with NFPA 99 incorporating extracted material in this section.
- The revisions clarifies that the tamper-resistant receptacle requirements apply to designated general care pediatric locations and not patient care areas.

Comment: 15-26
Proposal: 15-37

# Number of Receptacles – Critical Care Locations

## Code Language

**(B) Patient Bed Location Receptacles.**

**(1) Minimum Number and Supply.** Each patient bed location shall be provided with a minimum of 14 receptacles, at least one of which shall be connected to either of the following:

(1) The normal system branch circuit required in 517.19(A).

(2) A critical branch circuit supplied by a different transfer switch than the other receptacles at the same patient bed location.

*(See NEC for actual text)*

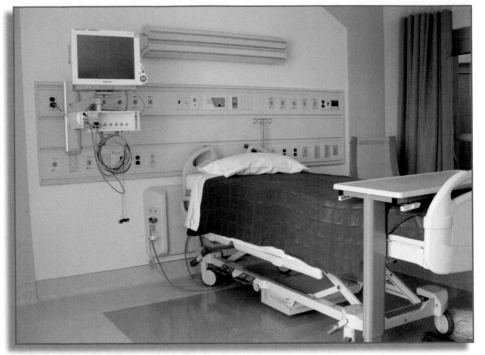

*Courtesy of Rick Maddox, Clark County, NV*

## Change Summary

- Section 517.19(B)(1) has been revised by changing the word "six" to "fourteen."

- The minimum number of receptacles required in a critical care patient bed location has increased to fourteen.

- These receptacles are required to be listed and identified as "hospital grade" and connected to an insulated copper equipment grounding conductor.

## Significance of the Change

The minimum number of receptacles required in a critical care patient bed location has been six for several years. This revision increases the minimum number required to align with the NFPA 99 standard. Advances in medical technology have resulted in more medical appliances and equipment being utilized in critical care patient bed locations to provide necessary care. NFPA 99-2012 *Health Care Facilities Code* has been revised by increasing the number of receptacles in critical patient care bed locations. This revision aligns 517.19(B)(1) with Section 6.3.2.2.6.2 (B) of NFPA 99. A minimum of fourteen receptacles must be installed in patient bed locations in critical care areas and they must be listed "hospital grade" and so identified. The equipment grounding conductor connected to the grounding terminal of these receptacles is required to be insulated, copper. At least one of the fourteen receptacles shall be connected to either the normal system branch circuit required in 517.19(A), or a critical branch circuit supplied by a different transfer switch than the other receptacles at the same patient bed location. The other revision in this section in list item (2) removes the term *essential branch* and replaces it with "critical branch."

Comment: None

Proposal: 15-39

## Receptacle Requirements for Operating Rooms

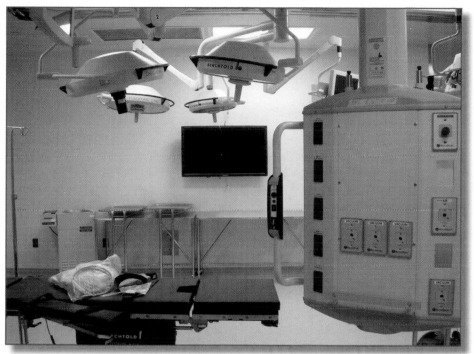

### Significance of the Change

Health care and advances in medical technology have resulted in significantly more medial appliances and equipment that are utilized in operating rooms to administer the necessary care. NFPA 99-2012 *Health Care Facilities Code* has been revised by increasing the number of receptacles in patient care locations of health care facilities, including operating rooms. This revision aligns the *NEC* with Section 6.3.2.2.6.2 of NFPA 99. New subdivision (C) has been added to require operating rooms be provided with a minimum of thirty-six receptacles and they must be listed "hospital grade" and so identified. The equipment grounding conductor connected to the grounding terminal of these receptacles is required to be insulated, copper, and must be connected to the reference grounding point typically provided in isolated power systems equipment that serve operating rooms. At least twelve of these receptacles are required to be connected to either the normal system branch circuit required in 517.19(A) or critical branch circuit supplied by a different transfer switch than the other receptacles serving the same operation room. The *NEC* was previously silent on this issue other than to require six receptacles in a critical care patient bed location, a defined term in 517.2.

### Code Language

**(C) Operating Room Receptacles.**

**(1) Minimum Number and Supply.** Each operating room shall be provided with a minimum of 36 receptacles, at least 12 of which shall be connected to either of the following:

(1) The normal system branch circuit required in 517.19(A)

(2) A critical branch circuit supplied by a different transfer switch than the other receptacles at the same location

**(2) Receptacle Requirements.** The receptacles required in 517.19(C)(1) shall be permitted to be of the single or duplex types or a combination of both.

All receptacles, shall be listed "hospital grade" and so identified. Grounding conductor...(See *NEC* text)

*(See NEC for actual text)*

### Change Summary

- New subdivision (C) titled Operating Room Receptacles was added to 517.19 and the balance of the section renumbered accordingly.
- The minimum number of receptacles required is increased from six to thirty-six.
- The revision provides direction on which system branch to which the receptacles must be connected and that they be "hospital grade" type.

Comment: None
Proposal: 15-41

# Application of Article 700

## Code Language

**517.26 Application of Other Articles.** The life safety branch of the essential electrical system shall meet the requirements of Article 700, except as amended by Article 517.

Informational Note No. 1: For additional information, see NFPA 110-2013, *Standard for Emergency and Standby Power Systems.*

Informational Note No. 2: For additional information, see 517.30 and NFPA 99-2012, *Health Care Facilities Code.*

*(See NEC for actual text)*

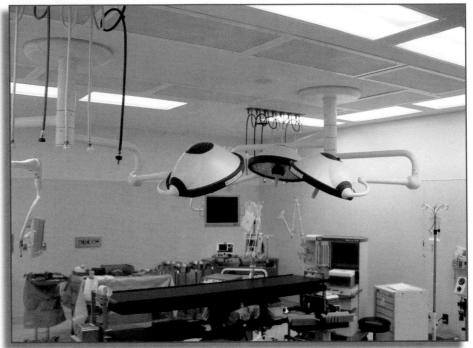

*Courtesy of Bill McGovern City of Plano, TX*

## Change Summary

- The entire essential electrical system is no longer required to comply with Article 700.
- The critical branch and equipment branch must meet the applicable provisions in Article 517.
- The life safety branch must meet the requirements in Article 700 and the specific requirements contained in Article 517.

Comments: 15-36, 15-39, 15-41,

Proposal: 15-48

## Significance of the Change

NFPA 99 *Health Care Facilities Code* is a performance-based standard that includes performance requirements that should be included in health care facility designs. The *NEC* is primarily a prescriptive-based standard that includes installation requirements. The performance requirements in NFPA 99 typically predicate the prescriptive installation requirements in the *NEC*. The performance requirements in NFPA 99 are the responsibility of the HEA-ELS technical committee. *NEC* Code-making Panel 15 is responsible for the technical requirements in Article 517 and ensuring that the two standards correlate. This revision removes the applicability of Article 700 to the equipment and critical branches of the essential system in health care facilities. There are specific amendments to Article 700 in chapter 6 of NFPA 99 to address performance requirements. This change is necessary to provide consistency between the two standards and Articles 517 and 700. Article 700 continues to apply to the life safety branch of health care facilities as a result of this change. A new informational note provides the reference to Chapter 6 of NFPA 99 for additional performance-based requirements. While the critical branch is not required to meet the provisions in Article 700, nothing prohibits designs from complying with those requirements.

## Hospital Essential Electrical Systems

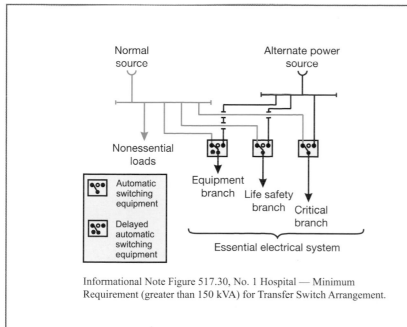

Informational Note Figure 517.30, No. 1 Hospital — Minimum Requirement (greater than 150 kVA) for Transfer Switch Arrangement.

### Code Language

**517.30(B) General.**

**(1) Separate Branches.** Essential electrical systems for hospitals shall be comprised of three separate branches capable of supplying a limited amount of lighting and power service that is considered essential for life safety and effective hospital operation during the time the normal electrical service is interrupted for any reason. The three branches are life safety, critical, and equipment.

*(See NEC for actual text)*

### Significance of the Change

The term *emergency system* has been removed from this section, associated figure, and all of Article 517. This revision has a history of standards development coordination between the NFPA 99 HEA-ELS and *NEC Code*-Making Panel 15, extending over a few development cycles. NFPA 99 *Health Care Facilities Code* includes performance requirements that predicate the installation requirements in the *NEC*. The term *emergency system* used throughout the *NEC* typically mandates Article 700 requirements. The performance requirements for essential electrical systems in hospitals or other health care facilities are covered in Chapter 6 of NFPA 99, and are not consistent with the prescriptive requirements in Article 700. NFPA Standards Council determinations in 2010 assisted the technical committees of NFPA 99 and NFPA 70 in establishing that the performance requirements in NFPA 99 must harmonize with the *NEC*. Removing the term *emergency system* from Article 517 continues that process and promotes consistency between NFPA 99 and Article 517 rules pertaining to the essential electrical system. It was contended the term *emergency system*, within Article 517, predicated requirements from Article 700. This revision clarifies that the essential electrical system consists of three branches designed to meet performance requirements in NFPA 99 and installation requirements in Article 517.

### Change Summary

- The word "emergency" has been removed from this section and from Informational Note Figure 517.30, No. 1.
- The essential electrical system is made up of the life safety branch, critical branch, and equipment branch.
- The critical branch and life safety branch are no longer referred together as the *emergency system* of a hospital.

Comment: None
Proposals: 15-51, 15-52

# Energized Receptacle(s) Identification Required

## Code Language

**517.30(E) Receptacle Identification.** The cover plates for the electrical receptacles or the electrical receptacles themselves supplied from the essential electrical system shall have a distinctive color or marking so as to be readily identifiable. [**99:**6.4.2.2.6.2(C)]

Nonlocking-type, 125-volt, 15- and 20-ampere receptacles shall have an illuminated face or an indicator light to indicate that there is power to the receptacle.

**517.41(E) Receptacle Identification...**See *NEC* text)...

*(See NEC for actual text)*

Note: **Subsequent NFPA Standards Council Action Pending**

The change in 517.30(E) was overturned by an appeal to the NFPA Standards Council. The change in 517.41(E) was _not_ appealed and therefore remains as a new requirement in 517.41(E) of the 2014 *NEC*. The result is that illuminated receptacles are required for receptacles connected to the essential branch in nursing homes and limited care facilities, but this is not a requirement for receptacles connected to the essential branch in a hospital.

*Courtesy of Hubbell, Inc.*

## Change Summary

- A new second sentence has been added to 517.30(E) and 517.41(E).
- Non-locking-type, 125-volt, 15- and 20-ampere receptacles must have an illuminated face or an indicator light.
- The requirement for an illuminated face or other indicator light applies to receptacles in the essential electrical systems for hospitals and nursing homes and limited care facilities.

## Significance of the Change

Receptacles supplied from the essential electrical system of a hospital, nursing home, or limited care facility must be clearly identified to insure that vital equipment and instrumentation continue to function in the event of power interruption. However, there was no requirement of indicating that these receptacles were supplying power to equipment. These sections have both been revised to require an energized indication. Information provided in the substantiation stated that the distinctive color or marking only identifies receptacles connected to the essential electrical system. An illuminated receptacle is ready evidence that the receptacle is providing power for essential loads. The increased visibility of an illuminated receptacle also helps ensure that energized receptacle can be quickly accessed in an emergency situation, especially when power failures result in diminished illumination by that portion of the patient care location that may not be illuminated by connection to the emergency system. Furthermore, reliance solely on some distinctive color in an emergency situation may be ineffective for personnel who are colorblind. This revision is also significant in that the number of receptacles required in these patient bed locations has increased substantially. The requirement for indicating the energized or de-energized state of receptacles is even more essential.

Comment: 15-57

Proposals: 15-64, 15-80

## Overcurrent Protective Device Coordination

*Courtesy of Schneider Electric*

### Code Language

**(G) Coordination.** Overcurrent protective devices serving the essential electrical system shall be coordinated for the period of time that a fault's duration extends beyond 0.1 second.

*Exception No. 1: Between transformer primary and secondary overcurrent protective devices, where only one overcurrent protective device or set of overcurrent protective devices exists on the transformer secondary.*

*Exception No. 2: Between overcurrent protective devices of the same size (ampere rating) in series.*

Informational Note: The terms *coordination* and *coordinated* as used in this section do not cover the full range of overcurrent conditions.

*(See NEC for actual text)*

### Significance of the Change

NFPA 99 the *Health Care Facilities Code* is a performance-based standard containing performance requirements for health care facility designs. The *NEC* is primarily a prescriptive-based *Code* that includes electrical installation requirements. The performance requirements in NFPA 99 typically predicate prescriptive installation requirements in the *NEC*. The performance requirements in NFPA 99 are the responsibility of the HEA-ELS technical committee and *NEC* CMP-15 is responsible for the requirements in *NEC* Article 517. The two standards must correlate. This change provides overcurrent protection coordination requirements that are consistent with those in NFPA 99. The NFPA Standards Council established that NFPA 99 HEA-ELS technical committee is responsible for electrical performance requirements in health care facilities. This committee has taken a different direction regarding the former requirements for selective coordination of overcurrent protective devices in essential electrical systems. As revised, overcurrent protective devices in the essential electrical system must at least be coordinated for a fault time duration extending beyond 0.1 second. Many engineering designs will continue incorporating the reliability of full selective coordination in essential electrical systems of health care facilities.

### Change Summary

- A new subdivision (G) titled Coordination along with exceptions and associated informational note have been added to 517.30.

- This new provision aligns with the overcurrent protection coordination requirements contained in NFPA 99.

- The informational note clarifies that overcurrent protection coordination in this section is different than selective coordination as defined Article 100.

Comment: 15-58
Proposal: 15-66

# Generator Set Accessory Loads

## Code Language

**(F) Generator Set Accessories.** Generator set accessories as required for generator performance. Loads dedicated to a specific generator, including the fuel transfer pump(s), ventilation fans, electrically operated louvers, controls, cooling system, and other generator accessories essential for generator operation, shall be connected to the life safety branch or to the output terminals of the generator with overcurrent protective devices.

*(See NEC for actual text)*

## Change Summary

- A new second sentence has been added to 517.32(F).

- The revision aligns with similar performance requirements contained in NFPA 99 Section 6.4.2.2.3.4.

- The new text clarifies and specifically calls out the types of associated generator loads that must be connected to the life safety branch of a hospital essential electrical system.

## Significance of the Change

The requirements in Part III of Article 517 must correlate with the performance provisions contained in NFPA 99 *Health Care Facilities Code*. The new text in this section clarifies the loads that are included in the phrase "generator set accessories." Previously, this section was very subjective as to the generator set accessory loads that must be connected to the life safety branch. Certain generator set accessories are essential for reliable generator operation and performance during interruption of normal power. As revised, the generator accessory loads that must be connected to the life safety branch include the fuel transfer pump(s), ventilation fans, electrically operated louvers, controls, cooling system, and other generator accessories essential for generator operation. This equipment is required to be connected to either the life safety branch or to the output terminals of the generator with suitable overcurrent protective devices that are properly sized. The additional text in this section is not extracted but is consistent with the performance language provided in NFPA 99 relative to generators and associated loads that are essential for generator performance.

Comment: None
Proposal: 15-70

# Definitions of Stage Equipment and Stage Switchboard

## Code Language

**520.2 Definitions.**

**Stage Equipment.** Equipment at any location on the premises integral to the stage production, including, but not limited to, equipment for lighting, audio, special effects, rigging, motion control, projection, or video.

**Stage Switchboard.** A switchboard, panelboard, or rack containing dimmers or relays with associated overcurrent protective devices, or overcurrent protective devices alone, used primarily to feed stage equipment.

*(See NEC for actual text)*

## Significance of the Change

Stage equipment is no longer limited to lighting equipment. In addition to lighting equipment, stage switchboards are required to supply a wide variety of production-related equipment. Modern stage lighting has moved rapidly from tungsten luminaires fed from dimmers to arc-source or LED luminaires fed from constant power and controlled by a data connection directly to the luminaire. Thus, a stage lighting switchboard used today is just as likely to be a circuit breaker panel as a dimmer system or relay cabinet with computer based control. Stage equipment and stage switchboards are no longer just manual controllers but are suitable to be computer controlled or orchestrated by specific production programs. Soon after industry acceptance of NFPA 1126: *Standard For The Use Of Pyrotechnics Before A Proximate Audience*, the use of pyrotechnics in the performing arts in conjunction with theatrical, musical, or similar productions in close proximity to the audience, performers, or support personnel is now relatively common. These pyrotechnic displays (sometimes referred to as special effects) are just another part of the production specific program that directly interfaces the stage equipment and is often coordinated with stage switchboards.

## Change Summary

- A new definition that applies specifically to modern *Stage Equipment* has been added to 520.2.

- A new definition that applies specifically to modern *Stage Switchboards* has been added to 520.2.

- These new definitions closely follow today's sophisticated theatrical equipment requirements of providing operator- and computer-based control of stage equipment and stage switchboards.

Comment: None
Proposal: 15-98

# 520.2

**Article 520 Theaters, Audience Areas of Motion Picture and Television Studios, Performance Areas, and Similar Locations**

**Part I General**

*NEW*

# Definition of Stage Lighting Hoist

## Code Language

**520.2 Definitions.**

**Stage Lighting Hoist.** A motorized lifting device that contains a mounting position for one or more luminaires, with wiring devices for connection of luminaires to branch circuits, and integral flexible cables to allow the luminaires to travel over the lifting range of the hoist while energized.

*(See NEC for actual text)*

## Significance of the Change

A new class of device has emerged in the past few years: the listed "packaged" stage lighting hoist. These devices contain a movable mounting position for one or more luminaires, a connector strip with wiring devices for connection of luminaires to branch circuits, and integral flexible round or flat cables to allow the luminaires and connector strip to travel over the lifting range of the hoist while energized. These cables are permanently connected at both ends and contained in a cable handling system that controls the path of the cable while gathering or folding as the hoist is raised or lowered. The installation requirements for this new product are contained within new 540.40 located in Part III, covering fixed stage equipment other than switchboards.

## Change Summary

- A new definition stage lifting hoist has been added to Section 520.2.
- This new definition is broad and covers many different types of motorized lifting devices with attached lighting and flexible cords and is capable of be operated while the lighting is energized.
- This new definition recognizes modern prepackaged stage lighting devices.

Comment: None
Proposal: 15-99

# Stage Lighting Hoist Assembly

## Code Language

**520.40 Stage Lighting Hoists.** Where a stage lighting hoist is listed as a complete assembly and contains an integral cable-handling system and cable to connect a moving wiring device to a fixed junction box for connection to permanent wiring, the extra-hard usage requirement of 520.44(C)(1) shall not apply.

*(See NEC for actual text)*

## Significance of the Change

The modern design of the stage lighting hoists often requires the use of a flat cable to insure a proper folding or gathering of the cable. Listed extra-hard usage flat cables are not available and testing by Underwriters Laboratories determined that flat cables of the required flexibility could not comply with all requirements for extra-hard usage cable. However, unlike the cords and cables referred to in 520.44(C)(1) that feed "non-hoist" connector strips, the cable handling system of a listed stage lighting hoist ensures that the cable is protected from contact with scenery or other equipment and gathers in a predictable and repeatable manner. Manufacturer's literature was provided with the substantiation as supporting material. These cables, typically an integral part of a listed product, are technically outside the scope of the *NEC*. Section 520.40 is necessary to avoid misapplication of the extra-hard usage requirements of 520.44(C)(1) to these devices. Requiring listed products and devices in the *NEC* ensures that product safety standards have been incorporated into these manufactured assemblies. Specification of listed products and devices also provides a known path for development of new designs and technologies and permits expansion into areas not presently available to the stage lighting industry of today.

## Change Summary

- "Packaged" stage lighting hoist assemblies are available, economical and safe to use.
- The extra-hard-usage requirement of 520.44(C)(1) do not apply provided the stage lighting hoist is listed as a complete assembly.
- Listed Stage Lighting Hoists will be without product safety concerns where they are installed and used in accordance with their listing and labeling requirements.

Comment: 15-77
Proposal: 15-111

# 547.9(A)(1) & 547.9(B)(3)(2)

**Article 547 Agricultural Buildings**

REVISION

## EGC Connected to Site Isolating Device Enclosure

### Code Language

**547.9 Electrical Supply to Building(s) or Structure(s) from a Distribution Point.**

**(A) Site-Isolating Device.** ...(See *NEC* text)...

**(1) Where Required.** A site-isolating device shall be installed at the distribution point where two or more buildings or structures are supplied from the distribution point.

**(B) Service Disconnecting Means and Overcurrent Protection at the Building(s) or Structure(s).**

**(3) Grounding and Bonding.** For each building or structure, ...(See *NEC* text) ... conditions shall be met:

(1) The equipment grounding conductor ...(See *NEC* text)...

(2) The equipment grounding conductor is connected to the grounded circuit conductor and the site-isolating device enclosure at the distribution point.

*(See NEC for actual text)*

### Change Summary

- The word "agriculture" was removed from 547.9(A)(1) to permit different purpose buildings at the same site.
- The term *site-isolating device* was changed to *site-isolating device enclosure* within 547.9(B)(3)(2).
- This exact term clarifies the requirement "The equipment grounding conductor is connected to the grounded circuit conductor and the site-isolating device enclosure at the distribution point."

Comment: None
Proposal: 19-20a, 19-21

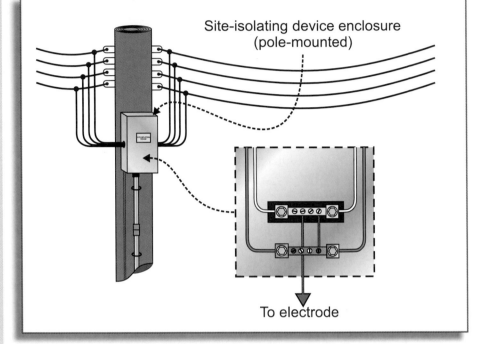

Site-isolating device enclosure (pole-mounted)

To electrode

### Significance of the Change

The proposal related to Section 547.9(A)(1) points out the term *agricultural buildings* is too limiting of a description, since the distribution point is allowed to serve structures and buildings other than strictly agricultural buildings. The word "agricultural" was dropped from the requirement since the distribution point may supply both agricultural and non-agricultural building on the same overall site. For 547.9(B)(2), the change is to replace a general and defined term with a more specific and accurate term. This section in the previous NEC required that the equipment-grounding conductor be connected to the grounded circuit conductor and the site-isolating device at the distribution point. As the submitter of the proposal points out, this requirement is not exactly accurate and the equipment-grounding conductor is actually required to connect to the enclosure of the site-isolating device. These two revisions clarify the requirements, improve technical accuracy and enhance usability and enforceability of these provisions.

## Required RV Labels

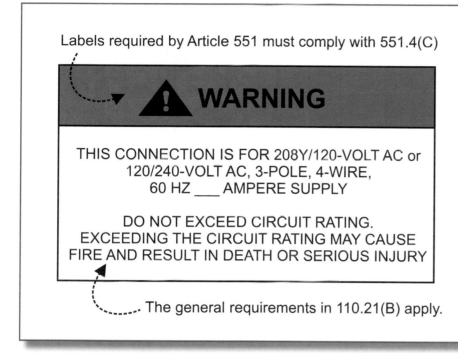

Labels required by Article 551 must comply with 551.4(C)

**⚠ WARNING**

THIS CONNECTION IS FOR 208Y/120-VOLT AC or 120/240-VOLT AC, 3-POLE, 4-WIRE, 60 HZ ___ AMPERE SUPPLY

DO NOT EXCEED CIRCUIT RATING. EXCEEDING THE CIRCUIT RATING MAY CAUSE FIRE AND RESULT IN DEATH OR SERIOUS INJURY

The general requirements in 110.21(B) apply.

### Code Language

**551.4 General Requirements.**

**(A) Not Covered.** ...(See *NEC* text)...

**(B) Systems.** ...(See *NEC* text)...

Informational Note: ...(See *NEC* text)...

**(C) Labels.** Labels required by Article 551 shall be made of etched, metal-stamped, or embossed brass; stainless steel; plastic laminates not less than 0.13 mm (0.005 in.) thick; or anodized or alclad aluminum not less than 0.5 mm (0.020 in.) thick or the equivalent.

Informational Note: For guidance on other labels criteria used in recreational vehicle industry, refer to ANSI Z535.4-2011, *Product Safety Signs and Labels.*

*(See NEC for actual text)*

## Significance of the Change

In the 2011 *NEC* there were four specific label requirements within Article 551 and located in Sections 551.46(D), 551.46(Q), 551.46(R) (4) and 551.46(S)(3). In the 2011 *NEC*, Section 551.46(D) identified "specific label criteria" and Sections 551.46(Q), 551.46 (R)(4) and 551.46(S) referred the user back to Section 551.46(D). In an effort to consolidate and simplify all this label information, this new proposal recommended all the 2011 *NEC* label criteria from 551.46(D) be relocated into a new first level subdivision (C) titled Labels in the Section 551.4. In the same section, a new informational note was added providing guidance for label criteria according to ANSI Z535, *Product Safety Signs and Labels.* Also of interest to the RV industry is that recent changes have been approved for NFPA 1192, Standard On Recreational Vehicles to require all signs and labels to comply with ANSI Z535. Therefore, common RV labels required by NFPA 1192 will now remain consistent with the electrical labels required by Article 551 of the *NEC*.

### Change Summary

- New Section 551.4(C) provides common essential materials and thicknesses for labels required by Article 551.
- Changes have been approved for NFPA 1192, Standard On Recreational Vehicles to require all signs and labels to comply with ANSI Z535.
- The label requirements of *NEC* Article 551 are coordinated with those of ANSI Z535 and NFPA 1192.

Comment: 19-23
Proposal: 19-50

# 551.71

**REVISION**

# Quantity and Types of Receptacles at RV sites

## Code Language

**551.71 Type Receptacles Provided.** Every recreational vehicle site with electrical supply shall be equipped with at least one 20-ampere, 125-volt receptacle. A minimum of 20 percent of all recreational vehicle sites, with electrical supply, shall each be equipped with a 50-ampere, 125/250-volt receptacle conforming to the configuration as identified in Figure 551.46(C)(1). Every recreational vehicle site equipped with a 50-ampere receptacle shall also be equipped with a 30-ampere, 125-volt receptacle conforming to Figure 551.46(C)(1). These electrical supplies shall be permitted to include additional receptacles that have configurations in accordance with 551.81. ...(See *NEC* text)...

*(See NEC for actual text)*

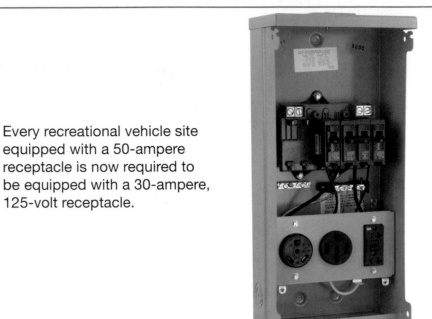

Every recreational vehicle site equipped with a 50-ampere receptacle is now required to be equipped with a 30-ampere, 125-volt receptacle.

*Courtesy of Milbank, Kansas City, MO*

## Change Summary

- Every recreational vehicle site equipped with a 50-ampere receptacle is now required to be equipped with a 30-ampere, 125-volt receptacle.
- This ensures one 30-ampere, 125-volt receptacles to at least 20 percent of the RV sites within an RV park.
- The electrical loads for modern recreational vehicles often demand a 30-ampere, 125-volt receptacle outlet.

## Significance of the Change

In the past, every recreational vehicle (RV) site with an electrical supply were supplied with at least one 125-volt, 20-ampere receptacle outlet, and minimum of 20 percent of the RV sites were required to be equipped with a 50-ampere, 125/250-volt receptacle outlet. Many modern RVs are manufactured with 30-ampere, 125-volt requirements. To facilitate these 30-ampere connections many campers were being sold "cheater" cords that adapt their 30-ampere, 125-volt RV supply cord to the 50-ampere, 125/250-volt recreational vehicle site receptacles. Since these "cheater" cords are never an acceptable solution, action by CMP-19 results in a requirement for an additional 30-ampere 125-volt receptacle at the same RV sites where 50-ampere 125/250-volt receptacles are required. This new addition of one 30-ampere, 125-volt receptacle to at least 20 percent of the RV sites within an RV park, where previously only a 50-ampere, 125/250-volt receptacle was in place, will be an equitable solution for the camper as well as campground owner. Although this action eliminates the need for "cheater" cords in newly wired recreational vehicle parks of the future, it does not generally impact existing parks. Generally *NEC* changes impact only new or upgraded RV parks or RV sites, but electrical professionals are encouraged to advocate for these safety upgrades.

Comment: None
Proposal: 19-77

# Marina and Boatyard Fuel Dispensing

## Significance of the Change

Article 555 entitled Boat Harbor Wiring first appeared in the 1968 edition of the *NEC*. In the 1971 *NEC*, Article 555 was renamed Marinas and Boatyards and the actual requirements for gasoline dispensing first appeared in Article 555 in the 1975 edition of the *NEC*. New for the 2014 *NEC*, electrical requirements for motor fuel dispensing stations previously found in Article 555, Marinas and Boatyards have been moved to Article 514, Motor Fuel Dispensing Facilities. The *NEC* Correlating Committee also noted that motor fuel dispensing stations are under the purview of Code-Making Panel 14, which has the jurisdiction of the electrical requirements for hazardous (classified) locations found in Articles 500 through 516. Previously located in 555.21 for the 2011 edition of the *NEC*, these requirements remain unchanged but are relocated in 514.3(C) titled Motor Fuel Dispensing Stations in Boatyards and Marinas. As a result of this relocation, Article 514 now contains all motor fuel dispensing station requirements related to hazardous (classified) locations. Moving these requirements from Article 555 within Chapter 5, Special Occupancies and into Hazardous Classified locations Article 514 adds to the usability of the *NEC* and facilitates enhanced *NEC* development work by CMP-14 regarding review and acting on all proposed revisions related to area classification, equipment and wiring for motor fuel dispensing facilities in boatyards and marinas.

## Change Summary

- Area classification requirements for motor fuel dispensing are located in Article 514.3.
- Section 555.21 retained only the reference to Article 514, while moving the area classification details to a new Section 514.3(C) for motor fuel dispensing in marinas and boatyards.
- See the information and material related to Section 514.3(C) in this textbook.

Comment: 14-71
Proposal: 19-108, 14-238

# Additional Construction Wiring Restrictions

## Code Language

**590.4(J) Support.** Cable assemblies and flexible cords and cables shall be supported in place at intervals that ensure that they will be protected from physical damage. Support shall be in the form of staples, cable ties, straps, or similar type fittings installed so as not to cause damage. Cable assemblies and flexible cords and cables installed as branch circuits or feeders shall not be installed on the floor or on the ground. Extension cords shall not be required to comply with 590.4(J). Vegetation shall not be used for support of overhead spans of branch circuits or feeders.

(Exception unchanged.)

*(See NEC for actual text)*

## Change Summary

- Cable assemblies, and flexible cords and cables installed as branch circuits or feeders must not be installed on the floor or on the ground.
- Extension cords laid on the floor are considered suitable for this use because they "extend" the GFCI protection of the outlet.
- Construction locations are almost always wet locations.

## Significance of the Change

This revision aligns the *NEC* requirements with existing OSHA requirements and address a serious safety issue with feeders and branch circuits installed on the floor or laying on the ground on construction sites. Generally, buildings under construction are all wet locations until the roof, exterior walls and windows are in place. Also during construction electrical lighting and receptacle power are required in most areas to meet the needs of the construction workers. Due to weather and incomplete exteriors, plus the fact that electrical circuits are laid on incomplete floors and pass through incomplete metal floors, walls and doorways, electrical shock is an ever present danger. This particular change addresses the fact that prohibiting electrical feeders and branch circuits from being laid on the floor or on the ground, a typical construction site could be a safer place to work. Accordingly OSHA Standards for the Construction Industry already recognizes this danger of shock and electrocution and prohibits cable assemblies, and flexible cords and cables installed as branch circuits or feeders from being installed on the floor or on the ground of construction sites. This change is a necessary step in protecting workers from the hazards of electricity.

Comment: 3-35
Proposal: 3-105

# NECA Code-Making Panel Members

### TECHNICAL CORRELATING COMMITTEE

**Michael J. Johnston,** [Chair]

**Stanley J. Folz,** [Alternate]

### CODE-MAKING PANEL NO. 1

**Harry J. Sassaman,** [Principal]

**Michael J. Johnston,** [Alternate]

### CODE-MAKING PANEL NO. 2

**Thomas H. Wood,** [Principal]

**Charlie Trout** [Alternate]

### CODE-MAKING PANEL NO. 3

**Stanley D. Kahn,** [Principal]

### CODE-MAKING PANEL NO. 4

**Ronald J. Toomer,** [Chair]

**Larry D. Cogburn,** [Alternate]

### CODE-MAKING PANEL NO. 5

**Nathan Philips,** [Chair]

**Jacob M. Howlett,** [Alternate]

### CODE-MAKING PANEL NO. 6

**Scott Cline,** [Chair]

**Michael W. Smith,** [Alternate]

### CODE-MAKING PANEL NO. 7

**Michael W. Smith,** [Chair]

**Wesley L. Wheeler,** [Alternate]

### CODE-MAKING PANEL NO. 8

**Larry D. Cogburn,** [Chair]

**Stephen P. Poholski,** [Alternate]

### CODE-MAKING PANEL NO. 9

**Wayne Brinkmeyer,** [Principal]

**Gregory A. Bowman,** [Alternate]

### CODE-MAKING PANEL NO. 10

**Richard Sobel,** [Principal]

### CODE-MAKING PANEL NO. 11

**Stanley J. Folz,** [Principal]

### CODE-MAKING PANEL NO. 12

**Thomas L. Hedges,** [Principal]

**William A. Brunner,** [Alternate]

### CODE-MAKING PANEL NO. 13

**Martin D. Adams,** [Principal]

### CODE-MAKING PANEL NO. 14

**Marc J. Bernsen,** [Principal]

### CODE-MAKING PANEL NO. 15

**Bruce D. Shelly,** [Principal]

**Don W. Jhonson,** [Alternate]

### CODE-MAKING PANEL NO. 16

**W. Douglas Pirkle,** [Principal]

### CODE-MAKING PANEL NO. 17

**Don W. Jhonson,** [Principal]

**Bobby J. Gray,** [Alternate]

### CODE-MAKING PANEL NO. 18

**Bobby J. Gray,** [Chair]

**Charles M. Trout,** [Alternate]

### CODE-MAKING PANEL NO. 19

**Thomas F. Thierheimer,** [Principal]

# Chapter 6

## Articles 600–695
### Special Equipment

# Installation Instructions for Listed Signs

## Code Language

**600.3 Listing.** Fixed, mobile, or portable electric signs, section signs, outline lighting, and retrofit kits, regardless of voltage, shall be listed, provided with installation instructions, and installed in conformance with that listing, unless otherwise approved by special permission.

**(A) Field-Installed Skeleton Tubing.** Field-installed skeleton tubing shall not be required to be listed where installed in conformance with this *Code*.

**(B) Outline Lighting.** Outline lighting shall not be required to be listed as a system when it consists of listed luminaires wired in accordance with Chapter 3.

*(See NEC for actual text)*

## Change Summary

- Retrofit kits for electric signs, section signs and some outline lighting systems must be listed and provided with installations instruction.

- With only limited exceptions, field-installed skeleton tubing and outline lighting must be provided with installation instructions.

- Listing requirements are in accordance with UL 48 *Electric Signs* and/or UL 879A *LED Sign and Sign Retrofit Kits*.

Comments: 18-43, 18-44
Proposals: 18-90, 18-91

## Significance of the Change

Recent advances in LED technology and energy conservation have significantly changed the electric sign and outline lighting industry. Rather than totally replacing electric signs, new retrofit kits allow updating existing signs to LED technology, thereby modernizing signs plus providing significant energy savings. Recently, UL 48, *Electric Signs*, updated required installation instructions to be delivered with the electric sign to the job site. The purpose of proposal 18-90 is to ensure that UL 48 requirements become mandatory and appear in *NEC* Section 600.3. The sign industry association desires strong language in Article 600 to ensure both electrical and structural safety. Now, safety-verified manufacturer's installation instructions are specifically delivered to the jobsite for the installer to use during the retrofit installation. The UL *White Book, Sign Conversions, Retrofit* (UYWU) describes UL's certification procedure under UL 879A, *Outline of Investigation for LED Kits*. UL's *Classified Kit* includes all the components and installation instructions to safely modify a sign. UL's *Product Guide to Inspections*, says, "Classification complies with the definition of "Listed" in model installation codes." These model installation codes refer to building codes, energy codes as well as the *NEC*. This strong new requirement builds on the present requirements of 110.3(B).

# Installation Marking Requirements for Most Signs

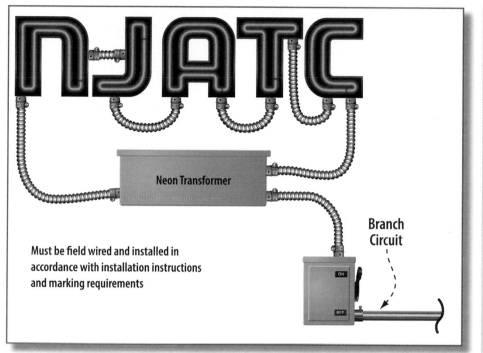

Neon Transformer

Branch Circuit

ON

OFF

Must be field wired and installed in accordance with installation instructions and marking requirements

## Code Language

**600.4 Markings.**

**(A) through (D)** ...(See *NEC* text)...

**(E) Installation Instructions.** All signs, outline lighting, skeleton tubing systems, and retrofit kits shall be marked to indicate that field wiring and installation instructions are required.

*Exception: Portable, cord-connected signs are not required to be marked.*

*(See NEC for actual text)*

## Significance of the Change

Many signs, outline lighting, skeleton tubing systems and associated retrofit kits are subjected to physical damaging conditions. Electric signs and related equipment can sometimes cause property damage and fires. Therefore, installation requirements and subsequent modification of installed electrical equipment is a serious safety concern that deserves close scrutiny by manufacturers as well as regulations within safety codes and standards. Section 110.3(B) requires listed or labeled equipment to be installed and used in accordance with any instructions included with the listing or labeling. With this change, the sign industry is raising the bar of installation integrity by requiring each listed sign, outline lighting, skeleton tubing systems and retrofit kits to be clearly marked that they must be field wired and installed in accordance with the installation requirements. This is not a subtle difference, but a challenging requirement for the installer, maintainer and repair worker of electric signs to perform the installation, modification and necessary field wiring in strict accordance with the manufacturer's and the listing agencies' instructions. Section 600.4(E) improves the usability and adds clarity for the marking and installation requirements of these sign products and changes in 600.12 also adds harmony for field-installed wiring for retrofit kit installations.

## Change Summary

- Previous marking requirements for section signs were changed to include installation marking requirements for all signs, and outline lighting within 600.4(E).
- Marking requirements apply to skeleton tubing systems and retrofit kits and do not apply to cord-connected and portable signs.
- Field-wiring instructions and installation instructions must be furnished with all equipment.

Comment: None
Proposal: 18-93

**NEW** **REVISION**

## Disconnect Required within Sight of the Sign

### Code Language

**600.6 Disconnects.** Each sign and outline lighting system, feeder circuit or branch circuit supplying …(See *NEC* text)…

**(A) Location.**

**(1) At Point of Entry to a Sign Enclosure.** The disconnect shall be located at the point the feeder circuit or branch circuit(s) supplying a sign or outline lighting system enters a sign enclosure or a pole in accordance with 600.5(C)(3) and shall disconnect all wiring where it enters the enclosure of the sign or pole.

*Exception: A disconnect shall not be required for branch or feeder circuits passing through the sign where enclosed in a Chapter 3 listed raceway.*

**(See NEC for actual text)**

### Change Summary

- A new 600.6(A)(1) has been added to 600.6(A) and previous subdivisions (1) and (2) have been changed to (2) and (3).
- Section 600.6(A)(1) is a significant worker safety issue requiring a sign disconnect where the circuit(s) enter the sign enclosure or pole.
- This safety-driven change simplifies worker compliance with both NFPA 70E and OSHA rules.

### Significance of the Change

The substantiation for this change points to a need for additional electrical safeguards for sign workers. In reality, sign supply conductors are often installed within a sign enclosure and run to the supply side of the randomly located disconnect mounted on the sign. These line-side supply conductors located within the sign enclosure remain energized whether or not the sign disconnect is turned off. Only the conductors from the load-side of the sign disconnect to the sign supply terminals are de-energized when the disconnect is opened. This practice exposes sign worker(s) to serious electrical hazards. Previous installation requirements did not specifically require all ungrounded conductors to be de-energized before entering a sign body or enclosure. Now, this new requirement of 600.6(A)(1) specifically requires the disconnecting means to be located at the point the feeder circuit or branch circuit(s) supplying a sign enters the sign enclosure or a supporting pole. Furthermore, the disconnecting means must disconnect all wiring where it enters the enclosure of the sign or pole. However, a practical and limited exception provides latitude to permit energized conductors within a sign only if they are installed using a Chapter 3 wiring method.

Comment: 18-47

Proposal: 18-99

For additional information, visit qr.njatcdb.org Item #1242

# Field-Installed Secondary Wiring

NECA Photo © Rob Colgan

## Code Language

**600.12 Field-Installed Secondary Wiring.** Field-installed secondary circuit wiring for electric signs, retrofit kits, outline lighting systems, and skeleton tubing systems shall be in accordance with their installation instructions and 600.12(A), (B), or (C).

*(See NEC for actual text)*

## Significance of the Change

Sign industry professionals again demonstrated their concerns by preparing many proposals and comments to add safety driven changes to the 2014 edition of the *NEC*. This change points out the importance of requiring product installation instructions be followed while installing field-installed secondary circuit wiring retrofit products. The installer must clearly understand that retrofit kit instructions are not a simple or optional guide to upgrade an existing product. The installer must realize that any deviation from the retrofit installation instructions is a serious *Code* violation. Instructions of retrofit kits are designed and specified to accomplish more than just the obvious "making it work." Therefore most considerations are with product safety, worker safety, and customer safety. Read, understand, and follow the installation instructions; these are the absolute *Code* minimum. The importance of following these requirements cannot be overstated. Industry standard UL 879A, *Outline of Investigation for LED Kits*, 22.1, describes the required content of installation instructions for retrofit kits. For many retrofit installers this is already standard practice. However, some industry workers are being served notices to upgrade their installation practices and to follow the installations instructions in a precise manner for the safety of all.

## Change Summary

- Retrofit kits for field-installed secondary wiring are specifically required to be installed according to their installation instructions.

- Secondary wiring retrofit kits must conform to either 600.31 for 1000 volts or less, or 600.32 for over 1000 volts, nominal.

- Retrofit kits using Class 2 secondary wiring must follow 600.12(C) and comply with 600.33.

Comment: None

Proposal: 18-109

# Article 605

Article 605 Office Furnishings

## Office Furnishings

### Code Language

**Article 605 Office Furnishings**

**605.1 Scope.** This article covers electrical equipment, lighting accessories, and wiring systems used to connect, contained within, or installed on office furnishings.

**605.2 Definition.**

**Office Furnishing.** Cubicle panels, partitions, study carrels, workstations, desks, shelving systems, and storage units that may be mechanically and electrically interconnected to form an office furnishing system.

**605.3 General.** ...(See *NEC* text)...

**605.4 Wireways.** ...(See *NEC* text)...

**605.5 Office Furnishing Interconnections.** ...(See *NEC* text)...

**605.6 Lighting Accessories.** ...(See *NEC* text)...

**605.7** through **605.9** ...(See *NEC* text)...

*(See NEC for actual text)*

### Change Summary

- Article 605 is now titled Office Furnishings.
- The scope and references replaced the term *wired partitions* with *office furnishings*.
- A definition for *office furnishing* is included in Article 605.
- The term *appliances* was revised to *utilization equipment* to correctly describe the type of equipment intended to be supplied by the office furnishing electrical system.

Comments: 18-52,18-54
Proposals: 18-125a,
18-126, 18-128, 18-129a

### Significance of the Change

Article 605 Office Furnishings (and subtitled as Consisting of Lighting Accessories and Wired Partitions) was first introduced into the 1984 edition of the *NEC*. This article continued to be used mainly in office construction and permitted the use of prefabricated and relocatable office partitions. These partitions most often included a wiring channel along the bottom of the assembly containing a pre-molded electrical and tele/data factory assembly using molded outlets. For 2014, this article was updated and revised in an effort to modernize, expand and permit a more complete line of office furnishing in lieu of simple pre-wired and relocatable office partitions. Manufacturers are moving away from traditional office panels to more modern offices featuring interconnected desks and storage systems and other furnishings. These office furnishings are powered with the same type of electrical distribution systems used in the office panels so that the furnishing system can be electrically interconnected and supplied by branch circuits and communications cables.

Chapter 6 • Articles 600–695

## Selective Coordination

*Courtesy of Bill McGovern/IAEI*

### Significance of the Change

For elevators and similar equipment, the requirement to selectively coordinate overcurrent protective devices used to protect an elevator driven machines first appeared in 620-51 of the 1993 *NEC*. Later clarified and moved into 620-62 for 1996 *NEC*, this twenty year old requirement has served our industry well, continuing to prevent short circuits or overloads on a single driven machine from affecting the power supply of another elevator or a bank of elevators supplied from the same feeder. This 2014 *NEC* significant change limits the application of selective coordination of elevator systems to professional engineers and qualified persons only. These professional engineers and qualified persons must engage primarily in the design, installation, or maintenance of electrical systems. Providing selective coordination of specific overcurrent protective devices requires specific manufacturer's technical knowledge as well as training. In addition, the selection of fuse characteristics and/or proper circuit breaker setting must be documented and made available to those authorized to design, install, inspect, maintain, and operate the elevator system.

### Code Language

**620.62 Selective Coordination.** Where more than one driving machine disconnecting means is supplied by a single feeder, the overcurrent protective devices in each disconnecting means shall be selectively coordinated with any other supply side overcurrent protective devices.

Selective coordination shall be selected by a licensed professional engineer or other qualified person engaged primarily in the design, installation, or maintenance of electrical systems. The selection shall be documented and made available to those authorized to design, install, inspect, maintain, and operate the system.

*(See NEC for actual text)*

### Change Summary

- Selective Coordination must be selected by a licensed professional engineer or other design, installation, or maintenance qualified persons engaged in the business.
- Technical documentation must be available to those authorized to design, install, inspect, maintain, and operate the particular system.
- These requirements ensure only professionals and qualified persons with select and document this coordination.

Comment: None
Proposal: 12-50

# Article 625

## Reorganization and Expansion of Article 625

### Code Language

**Article 625 Electric Vehicle Charging System**

**I. General**

**625.1 Scope.** The provisions of this article cover the electrical conductors and equipment external to an electric vehicle that connect an electric vehicle to a supply of electricity…(See *NEC* text)…

Informational Note No. 2: UL 2594-2013, *Standard for Electric Vehicle Supply Equipment*, is a safety standard for electric vehicle supply equipment. UL 2202-2009, *Standard for Electric Vehicle Charging System Equipment*, is a safety standard for electric vehicle charging equipment.

**II. Equipment Construction.** …(See *NEC* text)…

**III. Installation.** …(See *NEC* text)…

*(See NEC for actual text)*

### Change Summary

- Article 625 has been reorganized to provide a more logical layout and consistency with other articles in Chapter 6.
- New Informational Note No. 2 has been added following 625.1 and references UL 2594-2013 *Standard for Electric Vehicle Supply Equipment*.
- Part II has been re-identified as Equipment Construction and Part III has been identified as Installation.

Comments: 12-19, 12-20, 12-27a,

Proposal: 12-52

### Significance of the Change

Growth of electric vehicle production as well as the needs of the charging infrastructure have substantially increased in the last few years. To meet these needs, Article 625 has been reorganized and updated providing a practical layout and improved usability of present day electrical requirements. Also, as needed revisions and requirements were provided to accommodate evolving electric vehicle charging equipment technology. The scope was revised to include inductive charging systems and technology. A new informational note was added following the article scope and specifically references UL 2594-2013, *Standard for Electric Vehicle Supply Equipment*, and UL 2202-2009, *Standard for Electric Vehicle Charging System Equipment*. This note identifies the correct product safety standards to which this equipment is evaluated, tested and certified. The article parts have been rearranged for consistency and where necessary, the sections within those parts have been relocated and re-identified for clarity and usability. Various technical revisions were also incorporated into Article 625 as a result of two 2011 Tentative Interim Amendments (TIAs) and other proposals accepted by CMP-12. This updated arrangement should simplify application of the various electric vehicle charging by specifying designers and engineers, installers, and *Code* enforcers.

# Definition of Cable Management System for EVSE

Courtesy of EVSE, LLC

## Significance of the Change

A new definition of the term *Cable Management System* has been added to 625.2. Comment 12-20 introduced a concept of paralleling the definition of the term *Cable Management System* that is already included in Article 626 and defined in 626.2. This term was already included in 625.17(C) but was never defined within Article 625. Section 625.17 includes provisions covering cord and cable lengths and methods of protecting cables that are not part of a cable management system that is integral to the electric vehicle supply equipment. Including the new defined term that applies specifically to electric vehicle supply equipment will assist installers and inspectors in applying cable protection requirements. Some electric vehicle supply equipment is manufactured with a cable management system that is an integral part of the equipment. A good example of this type of EVSE is ceiling-mounted equipment. For this type of equipment, an automatic retractable cord system minimizes the possibilities of physical damage by controlling the cable length and exposure while connected and operational.

## Change Summary

- A new definition of the term *Cable Management System (Electric Vehicle Supply Equipment)* has been added to 625.2.

- This term is used in 625.17(C) and was undefined in previous editions of the *NEC*.

- This new definition parallels the same defined term used in 626.2 and will assist in addressing methods to protect EV connection cables.

Comment: 12-20
Proposal: 12-52

# Electric Vehicle Supply Equipment Circuit Rating

## Code Language

**625.41 Rating.** Electric vehicle supply equipment shall have sufficient rating to supply the load served. Electric vehicle charging loads shall be considered to be continuous loads for the purposes of this article. Where an automatic load management system is used, the maximum electric vehicle supply equipment load on a service and feeder shall be the maximum load permitted by the automatic load management system.

*Courtesy of EVSE, LLC*

## Change Summary

- Former 625.14 has been revised and relocated to 625.41 based on approved TIA 11-3 (SC 11-10-5/TIA 1038).

- A new last sentence that includes provisions for automatic load management systems has been added to 625.41.

- The maximum EVSE load on a service and feeder shall be the maximum load permitted by the automatic load management system.

## Significance of the Change

Electric vehicle supply equipment (EVSE) is considered as a continuous duty load. The load for Level 1 EVSE can be continuous for 8 to 12 hours to achieve full charge. For Level 2 EVSE, the load is also continuous, operating anywhere between 4 to 8 hours. Level 2 EVSE have a typical load profile of 30 to 50 amperes. This level of current running continuous, places considerable demand on electric services and feeders, especially for smaller residential services. The service or feeder is generally required to have capacity to supply the load served. Section 220.14 provides requirements for inclusion of EVSE in load calculations. This cycle, CMP-12 accepted a provision that recognizes an automatic load management system that limits the load on the service or feeder to their capabilities. The catch is that the load management system is automatic and limits the load on a service and feeder to the maximum load permitted by the automatic load management system. This new alternative will be useful for existing services and sources that are not quite capable of handling the additional continuous duty EVSE load. The automatic load management system provides the load shedding and limits necessary to protect the service or feeder from overload and eventual failure.

Comment: 12-27a

Proposals: 12-52, 12-63 TIA 1038

# Electric Vehicle Supply Equipment Connections

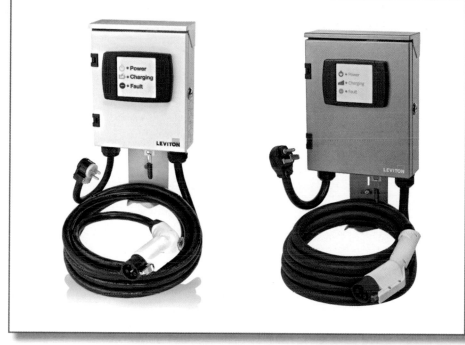

*Courtesy of Leviton Mfg. Co.*

## Code Language

**625.44 Electric Vehicle Supply Equipment Connection.** Electric vehicle supply equipment shall be permitted to be cord- and plug-connected to the premises wiring system in accordance with one of the following:

**(A) Connections to 125-Volt, Single-Phase, 15- and 20-Ampere Receptacle Outlets.** Electric vehicle supply equipment intended for connection to nonlocking, 2-pole, 3-wire grounding-type receptacle outlets rated at 125 V, single phase, 15 and 20 amperes or from a supply of less than 50 volts dc.

**(B) Connections to Other Receptacle Outlets.** Electric vehicle supply equipment that is rated 250 V maximum and complies with...(See *NEC* text)...

*(See NEC for actual text)*

## Significance of the Change

Part III of Article 625 covers electric vehicle supply equipment installations. In the 2011 *NEC*, there was confusion as to which EVSE was permitted to be cord-and-plug-connected and which units had to be direct wired to the individual branch circuit. The problem was significant enough to trigger a Tentative Interim Amendment TIA 11-2 (SC 11-10-4/TIA 1037) that provided the necessary clarification. As required by the NFPA Regulations Governing Committee Projects, the TIA was introduced as a proposal during the 2014 *NEC* development process. The result expanded provisions covering requirements for EVSE connections for both direct-wired types and cord-and-plug connected types. It should be noted that the EVSE is required to be listed and as such, should include installation instructions that provide the alternatives for direct connection or cord connection based on the listing of the product. Proposal 12-52 resulted in reorganization of Article 625 and the result is a relocation of 625.13 to 625.44 in Part III of the article. The revision not only improves usability, it addresses concerns expressed by EVSE manufacturers during the 2011 *NEC* cycle. The revision clarifies that EVSE above 125 volts but not exceeding 250 volts is permitted to be direct wired or cord-and-plug connected to an individual branch circuit where listed and identified.

## Change Summary

- Former 625.13 has been relocated to 625.44 and revised based on approved TIA 11-2 (SC 11-10-4/TIA 1037).

- Subdivision (A) covers cord-connected 125-volt electric vehicle supply equipment and (B) covers all others.

- The revision clarifies that Level 2 EVSE is permitted to be direct wired or cord- and plug-connected in accordance with 625.17(B)(1) through (4).

Comments: 12-31, 12-41, 12-39

Proposals: 12-52, 12-61,TIA 1037

**REVISION** | **RELOCATE**

# Electric Vehicle Supply Equipment Locations

## Code Language

**625.50 Location.** The electric vehicle supply equipment shall be located for direct electrical coupling of the EV connector (conductive or inductive) to the electric vehicle. Unless specifically listed and marked for the location, the coupling means of the electric vehicle supply equipment shall be stored or located at a height of not less than 450 mm (18 in.) above the floor level for indoor locations and 600 mm (24 in.) above the grade level for outdoor locations.

*(See NEC for actual text)*

*Courtesy of EVSE, LLC*

## Change Summary

- Former 625.29 has been relocated to 625.50 in Part III of Article 625 titled Installation.

- The revision incorporates inductive charging technologies and clarifies the locations permitted for the vehicle coupling means.

- The revision removes the 4-foot upper height limitation for indoor and outdoor EVSE and recognizes use of cable management systems.

Comment: None

Proposals: 12-52, 12-65, 12-77a

## Significance of the Change

Article 625 has been reorganized to provide a more logical layout. Part III now provides electric vehicle supply equipment (EVSE) installation requirements. The first sentence of 625.50 clarifies that the coupling means must be located for direct electrical coupling of the EV connector to the electric vehicle and applies to both conductive and inductive technologies. Currently, conductive connections are the most common means of coupling the vehicle charger to the EVSE, but indicative charging technologies are in development, as are applicable product safety standards. This section previously included upper height limitations for locating the vehicle coupling means for indoor installations. By incorporating outdoor provisions from former 625.30, this section now addresses location and storage requirements for both indoor and outdoor installations. The lower storage location height limitations remain at 18 inches for indoor locations, and 24 inches for outdoor installations. The previous upper height storage limit of 48 inches, derived from ADA guidelines, was subjective and seldom enforceable and has been removed. Modern EVSE technology has evolved to configurations that store the vehicle coupling means above 48 inches, such as those that are included in EVSE that has an integral cable management system located on a structure or ceiling.

# Arc-Welder Disconnecting Means

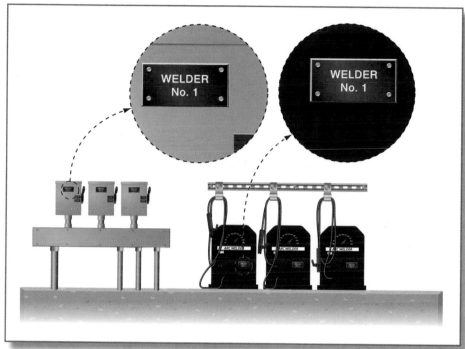

## Significance of the Change

In the past, the identification of each welder disconnecting means was sometimes confusing based upon the varied installations, especially using multiple welders. For temporary installations, the exact identification of each welder in a bank of welders was sometimes near impossible. The most common issue is how to specifically match a welder with the correct disconnecting means after additional welders are added or subtracted over time. This new change uses the words "The disconnecting means identity ..." to ensure that each and every welder disconnecting means is labeled with the correct identity or uniqueness from other disconnecting means nearby. The panel agreed, with the intent of the proposal, to identify the disconnecting means for each arc welder. In addition to revising the first sentence, CMP-12 added one additional sentence requiring compliance with the marking requirements of 110.22(A). This added requirement points to "...legibly marked to indicate its purpose ..." and the marking to be "...of sufficient durability to withstand the environment involved." From all points of view, a well defined and clearly marked identity label added to each arc welder disconnecting means provides additional safety on a project.

## Code Language

**630.13 Disconnecting Means.** A disconnecting means shall be provided in the supply circuit for each arc welder that is not equipped with a disconnect mounted as an integral part of the welder. The disconnecting means identity shall be marked in accordance with 110.22(A).

The disconnecting means shall be a switch or circuit breaker, and its rating shall be not less than that necessary to accommodate overcurrent protection as specified under 630.12.

*(See NEC for actual text)*

## Change Summary

- Each arc welder without an integral disconnecting means must be provided with a field installed supply-circuit disconnecting means.
- The identity of each arc-welder disconnecting means must be legibly marked to indicate its specific purpose.
- The required marking shall be of sufficient durability to withstand the environment involved.

Comment: 12-53
Proposal: 12-93

# IT Rooms Using Auxiliary Grounding Electrodes

## Code Language

**645.14 System Grounding.** Separately derived power systems shall be installed in accordance with the provisions of Part I and II of Article 250. Power systems ... (See *NEC* text )... 250.30.

**645.15 Equipment Grounding and Bonding.** All exposed non–current-carrying metal parts of an information technology system shall be bonded to the equipment grounding conductor in accordance with the provisions of Parts I, V, VI, VII, and VIII of Article 250 or shall be double insulated. Power systems derived within listed information technology equipment that supply information technology systems through receptacles or cable assemblies supplied as part of this equipment shall not be considered separately derived for the purpose of applying 250.30. Where signal...shall be installed in accordance with 250.54.

...(See *NEC* text)...

*(See NEC for actual text)*

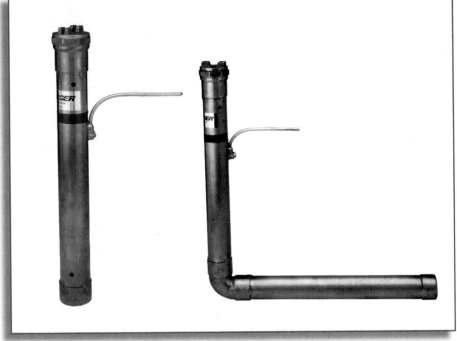

*Courtesy of Harger Lightning and Grounding*

## Change Summary

- A new last sentence requires all auxiliary grounding electrode(s) installed for information technology equipment to comply with 250.54.

- Specific bonding provisions and options are found within Parts I, V, VI, VII, and VIII of Article 250 or shall be double insulated.

- System grounding requirements from previous 645.15 were moved to new section 645.14 System Grounding.

Comment: 12-68
Proposal: 12-139

## Significance of the Change

CMP-12 agreed to divide the grounding requirements of 645.15 for the 2011 *NEC* into two logical sections: 645.14 System Grounding, and 645.15 Equipment Grounding and Bonding. Separating and providing comprehensive detailed requirements for each topic provides clarity and usability to the user. For the 2014 *NEC*, within 645.15, again CMP-12 chose to modify the requirements by providing the user with an all-inclusive list of parts related to the bonding requirements of Article 250. In regards to equipment grounding, a new last sentence requiring the use of 250.54 was added due to some existing confusion about what constitutes an isolated ground as it relates to computer installations. Installing a separate electrode connection to the earth that is not connected to the equipment grounding conductor of the branch circuits and feeders supplying information technology equipment is not a "*Code*-compliant" isolated ground and is a violation of the general requirements in 250.4(A)(5) and (B)(4) as well as 250.54. This new sentence provides clear direction and correlation for users about required connections between auxiliary grounding electrodes and equipment grounding conductors. The earth should never serve as an effective ground fault current path.

# Selective Coordination for COPS Data Systems

### Code Language

**645.27 Selective Coordination.** Critical operations data system(s) overcurrent protective devices shall be selectively coordinated with all supply-side overcurrent protective devices.

*(See NEC for actual text)*

## Significance of the Change

A Critical Operations Data System is described as an information technology equipment system that requires continuous operation for reasons of public safety, emergency management, national security, or business continuity. Since these systems are required to be operational by law or for business reasons, they are permitted to follow Article 645 unless specifically required to comply with more stringent requirements of Article 708, Critical Operations Power Systems (COPS). Throughout the *NEC*, selective coordination is an electrical engineering tool often specified and used to avoid a short circuit or overload in a single branch circuit from causing the automatic disconnection of other branch circuits and feeders. A lack of selective coordination reduces the reliability of these systems and negates the benefits of redundancy provisions that are typically designed into these systems. New for the 2014 *NEC*, selective coordination has been added to the requirements of overcurrent protective devices serving to protect the Critical Operations Data System from single circuit overloads and short circuits causing the interruption of critical feeders or wider outages.

### Change Summary

- *Critical Operations Data Systems* are defined as a continuous operation for reasons of public safety, emergency management, national security, or business continuity.
- Overcurrent devices of a critical operations data system must be selectively coordinated with supply side overcurrent protective devices.
- Coordination (Selective) localizes overcurrent conditions to restrict outages to circuits affected. See Article 100.

Comment: None

Proposals: 12-143

# Article 646

**NEW**

## Modular Data Centers

### Code Language

**Article 646 Modular Data Centers**

**I. General**

**646.1 Scope.** This article covers modular data centers.

**646.2 Definitions.** The definitions in 645.2 shall apply. For the purposes of this article, the following additional definition applies.

**Modular Data Center (MDC).** Prefabricated units, rated 600 volts or less, consisting of an outer enclosure housing multiple racks or cabinets of information technology equipment (ITE) (e.g., servers) and various support equipment, such as electrical service and distribution equipment, HVAC systems, and the like….(See *NEC* text)…

**646.3 Other Articles.** …(See *NEC* text )…

*(See NEC for actual text)*

### Change Summary

- A new Article 646 titled Modular Data Centers has been added to Chapter 6.
- Modular data centers are prefabricated units of information technology equipment and support equipment.
- Modular data centers are intended for fixed installation either indoors or outdoors.
- Article 646 closely follows Article 645, Information Technology Equipment and NFPA 75, Standard for the Protection of Information Technology Equipment.

Comments: 12-71, 12-74, 12-77, 12-80

Proposal: 12-147

### Significance of the Change

Modular Data Centers (MDCs) are important emerging trends in data center architecture. Their construction, installation and use results in a unique hybrid piece of equipment that falls somewhere in between a large enclosure and a pre-fabricated building. One informational note adds "A typical construction may use a standard ISO shipping container(s) or other structure as the outer enclosure." Placing modular data centers within ISO standardized shipping containers allow modular assemblies of data centers to be easily loaded and unloaded, moved, stacked, securely transported and tracked efficiency. Standardized containers permit distance shipping via truck, tandem trailer, rail and intercontinental shipping possible. Article 646 generally limits modular data centers wiring methods and materials by requiring only listed and labeled equipment to follow the requirements within the Article 646. Article 646 was added to the *NEC* because it is not always obvious which requirements in the *NEC* were applicable or how they should be applied, given the complexity, customization and scalability of modular data centers. This new article provides requirements that enhance safety, support the design and development of safe products and provide clarity for installers, end users and Authorities Having Jurisdiction (AHJs).

# GFCI for Single-Phase Pool Pump Motors

*Courtesy of Schneider Electric*

## Code Language

**680.21 Motors.**

**(A) Wiring Methods.** ....(See *NEC* text)...

**(B) Double Insulated Pool Pumps.** ...(See *NEC* text)...

**(C) GFCI Protection.** Outlets supplying pool pump motors connected to single-phase, 120-volt through 240-volt branch circuits, whether by receptacle or by direct connection, shall be provided with ground-fault circuit-interrupter protection for personnel.

*(See NEC for actual text)*

## Significance of the Change

This section no longer addresses a specific ampere rating for a single–phase 120 volt through 240 volt motor. Therefore, all single-phase 120 volt through 240 volt pool pump motors of any amperage, must be provided with ground-fault circuit-interrupter protection for personnel.

According to the substantiation of the proposal, a single 1.5 HP, 230 volt pool pump motor would be permitted to be installed on a 25 ampere branch circuit without GFCI protection whereas a 1 HP 230 volt motor would require a 20 ampere overcurrent device in addition to ground-fault circuit-interrupter protection for personnel. The substantiation continues by asking the simple question "If there is a shock hazard potential for 20 ampere branch circuits feeding pool pump motors, doesn't the same shock hazard apply to 25 ampere branch circuits or any size branch circuits feeding single-phase pool pump motors?" The *Code* making panel accepted this proposal without a statement.

## Change Summary

- The phrase "rated 15 or 20 amperes," has been deleted from this section.

- All single–phase 120-volt through 240-volt outlets supplying pool motors must have GFCI protection for personnel regardless of their ampere rating.

- These requirements apply to both receptacle connected and directly connected pool pump motors.

Comment: None
Proposal: 17-100

## Pool Pump Receptacle

### Code Language

**680.22 Lighting, Receptacles, and Equipment**

**(A) Receptacles.**

**(2) Circulation and Sanitation System, Location.** Receptacles that provide power for water-pump motors or for other loads directly related to the circulation and sanitation system shall be located at least 3.0 m (10 ft) from the inside walls of the pool, or not less than 1.83 m (6 ft) from the inside walls of the pool if they meet all of the following conditions:

(1) Consist of single receptacles

(2) Are of the grounding type

(3) Have GFCI protection

*(See NEC for actual text)*

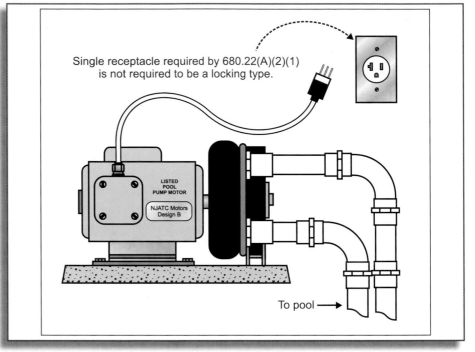

Single receptacle required by 680.22(A)(2)(1) is not required to be a locking type.

LISTED POOL PUMP MOTOR

NJATC Motors Design B

To pool →

### Change Summary

- 680.22(A)(2) list item "(2) Employ a locking configuration", has been deleted.

- Removing this locking configuration from 680.22(A)(2) matches existing requirements of Other Receptacles, Location not less than 6 feet from pool in 680.22(A)(3).

- Single receptacles of the grounding type and provided with GFCI protection for personnel are now considered sufficient safety measures for these locations.

### Significance of the Change

For the 2011 *NEC*, in wiring permanently installed swimming pools, receptacles outlets located for water-pump motors or other loads directly related to pool circulation, that are located less than 6 feet from the inside walls of the pool are required to be single receptacles of the grounding-type, have GFCI protection for personnel and be of the locking type. For the 2014 *NEC*, these receptacles are no longer required to be of the locking type. A proposal noted that similar outlets located less than 6 feet from the pool did have the same requirements except they did not have a locking configuration. The submitter presented a question to CMP-17 asking why is a receptacle for a circulation or sanitation system required to have the restriction of a locking configuration. The panel accepted the recommendation. *NEC* Code Making Panels are not required to provide a response for a panel action of Accept.

Comment: 17-31
Proposals: 17-101, 17-104, 17-105

# Bonded Conductive Surface in Direct Contact with Pool Water

## Code Language

**680.26 Equipotential Bonding.**

**(A) Performance.** ...(See *NEC* text)...

**(B) Bonded Parts.** ...(See *NEC* text)...

**(C) Pool Water.** Where none of the bonded parts is in direct connection with the pool water, the pool water shall be in direct contact with an approved corrosion-resistant conductive surface that exposes not less than 5800 mm² (9 in.²) of surface area to the pool water at all times. The conductive surface shall be located where it is not exposed to physical damage or dislodgement during usual pool activities, and it shall be bonded in accordance with 680.26(B).

*(See NEC for actual text)*

## Significance of the Change

The equipotential bonding requirements for permanently installed pools in Section 680.26(C) Pool Water have been rewritten for clarity and usability. The performance requirements for this section require pool water for permanently installed pools to be in contact with the metallic surface of bonded metal part(s) at all times thereby ensuring a difference in potential never exists between the pool water and any metal parts within or near a permanently installed pool. Some permanently installed pool designs and construction techniques preclude bonded metal parts from being in direct contact with pool water. Therefore CMP-17 is charged with writing requirements to ensure that pool water is in direct contact with an added bonded metal part. Accepted proposal 17-131 stated that the 2011 requirement was difficult to understand and recommended new *Code* language to replace the 2011 requirement. This new language contains detailed and accurate requirements, it is easily understood and clearly enforceable. The substantiation notes the proposal requirement of 9 in.² metal surfaces in direct contact with the pool water is technically valid based on previous action of the panel and these requirements provide the inspection community with the tools they need to enforce this provision as intended.

## Change Summary

- Where pool construction does not permit pool water to be in contact with bonded metal surfaces, an approved corrosion-resistant conductive surface that exposes not less than 9 in.² of surface area to the pool water at all times is required to be installed.

- This conductive surface must not be subject to physical damage.

Comment: None

Proposal: 17-131

# Bonding Outdoor Spas and Hot Tubs

## Code Language

**680.42 Outdoor Installations.**

**(A) Flexible Connections.**

**(B) Bonding.** Bonding …(See *NEC* text)… as required in 680.26.

Equipotential bonding of perimeter surfaces in accordance with 680.26(B)(2) shall not be required to be provided for spas and hot tubs where all of the following conditions apply:

(1) The spa or hot tub shall be listed as a self-contained spa for aboveground use.

(2) The spa or hot tub shall not be identified as suitable only for indoor use.

(3) The installation shall be in accordance with the manufacturer's instructions and shall be located on or above grade.

(4) …(See *NEC* text)…

Informational Note: …(See *NEC* text)…

*(See NEC for actual text)*

iStock Courtesy of NECA

## Change Summary

- This 2014 change originated as Tentative Interim Amendment 1005 for the 2011 *NEC*.

- Based on four specific criteria, spas and hot tubs listed for outdoor use may be exempt from the perimeter surfaces equipotential bonding requirements of 680.26(B)(2).

- The class of spas referred in this section is a self-contained outdoor/indoor rated UL1563 listed product.

## Significance of the Change

Unfortunately, outdoor self-contained spas that are manufactured "appliance" units tested and listed under UL 1563, designed and intended to be installed on or above grade, were required to follow the same *NEC* rules as custom in-ground spas and built-in swimming for perimeter bonding. In reality, the two categories have very different concerns of safety and enforcement. This difference was recognized for indoor spas and for storable pools, both of which are excluded from perimeter bonding requirements of 680.26. However, the application of 680.26 bonding requirements in the 2008 and 2011 *NEC* to outdoor spas created undue expense and difficulty for home owners who wish to install a listed portable spa in their back yard. This change began as a Tentative Interim Amendment (TIA) No. 1005 for the 2011 *NEC*. It provided interim relief for listed spas and hot tubs using a positive language exemption for listed equipment installed according to UL 1563, ANSI/UL 1563-2010, *Standard for Electric Spas, Equipment Assemblies, and Associated Equipment*. For the 2014 *NEC*, the existing TIA language was revised for enforceability and provided additional clarity to the four specific criteria items permitting the installation of listed indoor/outdoor spas without following the requirements of 680.26.

Comment: 17-46

Proposals: 17-142, 17-144

# Wiring Methods Supplying Indoor Spas and Hot Tubs

## Code Language

**680.43 Indoor Installations.**

A spa or hot tub installed indoors shall comply with the provisions of Parts I and II of this article except as modified by this section and shall be connected by the wiring methods of Chapter 3.

*Exception No. 1: Listed spa and hot tub …(See NEC text)…*

*Exception No. 2: The equipotential bonding …(See NEC text)…*

*Exception No. 3: For dwelling unit(s) only, where a listed spa or hot tub is installed indoors, the wiring method requirements of 680.42(C) shall also apply.*

**(See NEC for actual text)**

## Significance of the Change

Article 680.43 Indoor installations of spas and hot tubs requires that the provisions of Part I. General, and Part II. Permanently Installed Pools, be applied except as modified by 680.43 and shall be connected by the wiring methods of Chapter 3. But according to the proposal 680.42(C) Interior Wiring to Outdoor Installations contained less restrictive wiring requirements. CMP-17 accepted the proposed recommendation to use the wiring requirements of 680.42(C) allowing for common wiring requirements for all interior wiring supplying listed spas and hot tubs whether they were located indoors or outdoors. New Exception No. 3, by referencing 680.42(C), permits listed indoor spas and hot tubs in dwelling units be supplied by any Chapter 3 wiring method containing a copper equipment grounding conductor insulated or enclosed in the cable jacket not smaller than 12 AWG. This new exception now closely aligns the *Code* requirements with more clarity while remaining distinct between indoor and outdoor type installations.

## Change Summary

- New Exception No. 3 permits Chapter 3 wiring methods provided with an individual 12 AWG insulated or covered equipment grounding conductor to supply listed spas and hot tubs for dwelling units by referencing 680.42(C).
- New exception eliminates confusion in selecting interior wiring requirements.
- Reference to 680.42(C) also covers wiring requirements supplying underwater luminaires.

Comment: None

Proposal: 17-146

# Definition for Direct Current (dc) Combiner

## Code Language

**690.2 Definitions.**

**Direct-Current (dc) Combiner.** A device used in the PV source and PV output circuits to combine two or more dc circuit inputs and provide one dc circuit output.

*(See NEC for actual text)*

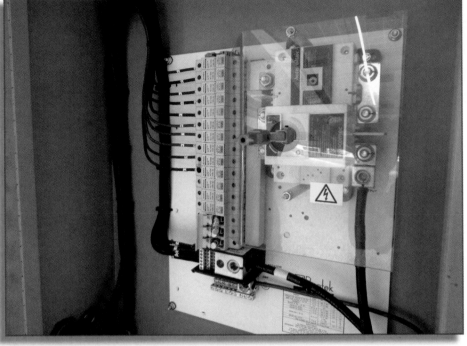

*Courtesy of San Diego Electrical JATC*

## Change Summary

- A new definition for *Direct Current (dc) Combiner* was added to Article 690 using common language for a specific product within the PV industry.
- Sections 690.4 requires a direct current (dc) combiner to be identified and listed for the application.
- All circuits in the direct current (dc) combiner require grouping and identification.

## Significance of the Change

Article 690-Solar Photovoltaic Systems was first introduced into the 1984 *NEC* to institute electrical safety requirements into a technical hobby of assembling batteries and solar arrays to provide lighting and heating from the sun. The Solar (PV) industry has made great strides by using modular systems, high efficiency panels, and participating in electrical safety standards over the past 30 years. Thus the systems of today are becoming more reliable and safer. Since the 2011 *NEC*, all wiring and equipment needs be installed only by qualified persons. For the 2014 *NEC*, changes continue to focus on reliability and safety. Older system combiners were originally splices inside a pull box with little or no wire markings and therefore difficult to identify during repairs. Different names were given to dc combiners such as a Source Circuit Combiners, Recombiners, Subcombiners, etc. Since the requirements should be the same no matter where in the circuit the combiner is located, there is now a single defined term that covers all dc combiners. Today, direct current (dc) combiners are required to be listed and identified. The wiring in and out from the direct current (dc) combiner devices require identification and grouping in accordance with 690.31(B).

Comment: 4-81
Proposal: 4-173

# Definition for Multimode Inverter

*Courtesy of Eaton Corporation*

## Code Language

**690.2 Definitions.**

**Multimode Inverter.** Equipment having the capabilities of both the utility-interactive inverter and the stand-alone inverter.

*(See NEC for actual text)*

## Significance of the Change

Inverters are used throughout the electrical industry and generally defined as equipment or a device that changes dc into ac. The general term inverter and specialized types of inverter definitions appear in Articles 100, 690 and 694 and 705. A simple stand-alone inverter is common and often generic for specified ratings within certain systems or as part of a simple UPS. A multimode inverter is a complex device allowing interconnection with a serving utility plus a separate interconnection to a standalone system. This more exact definition is necessary to define how a multimode inverter operates in order to clarify some of the connection and critical safety requirements. This definition was added in both Article 690 and Article 705 because a multimode inverter may interface with other equipment covered by requirements in both articles. As Solar Photovoltaic (PV) systems become more complex, it should be recognized that additional contractor and electrician training together with certification must be obtained to stay on top of this challenging electrical solar industry.

## Change Summary

- A new definition for *multimode inverter* was added to Article 690.
- This defined term now permits common language within the PV industry.
- Since a multimode inverter performs the function of a utility interactive inverter, this device must also comply with the specific utility requirements as well as the requirements of Article 705, Parts I and II.

Comment: None
Proposal: 4-181

# Warning Signs Comply With 110.21(B)

## Code Language

**690.5 Ground-Fault Protection.**

**(A) Ground-Fault Detection and Interruption.** ...(See *NEC* text)...

**(B) Isolating Faulted Circuits.** ...(See *NEC* text)...

**(C) Labels and Markings.** A warning label shall appear on the utility-interactive inverter or be applied by the installer near the ground-fault indicator at a visible location, stating the following:
WARNING
ELECTRIC SHOCK HAZARD
IF A GROUND FAULT IS INDICATED, NORMALLY GROUNDED CONDUCTORS MAY BE UNGROUNDED AND ENERGIZED
When the PV system also has batteries, the same warning shall also be applied by the installer in a visible location at the batteries. The warning sign(s) or label(s) shall comply with 110.21(B).

*(See NEC for actual text)*

## Change Summary

- A new last sentence was added to 690.5(C) Labels and Markings requiring compliance with 110.21(B) for warning signs located at the utility-interactive inverter, near the ground-fault indicator and at batteries for the photovoltaic (PV) system.
- Specific requirements apply to field-applied hazard markings or labels using signal words "danger", "warning", or "caution" as provided in 110.21(B).

## Significance of the Change

The existing text of 690.5 (A) through (C) has been retained. A new last sentence was added to (C) Labels and Markings to notify the user that warning signs must comply with 110.21(B). Warning signs are required within 690.5 for three specific locations. These areas of concern are at the utility-interactive inverter, near the ground-fault indicator and at batteries for the photovoltaic (PV) system. Also new for the 2014 *NEC*, Section 110.21(B) prescribes the requirements associated with field-applied hazard markings. Rules for field-applied markings require effective and consistent hazard warnings using appropriate colors, words, or symbols. This proposal is one of several coordinated companion proposals that now provide consistency of danger, caution, and warning sign or markings as required in the *NEC*. These changes promote a more consistent approach in developing and application of the hazard markings, labels, and signs for wiring methods and equipment that exist throughout the *NEC*. Mandatory references back to Chapter 1 also serve as a *NJATC Codeology* reminder that according to 90.3, latter chapters, such as Chapter 6, supplement or modify the general rules of Chapters 1 through 4.

Comment: 4-114
Proposal: 4-215

# Some PV Systems Raise Voltages to 1000 Volts

## Code Language

**690.7 Maximum Voltage.**

**(A) Maximum Photovoltaic System Voltage.** ...(See *NEC* text)...

**(B) Direct-Current Utilization Circuits.** ...(See *NEC* text)...

**(C) Photovoltaic Source and Output Circuits.** In one- and two-family dwellings, PV source circuits and PV output circuits that do not include lampholders, fixtures, or receptacles shall be permitted to have a maximum PV system voltage up to 600 volts. Other installations with a maximum PV system voltage over 1000 volts shall comply with Article 690, Part IX.

*(See NEC for actual text)*

## Significance of the Change

This proposal is the work of the High Voltage Task Group appointed by the Technical Correlating Committee. The Task Group identified the demand for increasing voltage levels used in wind generation and pV systems as an area for consideration to enhance existing *NEC* requirements to address these new common voltage levels. The task group recognized that general requirements in Chapters 1 through 4 need to be modified before identifying and generating proposals to articles such as 690 specific for PV systems. These systems have moved above 600 volts and are reaching 1000 volts due to standard configurations and increases in efficiency and performance. By not changing the 600 volts limitations for one- and two-family dwellings, CMP 4 has made it clear that one and two family dwellings should not be dealing with AC voltages above 600 volts. Therefore the 600 volt limit continues to apply to one- and two-family dwellings. However, the maximum voltage permitted in PV systems for other installations within Article 690 is now limited to 1000 volts. Other PV systems "over 1000 volts" shall comply with Article 690, Part IX.

## Change Summary

- The 600 volt maximum PV system voltage is retained for one and two family dwellings.
- The 600 volt maximum photovoltaic system voltage for other installations within the Article 690, Parts I through VIII was revised from a 600 to a 1000 volt limit.
- Other PV systems "over 1000 volts" shall comply with Article 690, Part IX.

Comment: None

Proposal: 4-223

# Stand-Alone System Back-fed Circuit Breakers

## Code Language

**690.10 Stand-Alone Systems.** ... (See *NEC* text)...

**(A) Inverter Output.** ...(See *NEC* text)...

**(B) Sizing and Protection.** ...(See *NEC* text)...

**(C) Single 120-Volt Supply.** ...(See *NEC* text)...

**(D) Energy Storage or Backup Power System Requirements.**

**(E) Back-fed Circuit Breakers.** Plug-in type back-fed circuit breakers connected to a stand-alone or multi-mode inverter output in stand-alone systems shall be secured in accordance with 408.36(D). Circuit breakers marked "line" and "load" shall not be back-fed.

*(See NEC for actual text)*

## Change Summary

- This change clarifies the use of plug-in type back-fed circuit breakers are strictly limited to stand-alone PV systems.
- Plug-in type back-fed circuit breakers in stand-alone systems must be secured in accordance with 408.36(D).
- Only listed circuit breakers without "Line/Load" markings are acceptable for use with connections reversed.

*Courtesy of Schneider Electric*

## Significance of the Change

Section 690.10 Stand-Alone Systems may not be easily understood unless the definition of a stand-alone system is understood and applied to stand-alone system *NEC* graphic of Figure 690.1(B). By definition, a stand-alone system is not connected to a utility and is not connected to another production source. However, a *stand-alone system* may be connected to a battery (energy storage) and supply either or both dc and ac loads. Moving to 690.10, there are two simple requirements followed by five (A thru E) positive language exceptions to *NEC* and listing requirements. Since all wiring must comply with the *Code* and listing agency instructions, subdivision (E) permits circuit breakers connected to field wiring to be back-fed, provided they are fastened-in-place using a screwed down clamp or similar fastener. Product marking within listing literature indicates that circuit breakers without line and load markings are the only circuit breakers permitted to be used in back-fed situations (input conductors connected to the load terminals of a circuit breaker).

Comment: 4-97
Proposals: 4-245, 4-246

# Rapid Shutdown of PV Systems on Buildings

## Code Language

**690.12 Rapid Shutdown of PV Systems on Buildings.**

PV system circuits installed on or in buildings shall include a rapid shutdown function that controls specific conductors in accordance with 690.12(1) through (5) as follows.

(1) Requirements for controlled conductors shall apply only to PV system conductors of more than 1.5 m (5 ft) in length inside a building, or more than 3 m (10 ft) from a PV array.

(2) Controlled conductors shall be limited to not more than 30 volts and 240 volt-amperes within 10 seconds of rapid shutdown initiation.

(3) through (5)...(See *NEC* text)...

*(See NEC for actual text)*

## Significance of the Change

During the 2014 *Code* cycle, three concerned industry groups representing fire fighters, solar energy and photovoltaic industries formed a single task group. Together, they successfully added major improvements for rooftop PV systems based on the safety concerns of the Fire Service during emergency operations on a PV-equipped structure. The proposal and associated comment addresses the deenergization of rooftop wiring leaving only the module wiring and internal conductors of the module still energized. To meet this requirement, disconnecting the photovoltaic module(s) at the source circuit level maybe one target and some form of a utility disconnect, or manual inverter shutdown may be the second target. However the task group stressed there are many ways to meet and achieve these objectives. The stakeholders decided the devices and methods of compliance should be left open to performance objectives within Section 690.12 and special products be developed to meet the future listed and identified requirements. The 2014 companion *NEC's* requirement for rapid shutdown of solar photovoltaic systems on buildings is found in 690.56(B).

## Change Summary

- Where the need for an electrical safety product or system is demonstrated, prescriptive operational and safety requirements are permitted in the *NEC* to stimulate industry into meeting that need.

- Limiting firefighter exposure to electrical shock is one of the safety requirements.

- Limited time to achieve a lower voltage level after shutdown is a system operational requirement.

Comments: 4-108, 4-113
Proposal: 4-253

# PV System Disconnects

## Code Language

**690.13 Building or Other Structure Supplied by a Photovoltaic System.** Means shall be provided to disconnect all ungrounded dc conductors of a PV system from all other conductors in a building or other structure.

**(A) Location.** The PV disconnecting means shall be installed at a readily accessible location either on the outside of a building or structure or inside nearest the point of entrance of the system conductors. …(See *NEC* text) …

**(B) Marking.** …(See *NEC* text) …

**(C) Suitable for Use.** …(See *NEC* text) …

**(D) Maximum Number of Disconnects.** …(See *NEC* text) …

**(E) Grouping.** …(See *NEC* text) …

*(See NEC for actual text)*

## Change Summary

- Revised 690.13 includes all requirements for disconnecting all dc conductors of a photovoltaic system from all other conductors in a building or other structure.

- The revisions clarify the PV disconnect requirements apply to all ungrounded conductors.

- These organized requirements mirror those of Part II in Article 225 and incorporate multiple revisions from many proposals.

Comments: 4-114, 4-127

Proposals: 4-254a, 4-255, 4-256, 4-263

## Significance of the Change

The reorganized requirements within Part III Disconnection Means of Article 690 apply to all PV system disconnecting means. The revisions of 690.13 are significant improvements, adding both clarity and usability to the disconnecting means requirements of PV systems. Matching the organizational structure of Article 225 Part II, the 690.13 changes simplify and organize the PV circuit disconnecting means requirements and their exceptions. Section 690.13 separates these distinctive requirements by using first level subdivisions organized by location, by marking, by suitability of use, by the maximum permitted number and by grouping the various disconnecting means. Correlating Article 690 PV disconnect requirements with Article 225 disconnect requirements provides additional clarity and usability allowing the manufacturer, designer, user and inspector to compare and contrast the minor differences significant to their unique design, project or inspection. This reorganization and improvement was accomplished by CMP-4 merging the work of several public proposals into two section, 690.13 and other sections and accepting additional and necessary comments.

For additional information, visit qr.njatcdb.org Item #1247

# Disconnecting Type

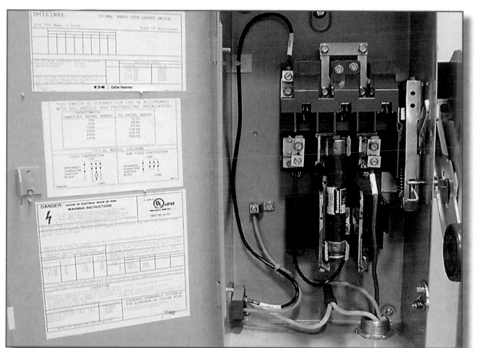

## Significance of the Change

For the 2014 *Code* cycle, CMP-4 did considerable organizational work consolidating requirement and building inclusive lists of acceptable equipment and acceptable installation methods. This detailed organizational work adds to the clarity, the usability, and the enforceability of the many requirements especially within Part III Disconnecting Means. This list of manually operated disconnecting means includes only listed equipment. The list also included dc rated equipment and PV system rated equipment. Each disconnecting means must be listed as either dc rated or PV rated. Some equipment on the list of ten devices may not yet be available, but when it is available, listed, and specifically dc rated or PV rated, it will be suitable for use. Environmental considerations for these disconnect enclosures are found in Section 110.31 and Table 110.31. Ever important is the required WARNING sign requirement of this section. Electrical workers must remember that all these disconnects, where used in certain PV systems, may remain live on both the line side and the load side all the while the disconnect is in the OPEN / OFF position. Wherever this is possible, a suitable warning sign complying with 690.17(F) must be posted on or adjacent to the disconnecting means.

## Code Language

**690.17 Disconnect Type.**

**(A) Manually Operable.** The disconnecting means for ungrounded PV conductors shall consist of a manually operable switch(es) or circuit breaker(s). The disconnecting means shall be permitted to be power operable with provisions for manual operation in the event of a power-supply failure. The disconnecting means shall be one of the following listed devices:

(1) A PV industrial control switch marked…(See *NEC* text)…

(2) A PV molded-case circuit breaker marked …(See *NEC* text)…

(3) A PV molded-case switch marked …(See *NEC* text)…

(4) A PV enclosed switch …(See *NEC* text)…

(5) through (10) …(See *NEC* text)…

*(See NEC for actual text)*

## Change Summary

- An inclusive list of suitable manually operable disconnects have been added to 690.17.
- Each of the ten different manually operable disconnecting means is required to be listed.
- In addition, each disconnecting means must be rated for use in a PV system or marked as suitably rated for dc.

Comments: 4-128, 4-129, 4-130, 4-131
Proposal: 4-278a

## Marking Roof Embedded PV Output Circuits

### Code Language

**690.31 Methods Permitted.**

**(A)** through **(F)** ...(See *NEC* Text)...

**(G) Direct-Current Photovoltaic Source and Direct-Current Output Circuits on or Inside a Building.**

**(1) Embedded in Building Surfaces.** Where circuits are embedded in built-up, laminate, or membrane roofing materials in roof areas not covered by PV modules and associated equipment, the location of circuits shall be clearly marked using a marking protocol that is approved as being suitable for continuous exposure to sunlight and weather.

**(2) and (3)** ...(See *NEC* Text)...

**(4) Marking and Labeling Methods and Locations.** The labels or markings shall be ...

*(See NEC for actual text)*

### Change Summary

- Marking requirements of embedded PV circuits hidden within roofing material have been upgraded.

- Hidden PV circuits must be clearly marked using an approved method suitable for the weather and continuous exposure to sunlight.

- This requirement is necessary to protect personnel from hazards that could arise from accidental contact with PV conductors embedded in roofs.

Comment: None

Proposals: 4-188a, 4-190, 4-204, 4-205, 4-207

**⚠ WARNING**

**LIVE WIRING EMBEDDED IN ROOF**

**NO WORK ALLOWED IN THIS AREA**

### Significance of the Change

Warning signs are an important safety feature of today's world. OSHA Standard for General Industry 1910.145 contains specifications for accident prevention signs and tags. All employees are instructed that danger and warning signs indicate immediate danger or other threatening hazards and that special precautions are necessary. Also in OSHA general industry 1910.335(b), OSHA requires employers to use alerting techniques (safety signs and tags, barricades, etc.) . . . to warn and protect employees from hazards which could cause injury due to electric shock, burns or failure of electric equipment parts. PV circuits maybe embedded in roofing materials not covered or blocked by PV modules according to 690.31(G)(1). These hidden circuits are a serious safety concern to workers examining, repairing, performing renovations or maintenance in and around embedded PV circuits. Within the NEC, field-applied ANSI caution, warning and danger signs have been recently upgraded and referenced 110.21(B). Since all field applied labels and signs must be suitable for environment where installed, for roof installations where wiring is embedded or hidden, signs may require free standing structures unless structural railing or other means are available to cordon-off the area of embedded or hidden wiring.

# GFP for Ungrounded PV Systems

*Courtesy of Rob Colgan, NECA*

## Code Language

**690.35 Ungrounded Photovoltaic Power Systems.**

**(A)** and **(B)** … (See *NEC* text)…

**(C) Ground-Fault Protection.** All PV source and output circuits shall be provided with a ground-fault protection device or system that complies with 690.35(1) through (4):

(1) Detects ground fault(s) in the PV array dc current-carrying conductors and components

(2) Indicates that a ground fault has occurred

(3) Automatically disconnects all conductors or causes the inverter or charge controller connected to the faulted circuit to automatically cease supplying power to output circuits

(4) Is listed for providing PV ground-fault protection

**(D)** through **(G)** …(See *NEC* text)…

*(See NEC for actual text)*

## Significance of the Change

This is a bold change for the PV industry in forcing new listed products to provide ground-fault protection (GFP), sometimes referred to as fire protection, to PV arrays. It is important to remember these GFP products are not GFCI protection for personnel but rather ground-fault protection for equipment which has a trip setting much higher than the 5 milliamperes required for GFCI's personnel protection. *Code* Making Panel 4 agreed to remove megohmmeter testing as a "requirement" but not as an acceptable practice. The electrical industry surely will continue commissioning PV systems by using megohmmeter testing. The committee indicated that once there are listed GFP products for PV equipment installed on working PV systems, they should prove to be most effective. At the present time there are no GFP devices specifically listed for protection of PV systems. But, as these products become available, this will allow the electrical inspector to rely upon product listings to provide the necessary safety and functionality to protect the PV system. This CMP-4 action also stimulates UL 1741 to be updated to ensure new functional requirements for GFP products of PV systems are met and to provide for the safety improvements of the *NEC*.

## Change Summary

- Ungrounded PV power systems no longer require specific megohmmeter testing prior to start-up and turn on.

- To achieve fire safety, PV industry safety groups prefer automatic disconnection of PV arrays by using ground-fault protection equipment products and devices.

- Required ground-fault protection equipment for ungrounded PV power systems must be listed for providing PV ground-fault protection.

Comment: 4-141
Proposal: 4-302

# Array Equipment Grounding Conductors

## Code Language

**690.46 Array Equipment Grounding Conductors.**

For PV modules, equipment grounding conductors smaller than 6 AWG shall comply with 250.120(C).

Where installed in raceways, equipment grounding conductors and grounding electrode conductors not larger than 6 AWG shall be permitted to be solid.

*(See NEC for actual text)*

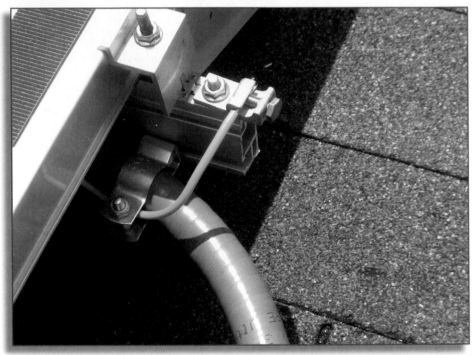

*Courtesy of Bill McGovern, City of Plano, TX*

## Change Summary

- Section 690.46 now permits a 6 AWG solid conductor within raceways as an equipment grounding conductor and as a grounding electrode conductor for PV system array grounding conductors.

- Chapter 6 is permitted to modify the general rules of Chapter 3 by permission in 90.3.

- Grounding and bonding at PV arrays maybe subject to physical damage.

## Significance of the Change

Section 90.3 Code Arrangement, displays the fact that Chapters I, 2, 3 and 4 apply generally, and Chapter 5, 6, and 7 are special chapters and amend or supplement the requirements of Chapters 1 through 4. This particular change 690.46 permits the use of a 6 AWG solid conductor installed in raceways and used as PV array equipment grounding conductors and grounding electrode conductors. The use of a 6 AWG solid conductor in a raceway is specifically prohibited for any purpose in Chapter 3, specifically 310.106(C). But, according to 90.3 is clearly permitted within these 2014 *Code* change requirements of 690.46, i.e. Chapter 6. The substantiation points to moisture at PV array electrical terminations. Using solid conductors prevents water migration and wire stranding degradation at terminations. Using solid 6 AWG as grounding conductors enclosed in raceways allows physical protection where necessary, and reduces inspectional issues. Permitting 6 AWG solid conductors in raceways allows an electrician to run an unspliced solid 6 AWG or smaller from the dc disconnect or combiner box to the array to bond all of the mounting components and even connect to any auxiliary grounding electrodes installed at the location of the array without a splice.

Comment: 4-150
Proposal: 4-309

# Combined DC and AC Grounding Conductors

## Code Language

**690.47(C)(3) Combined Direct-Current Grounding Electrode Conductor and Alternating-Current Equipment Grounding Conductor.** An unspliced, or irreversibly spliced, combined grounding conductor shall be run from the marked dc grounding electrode conductor connection point along with the ac circuit conductors to the grounding busbar in the associated ac equipment. This combined grounding conductor shall be the larger of the sizes specified by 250.122 or 250.166 and shall be installed in accordance with 250.64(E). For ungrounded systems, this conductor shall be sized in accordance with 250.122 and shall not be required to be larger than the largest ungrounded phase conductor.

*(See NEC for actual text)*

## Significance of the Change

PV grounding electrode system requirements are found in 690.47. These requirements are separated into ac grounding electrode systems, dc grounding electrode systems and systems with both ac and dc grounding requirements. Systems with both ac and dc grounding requirements are further divided into three sections for a combined dc grounding electrode/ac equipment grounding conductors. However, the great majority of ungrounded PV arrays will be connected to utility-interactive inverters and those inverters have common ac and dc equipment grounding terminals. The PV array dc equipment grounding conductors, when connected to such inverters, have the array dc equipment grounding conductors connected to earth through the ac equipment grounding system. Additional grounding electrodes and grounding electrode conductors are not required, but may be used. A new last sentence was added at the end of existing 690.47(C)(3) to acknowledge the use of an additional equipment grounding conductor for ground-fault sensing on ungrounded systems. This newly permitted conductor can be used to sense ground-fault current on an ungrounded systems and either notify operations that a ground fault current exists or trigger automatic disconnection of an array or a portion of an array.

## Change Summary

- A new last sentence was added to 690.47(C)(3) specifically permitting the use of an additional equipment grounding conductor for ground-fault sensing on ungrounded systems.
- Sections 250.66 and 250.166 are used to respectively size ac system and dc system grounding electrode conductors.
- Section 250.122 is used for sizing both ac and dc equipment grounding conductors.

Comments: 4-151, 4-152
Proposal: 4-310a

# Additional Auxiliary Electrodes for Array Grounding

## Code Language

**690.47(D) Additional Auxiliary Electrodes for Array Grounding.** A grounding electrode shall be installed in accordance with 250.52 and 250.54 at the location of all ground- and pole-mounted PV arrays and as close as practicable to the location of roof-mounted PV arrays. The electrodes shall be connected directly to the array frame(s) or structure. The dc grounding electrode conductor shall be sized according to 250.166. Additional electrodes are not permitted to be used as a substitute for equipment bonding or equipment grounding conductor requirements. The structure…(See *NEC* text)…

*(See NEC for actual text)*

## Change Summary

- The panel has reinstated and modified the 2008 *NEC* Section 690.47(D) because an auxiliary grounding electrode increases safety.

- The word "Auxiliary" notifies the user this grounding electrode is not required to be tied into the premises grounding electrode system.

- The electrode must be installed in accordance with 250.52 and 250.54 at the array location.

## Significance of the Change

Originally 690.47(D) was added to the 2008 *NEC* to mitigate the effects of lightning strikes near a PV array. Some technical issues were noticed and modifications to these requirements were suggested during the 2011 *NEC* cycle. However, there was no clear consensus with the existing requirements or the recommendations to change 690.47(D), so it was deleted. For the 2014 cycle, the panel reinstated some 2008 requirements and modified them as necessary. A consensus was achieved. First, the term *Auxiliary* was added to the title indicating that this grounding electrode is not required to be tied into the premises grounding electrode system and if multiple grounding electrodes are installed, they do not need to be bonded together by a dedicated bonding conductor. These clarifying statements are already found in Section 250.54 Auxiliary Grounding Electrodes, and this reference was added to 690.47(D). In addition, the original 2008 requirements mentioned multiple electrodes. For this cycle, multiple was changed to singular, indicating that multiple grounding electrodes are not necessarily a requirement. One grounding electrode may be all that is needed and this follows the requirements of 250.32. Finally, the reference to 250.166 and the warning in the last sentence were important and were retained.

Comments: 4-155, 4-156, 4-157

Proposal: 4-315

# Disconnects and Overcurrent Protection for Storage Battery Systems

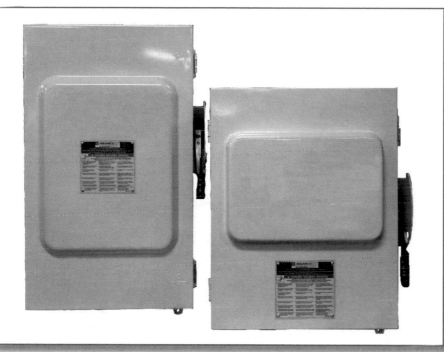

*Courtesy of Schneider Electric*

## Significance of the Change

Batteries and other energy storage devices may represent significant sources of short-circuit current (10,000 amps or more), and circuits connected to these sources must be protected with overcurrent devices. A switched disconnecting means is required to allow rapid disconnection of the batteries from the circuit because of equipment failure and during maintenance. Any penetration of a wall or partition necessitates the installation of a disconnecting means and overcurrent protection at the battery end of the circuit to protect the circuit as it passes through the wall and allows the battery to be disconnected at the source. Overcurrent protection is generally required at the battery or energy storage device end of the circuit since this is the source of the highest continuous currents and the source of the highest fault currents in the circuit. Where a wall is involved, disconnects may be required at each end of the circuit. The substantiation of this proposal indicated that PV residential systems are under development to operate above 300 volts dc and CMP-4 has set a "up to 600 volt" limit on these PV residential systems by the action in 690.7(C).

## Code Language

**690.71(H) Disconnects and Overcurrent Protection.** Where energy storage device input and output terminals are more than 1.5 m (5 ft) from connected equipment, or where the circuits from these terminals pass through a wall or partition, the installation shall comply with the following:

(1) A disconnecting means and overcurrent protection shall be provided at the energy storage device end of the circuit. Fused disconnecting means or circuit breakers shall be permitted to be used.

(2) Where fused disconnecting means are used, the line terminals of the disconnecting means shall be connected toward the energy storage device terminals.

(3) through (5) … See *NEC* text)…

*(See NEC for actual text)*

## Change Summary

- The 2014 *NEC* now requires overcurrent protection and disconnecting means for storage batteries used in solar PV systems.

- The line terminals of the battery disconnecting means must be connected toward the energy storage system (or battery).

- Another disconnecting means may be required where the disconnecting means is not "in sight from" the connected equipment.

Comment: None
Proposal: 4-325

# PV Systems Used To Charge Electric Vehicles

## Code Language

**X. Electric Vehicle Charging**

**690.90 General.** Photovoltaic systems used directly to charge electric vehicles shall comply with Article 625 in addition to the requirements of this article.

**690.91 Charging Equipment.** Electric vehicle couplers shall comply with 625.10. Personnel protection systems in accordance with 625.22 and automatic de-energization of cables according to 625.19 are not required for PV systems with maximum system voltages of less than 80 volts dc.

*(See NEC for actual text)*

*Courtesy of Rob Colgan, NECA*

## Change Summary

- A new Part X titled Electric Vehicle Charging Using PV Systems has been added to Article 690.

- Using PV systems to directly charge electric vehicles is a high efficiency charging operation.

- PV supplied charging systems will be provided with the same level of safety as other electric vehicle charging systems.

## Significance of the Change

A new Part X, Electric Vehicle Charging Using PV Systems, has been added to Article 690. While most electric vehicles will be recharged with alternating current, some vehicles will be charged directly from PV systems using direct current. The advantages of direct PV charging include a higher total equipment efficiency (no dc-ac inversion, and potentially a more efficient dc-dc charger), and a simpler system is permitted to be used since the charging can operate without grid connection thus minimizing the total length of required PV conductors in large parking areas. Industry experts imagine hybrid electrical systems will evolve, using ac-dc rectifiers with direct coupling of PV power to a dc charging bus. Of course, the design of these EV charging systems must provide the same level of safety as ac-fed systems as required in 625.10, 625.19 and 625.22. Therefore, it is important to define a basic maximum dc voltage level below which personnel protection and automatic de-energization is not required. For ac, the design voltage is limited to 120 volts and below. Since dc has a greater arc hazard, the design voltage is limited to 80 volts dc before arc-fault protection is required according to 690.11, Arc-Fault Protection (Direct Current).

Comment: None
Proposal: 4-331

# Article 694 Wind Electric Systems

## Code Language

**Article 694 Wind Electric Systems**

**694.1 Scope.** The provisions of this article apply to wind (turbine) electric systems that consist of one or more wind electric generators. These systems can include generators, alternators, inverters, and controllers.

Informational Note: Wind electric systems can be interactive with other electrical power production sources or might be stand-alone systems. Wind electric systems can have ac or dc output, with or without electrical energy storage, such as batteries. See Informational Note Figure 694.1(a), and Figure 694.1(b).

…(See *NEC* text)…

*(See NEC for actual text)*

## Significance of the Change

According to industry experts, experience with the 2011 *NEC* edition of Article 694 — Small Wind Electric Systems has shown that this article is a valuable and applicable addition to the *NEC*. From the past three years of experience, a single suggestion emerged that there is no significant difference between an electrical installation for a turbine sized less than 100 kW than for one rated above 100 kW. As far as industry experts are concerned, the *NEC* requirements developed for "small wind" can also be applied to intermediate and large wind electric systems, provided scope changes to Article 694 are made. The development process of UL standards for wind turbine electrical systems came to the same conclusion – there is no need to draw a distinction between small, intermediate and large wind electric systems. In addition, UL has developed two significant wind electric standards: UL/ANSI 6141, *Wind Turbine Converters and Interconnection Systems Equipment* and UL/ANSI 6142, *Small Wind Turbine Systems*. Therefore, for 2014 *NEC*, this article has been expanded and now applies to small, intermediate and large wind electric systems due to the elimination of the word "small" from the title, the requirements, and the informational notes of this article.

## Change Summary

- By eliminating the word "small" from Article 694, this article now applies to wind electric systems regardless of size.
- Very few changes were necessary to adjust Article 694 to apply to all wind electric systems.
- In concert with this 2014 change, UL has developed new product standards (UL/ANSI 6141 and UL/ANSI 6142) applicable to wind electric systems.

Comment: None
Proposals: 4-345, 4-346

# GFCI Protection For Maintenance Receptacles

## Code Language

**694.7(E) Receptacles.** A receptacle shall be permitted to be supplied by a wind electric system branch or feeder circuit for maintenance or data acquisition use. Receptacles shall be protected with an overcurrent device with a rating not to exceed the current rating of the receptacle. All 125-volt, single phase, 15- and 20-ampere receptacles installed for maintenance of the wind turbine shall have ground-fault circuit-interrupter protection for personnel.

*(See NEC for actual text)*

## Change Summary

- A new last sentence requires all 125-volt, single phase, 15- and 20-ampere receptacles installed for maintenance of the wind turbine to have GFCI protection for personnel.
- This new requirement provides protection from shock for maintenance personnel at wind electric systems.
- The *NEC* continues to expand the use of ground-fault circuit-interrupter protection of personnel.

## Significance of the Change

Section 210.8(B)(4) already requires all 125-volt, 15- or 20-ampere receptacles installed outdoors to be ground-fault circuit-interrupter (GFCI) protected. Without including an indoor requirement, 125-volt, 15- or 20-ampere receptacles installed inside for maintenance of the wind turbine would be exempt from being GFCI protected as it is not outdoors. For the 2014 *NEC*, a new last sentence in 694.7(E) requires all 125-volt, single phase, 15- and 20-ampere receptacles installed for maintenance of the wind turbine to have GFCI protection for personnel. This change ensures all 125-volt, 15- or 20-receptacles installed indoors for wind turbine maintenance be provided with GFCI protection for personnel. Examples may include a building installed near the wind turbine for the associated inverter as well as maintenance receptacles inside the tower. Often overlooked is the 210.8 requirement that all ground-fault circuit-interrupters, whether reset at the circuit breaker location, or on the receptacle itself, must be at a readily-accessible location. Extending GFCI protection into other areas where maintenance personnel will be using power tools or other maintenance related powered equipment is prudent. Installers and designers have provided GFCI protection in many areas for years, but GFCI protection for these areas is now required.

Comment: 4-180
Proposal: 4-351

# Support Poles for Wind Turbines Used As A Raceway

## Significance of the Change

Support structures are assumed to be safe and not a hazard, that is, until a support structure fails. Support structures, such as poles and towers, are designed by structural engineers and installed according to codes and standards. Safety concerns include strength and resistance to damaging winds and weather loads such as rain, wind, snow and ice, chemical agents and rust all while supporting their physical load with a built-in margin of safety. Anchor bolts, foundation and soil are critical to the safety of the structure. But poles and towers that contain and support electrical conductors must be of additional mechanical strength that prevents a structure failure due to electrical conductor weight as well as electrical short circuits and electrical cable fires. Many larger poles and towers are specifically fabricated and provide built-in supports suitable to fasten and support electrical cables or fasten and support electrical cable trays. Small poles may have a means to support a few small to medium-size multiconductor cables. In light of these concerns, the user of the Code should have a new vision as to a product evaluation and listing for metallic and nonmetallic poles and towers used as a raceway.

## Code Language

**694.7 Installation.** Systems covered by this article shall be installed only by qualified persons.

Informational Note: ...(See *NEC* text)...

**(A) Wind Electric Systems.** ...(See *NEC* text)...

**(B) Equipment.** ...(See *NEC* text)...

**(C) Diversion Load Controllers.** ...(See *NEC* text)...

**(D) Surge Protective Devices (SPD).** ...(See *NEC* text)...

**(E) Receptacles.** ...(See *NEC* text)...

**(F) Metal or Nonmetallic Poles or Towers Supporting Wind Turbines Used as a Raceway.** A metallic or nonmetallic pole or tower shall be permitted to be used as a raceway if evaluated as part of the listing for the wind turbine or otherwise shall be listed or evaluated for the purpose.

*(See NEC for actual text)*

## Change Summary:

• A metallic or nonmetallic pole or tower supporting a wind turbine is now permitted to be used as a raceway provided it is evaluated as part of the listing or otherwise listed or evaluated for the purpose.

• Metallic and nonmetallic poles and towers enclosing electrical conductors must be evaluated for suitability and especially fire rating.

Comment: None

Proposal: 4-356

# Wind Turbine Shutdown Procedures

## Code Language

**694.23 Turbine Shutdown.**

**(A) Manual Shutdown.** Wind turbines shall be required to have a readily accessible manual shutdown button or switch. Operation of the button or switch shall result in a parked turbine state that shall either stop the turbine rotor or allow limited rotor speed combined with a means to de-energize the turbine output circuit.

*Exception: Turbines with a swept area of less than 50 m² (538 ft²) shall not be required to have a manual shutdown button or switch.*

**(B) Shutdown Procedure.** The shutdown procedure for a wind turbine shall be defined and permanently posted at the location of a shutdown means and at the location of the turbine controller or disconnect, if the location is different.

*(See NEC for actual text)*

## Change Summary

- A wind turbine manual shutdown button or switch is required for all turbines with a swept area larger than 50 m² (538 ft²).

- This button initiates a shutdown procedure that parks (or slows) the turbine and disconnects the output circuit.

- A shut-down procedure must be adjacent to the button and both located in a readily accessible location.

Comment: None
Proposals: 4-364a, 4-365, 4-366

## Significance of the Change

This new requirement for 2014 *NEC* is similar to the international requirements for wind turbines. This is a safety driven change encouraged and supported by the wind turbine industry, manufacturers, contractors, electricians, inspectors and product testing companies. There is a need for a manual shutdown of all electric wind turbines to bring them to a stopped or safe and slow rotor condition and stop the export of power. Engineering design regularly includes safety relays and associated safety equipment with manual and automatic means to power-off equipment within wind electric systems. A manual power-off circuit is one of many possible inputs to the safety relay(s) that assure a safe and controlled turbine slow or stop and a disconnected power output circuit. Modern safety-relays often receive shut-down commands via automatic means, for such reasons as excessive wind, icing, other weather issues, vibration, rotor bearing heat and other mechanical issues. Even wireless command signals via radio, cell phones from boats, helicopters and planes are possible. This proposed requirement is consistent with the existing published IEC 61400-2, *Design Requirements for Small Wind Turbines* as well as UL 6142 *Standard for Small Wind Turbine System*.

# Equipment Grounding

## Significance of the Change

This major grounding and bonding revision for all electric wind system installations serves to simplify and clarify the language as well as the specific requirements and permissions. Concise informational notes were provided to warn of corrosive soil conditions and to point the user toward the lightning *Code* for other possible requirements. The panel noted the importance of stating the requirement for installing bonding to the premises grounding system as turbines are often located far from the premises and some installers may wrongly assume that grounding electrodes can perform the bonding function. The proposed language for (B)(3) Tower Connections, was retained In part to ensure that a reliable connection is made to the tower, and to maintain the important requirement for accessibility to connections (for inspection) which is not specifically included in Article 250. This revision provides very clear direction for users about grounding guy wires. Specifically, guy wires used to support turbine towers shall not be required to be connected to an equipment grounding or bonding conductor or to comply with the requirements of 250.110. In addition, an informational note points to an informative annex within NFPA 780-2011, *Standard for the Installation of Lightning Protection Systems*.

## Code Language

**694.40 Equipment Grounding.**

**(A) General.** Exposed non–current-carrying metal parts of towers, turbine nacelles, other equipment, and conductor enclosures shall be grounded in accordance with Parts IV, V, and VI of Article 250. Attached metal parts, such as turbine blades and tails that that are not likely to become energized, shall not be required to be grounded or bonded.

**(B) Tower Grounding and Bonding.**

**(1) Grounding Electrodes and Grounding Electrode Conductors.** A wind turbine tower shall be connected to a grounding electrode system. ...(See *NEC* text)...

**(2) Bonding Conductor.** ...(See *NEC* text)...

**(3) Tower Connections.** ...(See *NEC* text)...

**(4) Guy Wires.** ...(See *NEC* text)...

*(See NEC for actual text)*

## Change Summary

- Exposed non-current-carrying metal parts of electric system equipment shall be grounded in accordance with Parts IV, V and VI of Article 250.
- A wind turbine tower shall be connected to a grounding electrode system.
- Guy wires are not likely to become energized and don't require a connection to an equipment grounding or bonding conductor.

Comments: 4-185, 4-186
Proposal: 4-370a

# 695.1(B)(2) & (B)(3)

Article 695 Fire Pumps

## Jockey Pump Wiring

### Code Language

**695.1 Scope.**

Informational Note: ...(See *NEC* text)...

**(A) Covered.** ...(See *NEC* text)...

**(B) Not Covered.** This article does not cover the following:

(1) The performance, maintenance, and acceptance testing of the fire pump system, and the internal wiring of the components of the system

(2) The installation of pressure maintenance (jockey or makeup) pumps

Informational Note: For the installation of pressure maintenance (jockey or makeup) pumps supplied by the fire pump circuit or another source, see Article 430.

(3) Transfer equipment upstream of the fire pump transfer switch(es)

Informational Note: See NFPA 20-2010, *Standard for the* ...(See *NEC* text)...

*(See NEC for actual text)*

### Change Summary

- This revision clarifies that Article 695 Fire Pumps does not cover the installation of the pressure maintenance (jockey) pumps.

- The installation requirements of pressure maintenance (jockey) pumps are covered by Article 430, Motors.

- New language points out that transfer (switch) equipment upstream of fire pump transfer switch(es) are not covered by Article 695.

Comment: 13-32
Proposal: 13-48a

### Significance of the Change

Prior to 1996, the electrical requirements for the fire pump motor and associated fire pump transfer switch wiring were found only in NFPA 20, *Standard for the Installation of Centrifugal Fire Pumps*. In 1996, Article 695 Fire Pumps was first introduced into the *NEC*. Up until the 2014 *NEC*, Section, 695.1 contained essentially the same scope requirements. Revised for this *Code* cycle, the scope now clearly points out that pressure maintenance (jockey or makeup) pumps are not covered by Article 695, but rather covered by Article 430, regardless of whether these pumps are supplied by the fire pump circuit or another source. Pressure maintenance pumps are mentioned in Article 695 only as they relate to the electrical load on the fire pump and associated equipment circuit. In addition new text within the scope statement clearly states that transfer equipment upstream of the fire pump transfer switch is not covered by Article 695. Transfer between power sources specified within Section 695.3(B) is performed by a transfer switch supplying only those loads associated with the fire pump system.

# OCPD At 600% Of The Largest Fire Pump Motor Only

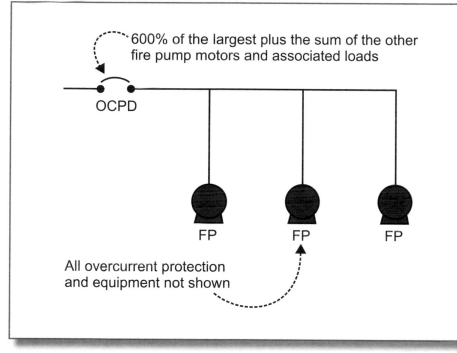

600% of the largest plus the sum of the other fire pump motors and associated loads

OCPD

FP   FP   FP

All overcurrent protection
and equipment not shown

## Code Language

**695.4(B)(2) Overcurrent Device Selection.** Overcurrent devices shall comply with 695.4(B)(2)(a) or (b).

(a) *Individual Sources.* Overcurrent protection for individual sources shall comply with 695.4(B)(2)(a)(1) or (2).

(1) Overcurrent protective device(s) shall be rated to carry indefinitely the sum of the locked-rotor current of the largest fire pump motor and the pressure maintenance pump motor(s) and the full-load current of all of the other pump motors and associated fire pump accessory equipment when connected to this power supply. Where ...(See *NEC* text)... with 240.6. The requirement to carry ...(See *NEC* text)... circuit(s). [**20**:9.2.3.4]
...(See *NEC* text)...

*(See NEC for actual text)*

## Significance of the Change

The technical requirements for sizing disconnect switches, fuses and circuit breakers for the protection of fire pumps and related equipment are found in *NFPA 20-2010, Standard for the Installation of Stationary Pumps for Fire Protection*. The *NEC* points to this explanatory material of NFPA 20 by using an informational note within 695.1. (See also 90.5(C), Explanatory Material.) The precise NFPA 20 reference is found in the bracketed text following 695.4(B)(2). The reference is {20:9.2.3.4}, that is NFPA 20, Chapter 9, Section 2.3.4. The proposal used to change this *NEC* requirement is a copy of the NFPA 20 revised text that occurred during the previous revision cycle of NFPA 20. This *NEC* change was accepted because the Fire Pump committee concluded that the upstream overcurrent protective devices do not need to carry the locked rotor current of all fire pump motors, only the largest. The possibility of all the fire pump motors being in a locked rotor condition at the same time is negligible. Two important past requirements were not changed; the locked-rotor current sizing does not apply to conductors or devices and the next (larger) standard overcurrent device continue to be sized in accordance with 240.6.

## Change Summary

- Past calculations sizing the disconnecting means and the overcurrent protective device included the sum of locked-rotor currents of all fire pump and jockey pump motors plus the full-load current of the remaining loads.

- Now the calculations include locked-rotor currents of only largest fire pump motor, plus the other motor and remaining loads.

Comment: None
Proposals: 13-57, 13-58

# Chapter 7

## Articles 700–760
### Special Conditions

# Definition of Automatic Load Control Relay

## Code Language

**700.2 Definitions.**

**Relay, Automatic Load Control.** A device used to set normally dimmed or normally-off switched emergency lighting equipment to full power illumination levels in the event of a loss of the normal supply by bypassing the dimming/switching controls, and to return the emergency lighting equipment to normal status when the device senses the normal supply has been restored.

Informational Note: See ANSI/UL 924, *Emergency Lighting and Power Equipment,* for the requirements covering automatic load control relays.

*(See NEC for actual text)*

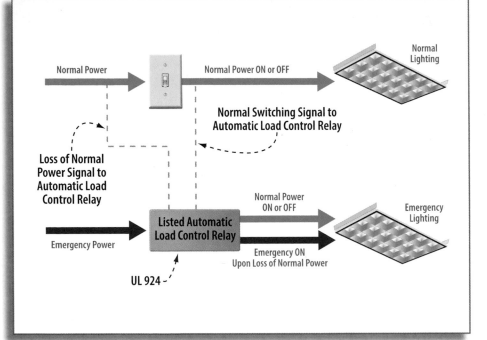

## Change Summary

- The definition of *automatic load control relay* was revised because less robust automatic load control relay system products were being used in the field.

- This safety-driven revised definition points directly to more reliable electrical equipment specifically rated for emergency lighting switching applications.

- The informational note was revised to comply with the *NEC Style Manual.*

## Significance of the Change

Emergency lighting systems are legally required and classed as "emergency" systems. They are required to be automatically energized, remain on for a predetermined period of time, and provide egress lighting and other necessary lighting essential for the safety of life during emergency conditions. All emergency lighting control equipment is required to be listed. For application within 700.24, Automatic Load Control Relay, only a listed load control relay in accordance with UL 924 may be used to bypass a switch or a dimmer to energize emergency lights. Also, a specific UL 924 listing may be applied to 700.23 dimmer system control equipment. All UL 924 products provide a by-pass function rather than a transfer function. However, only a UL 1008 listed transfer switch (specifically for emergency use) is permitted to be used to transfer emergency lights between a normal and an emergency power source. Providing an emergency transfer function requires a more robust product than providing an emergency bypass or emergency relay function; and products not specifically listed for emergency use are not allowed to automatically control emergency lighting loads. The revised informational note following this definition reflects the appropriate product standard, ANSI/UL 924, *Emergency Lighting and Power Equipment.*

Comment: None
Proposals: 13-88a, 13-92a

# Required Surge Protection Devices

Courtesy of Eaton, Cooper-Bussmann

## Code Language

**700.8 Surge Protection.** A listed SPD shall be installed in or on all emergency systems switchboards and panelboards.

*(See NEC for actual text)*

## Significance of the Change

Surge protective devices or SPD's are covered by the *NEC* in Article 285 Surge-Protective Devices (SPD's),1000 volts or Less; by Underwriters Laboratories in UL 1449, *Standard for Surge Protective Devices 3rd Edition* and by IEEE in C62.41 *IEEE Recommended Practice for Surge Voltages in Low-Voltage AC Power Circuits*. For the 2014 *NEC*, Section 700.8 now requires a voltage surge protective device must be installed in or on each emergency system switchboard and panelboard. The proper type and rating of the SPD must be suitable for the application. This requirement helps ensure that emergency electrical distribution systems will continue to deliver reliable power to vital life safety loads in the event of a voltage spike. Voltage surges resulting from lightning strikes or due to various sources within an electrical system, such as switching of power electronic devices, can destroy both the electrical distribution equipment and the loads it supplies. Electrical equipment damage can be from a single lightning strike nearby or the accumulative effects of multiple voltage surges from sources within an electrical system.

## Change Summary

- Voltage surge protective devices (SPD's) are required to be installed in or on all switchboards and panelboards of emergency systems.
- These surge protective devices and products must be listed.
- Requiring SPD's ensures emergency electrical distribution systems will continue to deliver reliable power to vital life safety loads in the event of a voltage spike.

Comment: 13-69
Proposal: 13-98

# 700.10(B)(5)

## Emergency Source Wiring Rules

### Code Language

**700.10(B) Wiring.** (1) through (4) ...(See *NEC* text)...

(5) Wiring from an emergency source to supply emergency and other loads in accordance with 700.10(B)(5)a, b, c, and d as follows:

a. Separate vertical switchgear sections or separate vertical switchboard sections, with or without a common bus, or individual disconnects mounted in separate enclosures shall be used to separate emergency loads from all other loads.

b. The common bus of separate sections of the switchgear, separate sections of the switchboard or the individual enclosures shall be permitted to be supplied by single ...(See *NEC* text)...

c. and d. ...(See *NEC* text)...

*(See NEC for actual text)*

### Change Summary

- All references to legally required and optional standby systems has been removed from 700.10(B)(5).

- This revised and clarified language clearly separates emergency wiring requirements from all other systems.

- The new defined term *switchgear* was introduced into the requirements as the common alternate product to switchboards.

### Significance of the Change

This change is a compilation of three proposals and one comment. The requirements for Article 700 apply to Emergency Systems only. However in 700.10(B)(5), previous text mentioned emergency systems, legally required systems as well as optional standby systems. One proposal indicated this existing language of Article 700, Emergency Systems could be misinterpreted to also set requirements for Article 701, Legally Required Standby Systems and Article 702 Optional Standby Systems. The panel agreed and decided to remove all mention of these other Chapter 7 systems. Now, this change clearly separates emergency wiring requirements from all other systems. In addition, some requirements in 700.10(B)(5)(a) implied that emergency loads must be separated from each other and the revised wording clarifies that separation of emergency from all other loads is the intent. In addition, CMP-9 retains the term *switchboard* but adjusted the language to be inclusive using the revised 2014 NEC defined term *switchgear* (previously referred to as *Metal-Enclosed Power Switchgear*).

Comment: 13-74

Proposals: 13-103, 13-104, 9-181e

# Outdoor Generator Disconnects

## Significance of the Change

New for 2014 *NEC* revision cycle, 110.25 Lockable Disconnecting Means, sets the standard for all disconnecting means required to be locked in the open position. 110.25 requires that the provisions for locking remain in place with or without the lock installed, but an exception permits the locking provisions of cord-and-plug connection to not remain in place. This new section was added as a mandatory reference within the requirements of 445.18. CMP-13 clarifies that a disconnecting means or the ability to shut down the driving means for the generator are permitted in Section 445.18. Also revised, 225.36 now requires disconnect switches that are "Suitable for use as Service Equipment" only where they are specifically applied to the exception of 250.32(B). In concert, all of these changes enhance the safety requirements and the reliability of operation while in some cases reducing the burden of requiring "Suitable for use as Service Equipment" switches on all outdoor emergency generators. This change repeats in 701.12(B)(5) and 702.12(A).

## Code Language

**700.12 General Requirements.**

**(A) Storage Battery.** ...(See *NEC* text)...

**(B) Generator Set. (1) – (5)** ...(See *NEC* text)...

**(6) Outdoor Generator Sets.** Where an outdoor housed generator set is equipped with a readily accessible disconnecting means in accordance with 445.18, and the disconnecting means is located within sight of the building or structure supplied, an additional disconnecting means shall not be required where ungrounded conductors serve or pass through the building or structure. Where the generator supply conductors terminate at a disconnecting means in or on a building or structure, the disconnecting means shall meet the requirements of 225.36.

*Exception: ...(See NEC text)...*

*(See NEC for actual text)*

## Change Summary

- To enhance safety, the disconnecting means of an outdoor emergency generator (set) must meet the requirements of 445.18 and 110.25.
- The disconnecting means for this generator must be located within site of the building served.
- This disconnecting means of 225.36 may not be required to be "Suitable for use as Service Equipment".

Comment: None
Proposals: 13-110, 13-111

# Emergency System Unit Equipment

## Code Language

**700.12(F)(2) Installation of Unit Equipment.** ...(See *NEC* text)...

**(1) and (2).** ...(See *NEC* text)...

**(3)** The branch circuit feeding the unit equipment shall be the same branch circuit as that serving the normal lighting in the area and connected ahead of any local switches.

Exception No. 1: In a separate and uninterrupted area supplied by a minimum of three normal lighting circuits, that are not part of a multiwire branch circuit, a separate branch circuit for unit equipment shall be permitted if it originates from the same panelboard as that of the normal lighting circuits and is provided with a lock-on feature.

*(See NEC for actual text)*

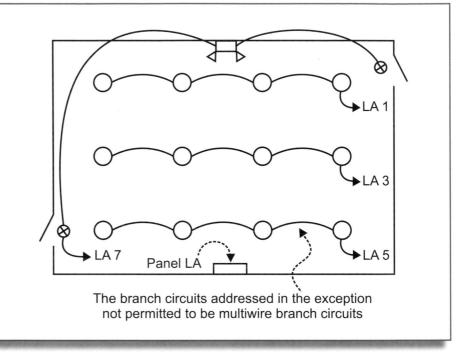

The branch circuits addressed in the exception not permitted to be multiwire branch circuits

## Change Summary

- An existing exception permitting unit equipment supplied by three or more normal circuits no longer permits multiwire branch circuits to serve the supplied area.

- Using normal multiwire branch circuits increases the risk of an area being without emergency lighting.

- Forbidding multiwire normal branch circuits in these specific instances provides additional safety during loss of normal lighting.

## Significance of the Change

Emergency lighting ensures egress illumination when the normal electrical supply is interrupted. Before emergency egress lighting operates, the loss of lighting must be automatically sensed or determined. Automatic action is then employed to insure emergency lighting is provided in proper areas. Where standard 1½-hour battery-unit equipment provides emergency lighting, these units normally sense loss of a single branch circuit or a single-phase of a feeder, such as 120- or 277-volt. For most egress areas, this power-loss sensing works well, but for 3-phase lighting circuit areas this is problematic. Section 210.4(B) requires each multiwire branch circuit be provided with a means to simultaneously disconnect all ungrounded conductors at the point where the branch circuit originates. This can be accomplished using multi-pole breakers or single-pole breakers with identified handle ties. If a multiwire branch circuit is used to comply with this exception, there is an increased possibility of leaving the area in total darkness if one circuit were to trip causing the others to open as a result. This revision seeks to improve consistency with other *NEC* rules that restrict multiwire branch circuits in areas where similar hazards have been identified, as in 517.18(A) and 517.19(A).

Comment: None
Proposal: 13-116

# Multiwire Branch Circuits

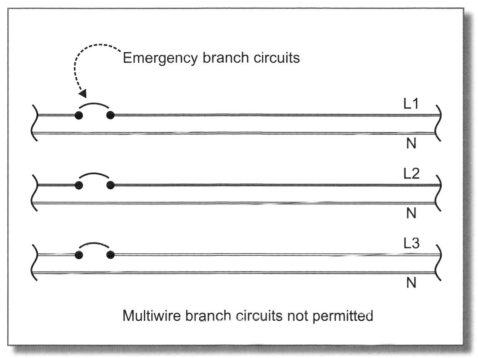

Emergency branch circuits

L1

N

L2

N

L3

N

Multiwire branch circuits not permitted

## Code Language

**700.19 Multiwire Branch Circuits.**
The branch circuit serving emergency lighting and power circuits shall not be part of a multiwire branch circuit.

*(See NEC for actual text)*

## Significance of the Change

This proposal is modeled after the requirements added to 517.18(A) and 517.19(A) in the 2011 *NEC*. The requirements were added to Article 517 to prevent the unnecessary opening of the other one or two poles of a multi-wire branch circuit because of an overload, ground fault, or short circuit on one pole of the multiwire branch circuit. Emergency power and lighting circuits have the same need for continuity of service. For example, reliability is certainly decreased when a short in a 277-volt lighting ballast takes out the other two poles of a 3-pole circuit breaker, knocking out the remaining 2/3 of the lighting. With this proposed requirement only the 1/3 of the lighting on the affected pole is out, leaving 2/3 of the lighting in operation. It should be noted that per 240.15(B)(3), a multiwire branch circuit supplying 277-volt lighting requires a common trip circuit breaker which results in the loss of multiple lighting branch circuits when one circuit is subjected to an overcurrent.

## Change Summary

- Article 700 no longer permits multiwire branch circuits protected by common trip circuit breakers to serve emergency lighting and power circuits.
- Emergency lighting and power could be unavailable during ordinary line-to-ground faults and other problems where common trip circuit breakers or handle ties are employed.
- Continued reliability of emergency circuits requires this change.

Comment: None
Proposal: 13-118

# Selective Coordination, Selection, and Documentation

## Code Language

**700.28 Selective Coordination.**

Emergency system(s) overcurrent devices shall be selectively coordinated with all supply-side overcurrent protective devices.

Selective coordination shall be selected by a licensed professional engineer or other qualified persons engaged primarily in the design, installation, or maintenance of electrical systems. The selection shall be documented and made available to those authorized to design, install, inspect, maintain, and operate the system.

*Exception: Selective coordination shall not be required between two overcurrent devices located in series if no loads are connected in parallel with the downstream device.*

*(See NEC for actual text)*

## Change Summary

- To achieve selective coordination, the responsible parties for determining the specific overcurrent protective device types, ratings, and settings are now identified.

- The responsible party must provide verification documentation to the AHJ that the overcurrent protective devices are selectively coordinated.

- Documentation must be made available to others involved in the life-cycle of the system.

Comments: 13-85, 13-92, 13-110

Proposals: 13-126, 13-139, 13-176

## Significance of the Change

For the 2014, the definition of *Selective Coordination (Coordination, Selective)* in Article 100 was clarified and new language was added to the requirements of 620.62, 700.28, 701.27 and 708.54. This change requires a professional engineer or other qualified person to choose the overcurrent protective device types, ampere ratings, and settings to achieve selective coordination. This responsible party must provide documentation to the AHJ that the selection of the overcurrent protective devices achieves the required selective coordination. This process will ensure selective coordination for a project without an additional burden on the AHJ. Documentation is required to be made available to others involved in the original construction process, or post installation, to ensure the system is installed, maintained, and modified with the knowledge of how the original system was selectively coordinated. A coordination study does not, by itself, ensure selective coordination is achieved. A coordination study may merely analyze the degree to which the system's overcurrent protective devices are coordinated (or have areas that lack selective coordination). The coordination study should state the analysis achieved selective coordination in compliance with 700.28. Full compliance is achieved when the selectively coordinated equipment is installed in accordance with the documentation.

# Separate Service For A Legally Required Standby System

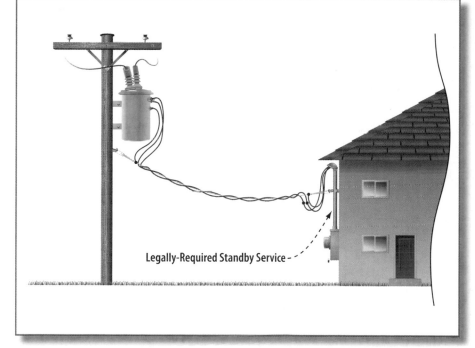

Legally-Required Standby Service -

## Code Language

**701.12 General Requirements**

**(A) Storage Battery.** ... (See *NEC* text)...

**(B) Generator Set.** ... (See *NEC* text)...

**(C) Uninterruptible Power Supplies.**

**(D) Separate Service.** Where approved, a separate service shall be permitted as a legally required source of standby power. This service shall be in accordance with the applicable provisions of Article 230, with a separate service drop or lateral or a separate set of overhead or underground service conductors sufficiently remote electrically and physically from any other service to minimize the possibility of simultaneous interruption of supply from an occurrence in another service.

**(E) through (G).** ... (See *NEC* text)...

*(See NEC for actual text)*

## Significance of the Change

During the 2011 *NEC* cycle, many defined terms applied to services were revised and clarified. The distinction continues to be made that the defined term *service point* is the point of demarcation between the serving utility requirements and the *NEC* requirements. The service point determines where the *NEC* requirements begin and where the serving utility requirements end. Article 701 permits a separate service to supply a legally required source of standby power. This separate service must comply with Article 230 and 701.12(D). A 2014 *NEC* change in 701.12(D) contains additional language that "a separate set of overhead or underground service conductors" must be located sufficiently remote, electrically and physically, from any other service. The terms *overhead or underground service conductors* refer to defined terms located on the customer side of the service point under the purview of the *NEC*. In addition, the utility wiring to the service point must be supplied by a service drop or a service lateral to the property. This wiring must also meet the important "... sufficiently remote..." requirements of 701.12(D). This combined and accurate language allows the AHJ to judge the suitability of a legally required standby system using a separate service.

## Change Summary

- The phrase "a separate set of overhead or underground service conductor" was added to 701.12(D) using current terminology within Article 230, Services.
- Service conductors overhead and service conductors underground, apply to conductors on the customer side of the service point.
- Service drop and service lateral apply to the utility side of the service point.

Comment: None
Proposal: 13-136

# Warning Sign at Power Inlet

## Code Language

**702.7(C) Power Inlet.** Where a power inlet is used for a temporary connection to a portable generator, a warning sign shall be placed near the inlet to indicate the type of derived system that the system is capable of based on the wiring of the transfer equipment. The sign shall display one of the following warnings:

WARNING:
FOR CONNECTION OF A SEPARATELY DERIVED (BONDED NEUTRAL) SYSTEM ONLY

or

WARNING:
FOR CONNECTION OF A NONSEPARATELY DERIVED (FLOATING NEUTRAL) SYSTEM ONLY

*(See NEC for actual text)*

## Change Summary

- New Section 702.7(C) requires a warning sign at the power inlet of a portable generator used as an optional standby system.
- Exact warning sign language is provided for both bonded neutral and floating neutral connections specific to the portable generator used.
- Section 702.7(C) requires a label and 110.21 provides the general requirements for all labels.

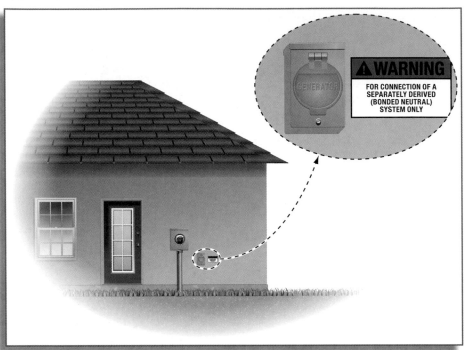

## Significance of the Change

Article 702 covers optional standby systems, which are those systems intended to supply power to public or private facilities or property where life safety does not depend on the performance of the system. Optional standby systems are intended to supply on-site generated power to selected loads either automatically or manually. The use of portable generators to supply standby power for these systems is permitted. The portable generators are not normally part of an electrical inspection, nor are they subject to inspection when an owner purchases a new one. Depending on the specific type of transfer equipment installed, this can lead to dangerous situations such as paralleling grounded currents on both the equipment grounding conductor and the grounded conductor or to cases where the system does not benefit from a system bonding conductor or one that acts as such. Therefore, safety signage at the portable generator inlet location is a necessary part of the safety requirements. This signage notifying the user that the power inlet requires either generator bonding or generator floating neutral based on the wiring of the transfer equipment within the property.

Comment: 13-96
Proposal: 13-146

# Small Outdoor Generator Sets

## Code Language

**702.12 Outdoor Generator Sets.**

**(A) Permanently Installed Generators and Portable Generators Greater Than 15 kW.** ...(See *NEC* text )...

**(B) Portable Generators 15 kW or Less.** Where a portable generator, rated 15 kW or less, is installed using a flanged inlet or other cord- and plug-type connection, a disconnecting means shall not be required where ungrounded conductors serve or pass through a building or structure.

*(See NEC for actual text)*

## Significance of the Change

During past CMP-13 deliberations that added portable generators to the scope of Article 702, a small portable generator connected by means of a flanged inlet and a flexible cord was not considered with regard to a disconnecting means at the building or other structure supplied required by 225.31. Small portable generators (mostly residential) are often installed without a disconnecting means where a flanged inlet and flexible cord is used as the connection means. During the last *Code* cycle, CMP-13 embraced this concept in the panel statement for Proposal 13-257. At that time, the panel noted, "A suitable disconnecting device is always available with a portable generator – the act of shutting it down." Revising this section to specifically permit a cord and plug connection to serve as a disconnecting means for portable generators 15 kW or less brings the requirements in line with typical installation practices of today without sacrificing safety. But remember, according to generator requirements of 445.18, the engine driving this 15 kW or less portable generator must be capable of being readily shut down.

## Change Summary

- An outdoor portable generator, 15 kW or less, supplying an optional standby system does not require a separate disconnecting means, provided a flanged inlet or other cord and plug type connection is used.

- However, 445.18 clearly requires the engine driving this portable generator to be capable of being readily shut down.

Comment: None
Proposal: 13-148

# Utility-Interactive Inverters

## Code Language

**705.12 Point of Connection.**

**(D) Utility-Interactive Inverters.** The output of a utility-interactive inverter shall be permitted to be connected to the load side of the service disconnecting means of the other source(s) at any distribution equipment on the premises. Where distribution equipment, including switchgear, switchboards, or panelboards, is fed simultaneously by a primary source(s) of electricity and one or more utility-interactive inverters, and where this distribution equipment is capable of supplying multiple branch circuits or feeders, or both, the interconnecting provisions for the utility-interactive inverter(s) shall comply with 705.12(D)(1) through (D)(6). …(See *NEC* text)…

*(See NEC for actual text)*

*Courtesy of Eaton Corporation*

## Change Summary

- There are multiple options to connect the utility-interactive inverter(s) to the load side of the service disconnect(s) and use of warning signs is included

- A safe and systematic approach for these connections is provided.

- A new informational note was added to inform users that fused disconnect switches, unless otherwise marked, are suitable for back-feeding.

Comments: 4-203, 4-204, 4-206

Proposals: 4-375a, 4-387, 4-402, 4-403, 9-181g

## Significance of the Change

This point of connection is an area of concern because it is supplied simultaneously by two or more sources of electricity. The key concern is the addition of a utility interactive inverter supply presents a potential overload condition for the feeder and main lug only (MLO) panelboards on the load side of the inverter interconnection point. By making sure that the ampacity of the feeder is sufficient for both sources, or by installing an overcurrent device on the feeder on the load side of the inverter interconnection point, the feeder is protected. The busbar of the MLO panelboard can be protected by the overcurrent device installed at the interconnection point or by installing a main overcurrent device on the panelboard to prevent busbar overcurrent. The requirement to protect busbar overcurrent is already in place. For taps and busbars, the word "load" was deleted from the language, to make it clear that any tap conductor, whether for loads or for an inverter output circuit, would be required to follow the tap rule when the tap rule sizing requirement exceeds the load of the tap or the supply of the inverter output circuit.

## Limiting Unbalanced Voltages

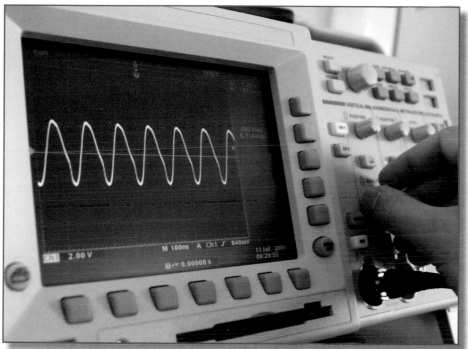

### Code Language

**705.100 Unbalanced Interconnections.**

**(A) Single Phase.** Single-phase inverters for hybrid systems and ac modules in interactive hybrid systems shall be connected to three-phase power systems in order to limit unbalanced voltages to not more than 3 percent.

Informational Note: For utility-interactive single-phase inverters, unbalanced voltages can be minimized by the same methods that are used for single-phase loads on a three-phase power system. See ANSI/C84.1-2011 *Electric Power Systems and Equipment — Voltage Ratings (60 Hertz).*

**(B) Three Phase.** ...(See *NEC* text)...

*(See NEC for actual text)*

### Significance of the Change

The intent of 705.100 is to prevent significant unbalanced voltages from occurring throughout a system of interconnected electric power production sources. In 705.100(B), for 3-phase systems, the requirements of operation for 3-phase inverters and 3-phase modules in interactive systems are clearly stated. Three-phase systems must either automatically deenergize or prevent significant unbalanced voltages from occurring. However, for 705.100(A) single-phase systems, the requirements were not as clear and it could be interpreted that single-phase inverters systems for hybrid systems and ac modules in interactive hybrid systems were simply not to be connected to 3-phase power systems. Revised for the 2014 *NEC*, single-phase requirements have been rewritten to clearly state that these single-phase inverters and ac modules "...shall be connected to 3-phase power systems in order to limit unbalanced voltages to not more than 3 percent." The new informational note points to ANSI/C84.1 *Electric Systems and Equipment — Voltage Ratings (60 Hertz)*. ANSI C84.1 recommends that electrical supply systems should be designed and operated to limit the maximum voltage unbalance to 3 percent when measured at the electric-utility revenue meter under no-load conditions. However, most utilities attempt to improve the voltage unbalance to less than 3 percent.

### Change Summary

- Single-phase requirements were rewritten to clarify single-phase inverters and ac modules must be connected to 3-phase systems to limit unbalanced voltages to not exceed 3 percent.

- A new informational note points to ANSI/C84.1 *Electric Power Systems and Equipment* for voltage calculations.

- This change corrects a misunderstanding in preventing significant unbalanced voltages in single-phase equipment.

Comment: 4-209
Proposal: 4-416

# 725.3(K) & (L)

## Protecting Class 1, 2 and 3 Cables

### Code Language

**725.3 Other Articles.** Circuits and equipment shall comply with the articles or sections listed in 725.3 (A) through (L). Only those sections of Article 300 referenced in this article shall apply to Class 1, Class 2, and Class 3 circuits.

**(A) – (J)** ... (See *NEC* text)...

**(K) Installation of Conductors with Other Systems.** Installations shall comply with 300.8.

**(L) Corrosive, Damp, or Wet Locations.** Class 2 and Class 3 cables installed in corrosive, damp, or wet locations shall comply with the applicable requirements in 110.11, 300.6, 300.5(B), 300.9, and 310.10(G).

*(See NEC for actual text)*

### Change Summary

- A new 725.3(K) was added to ensure that all Article 725 installations not be located in raceways or cable trays that contain any service other than electrical.

- A new 725.3(L) was added to ensure that all cables and equipment be protected from deteriorating agents above and below ground including corrosion, weather, chemicals and other substances.

### Significance of the Change

According to 90.3, Chapters 1 through 4 apply generally and they supplement or modify Chapters 5, 6 and 7. Following this rule, it may appear that there is no need to specifically mention Chapters 1 through 4 again within Chapter 7. However, the second sentence of 725.3 contains a positive language exception to the requirements of Article 300 stating "only those sections of Article 300 referenced in this article shall apply to Class 1, Class 2, and Class 3 circuits." As a result, prior to the 2014 *NEC*, many sections in Article 300 did not apply to Class 1, 2 and 3 cables. Now, with the addition of 725.3(K), all cables installed under Article 725 in raceways or cable trays shall not be run with any pipe, tube, or equal for steam, water, air, gas, drainage, or any service other than electrical in accordance with 300.8. And, the addition of 725.3(K), Class 2 and class 3 cables installed under Article 725 will be afforded the same protection required by most cables installed in corrosive, damp, and wet locations as covered by 300.5(B), 300.6, 300.9, and 310.10(G).

Comment: 3-46
Proposal: 3-122a

# 725.154 & 760.154

**NEW** / **REVISION**

## Cable Application Tables

Table 725.154 Applications of Listed Class 2, Class 3 and PLTC Cables in Buildings

| Applications | | CL2P & CL3P | CL2R & CL3R | CL2 & CL3 | CL2X & CL3X | CMUC | PLTC |
|---|---|---|---|---|---|---|---|
| | | **Wire and Cable Type** | | | | | |
| In Fabricated Ducts as Described in 300.22(B) | In fabricated ducts | Y* | N | N | N | N | N |
| | In metal raceway that complies with 300.22(B) | Y* | Y* | Y* | Y* | N | Y* |
| In Other Spaces Used for Environmental Air as Described in 300.22(C) | In other spaces used for environmental air | Y* | N | N | N | N | N |
| | In metal raceway that complies with 300.22(C) | Y* | Y* | Y* | Y* | N | Y* |
| | In plenum communications raceways | Y* | N | N | N | N | N |
| | In plenum cable routing assemblies | NOT PERMITTED | | | | | |
| | Supported by open metal cable trays | Y* | N | N | N | N | N |
| | Supported by solid bottom metal cable trays with solid metal covers | Y* | Y* | Y* | Y* | N | N |
| In Risers | In vertical runs | Y* | Y* | N | N | N | N |
| | In metal raceways | Y* | Y* | Y* | Y* | N | Y* |
| | In fireproof shafts | Y* | Y* | Y* | Y* | N | Y* |
| | In plenum communications raceways | Y* | Y* | N | N | N | N |
| | In plenum cable routing assemblies | Y* | Y* | N | N | N | N |
| | In riser communications raceways | Y* | Y* | N | N | N | N |

## Significance of the Change

CMP-3 decided that Article 725, Part III, Class 2 and Class 3 Circuits needed some reorganization. Revised 725.133 set the stage by requiring both application requirements and installation wiring requirements be separated and dealt with on an individual basis. After the wiring requirements were separated by other proposals, each application was expressed as simply as possible by using revised 725.154 (A) through (C) and its new associated Table 725.154, Applications of Listed Class 2, Class 3, and PLTC Cables.

CMP-3 made similar revisions within Article 760 Fire Alarm Systems, Part III, Power-Limited Fire Alarm (PLFA) Circuits for 760.154 (A) through(C) and its new related Table 725.154. As a result of these changes the cable applications and installation sections of Articles 725 and 760 will be editorially consistent with Articles 770, 800, 820 and 830.

## Code Language

**725.154 Applications of Listed Class 2, Class 3, and PLTC Cables.** Class 2, Class 3, and PLTC cables shall comply with any of the requirements described in 725.154(A) through (C) and as indicated in Table 725.154.

... (See *NEC* text)...

**760.154 Applications of Listed PLFA Cables.** PLFA cables shall comply with the requirements described in Table 760.154 or where cable substitutions are made as shown in 760.154(A)

... (See *NEC* text)...

*(See NEC for actual text and complete Table 725.154)*

## Change Summary

- The applications of Class 2, Class 3 and PLTC cables of Article 725 are now provided in table format.
- The applications of Power-Limited Fire Alarm Cables (PLFA) cables of Article 760 are now provided in table format.
- Articles 725 and 760 are now editorially consistent with Articles 770, 800, 820 and 830.

Comments: 3-60, 3-63, 3-104

Proposals: 3-154a, 3-202

# Article 728

**NEW**

## Fire-Resistive Cable Systems

### Code Language

**728.1 Scope.** This article covers the installation of fire-resistive cables, fire-resistive conductors, and other system components used for survivability of critical circuits to ensure continued operation during a specified time under fire conditions as required in this *Code*.

**728.2 Definition.**

**Fire-Resistive Cable System.** A cable and components used to ensure survivability of critical circuits for a specified time under fire conditions.

**728.3 Other Articles.** Wherever the requirements of other articles of this *Code* and Article 728 differ, the requirements of Article 728 shall apply.

**728.4 General.** Fire-resistive cables, fire-resistive conductors, and components shall …(See *NEC* text)…

*(See NEC for actual text)*

### Change Summary

- New Article 728 Fire-Resistive Cable Systems provides the necessary information required for the proper installation of fire-rated cables.
- Precise installation requirements for fire-resistive cables are critical components of fire egress and safety.
- Many buildings and specific areas require the continued use of electrical energy during fire and other emergency conditions.

Comments: 3-79, 3-80, 3-81, 3-83a, 3-83b
Proposal: 3-170

*Courtesy of VITALink MC Cable by RSCC Wire and Cable, LLC*

### Significance of the Change

The title of Chapter 7 is Special Conditions and since fire-resistive cables are considered special systems, fire-resistive cables became new Article 728. The application of Article 728, as with the entire Chapter 7, is explained in 90.3. Article 728, Fire-Resistive Cable Systems is a new article for the 2014 *NEC*. According to 728.1 Scope, this article covers the installation of fire-resistive cables, fire-resistive conductors and other system components used for survivability of critical circuits to ensure continued operation during a specified time under fire conditions as required in this *Code*. This article is not limited to just low-voltage cables and systems. As with many products required in the *NEC*, fire-resistive cables require proper installation to achieve their original purpose of providing electricity in a building during fire. As more fire-resistive cables are installed, this article will play a prominent role in these installations.

One information note indicates that "… the (mechanical) supports are critical for survivability of the (fire-resistive cable) system." Each system will have its support requirements. The product standard that ensures these systems are fire tested and listed is UL 2196, the *Standard for Tests for Fire-Restive Cables*.

**NEW**

## Energy Management

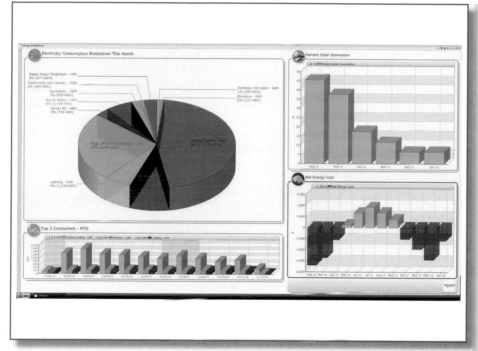

### Significance of the Change

*Courtesy of Schneider Electric*

New Article 750, Energy Management, was the work of the Smart Grid Task Group. Energy Management has become common place in todays electrical infrastructure through the control of utilization equipment, energy storage and power production. Yet, limited consideration is found in installation standards in actively managing these systems as a means to reduce energy cost or support peak power needs as it relates to a broader electrical infrastructure demand. Energy Management has two basic aspects, monitoring the system and controlling some portions of the system. These two basic elements must be separated in order to permit an energy management system to monitor and possibly restrict those areas of control that would adversely impact the electrical system or personal safety. The most important aspect here is to make sure an overall energy management system does not override a system specific to addressing load shedding for an alternate power source for fire pumps and emergency systems. Certain energy management systems become critical to ensure safety. For example, turning off ventilation systems for hazardous (classified) material or a moving walkway causing someone to fall, are examples of where load management controls need to be restricted.

### Code Language

**750.1 Scope.** This article applies to the installation and operation of energy management systems.

Informational Note: Performance provisions in other codes establish prescriptive requirements that may further restrict the requirements contained in this article.

**750.2 Definitions.** ...(See *NEC* text)...

**750.20 Alternate Power Sources.** ... (See *NEC* text)...

**750.30 Load Management.** Energy management systems shall be permitted to monitor and control electrical loads unless restricted in accordance with 750.30(A) through (C).

**(A) Load Shedding Controls.** ...(See *NEC* text)...

**(B) Disconnection of Power.** ...(See *NEC* text)...

**(C) Capacity of Branch Circuit, Feeder, or Service.** ...(See *NEC* text)...

**750.50 Field Markings.** ...(See *NEC* text)...

*(See NEC for actual text)*

### Change Summary

- New Article 750, Energy Management Systems defines and controls building systems while protecting the safety concerns of the *NEC* or building codes.
- With the application of the Smart Grid, premises energy management systems must be compatible with *NEC* safety concerns.
- Article 750 provides a safe and systematic approach for load shedding and disconnection of power.

Comment: None
Proposal: 13-180

# Fire Alarm Raceways Abovegrade in Wet Locations

## Code Language

**760.3 Other Articles.** Circuits and equipment shall comply with 760.3(A) through (L). Only those sections of Article 300 referenced in this article shall apply to fire alarm systems.

**(D) Corrosive, Damp, or Wet Locations.** Sections 110.11, 300.5(B), 300.6, 300.9, and 310.10(G), where installed in corrosive, damp, or wet locations.

*(See NEC for actual text)*

## Change Summary

• Section 300.9 was added to the requirements within 760.3, Other Articles, and adds new requirements for fire alarm wiring.

• Where raceways are installed in wet locations abovegrade, the interior of these raceways shall be considered to be a wet location.

• Insulated conductors and cables installed in raceways in wet locations abovegrade must comply with 310.10(C).

## Significance of the Change

According to 90.3, Chapters 1 through 4 apply generally to the *NEC* and Chapters 5 through 7 supplement or modify the general rules in Chapters 1 through 4. But, contrary to 90.3, Section 760.3 severely limits this general application of Chapter 3 to Article 760 by requiring "only those sections of Article 300 referenced in this article shall apply to fire alarm systems." Prior to 2014 *NEC*, 300.9 did not apply to fire alarm circuits since it is not referenced in 760. Now Section 300.9 is specifically mentioned within 760.3 Other Articels. This change is required for consistency in the *Code* so that the interior of a raceway installed in a wet location is considered a wet location where fire alarm circuits are installed. Interestingly, listing and marking requirements of both NPLFA and PLFA cables (760.176 an 760.179) already required cables used in a wet location to be listed for use in wet locations or have a moisture impervious metal sheath.

Comment: None
Proposal: 3-173

# Supporting Fire Alarm (CI) Cable

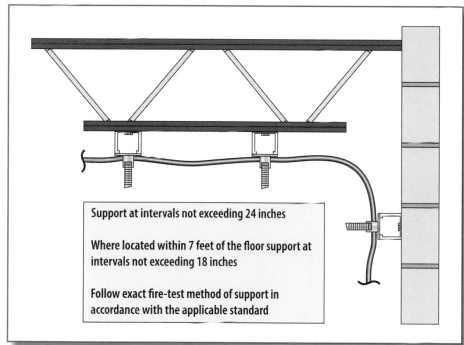

Support at intervals not exceeding 24 inches

Where located within 7 feet of the floor support at intervals not exceeding 18 inches

Follow exact fire-test method of support in accordance with the applicable standard

## Code Language

**760.24 Mechanical Execution of Work.**

**(A) General.** Fire alarm circuits shall be installed in a neat workmanlike manner. Cables and conductors installed exposed on the surface of ceilings and sidewalls shall be supported by...(See *NEC* text)...

**(B) Circuit Integrity (CI) Cable.** Circuit integrity (CI) cables shall be supported at a distance not exceeding 610 mm (24 in.). Where located within 2.1 m (7 ft) of the floor, as covered in 760.53(A)(1) and 760.130.(1), as applicable, the cable shall be fastened in an approved manner at intervals of not more than 450 mm (18 in.). Cable supports and fasteners shall be steel.

*(See NEC for actual text)*

## Significance of the Change:

Fire Alarm Circuit Integrity (CI) Cable provides additional reliability to fire alarm systems ensuring the operation of critical circuits during a specified time under fire conditions. The specified time of continued operation must be a minimum 2-hour when tested in accordance with UL 2196, *Tests for Fire Resistive Cables*. Fire Alarm Circuit Integrity (CI) cable (and electrical circuit protective systems) are used for fire alarm circuits to comply with the survivability requirements of NFPA 72-2010, *National Fire Alarm and Signaling Code*, 12.4.3 and 12.4.4. The listing requirements for Fire Alarm Circuit Integrity (CI) cable are located in 760.176(F). The new installation requirements in 760.24(B) Fire Alarm Circuit Integrity (CI) cable follow the exact fire-test method of support (distance of 2 ft) found in UL 2196. Within 760.24(B), the referencing of 760.53(A)(1) and 760.130(B)(1) provides direction to the user when installing circuit integrity cables in an exposed application located within 7 ft of the floor. Finally, the supports need to be steel because plastic or aluminum supports may melt under fire conditions.

## Change Summary

- New for 2014, 760.24(B) covers installation instructions for supporting Circuit Integrity (CI) fire alarm cable.
- Generally, CI cables must be supported at a distance not exceeding 24 in. by using steel supports and fasteners only.
- CI cables installed within 7 ft of the floor must be fastened at intervals of not more than 18 inches.

Comment: None
Proposal: 3-178

# Primary Protector For Outdoor Fire Alarm Circuits

## Code Language

**760.32 Fire Alarm Circuits Extending Beyond One Building.** Non-power-limited fire alarm circuits and power-limited fire alarm circuits that extend beyond one building and run outdoors shall meet the installation requirements of Parts II, III, and IV of Article 800 and shall meet the installation requirements of Part I of Article 300.

Informational Note: An example of a protective device suitable to provide protection is a device tested to the requirements of ANSI/UL 497B, *Protectors for Data Communications.*

*(See NEC for actual text)*

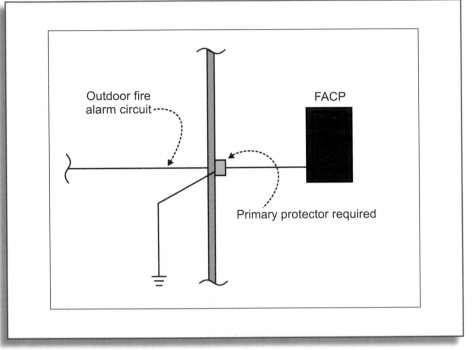

## Change Summary

- Fire alarm circuits extending beyond one building require a protective device similar to the primary protector of 800.90 for communications circuits.

- This requirement applies to all non-power-limited fire alarm circuits and power-limited fire alarm circuits overhead and underground.

- The device must be listed to the requirements of ANSI/UL 497B, *Protectors for Data Communications.*

## Significance of the Change

Section 760.32 covers installation of fire alarm circuits extending beyond one building. This section was modified by streamlining the language and combining the requirements for both power-limited and non-power-limited fire alarm wiring and by adding a new informational note. This new informational note reminds the fire alarm community that fire alarm circuits extending beyond one building are similar to many communication circuits extending beyond one building and require primary protectors. The substantiation for this proposal points to a new requirement in the 2013 edition NFPA 72 *Fire Alarm Code* in 12.2.4.2. The text of this section reads "All nonpower-limited and power-limited signaling system circuits entering a building shall be provided with transient protection." NFPA 72 has required all fire alarm wiring and equipment, including all circuits controlled and powered by the fire alarm system, to be installed in accordance with the requirements of the Article 760 of the *NEC*. It is interesting to note that before Article 760 Fire Alarm Systems came to the *NEC* for the 1975 edition, Article 800 Communications covered Fire Alarm wiring beginning in the mid1940s.

Comment: N/A

Proposal: 3-178a

For additional information, visit qr.njatcdb.org Item #1253

# IBEW Code-Making Panel Members

**TECHNICAL CORRELATING COMMITTEE**

Palmer L. Hickman, [Principal]

James T. Dollard, Jr., [Alternate]

**CODE-MAKING PANEL NO. 1**

Palmer L. Hickman, [Principal]

Mark Christian, [Alternate]

**CODE-MAKING PANEL NO. 2**

Donald M. King, [Principal]

Jacob G. Benninger, [Alternate]

**CODE-MAKING PANEL NO. 3**

Paul J. Casparro, [Chair]

Michael J. Farrell III, [Alternate]

**CODE-MAKING PANEL NO. 4**

Todd W. Stafford, [Principal]

Brian L. Crise, [Alternate]

**CODE-MAKING PANEL NO. 5**

Paul J. LeVasseur, [Principal]

Gary A. Beckstrand, [Alternate]

**CODE-MAKING PANEL NO. 6**

William F. Laidler, [Principal]

Todd Crisman, [Alternate]

**CODE-MAKING PANEL NO. 7**

Samuel R. La Dart, [Principal]

Keith Owensby, [Alternate]

**CODE-MAKING PANEL NO. 8**

Gary W. Pemble, [Pricipal]

Dan Rodriguez, [Alternate]

**CODE-MAKING PANEL NO. 9**

Rodney D. Belisle, [Principal]

Rhett A. Roe, [Alternate]

**CODE-MAKING PANEL NO. 10**

James T. Dollard, Jr., [Principal]

Richard E. Lofton, II, [Alternate]

**CODE-MAKING PANEL NO. 11**

James M. Fahey, [Principal]

Jebediah J. Novak, [Alternate]

**CODE-MAKING PANEL NO. 12**

Jeffrey L. Holmes, [Principal]

Dale Wion, [Alternate]

**CODE-MAKING PANEL NO. 13**

Linda J. Little, [Principal]

James T. Dollard, Jr., [Alternate]

**CODE-MAKING PANEL NO. 14**

John L. Simmons, [Principal]

Thomas E. Dunne, [Alternate]

**CODE-MAKING PANEL NO. 15**

Stephen M. Lipster, [Principal]

Gary A. Beckstrand, [Alternate]

**CODE-MAKING PANEL NO. 16**

Harold C. Ohde, [Principal]

Terry C. Coleman, [Alternate]

**CODE-MAKING PANEL NO. 17**

Randy J. Yasenchak, [Principal]

Brian Myers, [Alternate]

**CODE-MAKING PANEL NO. 18**

Paul Costello, [Principal]

Jesse Sprinkle, [Alternate]

**CODE-MAKING PANEL NO. 19**

Ronald Michaelis, [Principal]

Ronald D. Weaver, Jr., [Alternate]

# Chapter 8

## Articles 800–840
### Communications Systems

# Significant Changes
## TO THE *NEC®* 2014

# Communications Raceway Used as Innerduct

## Code Language

**800.2 Innerduct.** A nonmetallic raceway placed within a larger raceway.

**800.12 Innerduct.** Listed plenum communications raceway, listed riser communications raceway, and listed general-purpose communications raceway selected in accordance with the provisions of Table 800.154(b) shall be permitted to be installed as innerduct in any type of listed raceway permitted in Chapter 3.

*(See NEC for actual text)*

## Change Summary

- The new definition of *innerduct* is based on TIA and BICI dictionaries.

- Also new, listed communications raceways, including general-purpose, riser and plenum types, are permitted to be used as innerduct and placed within Chapter 3 raceways.

- These innerduct requirements include permission to use communications raceway as innerduct.

## Significance of the Change

For this *Code* cycle, CMP-16 submitted a group of coordinated proposals to align definitions and requirements within Chapter 8. First, a new definition of Innerduct was added to 800.2. This definition is based on information from other technical dictionaries of the Telecommunications Industry Association (TIA) and Building Industry Consulting Service International, Inc. (BICSI). The new definition of Innerduct correlates with the new installation permissions and requirements of 800.12, Innerducts. Section 800.12 now permits listed general-purpose, riser and plenum types of innerduct to be used and installed within any listed raceways permitted in Chapter 3, Wiring Methods. In addition, communications raceways, which are clearly permitted to be used as innerduct, are already available as general-purpose, riser and plenum types raceways. For this *NEC* change cycle and covered earlier in Article 100, the definition of communications raceway was expanded and moved from Article 800 into Article 100 since it now applies to both Chapter 7 and Chapter 8 wiring.

Comments: 16-8, 16-42
Proposals: 16-87, 16-97, 16-131

# Point of Entrance and Conduit Grounding

## Code Language

**800.2 Point of Entrance.** The point within a building at which the communications wire or cable emerges from an external wall, from a concrete floor slab, from rigid metal conduit (RMC), or from intermediate metal conduit (IMC).

**800.49 Metallic Entrance Conduit Grounding.** Rigid metal conduit (RMC) or intermediate metal conduit (IMC) containing communications entrance wire or cable shall be connected by a bonding conductor or grounding electrode conductor to a grounding electrode in accordance with 800.100(B).

*(See NEC for actual text)*

## Significance of the Change

For this *Code* cycle, CMP-16 submitted a group of coordinated proposals aimed at aligning the definitions and the requirements within Chapter 8. The change to 800.2 Point of Entrance and inserting a new 800.49 Metallic Entrance Conduit Grounding are some of the results of this task group. The definition of *point of entrance* contained requirements and required editorial improvements. First, the requirements were stripped from the definition and moved to new 800.49. The NFPA *Style Manual* specifically requires that definitions must not contain requirements. Secondly, the definition was editorially revised for clarity. For the new 800.49, exact and appropriate defined terms were used to require metallic conduits, which contain the "entering" communications cables, must be connected by either a bonding conductor or a grounding electrode conductor to the grounding electrode all in accordance with 800.100(B). These communications circuit requirements run parallel to some of the other grounding and bonding requirements in Article 250, Parts III and V.

## Change Summary

- The definition of *point of entrance* was revised to eliminate grounding and bonding requirements.
- The bonding and grounding requirements within the definition were moved to a new 800.49.
- New 800.49 is located within Part II Wires and Cables Outside and Entering Buildings.

Comment: None
Proposals: 16-88, 16-104

# Low Smoke Nonmetallic Cable Ties

## Code Language

**800.24 Mechanical Execution of Work.** Communications circuits and equipment shall be installed in a neat and workmanlike manner. Cables installed exposed on ...(See *NEC* text)... will not be damaged by normal building use. Such cables shall be secured by hardware, including straps, staples, cable ties, hangers, or similar fittings designed and installed so as not to damage the cable. The installation shall also conform to 300.4(D) and 300.11. Nonmetallic cable ties and other nonmetallic cable accessories used to secure and support cables in other spaces used for environmental air (plenums) shall be listed as having low smoke and heat release properties.

*(See NEC for actual text)*

## Change Summary

- CMP-16 added a new last sentence to 800.24, 770.24, 820.24 and 830.24.

- It requires nonmetallic cable ties and other nonmetallic accessories be listed as having low smoke and heat release properties where used in other spaces used for environmental air (Plenums).

- This complies with NFPA 90A, *Standard for the Installation of Air-Conditioning and Ventilating Systems.*

Comments: 16-16, 16-17, 16-20 and more

Proposals: 16-42, 16-99, 16-100 and more

## Significance of the Change

The NFPA Standards Council has assigned primary responsibility for combustibles, located within air handling spaces, to the Technical Committee on Air-Conditioning and the Standard, NFPA 90A, *Standard for the Installation of Air-Conditioning and Ventilating Systems.* Presently, NFPA 90A-2012 has requirements for cable ties in ceiling cavity plenums located in 4.3.11.2.6.5 and for raised floor plenums located in 4.3.11.5.5.6. Both of these sections require that all electrical equipment with combustible enclosures, including their assemblies and accessories, cable ties, and other discrete products, shall be permitted in the ceiling cavity plenum and raised floor plenums only where listed according to ANSI/UL 2043, *Standard for Safety Fire Test for Heat and Visible Smoke Release for Discrete Products and Their Accessories Installed in Air-Handling Spaces.* These air-handling spaces are called "Other Spaces Used for Environmental Air (Plenums)" in *NEC* 300.22(C). To comply with NFPA 90A, CMP-16 approved a new last sentence be added to 800.24 (and to 770.24, 820.24 and 830.24) requiring nonmetallic cable ties and other nonmetallic accessories to be listed as having low smoke and heat release properties. This action, and the action in 300.22(C)(1), brings the *NEC* in compliance and correlation with NFPA 90A.

# Fire Resistive Cable Listing Requirements

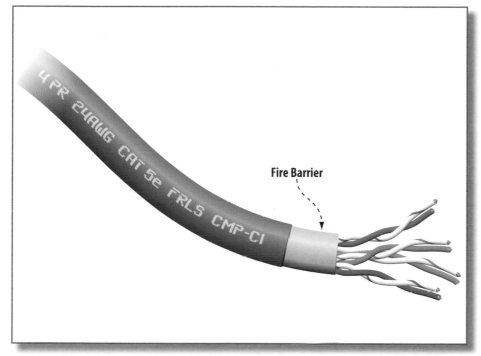

Fire Barrier

## Significance of the Change

Members of CMP-3 and CMP-16 formed a task group to reconcile differences among the various listing requirements of Circuit Integrity (CI) cable and Electrical Circuit Protective System installed for protection of circuits used within Articles 725, 760, 770 and 800. The exact *NEC* references include 800.179(G), 725.179(F), 760.176(F), and 770.179(E). The task group first agreed that common listing requirements be placed within each article as appropriate, then acted to ensure each article relied on common definitions and finally made certain that only these common listing requirements would be used to revise existing requirements or to become new requirements where necessary within each of the four articles. Revisions in Articles 725 and 760 included replacements actions such as "… suitable for use…" were deleted and the word "used" was added. The phrase "… installed in accordance with the listing of the protective system…" and the term *listed* was added to ensure proper installation and compliance with product standard and 110.3(B). New sections were added to Articles 770 and 800 allowing for their specific differences.

## Code Language

**800.179(G) Circuit Integrity (CI) Cable or Electrical Circuit Protective System.** Cables that are used for survivability of critical circuits under fire conditions shall be listed and meet either 800.179(G)(1) or (2) as follows: …(See *NEC* text)…

**(1) Circuit Integrity (CI) Cables.** Circuit integrity (CI) cables specified in 800.179(A) through (E), and used for survivability of critical circuits, shall have an additional classification using the suffix "CI". …(See *NEC*)…

**(2) Fire Resistive Cables.** Cables specified in 800.179(A) through (E) and 800.179(G)(1), that are part of an electrical circuit protective system, shall be fire-resistive cable identified with the protective system number … (See *NEC* text)…

*(See NEC for actual text)*

## Change Summary

- Common circuit integrity cable or electrical circuit protective system listing requirements were added to Articles 725, 760, 770 and 800.

- Listing information includes installation requirements to maintain the fire rating.

- Common requirements clarify what an electrical circuit protective system is and what type of circuit integrity cable is part of an electrical circuit protective system.

Comments: 16-40, 3-74, 3-109, 16-38
Proposals: 16-85a, 3-165, 3-208, 16-26a

## Listed Grounding Devices Required

### Code Language

**800.180 Grounding Devices.** Where bonding or grounding is required, devices used to connect a shield, a sheath, or non–current-carrying metallic members of a cable to a bonding conductor or grounding electrode conductor shall be listed or be part of listed equipment.

*(See NEC for actual text)*

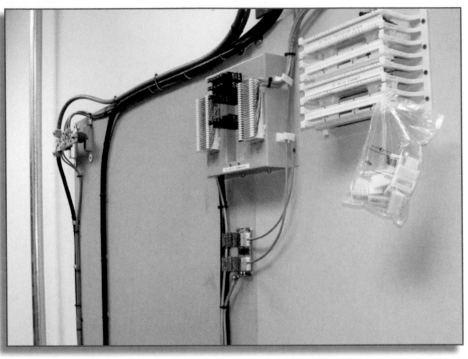

### Change Summary

- For the 2014 *NEC*, a single section was added to Articles 770, 800, 810, 820, 830 and 840.

- The common requirement is the use of listed devices or devices which are a part of listed equipment to achieve grounding and bonding connections.

- Except for Article 810, common numbering was used with the remaining proposals.

Comment: None

Proposals: 16-139, 16-80, 16-145, 16-211, 16-258, 16-285

### Significance of the Change

Section 90.3 permits Chapter 8 to stand alone and is not subject to the requirements of Chapters 1 through 7. When it comes to grounding and bonding, in some instances, this can be a serious issue especially where grounding requirements are different or nonexistent. Although requirements exist that specify when grounding or bonding of a shield, sheath or non–current-carrying metallic members of a cable is required, there was no requirement that devices used should be listed, which can result in poor connections due to questionable installation methods (e.g. wrapping the conductor around a cable sheath) or employing devices that do not have sufficient strength to maintain a solid connection or use materials unsuitable for the application.

Therefore the panel decided to require listed devices ensures the connection meets construction and performance criteria necessary for reliable bonding and grounding. Listed devices or grounding devices that are part of listed equipment comply with UL 467, *Grounding and Bonding Equipment*. Except for Article 810, common numbering (xxx.180) was selected and aligned with proposals submitted for Articles 770, 800, 820, 830 and 840.

# Antenna Lead-In Protectors

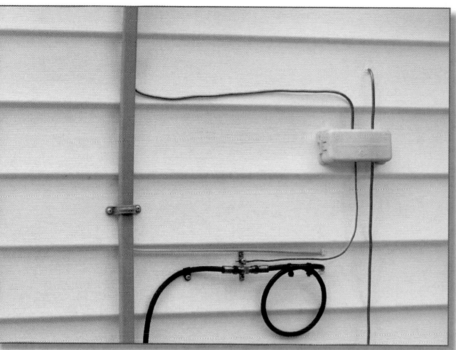

*Courtesy of ERICO International Corporation*

## Significance of the Change:

Article 810 covers wiring requirements for radio and television receiving equipment, including digital satellite receiving equipment for television signals, wiring for amateur radio equipment and citizens band (CB) radio equipment. Soon it may apply to outdoor WIFI and other data broadcast, receiving and antenna equipment. Where this equipment uses exterior antennas, there is a danger of bringing lightning and other atmospheric related surges into the building, which in many cases result in a fire. This new section deals with *antenna lead-in protectors*. These devices may be subject to high energy lightning surges in the range of 5-50 kA or higher. Listing and compliance with appropriate requirements ensure that the protector can withstand these surges without introducing a risk of fire or personal injury (from explosions) and the protector will continue to provide surge protection after being subjected to various environmental and surge conditions that may be expected in an typical installation.

## Code Language

**810.6 Antenna Lead-In Protectors.** Where an antenna lead-in surge protector is installed, it shall be listed as being suitable for limiting surges on the cable that connects the antenna to the receiver/transmitter electronics and shall be connected between the conductors and the grounded shield or other ground connection. The antenna lead-in protector shall be grounded using a bonding conductor or a grounding electrode conductor installed in accordance with 810.21(F).

Informational Note: For requirements covering protectors for antenna lead-in conductors, refer to UL Subject 497E, *Outline of Investigation for Protectors for Antenna Lead-In Conductors.*

*(See NEC for actual text)*

## Change Summary

- New for 2014, *Antenna Lead-In Protectors*, where used, shall be grounded using a bonding conductor or a grounding electrode conductor installed in accordance with 810.21(F).
- It must be a listed device and suitable for the cable used.
- The protector must be grounded using a bonding conductor or a grounding electrode conductor installed according to 810.21(F).

Comments: 16-74
Proposal: 16-144

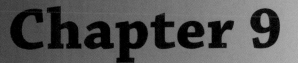

# Chapter 9

## Tables, Examples, Annexes

# Table 1, Note 7

**NEW**

## Maximizing Conduit and Tubing Fill

### Code Language

**Table 1 …(See *NEC* text)…**

**Notes to Tables**

(1) thru (7) …(See *NEC* text)…

(7) When calculating the maximum number of conductors or cables permitted in a conduit or tubing, all of the same size (total cross-sectional area including insulation), the next higher whole number shall be used to determine the maximum number of conductors permitted when the calculation results in a decimal greater than or equal to 0.8. When calculating the size for conduit or tubing permitted for a single conductor, one conductor shall be permitted when the calculation results in a decimal greater than or equal to 0.8.

*(See NEC for actual text)*

### Change Summary

- A new last sentence was added to Chapter 9, Table 1, Notes to Tables, Note 7.

- This allowance specifically permits single-conductor fill (53 percent) calculations to follow the same rules as multiple conductor fill percentage calculations.

- One sample calculation permits a single 500 kcmil bare copper conductor in a 1 in. rigid metal conduit.

### Problem:

Using the 2014 *NEC*, Chapter 9, Notes to Tables, Note 7, determine if it is possible to use a 1 in. rigid metal conduit for the installation of a single 500 kcmil bare copper conductor.

### Solution:

**Step 1.** Using Chapter 9, Table 4 for a 1 in. rigid metal conduit and using the 53% fill area column provides an area of 0.470 in.$^2$.

**Step 2.** Using Chapter 9, Table 8 provides the area of a bare 500 kcmil copper conductor to be 0.519 in.$^2$.

**Step 3.** Divide the conduit area (53% value) by the single bare conductor area

$$0.470 \text{ in.}^2 \div 0.519 \text{ in.}^2 = 0.906$$

### Answer:

Since the remainder of 0.906 is greater than 0.8, the next higher whole number of 1 (one single conductor) is now permitted to be installed in a 1 in. rigid metal conduit by new Note 7. This example reflects the absolute minimum.

## Significance of the Change

Since the 1971 *NEC*, an allowable practice of maximizing conduit fill was to use the 40 percent fill internal cross-sectional area of a single conduit or tubing and divide by the area of a single conductor, thus determining the exact quantity of conductors permitted. Where the quantity of single insulated conductors ended in a decimal greater than or equal to 0.8, the calculation allowed to be rounded up to the next larger whole number thereby allowing one more conductor. For the 2014 *NEC*, a new last sentence was added to Note 7 specifically including single conductor installations as well. Of course, such a calculation is not necessary where the Annex C fill tables already permit the fill desired. This Note 7 calculation for conduit or tubing fill, whether it be for multiple conductor or single conductor installations is somewhat similar to an exception. That is because the conductor fill is stretched to be slightly more than the required 53 percent, 40 percent or 31 percent of Chapter 9, Table 1. See the example above for a calculation using single 500 kcmil bare copper conductor within a 1 in. rigid metal conduit. While the example above reflects proper application of Note 7 to meet minimum raceway requirements, a better practice would be to use a larger sized raceway.

Comment: None
Proposals: 8-198, 8-199

**290**     Chapter 9 • Tables, Examples, Annexes

## Ease Of Use By Relocating Columns

### Article 358 — Electrical Metallic Tubing (EMT)

| Trade Size | Over 2 Wires 40% in.² | 1 Wire 53% in.² | 2 Wires 31% in.² |
|---|---|---|---|
| ½ | 0.122 | 0.161 | 0.094 |
| ¾ | 0.213 | 0.283 | 0.165 |
| 1 | 0.346 | 0.458 | 0.268 |
| 1¼ | 0.598 | 0.793 | 0.464 |
| 1½ | 0.814 | 1.079 | 0.631 |
| 2 | 1.342 | 1.778 | 1.040 |
| 2½ | 2.343 | 3.105 | 1.816 |
| 3 | 3.538 | 4.688 | 2.742 |
| 3½ | 4.618 | 6.119 | 3.579 |
| 4 | 5.901 | 7.819 | 4.573 |

### Code Language

**Table 4 Dimensions and Percent Area of Conduit and Tubing**
...(See *NEC* text)...

**Table 5 Dimensions of Insulated Conductors and Fixture Wires**
...(See *NEC* text)...

*(See NEC for actual text)*

### Significance of the Change

For the *Code* user, Chapter 9, Tables 4 and 5 are often referenced while performing or verifying conduit fill and wire (area) calculations, for both general applications and especially during licensing examinations. The previous table layouts often resulted in table lookup errors leading to calculation errors because the most used columns were located far apart. These two proposals and one comment result in relocation of the two most used columns in both of these Chapter 9 tables. For Table 4, Dimensions and Percent Areas for Conduit and Tubing, the most used column for "Over 2 wires 40%" has been relocated from the far right to a position adjacent to "Trade Size" (conduit or raceway). For Table 5, Dimensions of Insulated Conductors and Fixture Wires, the most used column "Approximate Area" has been relocated from the far right to a position adjacent to Size (AWG or kcmil) conductor. Both of these user friendly *Code* changes will greatly enhance the usability of the *Code* by lessening the amount of lookup errors and assist the users in performing more accurate *Code* calculations.

### Change Summary

• Both Tables 4 and 5 of Chapter 9 have relocated the two most used columns to be adjacent to one another.

• For Table 4, the "Over 2 Wires 40%" column was placed next to Column 1 "Trade Size" raceway.

• For Table 5, the "Approximate Area" column was placed next to Column 1 "Size (AWG or kcmil)".

Comment: 6-78
Proposals: 8-204, 6-113

**NEW**

# CU and AL Conductor Class B Stranding

## Code Language

**Table 10 Conductor Stranding**

... (See *NEC* Chapter 9, Table 10)...

ᵃ Conductors with a lesser number of strands shall be permitted based on an evaluation for connectability and bending.

ᵇ Number of strands vary.

ᶜ Aluminum 14 AWG (2.1 mm²) is not available.

With the permission of Underwriters Laboratories, Inc., material is reproduced from UL Standard 486A-B, Wire Connectors, which is copyrighted by Underwriters Laboratories, Inc., Northbrook, Illinois. While use of this material has been authorized, UL shall not be responsible for the manner in which the information is presented ... (See *NEC* text)...

*(See NEC for actual Table 10 and actual text)*

## Change Summary

- Table 10 of Chapter 9 now permits Class B stranding to have a lesser number of stands per conductor.

- This applies to Class B stranding for both aluminum and copper stranded conductors.

- This new *NEC* permissive language in footnote a matches UL 44 *Thermoset-Insulated Wires and Cables* and other UL wire and cable standards.

### Concentric Stranding

A concentric-stranded conductor consists of a central wire or core surrounded by one or more layers of helically laid wires. Each layer after the first has six more wires than the preceding layer. Except in compact stranding, each layer is applied in a direction opposite to that of the layer under it.

If the core is a single wire and if it and all of the outer strands have the same diameter, the first layer will contain six wires; the second, twelve; the third, eighteen; etc. The following 1959 diagram shows original this relation in convenient form.

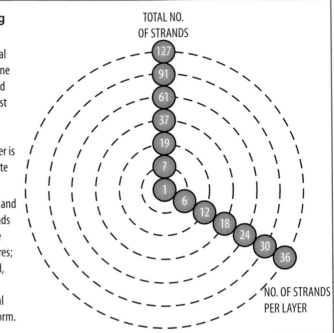

Adapted from The Simplex Manual, ©1959, Simplex Wire and Cable Co.

## Significance of the Change

Generally, concentric-stranded conductors consist of a central wire (or core) surrounded by one or more layers of helically laid wires. Each layer after the first has six more wires than the preceding layer. Except in compact stranding, each layer is applied in a direction opposite to that of the layer under it. This layering of "... six more wires..." leads one to believe only a specific number of strands, such as 7, 19, 37, etc are acceptable in Class B stranding. However, UL 44, *Thermoset-Insulated Wires and Cables*, as well as other UL wire and cable standards state that "... conductors with lesser number of strands shall be allowed based on an evaluation for connectability." So, for the *NEC* to reflect an accurate trade practice in manufacturing and listing wires and cable, *NEC* Table 10 of Chapter 9 has adopted similar language as the UL 44 standard governing listed wires and cables. For the 2014 NEC, Table 10 of Chapter 9 has incorporated a new footnote ᵃ stating that "Conductors with a lesser number of strands shall be permitted based on an evaluation for connectability and bending." This footnote applies to both copper and aluminum conductors using Class B stranding.

Comment: None
Proposal: 1-185a

# Example D3(a) Industrial Feeders in a Common Raceway

## Significance of the Change

This example was first submitted for use within the 2005 *NEC*. Originally used within NFPA *NEC* training, this example became a favorite among continuing education students of the *NEC* including engineers, contractors, instructors and electricians. The submitter of this proposal insisted upon retaining Annex D Example D3(a) due to its educational value. During the 2011 *NEC* revision cycle, the ampacity of the 90°C value of 1/0 AWG CU was revised from 150 amperes to 145 amperes. This 2011 change caused our example to lose a large proportion of its educational value. However, the submitter, by testing different load values, noticed the present example could be retained by changing the value of one single load. The only "given" information changed was the air compressor; it was reduced from 7.5 hp to 5.0 hp. Quoting the substantiation: "The changes in this proposal preserve the benefits of what was always a carefully contrived load profile that produces an actual change in conductor size if any of the variables are not processed correctly by a student." Industry instructors will be well served to take advantage of this meaningful load profile instructional example in the back of every new *Code* book.

## Code Language

**Example D3(a) Industrial Feeders in a Common Raceway**

An industrial multi-building facility has its service at the rear of its main building, and then provides 480Y/277-volt feeders to additional buildings behind the main building in order to segregate certain processes. The facility supplies its remote buildings through ...(See *NEC* text)...

Each of the two buildings has the following loads:

Lighting, 11,600 VA, comprised of electric-discharge luminaires connected at 277 V

Receptacles, 22 125-volt, 20-ampere receptacles on general-purpose branch circuits, supplied by separately derived systems in each of the buildings

1 Air compressor, 460 volt, three phase, 5 hp

... (See *NEC* text)...

*(See NEC for actual text)*

## Change Summary

- Example D3(a) was updated and revised to preserve its educational value.
- During the 2011 *NEC* revision cycle, the ampacity of the 90°C value of 1/0 AWG CU was revised from 150 amperes to 145 amperes.
- This example has retained its value by changing the size of the air compressor from 7.5 hp to 5.0 hp.

Comment: None
Proposal: 2-264

# Example D7

**NEW**

## Example for Sizing Dwelling Service Conductors

### Code Language

**Example D7 Sizing of Service Conductors for Dwelling(s)** *[see 310.15(B)(7)]*

Service conductors and feeders for certain dwellings are permitted to be sized in accordance with 310.15(B)(7).

If a 175-ampere service rating is selected, a service conductor is then sized as follows:

175 amperes × 0.83 = 145.25 amperes per 310.15(B)(7).

If no other adjustments or corrections are required for the installation, then, in accordance with Table 310.15(B)(16), a 1/0 AWG Cu or a 3/0 AWG Al meets this rating at 75°C (167°F).

*(See NEC for actual text)*

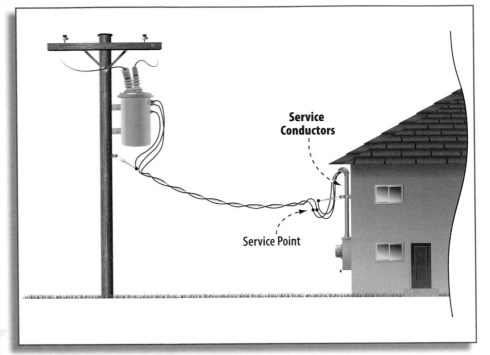

Service Conductors

Service Point

### Change Summary

- Table 310.15(B)(7) was deleted, text was revised and a new informational note was added pointing the user to Example D7 in Informative Annex D.

- Based on standard service ratings, an adjustment factor of not less than 83 percent is now used to determine the ungrounded service conductor ampacity.

- New example D7 is straight forward and simple.

### Significance of the Change

According to this CMP-6 proposal, during the 1956 Proceedings of the Sixteenth NFPA Annual Meeting, a factor of 84 percent was used to establish the aluminum residential service conductor size. However, based on trial calculations, if the panel used 84 percent in proposed new language, this would have resulted in larger sizes for some of the conductors, compared to the sizes in the 2011 *NEC*. Since the panel had no technical substantiation to justify these changes, a revised adjustment factor of 83 percent was used to maintain consistency with the sizes in the 2011 Table 310.15(B)(7). In order to address the various proposals submitted suggesting changes to 310.15(B)(7), the panel analyzed the existing language and determined that the conductor sizes in Table 310.15(B)(7) are equivalent to those that would be used if a 0.83 multiplier was applied to each service or feeder ampere rating. The resulting conductor size will be the same as existing text in Table 310.15(B)(7), if the same conductor types and installation conditions are applied. The informational note was added to clarify that adjustment and correction factors apply depending on conditions of use. See 310.15(B)(7) in this reference for further information.

Comment: 6-52
Proposals: 6-117a, 6-49a

## Annex J ADA Information

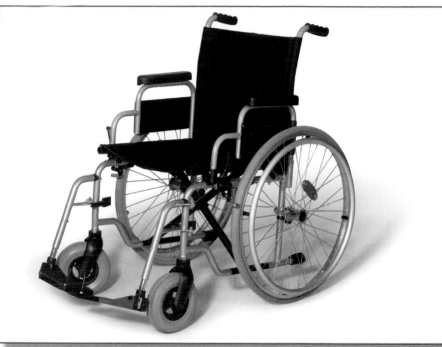

### Significance of the Change

The Americans with Disabilities Act (ADA) was signed into law in 1990 and was amended in 2008. Title II prohibits disability discrimination by all public entities at the local (*i.e.* school district, municipal, city, county) and state level. These regulations include physical access described in the ADA *Standards for Accessible Design*. According to the Department of Justice, compliance dates for new construction and alterations occurring on or after March 3, 2012 must meet the 2010 edition of ADA *Standards for Accessible Design*. Also, according to the substantiation for this *NEC* change, the *NEC* needed Annex J to comply with Federal Accessibility requirements for location of such electrical equipment such as devices, switches, receptacles, disconnects, controls, etc. Inclusion of this annex will assist installers and inspectors to understand and comply with these vital regulations. Annex J is intended to retain the ADA section numbering and it is not a complete set of requirements adopted by the US Department of Justice, but rather some of the sections that may be frequently used by the electrical industry.

### Code Language

**Informative Annex J ADA Standards for Accessible Design**

*This informative annex is not a part of the requirements of this NFPA document, but is included for informational purposes only.*

The provisions cited in Informative Annex J are intended to assist the users of the *Code* in properly considering the various electrical design constraints of other building systems and are part of the 2010 ADA Standards for Accessible Design. They are the same provisions as those found in ANSI/ICC A117.1-2009, *Accessible and Usable Buildings and Facilities.*

**J.1 Protruding Objects.** ... (See *NEC* text)...

**J.6 Forward Reach.** ... (See *NEC* text)...

**J.7 Side Reach.** ... (See *NEC* text)...

*(See NEC for actual text)*

### Change Summary

- New Informative Annex J, ADA Standards for Accessible Design was added to the 2014 *NEC*.
- Based on the Americans with Disabilities Act (ADA), the inclusion of this annex will assist the users of the *Code* during considerations of accessible design.
- Heavy in graphics, this Annex provides detailed illustrations including precise measurements of accessible design issues.

Comment: None
Proposals: 1-191

# Appendix A

## IBEW Code-Making Panel Members

**TECHNICAL CORRELATING COMMITTEE**
Palmer L. Hickman, [Principal]
James T. Dollard, Jr., [Alternate]

**CODE-MAKING PANEL NO. 1**
Palmer L. Hickman, [Principal]
Mark Christian, [Alternate]

**CODE-MAKING PANEL NO. 2**
Donald M. King, [Principal]
Jacob G. Benninger, [Alternate]

**CODE-MAKING PANEL NO. 3**
Paul J. Casparro, [Chair]
Michael J. Farrell III, [Alternate]

**CODE-MAKING PANEL NO. 4**
Todd W. Stafford, [Principal]
Brian L. Crise, [Alternate]

**CODE-MAKING PANEL NO. 5**
Paul J. LeVasseur, [Principal]
Gary A. Beckstrand, [Alternate]

**CODE-MAKING PANEL NO. 6**
William F. Laidler, [Principal]
Todd Crisman, [Alternate]

**CODE-MAKING PANEL NO. 7**
Samuel R. La Dart, [Principal]
Keith Owensby, [Alternate]

**CODE-MAKING PANEL NO. 8**
Gary W. Pemble, [Pricipal]
Dan Rodriguez, [Alternate]

**CODE-MAKING PANEL NO. 9**
Rodney D. Belisle, [Principal]
Rhett A. Roe, [Alternate]

**CODE-MAKING PANEL NO. 10**
James T. Dollard, Jr., [Principal]
Richard E. Lofton, II, [Alternate]

**CODE-MAKING PANEL NO. 11**
James M. Fahey, [Principal]
Jebediah J. Novak, [Alternate]

**CODE-MAKING PANEL NO. 12**
Jeffrey L. Holmes, [Principal]
Dale Wion, [Alternate]

**CODE-MAKING PANEL NO. 13**
Linda J. Little, [Principal]
James T. Dollard, Jr., [Alternate]

**CODE-MAKING PANEL NO. 14**
John L. Simmons, [Principal]
Thomas E. Dunne, [Alternate]

**CODE-MAKING PANEL NO. 15**
Stephen M. Lipster, [Principal]
Gary A. Beckstrand, [Alternate]

**CODE-MAKING PANEL NO. 16**
Harold C. Ohde, [Principal]
Terry C. Coleman, [Alternate]

**CODE-MAKING PANEL NO. 17**
Randy J. Yasenchak, [Principal]
Brian Myers, [Alternate]

**CODE-MAKING PANEL NO. 18**
Paul Costello, [Principal]
Jesse Sprinkle, [Alternate]

**CODE-MAKING PANEL NO. 19**
Ronald Michaelis, [Principal]
Ronald D. Weaver, Jr., [Alternate]

# NECA Code-Making Panel Members

**TECHNICAL CORRELATING COMMITTEE**
Michael J. Johnston, [Chair]
Stanley J. Folz, [Alternate]

**CODE-MAKING PANEL NO. 1**
Harry J. Sassaman, [Principal]
Michael J. Johnston, [Alternate]

**CODE-MAKING PANEL NO. 2**
Thomas H. Wood, [Principal]
Charlie Trout [Alternate]

**CODE-MAKING PANEL NO. 3**
Stanley D. Kahn, [Principal]

**CODE-MAKING PANEL NO. 4**
Ronald J. Toomer, [Chair]
Larry D. Cogburn, [Alternate]

**CODE-MAKING PANEL NO. 5**
Nathan Philips, [Chair]
Jacob M. Howlett, [Alternate]

**CODE-MAKING PANEL NO. 6**
Scott Cline, [Chair]
Michael W. Smith, [Alternate]

**CODE-MAKING PANEL NO. 7**
Michael W. Smith, [Chair]
Wesley L. Wheeler, [Alternate]

**CODE-MAKING PANEL NO. 8**
Larry D. Cogburn, [Chair]
Stephen P. Poholski, [Alternate]

**CODE-MAKING PANEL NO. 9**
Wayne Brinkmeyer, [Principal]
Gregory A. Bowman, [Alternate]

**CODE-MAKING PANEL NO. 10**
Richard Sobel, [Principal]

**CODE-MAKING PANEL NO. 11**
Stanley J. Folz, [Principal]

**CODE-MAKING PANEL NO. 12**
Thomas L. Hedges, [Principal]
William A. Brunner, [Alternate]

**CODE-MAKING PANEL NO. 13**
Martin D. Adams, [Principal]

**CODE-MAKING PANEL NO. 14**
Marc J. Bernsen, [Principal]

**CODE-MAKING PANEL NO. 15**
Bruce D. Shelly, [Principal]
Don W. Jhonson, [Alternate]

**CODE-MAKING PANEL NO. 16**
W. Douglas Pirkle, [Principal]

**CODE-MAKING PANEL NO. 17**
Don W. Jhonson, [Principal]
Bobby J. Gray, [Alternate]

**CODE-MAKING PANEL NO. 18**
Bobby J. Gray, [Chair]
Charles M. Trout, [Alternate]

**CODE-MAKING PANEL NO. 19**
Thomas F. Thierheimer, [Principal]

# Appendix C

## NECA NEIS Standards

**NECA 1-2010, Standard Practice of Good Workmanship in Electrical Contracting**
This is NECA's flagship NEIS and is the foundation of the NECA electrical workmanship standards. This standard describes what is meant by installing equipment in a "neat and workmanlike manner" as required by the National Electrical Code, Section 110.12.

**NECA 412-2012, Standard for Installing and Maintaining Photovoltaic (PV) Systems**
This standard describes the application procedures for installing and maintaining photovoltaic (PV) power systems and components.

**NECA 413-2012, Standard for Installing and Maintaining Electric Vehicle Supply Equipment (EVSE)**

This standard describes the procedures for installing and maintaining AC Level 1, AC Level 2 and fast charging DC (initially known in the industry as AC Level 3 and currently known in the industry as DC Level 2) Electrical Vehicle Supply Equipment (EVSE).

**NECA 701-2013, Standard for Energy Management, Demand Response and Energy Solutions**

This standard describes methods and procedures used for performing energy conservation surveys, controlling and maintaining energy consumption, implementing the smart grid and demand response, and developing, implementing and evaluation energy conservation measures for residential, commercial, and industrial applications.

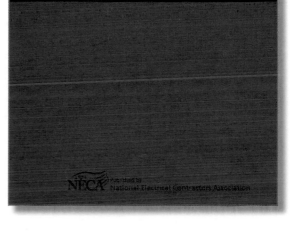